CW01216076

THE LIFE OF THE RED SEA DHOW

A Cultural History of Seaborne Exploration in the Islamic World

Dionisius A. Agius

I.B. TAURIS
LONDON · NEW YORK

Published in 2019 by
I.B.Tauris & Co. Ltd
London • New York
www.ibtauris.com

Copyright © 2019 Dionisius A. Agius

The right Dionisius A. Agius to be identified as the author of this work has been asserted by the author in accordance with the Copyright, Designs and Patents Act 1988.

All rights reserved. Except for brief quotations in a review, this book, or any part thereof, may not be reproduced, stored in or introduced into a retrieval system, or transmitted, in any form or by any means, electronic, mechanical, photocopying, recording or otherwise, without the prior written permission of the publisher.

Every attempt has been made to gain permission for the use of the images in this book. Any omissions will be rectified in future editions.

References to websites were correct at the time of writing.

ISBN (HB): 978 1 84885 806 0
ISBN (PB): 978 1 83860 342 7
eISBN: 978 1 78672 487 8
ePDF: 978 1 78673 487 7

A full CIP record for this book is available from the British Library
A full CIP record is available from the Library of Congress

Library of Congress Catalog Card Number: available

Typeset in StoneSerif by OKS Prepress Services, Chennai, India
Printed and bound in Great Britain

To Karmenu Agius, my godfather, who first awakened in me a love for material culture

CONTENTS

List of Illustrations ix
Abbreviations xiv
Acknowledgements xv
Preface xvii
Note on the Transliteration System xix

1. Cultural Memories of the Red Sea 1
2. 'Our life on the sea is gone but our stories will last forever' 7
3. The Geographic Context 27
4. Red Sea Corridor: The Early Modern Period 35
5. The Red Sea Sailing Dhow 43
6. On Building the Dhow: Sites, Skills and Techniques 48
7. Documenting and Remembering Old Dhows 59
8. The *Sanbūk*s of the Red Sea 66
9. The Dhow Landscape: The Northern and Southern Red Sea 82
10. 'Our life is the sea: The ship, the coast and the anchorage know us' 98
11. On Board the Dhow: Eating, Resting and Entertainment 113
12. This Dangerous Sea 124
13. 'You only ride the sea if you know the sea': Winds and Sails 134
14. 'We set forth with a favourable wind': The Red Sea Dhow Trade 153
15. 'We sail with the hope of a good catch': Fishing and Shell Collecting 175
16. The Dhow Hunt: The Slave Trade and Gun Running in the Southern Red Sea 193

17. The Dhow, the Coast and the Sea: Interacting with Nature, the Spirits and the Supernatural 206
18. Cultural Identities of a Red Sea Landscape: Recollections and Reflections 218

Glossary 233
Appendices 248
Notes 277
Bibliography 317
Index 332

LIST OF ILLUSTRATIONS

MAPS

Map 1 Places on the African and Arabian shores visited by the author between 2002 and 2013. 16

Map 2 Places visited by the author in the Gulf of Aden and Greater Aden area, 2009. 19

Map 3 The Farasan Archipelago, showing the islands visited by the author and the MARES team, 2010. 22

Map 4 Places visited by the MARES team in Eritrea, 2013. 23

Map 5 The sea route from Quseir to Jeddah, then returning north to Ras Muhammad and back to Quseir. 148

TABLES

Table 2.1 Occupations and ages of people interviewed between 2002 and 2013. 15

Table 13.1 Dhow sails. 138

Table 13.2 Winds of the northern Red Sea. 140

Table 13.3 Winds of the southern Red Sea. 142

Table 15.1 Sample *sahm* for an Egyptian Red Sea fishing trip. 189

FIGURES

Figure 2.1 Quseir's seafront in the 1920s. 17

Figure 2.2 Ummlejj harbour, 2013. 18

Figure 2.3 Chiara Zazzaro documenting the different types of dhow at Khor al-Ghureirah, 2009. 20

Figure 2.4 The author interviewing fishermen in the lagoon at Khor al-Ghureirah, 2009. 20

Figure 2.5 The MARES team at the Al Hafa dhow yard in Jizan, 2010. 24

Figure 2.6 Abandoned wooden dhows near the Kobri (causeway), Tuwaled, Massawa, 2011. 25

Figure 3.1 A coral-stone building in the Sur quarter, Yanbu al-Bahr, 2007. 31

Figure 4.1 Mocha harbour, 1680. 37

Figure 4.2 'The opening of the Suez Canal festival'. 39

Figure 4.3 Entrance to the Suez Canal. 40

Figure 4.4 Coaling at Port Said. 40

Figure 5.1 The port of Yanbu al-Bahr on the Hijazi coast, 1829–34. 44

Figure 5.2 Dhows with square and settee sails on the Red Sea, *c.*1890. 46

Figure 6.1 Dhow building at Ma'alla, Aden, in the 1940s. 50

Figure 6.2 *Lansh-sanbūk* built using the modern hybrid method, Suakin, 2004. 57

Figure 6.3 Laying planks edge to edge and securing by caulking in the Arabian style, Suakin, 2004. 58

Figure 7.1 Indian long chart of the Gulf of Aden. 60

Figure 7.2 A *quyāsa* anchored not far from the Muhafaza, Suakin. 64

Figure 7.3 *Quyāsas* entering an inlet, Suakin. 64

Figure 8.1 A *sanbūk*-like vessel with no overhang near Massawa. 69

Figure 8.2 A cargo *sanbūk* with a transom stern and slightly raised overhanging poop, Quseir, 1920s. 70

Figure 8.3 Vice-Admiral Pâris's portrait of a Red Sea double-ended *sanbūk*. 71

Figure 8.4 J. Brett's line-drawings of a square-stern *sanbūk*, Kamaran Island, 1935. 72

Figure 8.5 The scimitar-shaped stem piece of an Adeni *sanbūk*, Aden, 1940s or 1950s. 73

Figure 8.6 The transom-stern overhang of an Adeni *sanbūk*, Aden, 1940s or 1950s. 74

Figure 8.7 The *Sheikh Mansoor*, 1938. 75

Figure 8.8 Line drawings of a *gaṭīra* by Le Masson, a Suez Canal engineer, 1879. 76

Figure 8.9 Sketch of the *gaṭīra* in Quseir fort built by Atia Said Hussein Ali, 2002. 77

Figure 8.10 A double-ended *jurdī* built by Humaid Mani al-Muwallad of Rabigh and now on display at Yanbu al-Bahr, 2007. 78

Figure 8.11 An open-ended *za'īma* with an upper curved bow and a raised stern, Ras Ali, Djibouti, 2009. 79

Figure 8.12 Sudanese *sanbūks* at Flamingo Bay, north of Port Sudan, 1951. 80

Figure 8.13 A Gulf *sanbūq* in the 1960s. 81

Figure 9.1 A square-stern fishing *falūka*, Quseir, 2004. 84

Figure 9.2 A double-ended *'obrī*, Khor al-Ghureirah, 2009. 89

Figure 9.3 A square-stern 'winged' *hūrī*, Khokha, 2009. 91

Figure 9.4 Hamid Suleiman Hamid and two of his workers replacing parts of the garboard strakes, Tuwaled, Massawa, 2011. 94

Figure 10.1 A navigator's chart or *dīra*. 105

Figure 10.2 Sailors wearing the distinctive *ṣidriyya* and the long *'imāma*, Suakin, 2004. 110

Figure 10.3 Said Mohammad Alaiwa, a helmsman from Mocha, Yemen, wearing a *fūṭa* and a golden turban, 2009. 111

Figure 11.1 Pen-and-ink drawing of pilgrims in the hold of a dhow by F. George, 1875. 114

Figure 11.2 Singing and dancing to the rhythm of the drums and tambourines with cymbals on board the *sanbūk* in Farasan, 1950s. 120

Figure 12.1 A pirate *'obrī* off the coast of Somalia. 127

Figure 13.1 An Adeni dhow under sail in the 1930s. 141

Figure 13.2 Circular wearing, the preferred method of the Red Sea mariner. 149

Figure 13.3 Tacking technique: lateen/settee yard positions when sailing downwind. 151

Figure 13.4 Sailing with a *shamāl* tailwind. 151

Figure 14.1 A view of the busy port of Quseir in the nineteenth century. 159

Figure 14.2 The port of Dhuba with cargo dhows, nineteenth century. 161

Figure 14.3 A view of Dhuba from the restored fort overlooking the harbour, 2007. 161

Figure 14.4 A Royal Air Force photograph of the island town of Suakin, 1930. 164

Figure 14.5 The ruins of the island town of Suakin, 2004. 165

Figure 14.6 Coffee merchants at Mocha. 168

Figure 14.7 The *baghla Fatḥ al-Khayr.* 170

Figure 15.1 Fishing festival at Greater Farasan Island, 13 April 2012. 180

Figure 15.2 Sheikh Muhammad Hadi Al Rajhi weighing pearls with a *mīzān*, 2010. 190

Figure 16.1 The suppression of piracy and slave trading in the Red Sea, 1902. 198

Figure 16.2 An Arab slave ship in the Red Sea with a British cruiser in sight, 1874. 199

Figure 17.1 An *oculus* on the bow of a *mahadi*, Port de Pêche, Djibouti City, 2009. 208

Figure 17.2 Sheikh 'Alī Ibn 'Umar al-Shādhilī's tomb, Mocha, 2009. 216

Figure 18.1 Plan of Suakin's El Geyf district showing its six forts. 224

Figure 18.2 Poster in the mayor's office, Obock, Djibouti, 2009. 227

Figure 18.3 A fisherman with his catch, Jeddah. 228

Figure 18.4 Maritime sculpture, Quseir, 2004. 229

Figure 18.5 Monument at Ummlejj, Saudi Arabia, 2013. 230

PLATES

Plate 1 Dhow builder Mudassir Mousa Othman Mohammed of Nigerian origin, Suakin 2004 (photo by the author).

Plate 2 Former pearl diver Munawwar Aqili, Farasan Island 2010 (photo MARES by the author).

Plate 3 Fishermen from the Dahlak Islands at Sigalat Lamba, Massawa 2011 (photo MARES by the author).

Plate 4 Former dhow builder Muawwid Abd al-Raheem Mirbas with director of heritage, Awad al Subhi (standing) Yanbu al-Bahr 2007 (photo by the author).

Plate 5 Sea captain Mohammad Ahmed Zaid al-Anbari Khor al-Ghureirah 2009 (photo MARES by the author).

Plate 6 Boatswain Duwi Toufiq Mahmud, Quseir 2004 (photo by the author).

Plate 7 Singer Abd Allah Ibrahim Hasan playing the *simsimiyya*, Farasan Island 2010 (photo MARES by the author).

Plate 8 Sailors resting on board the dhow at Khor al-Ghureirah 2009 (photo MARES by the author).

Plate 9 Tying the sail to the yard on an Adeni *sanbūk* in the 1950s (photo courtesy Antonin Besse Jr).

Plate 10 Former sailor Muhammad Bukhayyit Alsinani, Ummlejj 2013 (photo by the author).

Plate 11 Former sea captain Abu Bakar Habib, Tadjourah 2009 (photo MARES by the author).

Plate 12 Former sea captain Hussein Abd al-Hamid Abd Allah, Suakin 2004 (photo by the author).

Plate 13 *Kukyān* diver Salim Salman Salim, Suakin 2004 (photo by the author).

Plate 14 Master dhow builder Ibrahim Ali Moosa, Quseir 2004 (photo by the author).

Plate 15 The fishing village people at Khor al-Ghureirah 2009 (photo MARES by the author).

Plate 16 Fisherman Idrees Daud Ali, Zula 2011 (photo MARES by the author).

ABBREVIATIONS

LANGUAGES

Ar.	Arabic
CA	Classical Arabic
DA	Dialectal Arabic
Dra.	Dravidian
Eng.	English
Er.	Eritrean
Far.	Farasani
Hin.	Hindī
It.	Italian
Kan.	Kanarese
Lat.	Latin
Mal.	Malaysian
Mar.	Marathi
MSA	Modern Standard Arabic
Per.	Persian
Port.	Portuguese
RSA	Red Sea Arabic
SA	Southern Arabian
Skt	Sanskrit
Sud Ar	Sudanese Arabic
Tur.	Turkish

LINGUISTIC SYMBOLS

√	root of a verb or noun
<	deriving from
>	becoming
*	a hypothetical word-mould

ACKNOWLEDGEMENTS

The fieldwork for this study was funded by the Arts and Humanities Research Council, the GoldenWeb Foundation, the Seven Pillars of Wisdom Trust, the Saudi Commission for Tourism and National Heritage (SCTNH) and King Abdulaziz University.

I owe a great deal to the many people who helped to make this book happen: my wife Anne, who read through each draft, making stylistic changes where necessary and to Philip Parr contributing many helpful comments; John P. Cooper, Steven Serels, Julian Whitewright and Chiara Zazzaro, who were invaluable in suggesting changes and improvements; the late Anthony Harrison and the late David Goddard, who drew my attention to a number of dhow-building and -sailing features; and the late Hassan Salih Shihab, who was generous enough to share with myself and the Maritime Ethnography of the Red Sea (MARES) team his knowledge and expertise on navigation in the Indian Ocean. I owe thanks to Paul Auchterlonie for compiling a complete index. I would like to express my gratitude to Alex Wright, formerly of I.B.Tauris and now Senior Executive Publisher at Cambridge University Press, who commissioned this book. My heartfelt gratitude goes to all these people.

My deepest appreciation goes to the late David Peacock and to Lucy Blue, who kindly invited me to join the Southampton archaeological team at Quseir; Laurence Smith, archaeologist of the Cambridge McDonald Institute of Archaeology; Michael Mallinson, architect at Mallinson Architects and Engineers Ltd, London, who invited me into their Suakin project; Simon Woodward, architect, and Aylin Orbasli, reader in Architectural Regeneration, Oxford Brookes University, who allowed me to participate in the Red Sea Towns project in the Hijaz; and Andrea Manzo of l'Orientale, Napoli, excavating with the Italian team at Adulis near Massawa. They all enabled me (the latter with John P. Cooper) to conduct ethnographic fieldwork in the areas mentioned. I would like to express my gratitude to Fahad Alsharif, senior researcher at the King Faisal Centre for Research and Islamic Studies in Riyadh, and Muhammad Alhazmi, associate professor at Medina University, who were instrumental in discussing linguistic, ethnic and social issues on the Arabian littoral.

My fieldwork would have been impossible without the assistance of the authorities in the countries visited. I offer my warmest thanks in particular to the secretary-general of SCTNH, HH Prince Sultan Bin Salman, for his kind invitation to conduct fieldwork in Jizan and the Farasan Islands, and his support during and after the ethnographic study; Ali AlGhabban, vice-president for Antiquities and Museums at SCTNH; and HH Sultan Abdoulkader Houmad Mahamad of Tadjourah, Djibouti, for allowing me to conduct fieldwork in the region.

I am also grateful to Abd al-Aziz al-Ghazzi, head of Research and Projects at SCTNH; Zahir Othman of the Turath Foundation; Awad al-Subhi, superintendent of Yanbu al-Bahr's Heritage; Abd al-Rahman Bin Muhammad Abd Al Haq, governor of the Farasan Islands; Sheikh Muhammad Hadi al-Rajhi of Greater Farasan; Sheikh Muhammad Abd Allah al-Rajhi of Khutub on Segid Island; MARES consultant Peter Harrigan; Zahi Hawass from the Supreme Council of Antiquities, Cairo; Sameh Ramses from the Archaeology Society of Alexandria; Khalid Balbikir El Karim, architect, and Bilsam Abd El Hamid, archaeologist, from the Sudanese National Cooperation for Antiquities and Museums, Khartoum; Muhammad-Nour Hedab, *omda* of the Ortega tribe in Suakin; Abdulla M. Bawazir, president, and Muhammad Taha al-Asbahi, director, of the General Organization of Antiquities and Museums (GOAM) at Sanaa, and Raja Batawil of GOAM in Aden; the president of l'Université de Djibouti, Abdilaahi Omar Bouhi; Président de Majlis Houmed Barkat Siradj of Tadjourah; Kamil Hassan, director of the Ministry of Education in Djibouti City; Jalludin Mohamed, director-general, and Omar Mahmoudi, director of science and the environment, at the Centre d'Étude et de Recherche de Djibouti; Josief Libseka, director of the National Museum at Asmara; Tsegai Medin, archaeologist, and Yohannes Gebreyesus, director, of the Massawa National Museum.

All of these people welcomed me as a researcher to their countries and provided the necessary permissions or assistance in order to facilitate my research. I record here my sincere appreciation and deep gratitude.

PREFACE

This book is the result of many years of fieldwork and research. I started by studying the maritime culture of the Arabian Gulf and Oman but came to realize that any such study of this area is incomplete without also including the Red Sea. Once I embarked on my research into the communities that inhabit both the African and Arabian shores, I quickly became fascinated by the still-vibrant maritime life I found there.

The traditional dhow, powered by sail and oar, was for centuries at the heart of the coastal communities who ventured onto the Red Sea. This was a time when merchants explored the sea in search of trade; fishermen searched for good fishing sites; and captains of pearling ships sought the best pearling beds. Then there were the many pilgrims who crossed the sea to perform *ḥajj*, an adventure that was, most probably, a once-in-a-lifetime event and one that would have brought them close to a landscape and seascape that they had never previously experienced. All of these journeys were forms of seaborne exploration.

This book is also a journey – one that documents the present but also uncovers the recent past of the communities of the African and Arabian Red Sea, with their diverse ethno-linguistic mix. Yet these communities have long worked and lived together, spoken an Arabic *lingua franca* and shared a maritime technology centred on the dhow. Another form of exploration came with the many European travellers who entered the Red Sea, initially in pursuit of trade, but later in a spirit of scientific enquiry, to explore the landscape, the seascape and the socio-cultural networks of the peoples who inhabit them, leaving behind a wealth of information upon which many a study has been based. This work utilizes that information but combines it with an ethnographic study, recording the voices of the Red Sea peoples themselves to gain a more direct understanding of their world. Although other ethnographic surveys have been conducted in local areas, this is the first to record and document both the African and the Arabian shores, uncovering the differences and commonalities of this maritime world.

NOTE ON THE TRANSLITERATION SYSTEM

I have adopted the Library of Congress Arabic Transliteration System for names of rulers and other religious and political figures. Years of death and reign are listed in the Islamic calendar followed by the Christian Gregorian calendar. Cited Arabic works and technical terms follow the Library of Congress system, but names of interviewees are given in the conventional writing of their respective countries. Arabic authors whose names begin with 'al-' are listed in the Bibliography under the first letter of their last name, so Al-Maqrīzī, Taqī l-Dīn is listed under the letter 'M', while Al-Shāfa'ī, 'Abd al-Qādir is listed under the letter 'S'.

CONSONANTS

'	ء	z	ز	q	ق
b	ب	s	س	k	ك
t	ت	sh	ش	l	ل
th	ث	ṣ	ص	m	م
j	ج	ḍ	ض	n	ن
ḥ	ح	ṭ	ط	h	ه
kh	خ	ẓ	ظ	w	و
d	د	'	ع	y	ي
dh	ذ	gh	غ		
r	ر	f	ف		

VOWELS

Long		*Short*	
ā	ا	a	ـَ
ū	و	u	ـُ
ī	ي	i	ـِ
ō		o	
ē		e	

Doubled

iyy (final form= ī)	ِيّ
uww (final form= ū)	ُوّ

Diphthongs

ay	َيْ
aw	َوْ

1

CULTURAL MEMORIES OF THE RED SEA

انا (كنت) ناخودة و تاجر اللوءلوء... (كنت) مالك سنبوك مصنوع في لحية
لخمسة عشرين سنة؛ السنبوك انقرض لا ينجبر، راح
الشيخ يحيى ابراهيم النجدي - جزيرة فرسان

'I was a sea captain, a pearl merchant; I owned a *sanbūk* built in Luheyya that lasted 25 years before it was damaged and finally, beyond repair, abandoned'.

Sheikh Yahya Ibrahim Bin Ibrahim Al Najdi Al Tamimi of Farasan Island.[1]

The voices of the Red Sea people and their narratives echo today as I write this book. With characteristic hospitality, those people welcomed a stranger who came to them with nothing to offer, yet they willingly engaged with my questions on their seafaring past, patiently explaining how things are made and work and enabling me, as an ethnographer and linguist, to build up a holistic picture of this still-vibrant maritime world.

This book, then, captures the cultural memories of the Red Sea people in all their diversity over the past 100 years. It covers Egypt, Sudan, Eritrea, Djibouti, Yemen and Saudi Arabia, with 166 interviews of people of varying ages and occupations conducted between 2002 and 2013. It reflects both continuity and change; the landscape and seascape have remained unchanged for thousands of years, but the lives of the people who inhabit them are subject to political, economic or demographic factors that enforce transformation.

The dhow is at the centre of this discourse, a unique blending of two different ecologies, the land and the sea.[2] The overarching aim is to understand the part it has played in the landscape of the Red Sea; how it enabled people to inhabit the coastline and navigate the seascape in Early Modern and more recent times. The name – 'dhow' – is a Western adoption to signify the traditional wooden sailing vessel that is typical of the western Indian Ocean.[3] With its characteristic features, the dhow is still part of the Red Sea landscape, just as it has been central to the lives of the maritime communities over many centuries. Its history of trading in the Red Sea region is well documented, as is the India trade that was pivotal to the commercial life of both the coastal and inland communities. Many dhows also served as pilgrim ships, making this one of the busiest maritime corridors in history. Moreover, for centuries dhows carried Africans and Arabians to the Red Sea's famous pearling beds, and then traded the divers' finds with Europe and India. Today, however, it is only the fishing dhows that survive, as poor fishermen persevere with the old technology of sails to save money on fuel and because a number of them want no part of the government-backed fishery cooperatives, which would tie them to loans and offer them much lower prices for their catches.

I wanted to know how the coastal and maritime people perceived this world of the dhow, to explore the physical and cultural landscape they experienced in the past and their current life at sea and along its shores. I wanted to learn about their lives more from examples than from principles, such as how to build a boat, be a mariner and navigate. My inquiry went forward to search for that cultural landscape where folk traditions from many centuries past, such as the songs of the sea and traditional rhythmic dances, are still found in some maritime communities, and to find explanations for why some folk beliefs and superstitions persist while others now exist only in the memories of older people.

Many questions arose as I began my journeys to and around the African and Arabian coasts, but I concentrated on just five in my fieldwork:

- How do the sea people perceive the Red Sea dhow?
- How do they engage with the physical and human geography of both shores of this sea?
- What remains of the maritime past in terms of human activity?
- The maritime identity is a composite of numerous ethnic and cultural practices, so is there a definitive Red Sea identity or merely many Red Sea identities?
- And how far can ethnographic inquiry supplement our understanding of the written word?

In answering these questions, this book aims to present a cultural history of the dhow and its people as well as the interplay of the human and non-human activities that have shaped the seascape and landscape of the Red Sea.

The ethnographic fieldwork is corroborated by the written reports and surveys of civil servants and the writings of travellers. There is no comprehensive written history about the maritime communities of the African and Arabian coasts over the past century (or earlier, for that matter) and no adequate account of the cultural life of the Red Sea dhow. The tangible and intangible culture that is documented here comes from the voices of the people themselves in an attempt to remedy this lacuna. The written sources of the Early Modern and Modern periods may be sparse, but we can, to a limited degree, reconstruct the socio-cultural history of the Red Sea by consulting the journals of a handful of Western travellers: John Ovington (fl. seventeenth century), chaplain to the English factory of the East India Company at Surat; Carsten Niebuhr (d. 1815), a German cartographer and explorer who, dressed as an Arab, joined a five-member Danish team in 1760 to study the human and physical geography of Suez, Jeddah and Mocha; a Catalan spy, Domènec Badia i Leblich, known as Ali Bey (d. 1818); a Swiss geographer, Johann Ludwig Burckhardt (d. 1817); and the British explorer Richard Burton (d. 1890). All of these men adopted Islamic names, and all performed the pilgrimage to Mecca and Medina. In addition, we have the works of the British politician George Annesley, Viscount Valentia (d. 1844); the US lawyer and judge Joseph B.F. Osgood (d. 1913), from Salem, Massachusetts; and the German physician Carl Klunzinger (d. 1914). All three recorded – sometimes in minute detail – the customs and practices of the people they encountered on their voyages through the Red Sea. More recently, the accounts of two travellers of the 1930s and 1940s – the Frenchman Henri De Monfreid (d. 1974) and the Australian Alan Villiers (d. 1982) – stand out. Both were experienced sailors who explored the southern region of the Red Sea, and their personal testimonies reveal that the indigenous people lived in harmony with nature and the sea. Also of note in the Early Modern period – up to and including the twentieth century – are those British colonial surveyors whose annotated reports have enriched our knowledge of the physical and human landscape: James R. Wellsted (d. 1842) of the Indian Navy; Captain F.M. Hunter (death year unknown), assistant political resident in Aden; and Cyril Crossland (d. 1943), director of the Sudan Pearl Fishery. Then there are the boat researchers and architects: Vice-Admiral François-Edmond Pâris (d. 1893), at one time head of the Musée National de la Marine in Paris; N.F.J. Wilson (death year unknown), port officer in Bombay; James Hornell (d. 1949), director of fisheries for the government of Madras; Alan Moore (d. 1959), a temporary medical officer in the Royal Navy; Richard LeBaron Bowen Jr (death year unknown), a nautical researcher; the New Zealander Clifford W. Hawkins (death year unknown), who was particularly knowledgeable about ocean-going sailing ships and dhows; Alain Rouaud, Henri Perrier and Ṣāliḥ Ḥasan Shihāb (d. 2013), all of whom have contributed much to our technical knowledge of the dhow world.

A CULTURAL LANDSCAPE

'Culture' is difficult to define, but perhaps D. Matsumoto and L. Juang's definition is the closest to fitting the framework of this book. They sum it up as: 'the set of attitudes, values, beliefs, and behaviors shared by a group of people, but different for each individual, communicated from one generation to the next'.[4] I would refine this definition to include the material and non-material practices and their engagement with the environment that form part of a landscape, in this study represented by the infrastructure of a coastal anchorage or port, harbour activity, merchant houses, the market, workshops, dhow building yards, sailing, fishing and pearling, or any other activity undertaken by the community. Thus, that landscape that a 'people' modifies is called 'a cultural landscape',[5] and the cultural landscapes of the Red Sea vary from one region to another, though they also share common maritime features and structures found on the African and Arabian shores.

To understand the landscape is to go out in the field and experience it for oneself through 'the sensual and sensing body', as Tilley and Cameron-Daum put it.[6] They explain that landscape is part of our life and, therefore, 'we cannot think of it in any way we like'.[7] By being present in the environment, the mind and body are engaged with the physical and cultural life of the landscape, together with the people, their work and their mental process of perception. Nature and culture are intertwined, as I found from my informants, who tell of the hard lives they experience just for survival, their everyday needs and worries, particularly when out at sea.

The sea, for mariners, wrote Brian Fagan, is everything, 'their company, their adviser, their friend'.[8] The companionship and friendship that my informants have known is in one sense lost in old age, but, although 'the sea is gone [...] its stories, surprises and secrets remain [in our memories]', exclaimed the Jeddawi fisherman Muhammad Said al-Ahmadi.[9] The people of the sea are still bonded together with their landscape and seascape in a harmonious relationship they once knew at first hand, and which remains alive in their collective memory today.

Natural forces – the climate, winds, waves, currents and tides – shape the coastal landscape. Organisms such as corals and algae can erode or build parts of the coast that are predisposed to contain inlets or creeks. People perceive this landscape and the sea by acting and interacting with the natural elements to create a cognitive cultural landscape; 'Everywhere along the coast', elucidates Brian Fagan, 'people live amid what one might call seascapes of memory, amid waters that are alive, at one with human actors'.[10]

THE MARITIME COGNITIVE CULTURAL LANDSCAPE

The term 'cognitive' may be understood as 'of or relating to the mental processes of perception, memory, judgment etc.'.[11] The communities of the African and Arabian coasts share cultural identities that are deeply embedded in the past but still alive today. Looking at the 'sea and its resources', the topography in relation to the sea, sailing and navigational techniques, the people, their oral literature and practices,[12] is a way to conceptualize what Christer Westerdahl has called the 'maritime cultural landscape'.[13] He sums it up as: 'the whole network of sailing routes, with ports, havens and harbors along the coast, and its related constructions and other remains of human activity'.[14] It should be noted here that 'port' or 'harbour', as Himanshu Prabha Ray purports, should not be construed as a loose term for 'a coastal centre'.[15] It is specifically a landing place where taxes are levied, but it can be understood only in connection with the sea and the people.

Westerdahl's summation points to two essential factors: topographical and cultural. The former covers the physical conditions of the coast, its relation to the sea and the people, while the latter is associated with the cognitive use of the landscape, which includes the people's ritual and spiritual elements.[16] But such conceptualizations of topography and culture give an 'erroneous' impression, posits David Berg Tuddenham.[17] The cultural landscape, he argues, is both physical and cognitive, encompassing the coastal environment, the coastal society and the cultural space (social practices), and he coined the term 'maritimity' to explain this multifaceted relationship between the land and sea. He admits that this is a complex solution to a complex question. Land and sea remain dichotomic, so he suggests looking at a 'landscape through a human and non-human dichotomy'.[18] Jorge Vaz Freire, an archaeologist, refined this idea when advocating the study of 'maritime spaces in a global context through the multiplicity of elements related to navigation and human occupation of coastlines'.[19] His approach is even wider, though, as it includes the physical, the cognitive and the interplay of human and non-human elements (nature, the environment and the spirit world), all of which are contained in the framework of this book, enabling a better understanding of the interconnectivity, mentality and, to some extent, commonality of the African and Arabian peoples, notwithstanding the many ethnic groups with their differing traditions and customs who inhabit the two shores of the Red Sea. This maritime culture, however, does not preclude the relationship of the coast to the hinterland, where goods are manufactured and transported by camel across the desert to reach the dhows moored at their anchorages. That relationship is also essential to our understanding of the maritime cultural landscape and seascape.

My own ethnographic fieldwork and the written accounts of the Early Modern and Modern periods – the core of the present study – capture the last days of a maritime culture as remembered by the older generations, but this book also documents the present-day activities of a traditional maritime world. Moreover, it has an even broader perspective, one that I previously employed in *Seafaring in the Arabian Gulf and Oman* (2005 and 2009), to include Braudel's fundamental truth that time works on a variety of 'zones', one of which is the *longue durée* – a long-term reality of interaction with the environment[20] represented by the coast, its people, their skills and knowledge, trade and local fishing activity – which Johan Rönnby describes as 'the history of the almost unchanging structures in mentality, technologies and landscape'.[21] In the context of the Red Sea many people are still engaged in a number of maritime activities; fishermen continue to utilize traditional techniques; Egyptian and Sudanese craftsmen build wooden vessels in much the same way as their forefathers did; dhows are still repaired with planks from older vessels; and pearl-diving continues, although it is now limited to a few amateur, part-time divers around the Farasan Islands, and new techniques have supplemented the old to aid the collection of beautiful pearls that are much desired in Bahrain, India and Europe. It is true that over the past 20 years many mariners, traders and craftsmen have moved away from the sea and the coasts to inland regions or even abroad in search of new livelihoods as the traditional maritime industries have declined, but enough remains to demonstrate a continuum that reaches deep into the past.

By recording the voices of the people themselves and their directly experienced knowledge, and then collating that information with written accounts and reports, we gain a deeper understanding of the dhow world. As Ole Henrik Magga concludes: 'indigenous knowledge systems, at least in some ways, are equal and sometimes even superior to western scientific ways of understanding the same realities'.[22]

2

'OUR LIFE ON THE SEA IS GONE BUT OUR STORIES WILL LAST FOREVER'[1]

هو االذي يسيركم في البر والبحرحتى اذا كنتم في الفلك و جرين بهم بريح طيبة وفرحوا بها

'He it is who enableth you to traverse through land and sea; so that ye even board ships; – they sail with them with a favourable wind, and rejoice thereat.'

Sūrat Yūnus, 10: 22[2]

An ethnographic study necessitates a balance of informants, selected for interview on the basis of their occupation and ages. But what is ethnography and what does it entail in this study? How does one go about finding informants and initiating the necessary meetings and conversations?

MARITIME ETHNOGRAPHY

'Ethnography' has different definitions depending on the scope and nature of the research. The focus in the present study is maritime, as it entailed collecting data from people living on the coast and those with seafaring experience. This incorporated an examination of the coastal landscape and the seascape of the region, documenting activities among the communities and those engaged at sea as well as their recollections of the past and their opinions of life today. The geographic context (Chapter 3) is highly relevant as it is the study of people in a particular time and place, collecting data on their material (tangible) culture, their skills and knowledge (intangible) culture and their folk practices and beliefs. It was essential to remain objective while conducting fieldwork on the coastal communities' behavioural situations and noting their memories. Where possible, oral accounts and practices were complemented or supplemented with albeit subjective information from the authors mentioned in Chapter 1. Of course, the data collected from the interviewees is similarly subjective, but evaluating both the written and the oral evidence can be helpful when deciding what to include or exclude. Maritime ethnography is a valuable tool that provides both questions and answers to historians, archaeologists and social scientists who are seeking an understanding of behavioural patterns and cultural memories.

The ethnographic fieldwork was conducted from 2002 to 2013 (albeit with none undertaken in 2012). From 2002 to 2007, and again in 2013, I worked alone, visiting Egypt, Sudan and Saudi Arabia; between 2008 and 2011, I led the Maritime Ethnography of the Red Sea (MARES) project team at Exeter,[3] which included John P. Cooper, Chiara Zazzaro, Lucy Semaan[4] and Julian Jansen Van Rensburg.[5] Drawing on ethnography, history, semantics and archaeology, the aim of the MARES project was to analyse the human and non-human interactions of the maritime cultural landscape with the objective of understanding how people inhabited the landscape and navigated the seascapes from antiquity to the present time. My work throughout the period covered tangible and intangible maritime culture. I coordinated some interviews with John P. Cooper, while he and Chiara Zazzaro conducted surveys, measuring the watercraft's lines and profile sections. (Their findings will be published in a forthcoming work.) Together with Lucy Semaan, they also collected samples of the different types of timber used in dhow construction; all three drew on both ethnography and archaeology.

Working through my field notes and audio/video recordings, a number of issues came to the fore. First, there are no prescribed rules regarding how to conduct interviews and how to sift through the material. Each situation to some extent dictates its own, so the researcher has to be prepared to be opportunistic. Observation is crucial when noting the environmental landscape and the work or event that is taking place. Thus, I watched with eagerness as the sailors at Djibouti harbour loaded a dhow with a cargo of food and domestic items; I sailed on a dhow with passengers from Tadjourah to Rassali in Djibouti; at Khor al-Ghureirah, south of Yemen, I saw the crews cleaning and repairing their dhows; I listened to the chanting of the conch fishermen in Suakin, Sudan, as they pushed their dhow on to the shore; on board a dhow at Safaga, Egypt, the *rayyes* (captain) explained the hoisting of the yard and sail and the various rigging ropes; and meeting a fisherman at the Cave of the Jinns on Greater Farasan Island, off the Saudi coast, was an experience that illuminated the spiritscape of the Arabian Red Sea. Other experiences unrelated to what I was studying are interesting to note. At Tadjourah quay in Djibouti a crowd made up of both young and old seemed to cheer the MARES team as we arrived. Alas, it soon became apparent that the crowd was not there to welcome us; rather, they were eagerly awaiting a consignment of *qat* (an amphetamine-like stimulant contained in the leaves of the *Catha edulis* shrub) that was also on the dhow we had taken from Djibouti City. The chewing of *qat*, of course, is an integral part of the cultural life of these maritime communities.

The time spent talking with these people provided ample opportunities to observe their relationships with the wider maritime community and try to understand their perspectives and behaviours. Noting the information, observing how the interviewees spoke and interpreting their body language was one thing, but it was also necessary to reflect on their different perceptions of the landscape and seascape, how they went about their daily business and why they behaved in particular ways. All of the interviewees were male with the exception of Ruqayya Hassan Mahalla,[6] the 83-year-old widow of a sea captain by the name of Abdalla of Obock. It is difficult for a man to interview a woman on the shores of the Red Sea; as Lorenzo Ricciardi wrote in 1980, 'the world of the dhows is a man's world'.[7] It must be said that my interview with Ruqayya was conducted in company of a dozen men and boys, all of whom seemed rather uncomfortable at her candour when revealing details of her husband's slave-trafficking activities. Clearly, women are a great untapped repository of information in the region, and more female researchers are needed to unlock this.

The question of what people say and how they say it is crucial to this inquiry. Interpreting people's experiences and opinions through the prism of one's own cultural expectations is a trap to be avoided at all costs. Here, knowledge of the target language – Arabic, in this case – is a great asset, as it enables the researcher to move much closer to his subjects.

Interpreting the data is not straightforward. For example, at Khokha, Yemen, we found partially constructed wooden dhows that had been left unfinished for many years. When asked for an explanation, our informants mentioned the cost of wood, loss of skills, migration and so on. However, we conjectured that the real reason might be that the Yemeni Government was sponsoring the building and purchase of fibreglass boats, with additional financial aid in the form of discounted fuel and fishing equipment. Although this could not be confirmed, it was a strong possibility as this was the situation elsewhere in the Red Sea. Our informants' reticence was no doubt due to their reluctance to imply any criticism of the government – another widespread phenomenon in the region. Maritime ethnography may shed light on an area where there is no or little written evidence because we, as researchers, have access to the words of the people and their surviving practices. We have a responsibility not only to document those words but to understand and interpret them.

IN THE FIELD

A qualitative (socio-cultural ethnographic) approach was applied in this inquiry to gain an understanding of the tangible and intangible culture of the dhow and its people, and to search for answers as to how and why certain practices and behaviours were adopted and developed. Most of the meetings were conducted on a one-to-one basis, though sometimes I met groups of people. The latter proved to be beneficial, as some individuals' comments steered the discussion into topics that I had not previously thought to explore. In such gatherings the usual custom is for the sheikh or the most senior man in terms of age to do the talking, while the rest listen in silence. Sometimes, though, if one of the less-senior elders interjected, the conversation could take a different turn. On one or two occasions, sitting in a circle with a number of elderly people, I lost track of the subject under discussion as several of them argued among themselves about who should provide the information I needed. Tact and patience were often required, but eventually my questions – and more besides – would be answered.

Some 80 per cent of the informants were either semi-literate or illiterate, although some were impressively articulate. With the exception of a few informants who spoke Bejāwī in Sudan, Afari in Djibouti and Tigrinya in Eritrea, knowledge of spoken Arabic helped me to communicate with the majority of the people on the African and Arabian coasts, who, as I gradually learned, spoke a Red Sea *lingua franca*. Ethnographers who do not speak the target language are always at a disadvantage, which can lead to the misrepresentation of facts in both the original study and subsequent citations. A sound maritime technical register of Arabic, which I have acquired over 40 years of ethnographic fieldwork, gave me access to all the places I visited. Gatekeepers, people who travel ahead and make the necessary contacts, and guides were occasionally surprised that I could converse fluently with the informants as they themselves lacked the necessary technical maritime Arabic. However, the guides during my 2007 field trip – Awad al-Subhi in Yanbu al-Bahr, Ibrahim al-Sharif and Rashid al-Balaw in El Wejh and Abdallah al-Qahtani of Ummlejj – were familiar with the dhow world and could convey the reason for my research to the people they contacted.[8] Their introductions helped the interviewees and I to understand each other. Wandering in alone, without a guide, can cause serious difficulties in this part of the world.

My essential tools in the field were a notebook, an audio recorder and a camera. Prior to each visit, I would enlist the help of a gatekeeper or guide, preferably someone I knew personally, who would prepare a schedule and obtain the necessary permits with the local sheikhs and mayors. For example,

Fahad Al-Sharif from Jeddah, who introduced me to a number of people in Qunfudha, Saudi Arabia, in 2013,[9] was instrumental in explaining my role as an ethnographer and my maritime interests to the interviewees. This made a significant difference as they were able to understand my work as chronicling a maritime heritage that is fast disappearing.

Ethnographic research requires patience and perseverance as obtaining permits and contacts can be a slow process. I always tried to clarify each individual situation with the guide and establish a sense of mutual trust between us. It is far easier to observe behavioural patterns after the guide has explained some of the unique attitudes and practices of the host places. Such discussions turned out to be extremely helpful throughout my research.

Security is a prime concern in coastal regions and a foreign visitor always experiences keen scrutiny, but the police were generally helpful provided they were informed of my movements. In Yemen a soldier kept guard wherever the MARES team visited and during interviews in Khor al-Ghureirah in 2009. Having a soldier looking over one's shoulder is not easy for either the interviewer or the interviewee; I could see suspicion in the latter's eyes. But the military presence was deemed a necessity for the protection of foreigners. The Egyptian Red Sea coast is guarded by mounted camel police to monitor, among other things, illegal fishing. Once, in 2003, they spotted me and my guide, Mohammed Gaballah Musaid, during an interview with some fishermen on the shore outside Quseir. They came over to interrogate us as to our business. Mohammed endeavoured to explain the purpose of my work, but permission was revoked even though my papers were in order and we were politely escorted back to the road.

Fishermen are generally wary of the police and soliciting information from them has to take this into account; all in all, though, I found local policemen to be courteous and helpful. In 2007 one of them, unprompted, greatly enhanced my interview with the fisherman Marzuq Muhammad al-Ilaj by asking a series of interesting and appropriate questions.[10] I asked the policeman how he knew so much about the subject and it turned out that his father was a fisherman. He was happy to get involved, but I am not so sure about the fisherman, who was left rather intimidated and suspicious.

All of the interviewees were asked if they were willing to have their voices recorded and their names documented. The interviews themselves were semi-structured; I wanted people to feel relaxed and free to discuss any subject they wished, rather than think that they had to answer all of my prepared questions. This is good practice that I have followed for the past four decades. In certain regions, however, there are some topics about which an ethnographer is advised to exercise a degree of caution. For instance, many Egyptians, Yemenis,

Djiboutians and Farasanis believe in *jinns* (good and evil spirits), but they rarely wish to talk about them. Similarly, in Suakin, Sudan, the Beja and other sub-groupings are firm believers in magic (*siḥr*) and show this by wearing amulets (*ḥijābs*) with Qur'ānic writing or magical figures, but all of the information they provided was disclosed in secret, as they were afraid of persecution by the authorities. Talking about slaves was also problematic; in general, neither Sudanese nor Saudis were willing to discuss this subject, though Farasan Island was an exception, but the Eritreans and Djiboutians were more relaxed and provided some interesting information (see Chapter 16).

The question of the reliability of information gathered is quintessential to any ethnographic inquiry. Red Sea Africans and Arabians are polite and do their best to provide useful details, although patience is required when they run off at tangents and it can be difficult – or even impossible – to get a straight answer to a straight question. If the informant is an old man, there is always the risk that he does not remember clearly, has misunderstood the question or has trouble hearing it. Failing memory is a recurrent problem but may be resolved by asking the same question in different ways and at different times. There is also the danger that some informants will tell you what they think you want to hear, will try to direct the conversation to what they think you ought to know, or will remain selective about what they disclose for many reasons, be they political or ethnic. For instance, in 2004 the Rashayda, originally from Saudi Arabia, were keen to assert that they were the only dhow builders of any consequence in Suakin, whereas 13 years later the Hadandawa from the same port town told another ethnographer that they had been engaged in boat building for many centuries and still practised it to that day.[11] Hence, it is wise to be wary of exaggeration. All this, of course, is a natural part of human behaviour. Anecdotes may be embellished, particularly when the subject is *jinns* or a gale that supposedly almost claimed the life of the interviewee. An experienced ethnographer learns to sift through material carefully, with some sceptical reservations, as some data may be patchy or contradictory.

Stories are told down the generations, but while the informants could often remember their fathers' and uncles' tales, very few could recall those related by their grandfathers. The source material was simply too remote. Their own recollections were, of course, much clearer, but memory can be a fickle instrument and it is easy to forget, perhaps through neglect or losing contact with the past.[12] My presence often acted as a catalyst, triggering recollections because of my questions. The lack of relevant material culture from the past – such as photographs, nautical instruments or diving equipment – was disappointing but understandable in poor fishing and trading communities. However, there was still an abundance of maritime material culture on the coast and in dhow-building yards, which helped me to understand the informants' current relationship to the coastal landscape and the sea. These artefacts and others were important 'vehicles of communal memory and memory-transmission',[13] as I will show in Chapter 18.

Repetitive information may lead down a cul-de-sac, but each interview usually generates something new. Such was the case with the 77-year-old skipper Youssef Omar Mohamed of Obock, Djibouti, a man of great experience.[14] I interviewed him several times in October 2009 because he invariably provided extra information on winds, navigation, life on board ship, port protocols and so on. And there was the added bonus that he was always keen to sing, with a powerful voice, a variety of sea songs.

On some occasions I reached saturation point and work came to a halt as there seemed nobody else to provide new information. Then there was a sense of frustration when contacts failed to show up or the content of interviews proved to be worthless. An ethnographer has to be ready to deal with such disappointments. Sometimes you wish you had more time. On our last day in Massawa in 2011, a middle-aged sea captain, Muhsin Saud Muhsini, came forward to talk to John P. Cooper and myself about the rising and setting of stars, how this is used to predict the pearling season, and sailing in the inter-monsoon period.[15] It was a very productive meeting and at the end Muhsin told us that a very old acquaintance of his was even more knowledgeable on these subjects. Unfortunately, it was too late in the day to arrange a visit and we had to leave for Asmara, the capital, the following morning, so we never benefited from that knowledge.

During research, quality wins out over quantity every time. In 2009 I met a fisherman from Mocha who was curious to see a stranger and particularly one chasing dhows. Now in his 60s, his name was Said Mohammad Alaiwa and he had worked for many years as a boatswain, having first set out for sea at the age of 20.[16] We spoke for no more than ten minutes, but his information was so precise and detailed that I longed for more time with him. He managed to sum up topics with great concision while making some interesting comments on seamanship. Such a good informant cancels out all the frustration and makes all the hard work seem worthwhile.

Interviews were held in various locations, from private residences to public places: in the souq, on the shore, at dhow yards, outside mosques and under trees after *'aṣr* (afternoon) or *'ishā'* (evening) prayers. As mentioned earlier, the Red Sea peoples are kind and often go out of their way to help (see Plate 15). They are also enthusiastic when talking about their maritime heritage, though sometimes I could tell they were wondering why on earth this stranger had travelled thousands of kilometres to talk to them about their folk traditions and practices, especially as all of the maritime professions tend to be badly paid and held in low esteem.

Of those who were willing to share their knowledge, I always tried to note the name, age and occupation of the person I was interviewing (see Table 2.1). Sometimes, however, this was impossible because the informant, having offered his testimony, would simply retreat back into the crowd. For instance, an old sea captain from Khor al-Ghoreirah approached me and volunteered some valuable information on the maritime calendar but disappeared before I could learn either his name or his age.[17] He seemed a particularly interesting person and the episode has stuck in my mind. One of the great joys of ethnography is that the research process provides countless opportunities to meet a wide variety of people, and I feel particularly fortunate in being allowed access to their world.

PLACES VISITED

I interviewed 166 informants, ranging in age from early 20s to over 100,[18] in 31 different locations (see Table 2.1 and Maps 1, 2, 3, and 4).

Egypt: Quseir, Safaga and Mersa Alam

The ethnographic fieldwork on the Egyptian Red Sea coast was undertaken in Quseir and two neighbouring fishing towns, Safaga and Mersa Alam, in three consecutive trips (March 2002, March and April 2003 and February 2004). The first of these was a pilot field trip whereas the subsequent two were much longer.[19] Quseir was chosen because of its historical links with the Nile and the Hijazi coast, and the chief aim was to record and document mariners' experiences at sea, trading and fishing practices and dhow-building methods (see Figure 2.1). Quseir was a busy pilgrim port for more than 150 years while the sea trade with the Sudan and the Hijazi coast flourished, but both of these functions dwindled as the days of sail drew to a close. Today, it is a fishing town with an estimated population of 24,653.[20] Its port is located to the south-east of the town, where fishing craft dominate the small harbour quay (*sigāla*). Most of the vessels are wooden and motorized, though a small but significant minority still use sails.

Of the 33 people I interviewed in Quseir, Safaga and Mersa Alam, most were members of the Arabic-speaking 'Ababda tribe of Beja origin[21] and 23 were mariners with considerable sailing experience across the Red Sea. Safaga, which lies 86.6 km to the north of Quseir and has a population of around 35,000, was once a commercial port and is now an active fishing town with some boat-building activity. It is known for its phosphate mines and export trade, and it continues to ferry pilgrims and workers to the Arabian coast.

TABLE 2.1 Occupations and ages of people interviewed between 2002 and 2013.

Occupation	**Age 20–40**	**Age 41–60**	**Age > 61**	**Age unknown**	**Number of informants**
Dhow owner	–	1	2	1	4
Dhow builder	5	12	7	–	24
Dhow model maker	–	1	–	1	2
Sea captain	–	16	12	1	29
Sea captain's wife	–	–	1	–	1
Boatswain	–	3	2	–	5
Mariner/fisherman	7	18	22	5	52
Head of fisheries	–	–	–	2	2
Pearl diver/ shell or conch collector/fisherman	2	3	9	1	15
Pearl merchant	1	1	1	–	3
Camel driver	1	–	4	–	5
Rope maker	–	1	–	–	1
Blacksmith	–	1	–	–	1
Gate guard	–	1	–	–	1
Porter	–	–	1	–	1
Coal trader	–	–	1	–	1
Shop owner	–	–	2	–	2
Boat researcher	–	–	1	–	1
Senior police officer	–	–	–	1	1
Folklorists/historian	2	2	2	6	12
Archaeologist	1	–	–	–	1
Museum director	1	–	–	–	1
Researcher (eco-marine culture)	–	1	–	–	1
Total	20	61	67	18	166

Mersa Alam, 141.2 km to the south of Quseir, is a small fishing town where traditional dhows still form part of the landscape. However, its main industry is phosphate mining, with tourism perhaps in second place.

The Hijazi coast: Yanbu al-Bahr, Ummlejj and El Wejh

Egyptian and Hijazi merchants and skippers shared a life on both coasts as they traded commodities and transported pilgrims back and forth. My first trip to the Hijazi coast was a short pilot study in 2007, but it opened my eyes to the way the landscape had changed, as I saw the ruins of merchants' houses and storehouses

MAP 1 Places on the African and Arabian shores visited by the author between 2002 and 2013 (cartography by Anna Sirica).

FIGURE 2.1 Quseir's seafront in the 1920s, showing a camel caravan and passengers either setting off for or returning from the Arabian coast, with a *sanbūk* in the background (photo by Henri R. Maurer, courtesy of the Archaeological Society of Alexandria).

close to the seafront.[22] I revisited the region in 2013 with the aim of collecting data on fishing activities and recording sea shanties in Yanbu al-Bahr, Ummlejj and El Wejh (see Map 1). The region is a centre of sea songs, a tradition that is sufficiently important to include as part of the maritime cultural landscape, particularly as knowledge of it is decreasing rapidly as the older seamen pass away. I was accompanied by the ethno-linguist Muhammad Alhazmi, a native of the Hijaz,[23] and we interviewed 26 informants, many of whom were fishermen.

Yanbu al-Bahr, north-west of Jeddah, is the largest port town with a population of 188,430 in the 2004 census.[24] It has provided a good harbour for both trade and pilgrim ships for centuries. Ummlejj, which lies 438 km north of Jeddah, is a smaller port town with a long maritime tradition. No traditional watercraft are found in the harbour, which is now full of fibreglass boats (Figure 2.2). About 250 km further north is El Wejh, a harbour town in Tabuk Province; it has a

FIGURE 2.2 Ummlejj harbour, dominated by fibreglass boats, 2013 (photo by the author).

good anchorage and an active fishing community among the population of 30,512.[25] Dhow building was once well-known in all three towns, but there is no evidence of it today.

Sudan: Suakin

The Sudanese coast has good fishing grounds that were much visited by Egyptian fishermen until the 1970s. I chose to visit Suakin in 2004 because it is a unique centre of conch collecting and dhow building. The fieldwork comprised interviews with 21 people, mostly from the Hadandawa and Rashayda tribal groups.[26]

Today's city developed from an old island town that was populated by a few thousand merchants and traders until the 1920s – a period that some elderly sea captains could still recall in some detail. Suakin had an estimated population of 42,456 in 2008[27] consisting mainly of very poor nomads and herders, a small percentage of whom work seasonally on the land and/or at sea. The dhow-building site is located around a large semicircular *mersa* (coastal inlet) south-west of the old town.

Yemen: Aden, Khor al-Ghureirah, Khokha and Mocha

The Yemeni fieldwork of February 2009 was my first collaborative work with two members of the MARES project team, John P. Cooper and Chiara Zazzaro. We visited Aden and neighbouring Khor al-Ghureirah, Khokha and Mocha, before Cooper and Zazzaro continued further north, to Hodeidah and al-Salif. Our original plan was to undertake a preliminary investigation in order to conduct a more detailed one in the future. However, we never made the second trip as the political situation deteriorated over the ensuing years and access to the coast became ever more difficult. My colleagues' work in Yemen and other parts of the southern Red Sea coast produced orthographic drawings of the dhows, while I continued to collect data on seafaring, trade and fishing. In total, I interviewed 15 people in Yemen.

Our fieldwork started in Aden, some 170 km east of the strait that separates the Red Sea from the Gulf of Aden – Bab el-Mandeb. The city's population was estimated at 760,923 in 2012.[28] We conducted work at Dokkat al-Ghaz, in an area called Ma'alla, a well-known dhow-building centre, but also made a series of day trips to fishing sites – Kheesa, Seera, Bir Fuqum and Bureiqa – gathering data on dhow typology, dhow building and fishing (see Map 2).

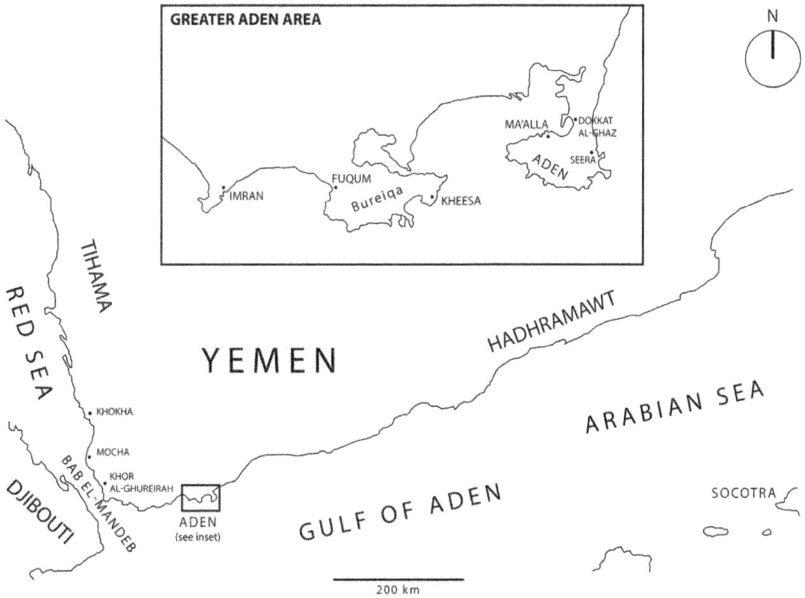

MAP 2 Places visited by the author in the Gulf of Aden and Greater Aden area, 2009 (cartography by Anna Sirica).

FIGURE 2.3 Chiara Zazzaro documenting the different types of dhow at Khor al-Ghureirah, 2009 (photo MARES by John P. Cooper).

FIGURE 2.4 The author interviewing fishermen in the lagoon at Khor al-Ghureirah, 2009 (photo MARES by John P. Cooper).

Heading westwards, we proceeded to the fishing village of Khor al-Ghureirah, about 5 km north-east of Bab el-Mandeb. The general landscape and topography of the region are impressive, and it provides a safe haven for dhows heading for or leaving the Red Sea (see Figures 2.3 and 2.4).

From Khor al-Ghureirah we travelled north to Mocha, an old coffee-trading port that once hosted large ships from India as well as Ottoman, Egyptian and European East India Company vessels. It was the hub of the Red Sea for several centuries, but all that remains of the once-bustling port are the ruins of merchants' houses, craftsmen's workshops and storerooms. Further north, at Khokha, many vessels had been dragged on to the lagoon's shore; some may have been operative, but others were unfinished or abandoned[29] (see Chapter 9).

Yemen proved to be an invaluable location in which to study dhows. Although no dhow building takes place there now, the older people were involved in repair work, and the unfinished and abandoned dhows that were lying along the coast provided plentiful information about methods of construction, including one technique that is unique to the Red Sea. Meanwhile, the working dhows, both trading and fishing, enabled us to build up a holistic picture of current activity in the south of Yemen (see Chapter 9).

Djibouti: Djibouti City, Tadjourah and Obock

The Republic of Djibouti is on the opposite shore of Bab el-Mandeb from Yemen. It is a small country with a coastline of just 314 km and an estimated population of 810,179 in 2014.[30] My research colleagues and I spent three weeks there in Ocotber 2009, visiting Djibouti City, Tadjourah (about 173 km to the north-west on the northern shore of the Gulf of Tadjourah) and Obock (in the north-east of the country). Tribal Afar and Issa (Somali), both Cushitic speakers, have lived in this area since antiquity;[31] they are primarily cattle herders and farmers. A third ethnic group – Yemenis of the Ḥaqmī and Mashlīḥī tribal groups – work seasonally, cultivating the land, fishing and/or in the maritime trade. Around half of the 35 people I interviewed were members of the Afar group, while the other half were Yemeni.

Djibouti City's port occupies a prime strategic position for both Red Sea and Indian Ocean sea traffic. The fishing town of Tadjourah, which was an important medieval urban centre,[32] is today the residence of Sultan Abdoulkader Houmed Mohamed (r. 1985–). Obock, 62 km to the north-east of Tadjourah, is a small fishing village; a number of its citizens are of Yemeni origin and practically all are engaged in the fishing industry, although some, not necessarily Yemenis, are involved in animal husbandry (see Map 1).

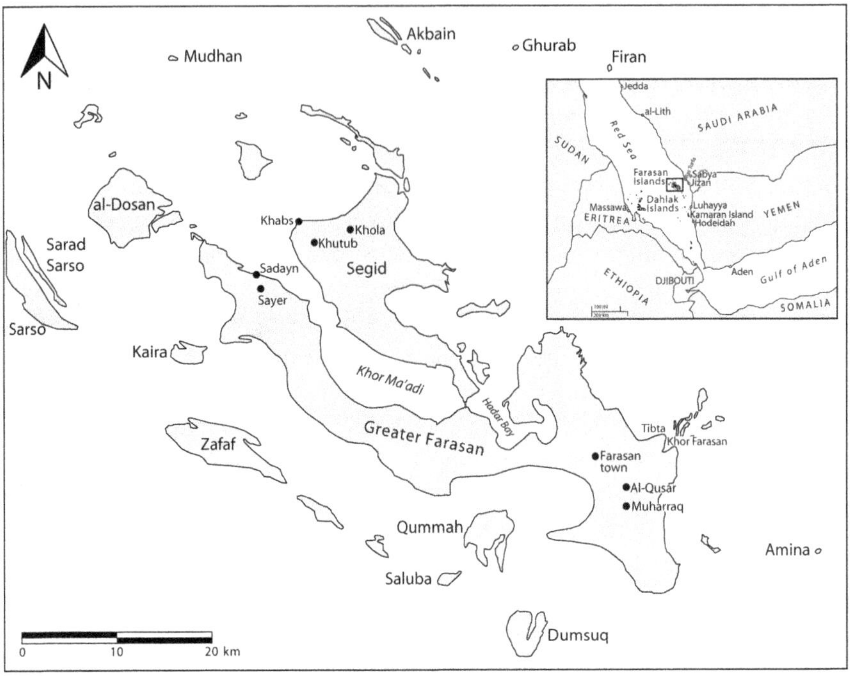

MAP 3 The Farasan Archipelago, showing the islands visited by the author and the MARES team, 2010: Greater Farasan, Segid and Qummah (cartography by Chiara Zazzaro and John P. Cooper).

Saudi Arabia: The Farasan Islands and Jizan

Pearl diving has been practised in the Red Sea since ancient times. While there are many accounts of harvesting oysters for pearls in the Dahlak Archipelago, Eritrea, not much is known about this activity in the Farasan Archipelago, 40 km due west of Jizan in Saudi Arabia, which was why we organized a field trip to the region. I undertook a pilot visit to the islands with John P. Cooper and Peter Harrigan, an independent researcher, in January 2010 before returning to conduct the fieldwork from 11 to 29 May 2010.

Although our focus was on pearl diving in the archipelago, we extended our study to include Jizan (see Map 3 inset) because of its dhow-building activity. A port town, Jizan had a population of 127,743 in 2014.[33] At the Al Hafa dhow yard, Cooper and Zazzaro documented dhow-building techniques and made line drawings of racing dhows,[34] while I collected information from the master dhow builders on maritime trade and life at sea (see Figure 2.5). Lucy Semaan, who joined us for this fieldwork, collected timber samples and studied their use in boat building.[35]

The Farasan Islands are noted for their corals and shells. The archipelago consists of 84 islands, although only three are inhabited by the 1,000-or-so residents:[36] Greater Farasan (57 km long and more than 20 km wide); Segid (109 sq. km), which is connected to the large island by a causeway; and a much smaller island, Qummah (14.3 sq. km), which is surrounded by unusually clear waters and boasts a cave system that has long provided shelter for fishermen (see Map 3).[37] Most of the islanders are fishermen who also work as farmers during the date harvesting season, some herdsmen graze their goats, and a large number of people work for the governorate of Jizan Province. Our data-collection included gathering information from fishermen, divers on dhow pearling trips, life on board the dhows, oyster and shell collecting, the pearl merchants, the weighing of pearls and pearl trading.[38] Part of the fieldwork involved observing and photographing the divers at work on the pearl beds (see Chapter 15). I interviewed a total of 26 informants, sometimes with the help of John P. Cooper and Robert Carter from University College London at Doha, who joined us for a week as an observer.[39]

MAP 4 Places visited by the MARES team in Eritrea, 2013 (cartography by Anna Sirica).

FIGURE 2.5 The MARES team at the Al Hafa dhow yard in Jizan, 2010. Rear (left to right): Abdou Ibrahim Bilghaith (master dhow builder's son), Muhammad Hadrami Abdo (assistant dhow builder), the author, Lucy Semaan, Abdo Mohammed Aqili (our guide), Chiara Zazzaro. Front (left to right): Majid Ibrahim Bilghaith (master dhow builder's son), Ibrahim Ahmed Bilghaith (master builder), John P. Cooper (photo MARES).

Eritrea: Massawa

Our next field trip was to Massawa, Eritrea, in 2011, which covers an area of 477 sq. km and had an estimated population of 36,700 in 2016.[40] John P. Cooper and I planned to investigate the tangible and intangible maritime culture by asking questions relating to seafaring, fishing and trade in the region.[41]

In the Islamic medieval period and earlier, Massawa stood at a significant strategic crossroads in the trade network of the northern Red Sea, Yemen and India. Moreover, for several centuries, the Dahlak Archipelago (over 200 islands), off the Massawa coast, boasted a flourishing pearling trade.[42] More recently, World War II and Eritrea's 30-year fight destroyed the infrastructure, but the town is gradually recovering and transforming itself into a modern port with a dockyard, boosted by burgeoning trade with Saudi Arabia. However, fishing also continues to sustain the coastal economy. Causeways connect mainland Massawa to two islands: Tuwaled and old Massawa.

FIGURE 2.6 Abandoned wooden dhows near the Kobri (causeway), Tuwaled, Massawa, 2011 (photo MARES by the author).

We conducted most of our 23 interviews in Massawa's fishing dhow harbour – Sigalat Lamba – where we spoke to a pair of dhow builders as well as the fishermen. Many of the latter were from the islands of Dihil, Dese and Dahlak Kebir in the archipelago (see Plate 3), while a few were natives of three villages to the south-east of Massawa – Afta, Zula and Malkato (see Map 4) – which have mixed economies based on cattle herding, farming and fishing. The Afta and Zula villagers mainly spoke Tigrinya, but many of them could converse fluently in Arabic because of their Yemeni origins or dealings with Arabic speakers.[43]

No dhows are built in any site we visited, although a number were undergoing repair or lying disused at Tuwaled and elsewhere (see Figure 2.6). A similar picture of abandoned dhows is seen in Djibouti. The landscape of traditional dhows is gradually fading away as ever more African countries switch to motorized vessels.

Saudi Arabia: Jeddah and Qunfudha

Eight interviews were scheduled for Jeddah and Qunfudha in 2013. Jeddah has been Saudi Arabia's main pilgrim port for many centuries, so I was expecting to see some traditional trading and pilgrim dhows near the quay. Unfortunately, there was nothing except for a few old, abandoned dhows on the shore. The old port has also disappeared to make way for new port facilities that cater for the thousands of pilgrims who make their way to Mecca each year. Some traditional houses survive in an old quarter of the city, but they are almost lost among the new tower blocks. Steam ferries carrying pilgrims still arrive in Jeddah and return to Egypt, Sudan, Eritrea and Yemen, but it is a different world to the one described by the old fishermen I met at the city's Bangala fish market. An early-morning fish auction proved to be especially informative as it revealed the wide variety of fish caught in different parts of the Red Sea. Qunfudha, 335 km to the south of Jeddah, was my final stop in April 2013. In the past its harbour was visited by large vessels from the western Indian Ocean as it was well connected with the caravan trade routes across the Arabian Desert. Here, the focus was on sea shanties, and I recorded three singers (see Chapter 11).

THE PLEASURE AND PAIN OF FIELDWORK

My fieldwork took me to a number of key places where communities still survive on fishing and small-scale coastal trading. Many of my informants had vivid memories of the days of sail, a time of hardship and poverty and, in some circumstances, courage and heroism. As well as the excitement of collecting new data, the field trips provided wonderful opportunities to discover new places, communicate with new people and appreciate the Red Sea landscape. Some aspects were not so welcome – sleeping rough in tents; encountering scorpions and spiders; listening to the howling of hyenas and desert dogs in the middle of the night – but on the whole it was a positive experience.

It is interesting to note that oral history is gaining momentum in the Middle East, among folklorists, newspaper journalists and media correspondents on television and radio. It is very encouraging to see a wealth of material collected on the Saudi coast, some of which has been published in print or uploaded online. Of note are the works of: Khālid Muḥammad Bāṭarfī of Jeddah,[44] Ṣāliḥ Bin 'Abd al-Laṭīf 'Alyān Al-Sayyid of Yanbu al-Bahr,[45] Ibrāhīm Muftāḥ of Greater Farasan[46] and M.S. Ḍirār[47] and Shadia Taha of Sudan.[48] Their ethnographic research provides substantial data on much that was not known before; importantly, it gives valuable insights into the day-to-day lives of the current and older generations of mariners and their experiences at sea in the coastal landscapes and seascapes of the region. These recollections are all the more vital as technology has changed their lifestyles forever, and the younger mariners have little or no understanding of the hardships endured by previous generations.

The need for ethnography is pressing, and I hope that my contribution will enhance this corpus of material. Several of the people I interviewed will surely be dead before this book is published, but I trust that their memories will live on in these pages.

3

THE GEOGRAPHIC CONTEXT

ما يزال البحر غافيا في سكينة شاملة
ثم يسري شفاع شمس فيهم الليل بالرحيل
وتتموج صفحة الماء برقة بالغة
وفي الضوء الخافت يستيقظ النهار

'The sea still slumbers in deepest peace
A sudden sunbeam and night takes flight
The waves so gently now do tremble
In the soft light the day awakes'.
Anonymous, 1920s–1940s.[1]

GENERAL PHYSICAL FEATURES

The Red Sea connects to the Mediterranean through the Gulf of Suez in the north and to the Indian Ocean through Bab el-Mandeb and the Gulf of Aden in the south. It is approximately 1,900 km long and 300 km wide, with a surface area of about 450,000 sq. km.[2] The narrowest point is Bab el-Mandeb, at just 12 km wide. The western (African) littoral, which includes the southern coast of the Sinai Peninsula, is 2,450 km in length, while the eastern (Arabian) shore is roughly 2,640 km.[3] There are three distinct depth zones: shallow coral reefs, down to about 50 m; the seabed, which slopes from 500 m to 1000 m; and the median trench, which reaches a depth of 3,040 m.[4] The sea is predominantly blue-green due to the presence of blooms of the algae *Trichodesmium erythraeum*, which 'turn the sea a reddish brown colour'[5] when they die. Coastal Arabians use the word *ṭihār* to describe the dark blue of the deep sea, *biṭān* when referring to the greener, shallower waters and *jadra* when discussing the distance between the land and the deep sea area.[6]

CLIMATE

The Red Sea is 'one of the hottest and saltiest bodies of seawater in the world',[7] with an average salinity of 42 per cent,[8] compared to 38 per cent in the Indian Ocean,[9] and both coasts suffer from an inhospitable climate. In the north the surface water reaches an average temperature of 26°C in the summer, while in the south the average is 30°C. The heat and humidity on the coasts are oppressive, especially for visitors; one source reports that 'over 70 [per cent humidity] generally implies uncomfortable conditions and one over 80 per cent ... becomes] dangerous to health'.[10] One place that experiences particularly perilous temperatures is the low-lying Tihama (lit. 'intense heat') region, from Qunfudha, Saudi Arabia, to the south of Yemen at Bab el-Mandeb. This area 'is exposed to the burning heat of the sun'[11] throughout the year, according to the Finnish explorer G.A. Wallin (d. 1852). Slightly further north, as Angelo Pesce wrote, 'The Jeddah climate [...] [is] remarkable for the discomfort it caused unaccustomed people [...] [This] is related to the city's location on the Red Sea on the line between the Mediterranean and the monsoon type of climate'.[12] Yet, the local people are remarkably acclimatized to the hot, humid weather. Indeed, they seemed bemused when I asked how they coped before the advent of air-conditioning, which was introduced only around 50 years ago. For me, the heat and humidity were unbearable, even in a shaded room with fans.

The prevailing winds blow parallel to the shores. The wind in the north, at a latitude of 20°N, blows north-north-west throughout the year at an average speed of 7–12 km/h, but it can reach gale force in the Gulf of Suez and northern parts of the Red Sea during summer: 'The neighbourhood of Ra's Muḥammad, the southern tip of the Sinai peninsula, [is] especially feared because of the meeting of winds from the Gulfs of Suez and 'Aḳaba'.[13] From October to May, however, the wind sometimes blows from the south as a result of Mediterranean 'coastal depressions'. Heading south of 20°N, the winds are more predictable but seasonally reversible; from October to April, the prevailing wind blows south-south-east, while from May to September it blows north-north-west. In the Gulf of Aden the prevailing wind along the coast is south-easterly; the wind here coincides with the south-west monsoon that blows steadily from June to September.[14] The navigators' techniques for coping with these variable winds are discussed in Chapter 13.

The average annual rainfall in the Red Sea region is just 0.06 m. So, in general, the moisture in the air does not produce rain, but it is evident in dews and mists.[15] The Arabian shores experience 'high atmospheric humidity' but rain is scarce in the coastal region; the same is true of the Eritrean and

Djiboutian coasts, which share a desert climate – hot and arid. By contrast, even though the Sudanese coast forms part of the Eastern Desert, it consists of 'salt marsh' and 'semi-desert' areas that experience significant rainfall in winter.[16] Indeed, the rain can be torrential on the coastal hills. The Egyptian Red Sea littoral has a similar landscape, with hills running parallel to the coast, but it is very dry. During our conversation, Saad Abdallah Jouma, a camel driver from Tundura, near Mersa Alam, lamented: 'No rain since the eleventh month of 1996!'[17] Several other Egyptians told me that they expected to see rain only once a decade; but when it does rain, there are floods. In the mountainous region from Quft on the Nile to Quseir the water 'is occasionally precipitated with extraordinary suddenness and copiousness, and from the absence of soil on the rocks, it rushes off with exceptional violence', according to the traveller E.N. Buxton.[18] On desert coastal plains, such as those of Egypt and the Hijaz, 'Flash flooding [is] the main natural hazard posing [a] greater threat [to] life, constructions and even marine life', according to M.A. Azab in his report on the Egyptian Red Sea coast.[19]

Although long stretches of the coastline – the *sāḥil* – are sparsely populated, 'behind these barren coasts [lie] the rich Nile Valley, the fertile Ethio-Eritrean and Yemeni highland plateaus, and the Hijazi range of mountains with its oases'.[20] These fertile hinterlands give life to the arid coastal areas. Consider Quseir on the Egyptian Red Sea littoral, a five-day desert crossing from Quft and its supplies of grain and water. The Ethiopian highlands experience rain from May to October, yielding good crops.[21] Yemen has high fertile plateaux watered by the monsoon. In many parts of the southern region the coffee bushes grow in terraced fields. The coffee industry was once important for the coastal people as it was a trading staple, although recently the more profitable *qat* has become the dominant crop in the region. Of course, these people have never been entirely dependent on the hinterland; there has always been a good deal of sea traffic, importing and exporting, trading goods both regionally and as far as India.

THE CORAL REEF

The Red Sea is noted for its exceptional coral reefs; 'the richest biotopes in the world' and 'some of the finest examples' are found here.[22] The entire coral reef complex stretches to roughly 2,000 km of the shoreline and includes 15 different 'reef-building corals'.[23] Morphologically, the majority of the coral reefs are 'fringing reefs'. Thousands of years old, these develop just metres from the coastline.[24] Their growth is stimulated by 'warm sea-water and a generally steep sloping sea-bed where little sediment accumulates, together with moderate winds and a reduced tidal range'.[25] In total, around 180 to 200 types of coral are found in the Red Sea.[26] 'Soft or stony' coral grows slowly to a depth of some 55 m.[27] In the Farasan Islands, which are formed of 'fossil coral-reefs', there is a profusion of 'well-preserved' corals and shells.[28] The local navigators know these reefs well and proceed cautiously through often narrow channels.

The coral reefs on the Egyptian coastline are concentrated mainly in Hurghada, Safaga, Quseir and Mersa Alam, and at Ras Nosrany, Dahab and Nuweiba in the Gulf of Aqaba. Saudi Arabia's 'pristine' reefs are found at Haql, Maqna, Dhuba, Ummlejj, Matura, Lith, Hali and the Farasan Islands, while 'coastal development' around the industrial areas of Jeddah and Yanbu al-Bahr have caused some damage.[29] Sudan's reefs have 'the highest diversity of habitats and species in the region'.[30] In Djibouti, at the western end of the Gulf of Aden, the best-known reef area is around the Sept Frères Islands, which boast 'stunningly colourful soft corals', while 'maritime transport, port related activities, and other anthropogenic coastal pressures' have had a detrimental impact on the reefs in the Gulf of Tadjourah.[31] In a 2009 report, the Regional Organization for the Conservation of the Environment of the Red Sea and Gulf of Aden (PERSGA) stated: 'what makes Djibouti unique as an ecosystem is the profuse marine life' due to the mixing of Red Sea and Indian Ocean water.[32] The seawater in the Gulf of Aden itself is full of nutrients, but the hot climate and monsoonal winds are not conducive to the growth of coral, so 'fringing reefs' run parallel to just 5 per cent of the gulf's coast.[33] However, a number of offshore islands have 'healthy reefs', according to the PERSGA report.[34]

Recently, coral has been employed to treat multiple sclerosis, cancer and other chronic diseases,[35] and it has been used as 'a bone graft substitute to treat a wide range of bone-related problems'.[36]

Many of the nineteenth-century merchants' houses and mosques in the sea towns of Suakin,[37] Massawa, Jeddah, Hodeidah, Luhayya and the Farasan Islands were built out of coral stone (see Figure 3.1).[38] Angelo Pesce remarked that these buildings are 'naturally dictated by the characteristics of local building materials and by the demands of climate'.[39] Aylin Orbaşlı, a researcher in architectural regeneration, has suggested that 'Coral stone is light, relatively soft and therefore easy to work, and its porous irregular surfaces can provide a good key for mortars and rendering'.[40] Unfortunately, though, the region's high humidity means that coral buildings are relatively short-lived.[41]

Under normal circumstances, coral thrives in the Red Sea, but 'sudden rainfall; storms which may break-up shallow water corals; siltation [...] and of course natural predation' can all harm the delicate reefs.[42] Among the predators are butterfly fish and particularly parrotfish, which inflict damage by 'breaking-off large chunks of coral'.[43] Since the advent of human civilization in

FIGURE 3.1 A coral-stone building in the Sur quarter, Yanbu al-Bahr, 2007 (photo by the author).

the region, many reefs have also been disturbed and damaged by anchoring, the harvesting of coral and ever-increasing pollution.[44] The 'lack of mooring systems in [the Red Sea region] [...] increases the probability of coral damage from poor anchoring practices',[45] while oil leaks and dredging both contribute to marine pollution.[46] Moreover, some developers have deliberately destroyed coral reefs when building their industrial or even tourist projects.

MARINE BIODIVERSITY

Nevertheless, marine flora and fauna remain abundant in the Red Sea.[47] The coral reefs 'have given rise to an extraordinary range of ecosystems and biological diversity',[48] including mangroves, beds of seagrass, algal reefs and intertidal habitats.[49] Mangroves grow in areas that have 'waterlogged and saline soils of the intertidal zone'. There are two species: *Avicennia marina* (*shūra*), which is very common, and *Rhizophora mucronata* (*gandal*), which is found at only a few sites on the Red Sea.[50] Egypt has a small population of *Avicennia*, found in a number of inlets. There are 14 places along the Sudanese coast where *Avicennia* grows, with other species reported in the past. An ideal place for the growth of mangroves is the region between Port Sudan and Suakin, which is 'rich in tidal inlets especially at the seaward end of drowned valleys'. Meanwhile, south of Suakin to the border with Eritrea, the inlets are 'rich in alluvium' as a result of floodwater from the hills, which also aids the development of mangroves.[51] Both species are found along the El Wejh coast and its offshore islands in Saudi Arabia, whereas on the coast between Yanbu al-Bahr and Jeddah they are much less common due to oil and sewage pollution.[52] Greater Farasan offers fertile grounds for both *Avicennia* and *Rhizophora*, and other species have been recorded on the beaches.[53] Yemen's Red Sea littoral from Midi to Luheyya has a 'very flat *sabkha* [plain covered with salt] coastline'[54] with several narrow inlets where *Avicennia* grows. There is another rich mangrove site around Kamaran Island, with both species growing in lagoons and inlets.[55] Other mangrove forests are found around the small islands near the Hodeidah shoreline. At Khor al-Ghureirah, opposite Bab el-Mandeb, *Avicennia* grows densely in the upper channel of the bay.[56] In Djibouti there are mangroves at Ras Siyyan, Khor Angar, Godoria, Obock, Gaan-Maan and the Moucha and Maskali islands, with both species still found in abundance at Khor Angar and Godoria.

Mangrove forests protect the coastline from erosion by binding the soil together and reducing the impact of storms. They also provide a home for a variety of plants, animals and shorebirds as well as copious food for coastal fish. Moreover, for centuries, mangrove timber was used for boat building. However, in recent years the forests have suffered as trees have been felled for firewood, while camel grazing 'reduces the height of mangrove trees, their productivity, and their reproductive capacity'.[57]

Seagrass is generally found in inlets and lagoons 'because of the soft-bottom sediments' in such places. There are 11 species in the Red Sea, all but one of which are found along the coast of Saudi Arabia. They are considered 'the most productive habitats in the coastal environment' as they contribute to 'a highly productive ecosystem'.[58] Turtles, dugong, fish, crustaceans and seabirds all live in seagrass beds in shallow water, but these beds are being destroyed by urbanization and the increasing use of dredging by the fishing industry.[59] Seaweed is a valuable resource for reef building as it provides food for invertebrates and fish.[60]

There are some 1,350 species of fish in the Red Sea,[61] falling into two broad categories: reef fish and pelagic fish. The 300-or-so species of reef fish are small to medium-sized and usually brightly coloured.[62] They include snappers (*Lutjanidae*), groupers (*Serranidae*), parrotfish (*Scaridae*), squirrel fish (*Holocentridae*) and goat fish (*Mullidae*). The pelagic fish, such as sharks, spend most of their time in the deep sea and are 'mostly carnivorous'.[63] There are 54 species of shark in the Red Sea, with the most common 'the whitetip reef shark and the blacktip reef shark'.[64] These fish play an important role by maintaining 'the balance of reef-life' as they eat unhealthy creatures. Fishing for sharks is widespread in the southern Red Sea and their numbers are declining in consequence, leading to 'a gradual deterioration in the entire ecosystem'.[65] Other common sea creatures are: lobsters (*Panulirus homarus* and *P. versiclour*), deep sea lobsters (*Periulus semelli*)[66] and sea urchins (Echinoidea).[67] We shall look at Red Sea fishing in detail in Chapter 15.

The Red Sea archipelagos have 'a high diversity of marine biotopes, and many internationally important vertebrate groups',[68] including mammals and breeding turtles. There are 13 cetacean species, 'including dolphins, toothed and baleen whales', and about 4,000 dugong (*Dugong dugon*) – 'quiet harmless' mammals that feed on seagrass beds.[69] The latter are not commonly seen in either the Gulf of Aqaba or along the Sudanese coast, though they have been spotted in the Wejh Bank, Lith and Jizan.[70] Unfortunately, they tend to get entangled in trawlers' nets, so their population is in decline.

A PERSGA report lists three types of turtle in the Red Sea: 'the green (*Chelonia mydas*), hawksbill (*Eretmochelys imbricata*) and loggerhead (*Caretta caretta*)'. These are found in the Tiran Islands, the Wejh Bank and the Farasan Islands, Saudi Arabia; off the coast of southern Sinai in Egypt; around the Dahlak Islands in Eritrea; and near Ras Sharma and Dhobah, Yemen.[71] They are hunted for their meat, oil and eggs, while tourists continue to buy products made from their shells.

There are significant seabird 'nesting and feeding grounds' in Mait Island, Aibat, Saad ad-Din Island and Saba Wanak in the Gulf of Aden, the Farasan Islands in Saudi Arabia and Aden in Yemen.[72] The Farasan Islands in particular attract a number of shorebirds, *nawraz* 'seagulls' and *qumārī*, 'a variety of turtle doves'.[73] Seabirds' guano is harvested and turned into high-quality fertilizer.

THE ANCHORAGES

Many of the anchorages along the African and Arabian coasts provide 'convenient halting-places for the boats and vessels in their progress up and down the sea'.[74] With sand and/or coral bottoms to depths of 15–20 m, they are 'sheltered from sea and swell but because the land is usually low, not protected from the wind'.[75] There are two distinct types of anchorage in the Red Sea: the *mersā* and the *sherm*. The former (a dialectal form of the Arabic *marsā*) refers to 'natural bays, sometimes with creeks leading off them'.[76] These natural embayments are found on the western coast, notably at Mersa Alam, Mersa

Sha'ab and Mersa Haleib in Egypt, though they are rather less common south of Eritrea.[77] The word derives from *rasā* ('to cast anchor') and *arsā* ('to ground the ship'), giving the term *mirsā(h)* ('anchor of a ship').[78] *Sherm* (dialectal usage of the Arabic *sharm*) is also used to mean an inlet that is 'narrow, deep, often winding and push[es] several kilometres inland or into the fringing reef'.[79] In essence, the term means 'a canal' from the deep sea, a 'creek', deriving from *sharam* ('to slit or cut').[80] The two best-known *sherms* are at Port Sudan and Suakin on the African coast. The word is also applied to somewhat fewer anchorages on the Arabian coast, such as Sherm Wejh, Sherm Antar and Sherm Yanbu,[81] while further south both Jeddah and Jizan are well situated.[82]

At 60–92 m in depth, Suakin's channel is still sufficiently deep to accommodate large sailing vessels, but over the centuries it has continued to narrow due to the growth of coral reefs on both banks. As a result, steamships were unable to make their way up the inlet,[83] which allowed Port Sudan (built between 1905 and 1909) to become the Sudan's new centre of international trade by the 1920s.

Until recent years, Sherm Wejh and Sherm Yanbu were the two busiest harbours on the Arabian coast. Yanbu al-Bahr has 'a broad open harbour [...] of rather irregular shape', while El Wejh has 'a broader inlet, more rounded in outline'.[84] South of Jeddah, the term *khōr* is sometimes used in place of *mersā* or *sherm*, as at Khor Nohud, Khor al-Birq and Khor al-Wasm on the Saudi coast; Khor Segid and Khor Hasayif on the Farasan Islands;[85] and Khor al-Ghureirah in Yemen. This word is more commonly used to mean a bay, inlet or lagoon in the Arabian Sea and the Arabian–Persian Gulf regions.

IN CONCLUSION

Geographically, the Red Sea has a unique marine environment with varied natural habitats, coral reefs and numerous species of fish and other wildlife. The reefs are highly beneficial for the local human population, while the mangrove forests protect the coastline, encourage the growth of numerous plant species and provide shelter for animals and birds. Central to this marine environment is the dhow and the coastal people who have inhabited the landscape and seascape for thousands of years. The traditional wooden boats, which are designed to work in harmony with this environment, are far less liable to damage fragile marine ecosystems than modern fibreglass vessels and metal-hulled trawlers. Fishing remains a vital industry among many of the Red Sea communities that continue to sail these traditional craft, just as it was for their ancestors. It is their world – a world that now seems on the verge of extinction – that I document in the following chapters.

4

RED SEA CORRIDOR: THE EARLY MODERN PERIOD

عاشق النبي يصلي
هي حول هي حول
عاشق النبي يصلي

'For the love of the prophet;
heave, heave, heave
for the love of the prophet.'
Egyptian prayer/sea song.[1]

Since antiquity, the Red Sea has always been alive with commercial activity on both coasts, connecting the Mediterranean with the western Indian Ocean. Vital to this cross-regional activity were the commercial agents of the African and Arabian coasts who linked the camel-caravan land trade with the seaborne trade managed by the dhow owners and skippers at every port.[2] They traded goods regionally and in many respects 'complemented each other' at various times dictated by 'political and economic conditions'.[3]

THE TWO TRADING SEA ZONES OF THE RED SEA

From the mid-seventeenth century, the Red Sea was, in André Raymond's words, a 'divided sea',[4] demarcated by two distinct trading zones: the northern region, which stretched from the Egyptian ports to Jeddah and was controlled by the merchants of Cairo; and the southern region, with Mocha as the centre of the coffee trade, which was in the hands of Gujarati merchants.[5] In the latter area, the ships of Calcutta, Surat and Sumatra would arrive laden with 'spice, muslin and other fine stuffs [...] for the European market'.[6] Jeddah, on the dividing line between the two zones, was the entrepôt of transoceanic trade and, seasonally, the main pilgrim port. According to many sea captains I interviewed on the Egyptian, Saudi and Eritrean coasts, this division still existed until some 100 years ago. Captains and/or ship owners from the Hijaz and Yemen, some of whom also acted as merchants, are said to have settled on the African coast to manage their commercial affairs, north and south. Moreover, as Daniel Van Der Meulen (d. 1989) – for many years the Dutch consul in Jeddah – noted, the pilgrim activity in the north was 'the bread of the Hijaz',[7] as thousands reached the coast from Suez, Quseir, Safaga and Mersa Alam.

There is no doubt that the trans-regional commercial activity of the Early Modern period, accentuated by the annual pilgrimage to Mecca via Jeddah, made the Red Sea corridor one of the most dynamic shipping zones in the world. Egypt supplied grain from the Nile Valley to the barren lands of the Hijaz, while rice and grain were shipped from India to Yemen and the south-western Red Sea coast. Foodstuffs from the Sudanese Nile and the Ethiopian highlands reached the ports of Arabia, textiles came from Egypt and India, while metal, copper and manufactured products reached the African and Arabian coasts via Egypt. Many of the voyages from the seventeenth to the nineteenth century were undertaken by coffee exporters. The coffee trade animated the Red Sea, with the Ottomans controlling the market until Europeans – especially the Dutch and the English – entered the global competition with their East India companies[8] (see Figure 4.1).

In addition to coffee, pearls and mother of pearl from the Dahlak and Farasan archipelagos, gold and ivory from the highlands of Ethiopia and frankincense from Somalia were all shipped to Europe, India and the Middle East, while slaves from the north-east African coast were transported to Arabia and the Arabian–Persian Gulf.[9] Throughout the nineteenth century, the African ports of Quseir, Suakin and Massawa flourished, as did Djibouti and Berbera in the Horn of Africa. The latter, ideally located on the Gulf of Aden, hosted a famous annual fair at which sailing dhows from the lower Red Sea ports and Oman purchased products transported from the interior.

Much of this trade is attributed to the shrewd commercial management of the Ottomans, who controlled the Red Sea ports for 400 years (akin to what the Romans achieved in the first few centuries CE), and to the colonizing ambitions of Europe's Great Powers in the nineteenth century. The battle for European supremacy, in which the English, the French and the Italians were the main protagonists, eventually brought about political and economic transformation in the southern Red Sea region, while the Egyptians remained the dominant influence on the African and Arabian coastal towns. Although

FIGURE 4.1 Mocha harbour, 1680: galleys and Dutch East India Company ships with the Dutch and English factories in the background (from an engraving by the Dutch geographer Olfert Dapper).[10]

there was certainly some tension between the Europeans and the Egyptians, not to mention among the Europeans themselves, all sides were prepared to cooperate in the interests of stimulating trade through the Red Sea.

OPENING UP THE RED SEA

In the eighteenth century, European merchants' attempts to venture beyond the Mediterranean to the Red Sea were fraught with difficulties, as travel to this region was severely restricted by the Ottoman governors.[11] Nevertheless, in 1762, a Danish mission comprising five scientists managed to travel from Cairo to Suez, where they boarded a large dhow laden with pilgrims. They landed in Jeddah on 29 October and then proceeded south to Yemen, but four of the party died during the course of the expedition. The only survivor was Carsten Niebuhr (d. 1815), who kept a diary throughout his time in the region.[12] The most significant scientific discoveries were those of Peter Forsskål (d. 1763), a naturalist, whose research in the field of marine biology was pioneering.

Several decades later, during Muḥammad ʻAlī's reign (r. 1805–48), 'the windows of Egypt [were] thrown open' to Europe.[13] German scientists and explorers C.G. Ehrenberg (d. 1876) and F. Hemprich (d. 1825) investigated the marine life of the Red Sea, while their countryman E. Rüppell (d. 1884) 'laid down the foundations for our knowledge of [its] sea fishes'.[14] C.B. Klunzinger

(d. 1914), a medical doctor, worked as a sanitary inspector in Quseir for the Egyptian Khedive government from 1863 to 1869 and 1872 to 1875.[15] His research into the socio-cultural life of the Egyptians is renowned for its clear-sighted observations and ground-breaking interpretations.

When the Egyptian Khedive sultan Sa'īd Pasha (r. 1854–63) invited Ferdinand de Lesseps (d. 1894) to construct a canal between the Mediterranean and the Gulf of Suez, he paved the way for his country's economic growth and ushered in a new era of commerce to and through the Red Sea.[16] After much 'frustrating negotiation' with Sa'īd's successor Ismā'īl Pasha (r. 1863–79), de Lesseps finally completed the project in 1869 (see Figure 4.2).[17] The 192-km canal from Port Said to Port Suez may have been engineered by the French, but it was dug by Egyptians, and 120,000 of them perished in the course of its construction.[18] Unexpectedly, it was Britain that benefited most from the new waterway: 'British tonnage comprised 60 per cent of the total transiting the canal in its first year, three times that of French ships'.[19] Previously, British ships had travelled to and from India via the Cape of Good Hope, with a journey time of six months. The opening of the Suez Canal cut the duration to just eight weeks.[20]

Three great seas – the Mediterranean, the Red Sea and the Indian Ocean – were now connected. Therefore, the opening of the canal, which would prove to be 'of great commercial and strategic importance', no doubt also served as an incentive for colonial expansion.[21] For economic reasons, the Middle East and North Africa had finally opened at least some of their doors to the West. In the wake of the European merchants, Catholic and Protestant missionaries ventured into the poorer countries – Egypt, Sudan, Ethiopia, Yemen and Somalia – as well as the Levant. They presented themselves as educators or providers of medical care, but their true intention was to convert the locals to Christianity. In that respect, their missions were far from successful.

THE ARRIVAL OF THE STEAMSHIPS

The other great expansion of the Red Sea occurred with the invention of steam propulsion. Previously, a dhow voyage from Suez to Jeddah and Aden had been tortuous, as the journals of the Swiss Johann Ludwig Burckhardt (d. 1817), the Catalan Domènec Badia i Leblich (d. 1818) and the Englishman Richard Burton (d. 1890) all relate.[22] After 1869, the steamship brought both political and commercial changes to the Red Sea ports; Suez was now directly linked to the Mediterranean, a line of communication that accelerated the speed with which goods could be traded from the Mediterranean to the ports of the Indian Ocean and back,[23] whereas previously all goods had arrived in Suez from Cairo or

FIGURE 4.2 'The opening of the Suez Canal festival: the Arab Sheikhs and their followers listen to the performance' at Ismailia on the west bank of the canal, 1869 (courtesy Devon and Exeter Library).[25]

Quseir via the Nile.[24] Moreover, by setting up a telegraph office on Suakin Island in 1872,[26] the British transformed communications from India to Europe. Mail was carried by Peninsular and Oriental Steam Navigation Company (P&O) liners from Southampton to Alexandria via Gibraltar and Malta, and some carried passengers through the Red Sea en route to India.[27]

The combination of the Suez Canal and the new, faster steamships led to an exponential increase in the number of foreign visitors to the Red Sea region. They travelled on the steamers from Europe to India via the canal and would usually pause at one or more sea towns; Quseir, Suakin, Massawa, Hodeidah or Aden were favourite stops. Dhow hawkers would approach the passing steamers at Suez to sell artefacts to both crew and passengers,[28] although Valeska Huber points out that the 'Western travellers seldom had contact with the dhows'.[29] The majority of them 'contented themselves [...] with curiously observing these [wooden boats]'[30] with their lateen sails as they tacked alongside (see Figures 4.3 and 4.4). The passage down the Red Sea took four days, and the unacclimatized passengers frequently found the heat and humidity oppressive until the ship finally steamed through Bab el-Mandeb and into the open waters of the Gulf of Aden.[31]

Britain played a significant political and commercial role in the region due to its acquisition of Aden in 1839, Perim Island (Ar. Mayyun; a volcanic island

FIGURE 4.3 Entrance to the Suez Canal (postcard by Raphael Tuck & Sons, late nineteenth/early twentieth century).

FIGURE 4.4 Coaling at Port Said (postcard by Raphael Tuck & Sons, late nineteenth/early twentieth century).

in Bab el-Mandeb) in 1857 and increasing involvement in southern Arabia, whereas France and Italy 'confined their attention to the African shores'.[32] Mocha, once an international entrepôt which boasted Dutch and British East India Company factories (see Figure 4.1), was soon superseded by both Aden and Jeddah. Aden, which lies roughly halfway between Suez and Bombay, became a strategically important and vibrant port both transregionally and transoceanically, particularly after the British established a coaling station there. They built another in Port Said, at the Mediterranean end of the canal,[33] and created Port Sudan between 1905 and 1909, much to the detriment of the previously dominant port of Suakin. Meanwhile, the French founded Djibouti City, which became an international port, and the Italians used Massawa and Assab to develop their links with the Indian Ocean. Indian migrants started to gravitate towards the Red Sea ports as Britain strengthened its grip on the subcontinent, while the Arabian–Persian Gulf became a British protectorate, governed through Bombay.

THE STEAMER AND THE DHOW

Jeddah developed into a key port as the number of pilgrims using steamers increased throughout the nineteenth century. By the late 1860s, Egyptian and Ottoman steamships were picking up pilgrims from the ports of Suez, Quseir, Suakin and Massawa, while the trading dhows continued to sail up and down the Red Sea and into the Indian Ocean. Huge numbers of large Indian vessels would arrive at the port of Jeddah with foodstuffs and other commodities,[34] but this hectic traffic and the unsanitary conditions on board have been blamed for four major cholera epidemics in the city.[35] The 1835, 1865 and 1893 epidemics claimed the lives of thousands of pilgrims, particularly those travelling from India and South-East Asia.[36] Isabel Burton (d. 1896) reported that 'five hundred *per diem* died at Mecca' in the 1865 outbreak.[37] It seems highly probable that the Indian dhows carried the disease to Jeddah, and Mecca was certainly 'a spot for germination',[38] but the sea route to the Hijaz remained open. Burton reported that 600 *sanbūk*s and 30–40 steamships carried 80,000 pilgrims in 1869 alone.[39] Although there is a lack of written evidence, the pilgrims must have been especially vulnerable to disease while travelling in what must have been very cramped conditions on board ship. One source reports that hundreds of them died of infections en route back to Suez after completing the *ḥajj* in 1865.[40]

Other economic and political upheavals in the nineteenth and the first half of the twentieth century may have had an impact on both the steamship and the dhow. Consider the Mahdist Revolt against the Egyptian Government and

British colonial rule (1881–5), which brought great disruption to Suakin, generating an economic crisis that left the harbour paralyzed. Then, in 1948, the Red Sea ports suffered another serious economic blow when the Egyptian Government closed the Suez Canal to all sea traffic.

The steamer was certainly 'superior' to the dhow. As Dubois explains, it was 'less expensive, bigger, and could travel without refuelling for 2000 kilometers'.[41] Steamships also did not rely on seasonal trade winds, so their departure from ports was not dictated by these winds; nor were they delayed by the traditional methods of loading and unloading cargo. Moreover, they could steam straight through the Red Sea during high winds whereas the dhows would have to wear constantly, adjusting their sails in one direction or the other.

Yet the traditional sailing dhow continued to flourish, as we shall see in the next chapter.

5

THE RED SEA SAILING DHOW

على الشواطئ ترسى السفن
وعلى القلوب ترسى الذكريات

'Off the coast the boats drop anchor while in [our] hearts lay memories.'
Script on a dhow's stern, Suakin, 2004.

The dhow, a central part of the physical and cultural landscape described in the preceding chapters and integral to the lives of the maritime communities of the Red Sea, has a long history of continuity, going back centuries, albeit with adaptations to specific climatic and coastal conditions. Before exploring the life of the Red Sea dhow and its typology in the following chapters, a general overview of the traditional wooden craft is presented here, together with the answer to why it survived in spite of the encroachment of the modern world.

Seagoing cargo and pilgrim vessels (*marākib lis-safar*) traditionally left Suez between January and September, using the north-westerly winds to head for Jeddah on the Arabian coast, or travelling from Egyptian Quseir across the Red Sea to Arabian El Wejh or Yanbu al-Bahr (see Figure 5.1). Meanwhile, other cargo–pilgrim boats shuttled back and forth between Jeddah and Suakin or Massawa on the African coast. The return voyage to Suez or Quseir was made with the assistance of the prevailing north-north-east winds between October and March. At all of the ports, passengers would embark and disembark, goods were exchanged, and larger vessels would then proceed to Mocha, on through Bab el-Mandeb to the Gulf of Aden, and from there to the Indian Ocean. The harbours of the southern Red Sea were slaves to the north-east (winter) and south-west (summer) monsoons. Much of the outbound traffic to East Africa, the Arabian–Persian Gulf and the west Indian coast travelled between July and September, while the homebound ships made their voyages between October and December. There were 'transition periods' every spring and autumn 'as one

FIGURE 5.1 The port of Yanbu al-Bahr on the Hijazi coast, 1829–34 (watercolour by Captain Robert Moresby, courtesy of the Victoria & Albert Museum, London).

monsoon comes to a close and the other begins at which time the wind ceases to be fixed and turns variable until the new monsoon takes hold'.[1] The wind regimes in the Red Sea and around the Horn of Africa are complex, as we shall see in Chapter 13, but generally predictable.

Dhows continued to traverse the routes to Jeddah alongside steamers long into the 1970s. Sea transport for Muslim pilgrims and merchants was the only viable option until air travel became more frequent, and sea crossings by steamer from Safaga and Suakin are still available for poorer travellers.

Skippers knew their anchorages intimately and would island-hop to find the safest moorings. Each long-distance journey could take up to six months, so dhows would sometimes stay weeks in a port. Young boys, apprenticed to become skippers, accompanied their fathers and grandfathers on these voyages, learning 'about stars, swell patterns and birds'.[2] But the youngsters acquired far more than practical knowledge; they were also taught to trust in Allāh, learned countless prayer (work) songs and participated in the many rituals to ward off evil spirits.

The pace of a cargo–pilgrim journey was slow, as the dhow would stop at almost every 'desolate creek'.[3] Moreover, life on board a ship with limited space and few or no home comforts was not a pleasant experience, especially in the heat of the day or during the cold nights of winter. Then there were the swarms of insects that were drawn to the boat, the smell of passengers' vomit splashing in the bilge and the squeaks of rats scurrying around the cargo in the hold. Rough seas could lead to such panic among the passengers that they might destabilize the dhow if it were not weighed down with ballast.

Traditional dhows carried a single square sail, which skippers used alongside the familiar lateen or settee sail (see Figure 5.2). The sails' fittings and riggings were strong and heavy. You still occasionally see a traditional dhow with a lateen or settee sail rather than a motor to save on diesel. The small and medium-sized dhows hugged the coast, which meant they could sail only by day if they were to avoid the coral reefs and submerged rocks. On larger dhows, which crossed the sea, the navigators plotted their routes by stargazing and could even tell when they were entering deep and wide coral reefs by the positions of the stars. They were aided by fires that were lit on the shore to guide them into port.

None of the skippers I interviewed had ever consulted a portolan, and there is no record of their use in the Red Sea. Similarly, few dhows are equipped with lead or line, let alone a compass. Instead, the mariners have tended to rely on 'their sea sense'.[4] Empirical knowledge and experience have long been the essence of good seamanship. Meanwhile, 'bad' seamanship is not necessarily attributable to mariners' incompetence. Rather, it could be due to poor construction. 'There are no instruments to measure stresses, strains or breaking-points', Lorenzo Ricciardi observed when sailing on a dhow in the 1970s. 'The "instruments" to test a dhow are storms, waves and reefs, and they do not give a second chance.'[5] Egyptian, Yemeni and Eritrean captains all echoed these sentiments when I interviewed them in 2004, 2009 and 2011. Richard LeBaron Bowen Jr, a nautical researcher, noted that leakages are caused by poor seams but also storms, heavy rain and open space, as many dhows have no decks. Some tow a ship's boat, known as a *hūrī*, which could serve as a lifeboat if the dhow were to sink, but in general that is the only piece of safety equipment.[6] Nevertheless, there have been far more successful voyages than disasters. Carl Klunzinger (d. 1914), a great observer of the cultural life at the port of Quseir, where he lived for many years, insisted: 'There is more safety in a *sanbūk*, miserable as it appears, than in a fine European steamer, constructed and fitted in the most substantial manner.'[7] Indeed, he claimed that it was rare for any Arabian vessel to founder. We will explore the truth of this statement in the next chapter and Chapter 13.

In spite of the many miseries endured on a long sea voyage and the difficulties and dangers during heavy seas, the sailors were fiercely proud of

FIGURE 5.2 Dhows with square and settee sails on the Red Sea, *c.*1890 (courtesy Getty Images, Universal History Archives).

their vessels. When the Australian adventurer and experienced sailor Alan Villiers (d. 1983) sailed from Ma'alla to Jizan on the *Sheikh Mansoor* in November 1938, he reported:

> I noticed that the sailors from the [*nākhōda*] down had a great affection for their ship, and though we saw no long-voyage *sanbūk* which did not look better than she did, they failed to notice this and would hotly contest the statement. The *Sheikh Mansoor* was their home and their living, and they were proud of her.[8]

Similar pride was obvious among the mariners I interviewed. The older men spoke nostalgically of 'belonging' to the sea – a landscape they knew and loved – but, above all, of their attachment to the wooden vessels of their youth.

As Colette Dubois rightly points out, although the arrival of the steamships and the opening of the Suez Canal were the two main factors in uniting the northern and southern zones of the Red Sea, they did not completely obliterate the sailing dhow.[9] Admittedly, the old maritime cultural landscape in ports with landing places, caravan halting areas, customs houses, sanitary offices and infirmaries, ferry boats and markets was ultimately transformed, but it lives on in the memories of older generations of mariners. The dhow trade that existed in the days of sail is now limited to just a few anchorages, from which (usually) motorized vessels depart with small cargoes of clothes, food and other commodities. Yet the old skippers still remember the sailing vessels of their youth with great affection: the large cargo dhows of Yemen that sailed to India and East Africa; the pearling dhows of Eritrea and the Farasan Islands; the gun-running and slave-trafficking dhows of Djibouti and Yemen; and the pilgrim dhows operated by the Egyptians and Sudanese. These ships formed an integral part of the seasonal traffic and general landscape of the Red Sea for centuries. And while the advent of faster modes of sea travel may have curtailed the role of the traditional dhow, it has not precipitated its total demise. Even the recent preference for fibreglass dhows, although a serious blow, has not killed off all of the wooden vessels. Indeed, there is still a thriving, if diminished, traditional dhow culture in the Red Sea. In contrast to the Arabian–Persian Gulf and Oman, the story of the traditional wooden Red Sea dhow is one of survival; in Saudi, Sudan and Egypt these boats are still built to suit different purposes, and some still operate under sail, primarily to economize on fuel. Repaired wooden dhows continue to ply their trade in Eritrea and Yemen; others are still used as fishing vessels up and down both coasts as well as far out to sea. And trading dhows, albeit in far fewer numbers and along shorter routes than previously, still brave the wind and waves in the north and south of the Red Sea and the Gulf of Aden, just as they have for centuries.

6

ON BUILDING THE DHOW: SITES, SKILLS AND TECHNIQUES

وكان حولنا معلمين كبار وعظام علمونا ادق اسرارها
الشيخ احمد ابرهيم خياط ، جدة

'We were in company of great master [builders] who taught us [the] secrets [of building dhows] with such perfection.'

Master builder Sheikh Ahmad Ibrahim Khayyat of Jeddah.[1]

Having conducted an extensive study of the dhows of the Arabian Gulf and Oman,[2] I was acutely aware of the need to document Red Sea dhows long before I embarked on fieldwork in the places described in Chapter 2, first on my own and then in the company of John P. Cooper, Chiara Zazzaro and Lucy Semaan of the MARES team. We conducted surveys of the craft we found and published our preliminary findings between 2010 and 2016,[3] and we intend to present our line-drawings and technical observations in a forthcoming publication.

Any inquiry into the world of the Red Sea dhow presupposes the need to look at the different types of craft that have plied these waters throughout history. Such an inquiry must ask if there is any correlation of designs with the region where the dhows are built. Furthermore, what characteristic features do we find when comparing one dhow type with another? And what are the reasons for these features? I will attempt to answer these and other questions in Chapters 7, 8 and 9.

RECOGNIZING DHOWS

Categorizing dhows on the basis of hull design has often proved difficult. The main problem is that one finds oneself in a labyrinth of different names for the same type or the same name for different types. Furthermore, as Hornell noted, 'any particular type of craft is liable to show variation between port and port, often in small details, occasionally in major features'.[4]

The Red Sea communities, as in the Gulf and Oman, tend to recognize dhows by the stem and stern posts (straight or raked), the poop (low or high) and so on. The common perception, therefore, is that dhows are categorized by their shape, not by their rigging, as is customary in the West (brig, cutter and so on). Hence, dhows fall into two main categories: double-ended (*abū-samaka*) and square-sterned (*bil-gadaḥ*). The term *samaka* is used because the shape of the craft resembles a fish. Both bow and prow are pointed, or, as builders and sailors often say: 'Fore and aft are one alike' (*warā wa guddām wāḥid*). A double-ended vessel may also be termed a *zāy el-hūrī*, simply 'like the *hūrī*', in reference to the open-ended shape of dugout boats that are often seen along the Red Sea coasts. All dhows have a raking stem post, sometimes with a curve at the upper part. Generally, 'all dhows are open amidships', with fore and aft decks.[5] Finally, it should be mentioned that such craft are also identified by their size, not by their mode of construction, as Alan Moore has rightly observed.[6]

DHOW-BUILDING SITES

When John Ovington (d. 1731), chaplain of the East India Company, visited Suez, he noticed 'some vessels of very good burthen',[7] probably a reference to large craft. Several decades later, the German traveller Carsten Niebuhr noted 'the chief employment of the inhabitants of Suez' was shipbuilding, with the materials brought on camel from Cairo.[8] Suez became better known for its shipbuilding at the start of the nineteenth century, and though many vessels were built around the same time in Bombay and Muscat, the Suez market for dhow building was relatively steady, according to J.L. Burckhardt, the Swiss traveller and geographer.[9] Rather later, and further south, Captain F.M. Hunter, assistant political resident in Aden in the 1870s, recorded dhow-building yards at Hodeidah, Luheyya, Mocha and Aden, all active ports under the Ottoman administration in Yemen. Seagoing vessels, such as the *baghla*, *ghanja* and *za'īma-sanbūk*, were built in this region at a time when large Indian vessels were constructed on the west Indian coast. The characteristics of the *baghla* and *ghanja*, according to Hunter, were a 'long overhanging stem, square stern with quarter galleries, [and] two masts', with a weight capacity of 50 to 400 tons.[10] The smaller *za'īma-sanbūk* had a lower raked aft and was characterized by its upper curved stem post;[11] its capacity ranged from just 2 to 50 tons.[12] Both the *baghla* and the *ghanja* had Indian origins, and it is known that Indian master builders worked alongside Arabians and Iranians in the shipyards.

A shortage of timber had a significant impact on dhow building in Suez, as Richard Burton recorded during his stay in the port in 1853.[13] This shortage persisted for many decades, and some of my interviewees recalled that it was still an issue 50 years ago. With the decline in dhow building and the rise in political and tribal conflict in the late nineteenth and early twentieth centuries, a number of Arabian carpenters (s. *najjār*) left the Hijazi coast for Egypt and Sudan. Meanwhile, Yemeni shipbuilders (s. *mu'allim*) migrated to Eritrea and Djibouti to improve their economic prospects as commercial links with the Indian Ocean grew steadily. They settled in Massawa, the Dahlak Islands, Djibouti City, Tadjourah and Obock.[14] Notwithstanding this exodus to the African coast, Aden and Hodeidah continued to operate for more than a century. In the 1940s James Hornell asserted that the African dhow-building towns of Suakin, Port Sudan, Massawa and Djibouti were still active,[15] and several of my interviewees confirmed that these sites were relatively prosperous in that period. Travellers and informants alike asserted that the workshops in Aden's Ma'alla port were particularly vibrant, just as they had been for hundreds of years (see Figure 6.1). A Naval Intelligence survey collated in the1940s reported that Aden 'produces about seven dhows a year',[16] although it provided no details about their size. The British Government viewed Aden as a safe haven for vessels travelling between the Mediterranean and the west coast of India, just as the Romans had almost 2,000 years earlier.

FIGURE 6.1 Dhow building at Ma'alla, Aden, in the 1940s.[17]

Understandably, the port's natural harbour had always provided a good refuge for shipbuilders and merchants. According to the explorer Freya Stark (d. 1993), Parsee ship owners arrived in Aden with British troops from Bombay in 1839 and settled there.[18] They were subsequently joined by Parsee shipbuilders and mariners. It is unclear whether they worked independently of Adenis and other Yemenis, but the Parsee presence must have boosted the dhow and trade economy of the city. Some 100 years later, the Besse family moved to Aden from France and opened a dhow- and shipbuilding company – Halal Shipping – in the Crater district, which prospered until the 1960s. Dhows built there ranged from 50 to 465 tons.[19] It should be noted that, while I speak of Yemeni carpenters, several of the interviewees were natives of Hadhramaut, a region that is renowned for its shipbuilding and seafaring traditions.

Hornell asserted that Jeddah was another active dhow-building area in the 1940s, and several interviewees from the Hijaz and Tihama confirmed this. One place that was rarely mentioned was Jizan, on the Tihama coast. However, the 55-year-old master builder Bilghaith insisted that there were six dhow yards in the town in his youth. Only one – his own workshop at Al-Hafa – remains active today. He recalled: 'I started working in the dhow building yard as a boy with my father and grandfather; when I was old enough I built about one hundred and thirty dhows in ten years.'[20] These would have been vessels of various sizes, constructed with the assistance of a number of carpenters. Until 1991, Bilghaith hired Yemeni dhow builders, but he was forced to dismiss them and change his working practices when relations between Yemen and Saudi Arabia deteriorated. From this information, we drew the conclusion that Bilghaith had relied on the Yemeni builders' skills to construct these particular dhows.[21] When they left, he hired Egyptian carpenters and introduced a different design for his wooden fishing vessels that followed the Egyptian tradition – the skeleton-first construction sequence (see below). One of these boats was under repair in his workshop when we visited in 2009. Despite their different design, Bilghaith still called them *sanbūk*s – the generic term for oceangoing dhows. Some 15 years ago, however, Turkish metal fishing vessels started to appear in the Red Sea, to the detriment of the traditional wooden boat industry. So Bilghaith switched to building metal vessels employing Egyptian builders. These vessels are still being built today and Bilghaith is assisted by his two sons, Abdou and Majid (both in their 30s), and Muhammad Hadrami Abdo (in his 50s).

For decades, dhow building on the Sudanese coast was concentrated in Port Sudan[22] and Suakin,[23] where the best examples of oceangoing *sanbūk*s measuring 20–30 m long by 5–7 m wide were built. These vessels functioned mainly as cargo and pilgrim ships during the *ḥajj* season,[24] but a change in Sudanese Government policy in the 1980s following reports of gun-running and alcohol trafficking curtailed their construction. Thereafter, the government restricted all new vessels to just 12 m in length.[25] This ordinance was issued at a time when large wooden dhow owners and builders were already finding it difficult to cope with the increased cost of timber from India and Europe, high import duties and competition from new lighter, mechanized ferries and fishing launches. All of these issues, together with the dhows' unfortunate association with smuggling, meant the shift to constructing smaller craft became inevitable.

In the 1990s Henri Perrier conducted a survey of dhows in Djibouti. Interviews with boat builders and written records on dhow building at the Direction des Affaires Maritimes revealed that shipyards in Tadjourah and Djibouti City had been building large *sanbūk*s for more than a century.[26] Almost all of the dhow builders were descendants of Yemenis who had settled in Djibouti in the nineteenth century or earlier. In the 1960s Jean-Marie Pujo documented large trading *sanbūk*s ranging between 25 and 40 m in length.[27] The largest of these vessels would have had a weight capacity of some 500 tons, according to 60-year-old Abdou Suleiman of Obock.[28] (The average capacity was between 200 and 300 tons at the time.) However, dhow building in Djibouti declined from the 1960s until the 1990s. In 2009 we found only one builder in the country, a 45-year-old fisherman named Ahmed Jaber, who had learned his construction techniques as a hobby. As Perrier rightly reported, none of the descendants of the early migrant carpenters from Yemen seemed to have any interest in preserving their ancestors' boat-building skills.[29]

Yet, dhow building is still practised in Safaga and Quseir (Egypt), Yanbu al-Bahr and Jeddah (Saudi Arabia) and Suakin (Sudan). Particularly worthy of note is Suakin, where a dozen-or-so fishing boats are still built every year. The dhow-building yards lie around a large semicircular *mina* (harbour), south-west of the old ruined island town. Of all the sites I have visited in the Red Sea, Suakin is the only one where carpenters work only with hand tools (because they have no access to electricity). Alongside the native Suakin boat builders (the Rashaydas and Hadandawis),[30] there are a few Nigerian builders (see Plate 1), all trained locally, whose fathers had settled in the town after completing the *ḥajj*.

Suakin offers hope to carpenters who still work in the traditional way, even though the tide is clearly turning against the building of wooden craft as governments throughout the region offer financial incentives to young dhow builders to switch to fibreglass. Moreover, the Egyptian Government has refused permits to fishermen with wooden vessels in the hope of forcing them to abandon them in favour of fibreglass boats.[31] But governments do not always have everything their own way. Two decades ago, the Sudanese Fisheries Department encouraged the country's dhow builders to form a cooperative, but Hussein Ibrahim Muhammad, a 72-year-old master builder, recalled that he and the other dhow builders refused to be bullied: 'If we had agreed, we would have been obliged to conform to the government's regulations and pay taxes'.[32]

All of the government intervention has undoubtedly had an impact on wooden dhow building throughout the Red Sea, yet the industry has survived in the northern region at least. Shipbuilders in Quseir and Suakin told me that timber for planks is still imported from Europe, while local wood is used for other parts of the dhow. As for the southern region, the dhow-building industry finally died out a few decades ago. It had long relied on timber from western India and East Africa, particularly teak, but prices soared in the 1970s when India imposed export restrictions in a bid to counteract deforestation in Kerala.[33] The Red Sea builders continued to buy teak from Indonesian and Malaysian suppliers for a few years, but eventually the benefits of moving to fibreglass construction became irresistible, especially when government grants were introduced.

DHOW-BUILDING SKILLS

Antonin Besse Sr (d. 1951) described dhow building as 'empirical experience'; in other words, the master builder follows the traditional methods of construction and hones his skills over many years. The Besse family's dhow yard in Aden employed a number of builders prior to its closure in the early 1960s,[34] at the height of the political unrest before the British withdrawal from the colony in 1967.

During interviews, Egyptian and Sudanese carpenters repeatedly stressed the importance of a good master builder–owner relationship, as there must be complete understanding of each other's expectations. For instance, whenever a ship owner orders a dhow, he will discuss a number of issues with the master builder: how the craft will be used; which ports and/or fishing grounds it will visit; whether any long-distance travel is envisaged. On the basis of this information, the master builder will calculate the best width for the vessel – the beam – and then picture the ideal shape of the hull in his mind. Typically, there will be no drawn or written plan.

Therefore, the design of a purpose-built boat is realized by an experienced and skilled craftsman. The coastal landscape and seascape dictate the design of each dhow. When one considers their exposure to northerly winds, the vessels' hulls must be able to perform well when sailing windwards, and the region's regular but unpredictable squalls must be taken into consideration, too.[35] The dhow must be strong enough to 'stand up to the pounding of short, choppy waves created by the tide and current rebounding off the reefs and the inevitable knocks from the reefs themselves'.[36] A shallow draft is essential if a dhow is to have any chance of negotiating the reefs and numerous sandbanks of the Arabian coast, but the vessel 'must be keeled in order to counteract the pull of the current' far out to sea and in some of the deep channels, as Kentley explains.[37]

Given these requirements, clearly the dhow builder must have excellent carpentry skills. A trainee usually starts his apprenticeship at about ten years of age under the supervision of the master builder, who is often his father or uncle. He must develop a good eye to calculate the correct curve of the planks and other parts of the boat, just as his ancestors have done for centuries. As Alan Moore has so rightly pointed out, Red Sea carpenters 'manage with what they have and, if it serves, why use other?'[38]

As mentioned earlier, Hadhrami carpenters were particularly renowned for their fine woodworking skills. In his youth, 65-year-old Muhammed al-Ghaili, an experienced Hadhrami carpenter living in Aden, knew many of Ma'alla's dhow builders: 'They all came from Hadhramaut', he remembered, 'but they have all now passed away.' Now retired himself, Muhammed was living in a wooden shack at Dakkat al-Ghaz, 'pushed out of work as the fibreglass craft replaced our wooden vessels'.[39] He told me that Ma'alla's last wooden dhow was built in the late 1980s.

Jeddawi carpenters were similarly famous for their boat-building skills: 'we were in the company of great masters who taught us their secrets to perfection', commented Sheikh Ahmad Ibrahim Khayyat.[40] Jeddawis have a saying: *ṣanā'at abūk lā yaghlabūk*, which translates roughly as 'nobody surpasses the skills of your father'; in other words, the best dhow-building skills are passed down through the generations.[41] The Al Sayyid family in the Hijaz had a long tradition of building *sanbūk*s, as Muhammad Hamid Alsinani, a municipal council employee, and Abd al-Karim Khayaya, a 52-year-old fisherman, both recalled when I interviewed them in Ummlejj.[42] Other interviewees in Quseir confirmed that a great number of the old *sanbūk*s were built there in the early to mid-twentieth century. Ibrahim Ali Moosa, a 72-year-old master builder who represented one of five generations of a single dhow-building family, remembered his grandfather building large (20 × 5-m) transom-stern craft.[43]

The robustness of these vessels is a question that has vexed Western observers for decades. The first time I saw a Gulf *sanbūq*[44] under construction in a yard at Doha, Kuwait, in January 1985, I said to myself: 'My God, how on earth will it hold together?' I expected to see scaffolding – metal poles standing vertically and holding the dhow horizontally – but it was simply propped up on wooden poles. The whole thing seemed sure to collapse, but there it was, perfectly balanced in spite of its size. The Kuwaiti builder standing next to me merely laughed and said: 'My fathers and grandfathers have been building dhows like this for centuries and they have survived the test of time'.[45] Years, later, several Yemeni builders displayed similar reactions when I queried their dhows' seaworthiness.

There is ample evidence to suggest that oceangoing dhows do indeed survive to ply the seas for many years. Nevertheless, for two centuries, Western travellers' accounts have been marked by scepticism towards these supposedly rickety vessels. For instance, Thomas Machell (d. 1863), a midshipman in the merchant navy and indigo planter, voyaging on a *baghla* from Oman to Jeddah in 1848, remarked that it was 'clumsily shaped and badly built'.[46] The *baghla* was the largest type of dhow at the time, with two or three masts, a low bow and an overhanging transom stern.[47] Later, the Anglo-American spy William Makin (d. 1944), who sailed on the Red Sea in the 1920s, insisted that dhows were unfit for long-distance journeys: 'beamy and deep' with small keels and 'none of them is any good at beating to windward'.[48] Finally, a couple of decades ago, Hugh Millar, writing about Adeni dhows, expressed his dismay at the way the hull was constructed.[49] Although he had no issue with the individual components of the craft, he asserted that the 'method of construction' always introduced weakness, which was revealed whenever a dhow, beached after a storm, 'started to break up almost at once'.[50] Millar's manuscript was never published.

More expert eyes – such as those of Moore, Hornell and Perrier – have been rather more complimentary when discussing the master builders' construction methods. In 1909, N.F.J. Wilson, a port officer in Bombay, declared that Red Sea vessels looked 'rough' but 'sail[ed] well'.[51] Having surveyed a number of dhows in the southern Red Sea, the MARES team concluded that the methods used to fit and strengthen the ships' planks reflect sound builders' skills and produce vessels that are sturdy and sufficiently seaworthy to stand up to the rigorous conditions they must face.[52]

BUILDING TECHNIQUES

The first stage in building a dhow is to clear a site and prepare it for the laying of the keel and erection of the posts. The site may be shaded with sackcloth or other material, and it is often shared with goats, cats and other animals. Woodchips (*nishāra*) are used to make fires on which water is boiled for tea and coffee.

The hull is carvel-built with edge-joined planking. In 1909, Wilson wrote that 'roughly adzed planks of teak or jungle wood [...] are nailed and trenailed to the ribs in a somewhat rough manner',[53] although we never saw planks trenailed. By 'rough', Wilson meant that the dhow builder decides where everything goes by eye. It is his ability to decide which particular piece of wood best fits another that ultimately produces a balanced and seaworthy craft.

In the past, dhow builders followed a shell-first construction sequence – a well-known technique from Aqaba to Basra on the Arabian Peninsula that 'requires considerable skill at all stages'.[54] Once the planks had been laid and fitted edge to edge, the ribs were rebated and fixed to them. Measurements were taken when needed, a technique that probably developed because 'it was the only method of creating a fair shape that shipwrights knew'.[55] Dowels were used on smaller craft 'to set the below-the-waterline part of the hull into shape' before the framing-up was set.[56] The late David Goddard, an experienced sailor on traditional vessels, recalled seeing carpenters in Bahrain in the 1960s fitting the planks and making minor changes and adjustments over the course of many days before beginning the second stage – the installation of the frames.[57] The process took so long because the builders worked solely with hand tools. There was much twisting and turning as the timber was flexed with fire and bent with an iron or wooden rod. Historically, the shell-first sequence was used when building sewn-planked vessels because it was impossible to lay the ribs unless the planks were first tightened with wooden pegs and then held firmly in place by stitching them together with rope.[58] Ibrahim Muhammad Al-Anbari, a one-time dhow builder from Khokha, recalled, 'Those pegs served better in the long run. Of course, they would hold better in water than if you had iron nails, which rust'.[59]

An alternative to the shell-first sequence is the skeleton (or frame-first) method, which entails fitting the frame to the keel and then planking the hull. However, 'Frame-first ships required that the shipwright knew how to predict the eventual shape of a ship and set up frames which had been prefabricated'.[60] According to Richard Burton, the Greek carpenters that Muḥammad 'Alī Pasha (r. 1805–48) brought to Suez used this technique and then passed it on to their descendants.[61] More than 150 years later, a number of Egyptian shipbuilders of Greek origin are still utilizing the Mediterranean skeleton technique. Furthermore, over the past 25 years, it has started to appear in other boat-building centres, such as Quseir, as local or foreign companies have hired carpenters from further afield to construct their dhows. For instance, in 2003 I interviewed Mohammed Saeed al-Sabbagh, who had relocated to Quseir from Alexandria, where he had learned his skills from his father and grandfather. In Quseir, he had been commissioned to build *falūka*s for the tourist industry.[62] It was around the same time that I also met the aforementioned Ibrahim Ali Moosa (see Plate 14), who had lived all his life in Quseir and therefore knew nothing of the skeleton technique.[63]

FIGURE 6.2 *Lansh-sanbūk* built using the modern hybrid method, Suakin, 2004 (photo by the author).

Recently, a hybrid approach has developed, whereby the builder lays the garboard strakes and upper planks simultaneously with prefabricated frames. In any case, in both old and new methods, the builder always lays the keel before fitting the stem and stern posts, rebating the garboard strakes to the keel and finally fitting the planks to the posts and frames (see Figures 6.2 and 6.3).[64] In general, then, it may be said that a dhow's construction remains a 'simple and practical' process,[65] because, as noted earlier, in Suakin carpenters still use hand tools as they do not have access to electricity.[66]

We observed some remarkable variations in building techniques in 2009 in Yemen. For instance, in Khokha we saw large transom-stern 'winged' *hūrīs* that had been built using a novel construction sequence.[67] The carpenters had fitted the keel, stem and stern posts at the end after first framing the timbers and fixing the planks. Whichever technique is used, though, the edge-joined planks are always secured by caulking with coir dipped in shark-liver oil in order to fill any gaps between the planks (see Figure 6.3). Interestingly, the 'winged' *hūrīs* had been left in an unfinished state, possibly because timber had become unaffordable for the builders.

FIGURE 6.3 Laying planks edge to edge and securing by caulking in the Arabian style, Suakin, 2004 (photo by the author).

IN CONCLUSION

Building a traditional dhow demands an accurate eye, a wealth of experience and access to the knowledge of previous generations of craftsmen. Although most dhows seem much the same to onlookers, the builders and mariners always notice distinctive features in each vessel. Nevertheless, while adaptations have been incorporated over the decades, these have developed slowly and for the most part the dhow has remained unchanged for years.[68]

In recent years, the art of wooden dhow building has been threatened as fishermen have come under increasing pressure from governments to opt for cheaper fibreglass boats instead. As a result, ever fewer traditional dhows are being built. The decline is most marked in Djibouti, where there is now almost no dhow-building activity, and in Yemen and Eritrea, where only routine maintenance takes place. And yet, small communities of Egyptian, Sudanese and Saudi carpenters have managed to preserve the practice of wooden dhow building using traditional techniques. And we should be thankful that they have, because their skills, designs and workmanship are unrivalled.

7

DOCUMENTING AND REMEMBERING OLD DHOWS

هيلي سفر قلا
عش جابك بلادنا ؟
جابوني مصالحة
حملوني حمل الجمل
يوسف عمر محمد ، ناخودا من ابك جبوتي

'We rejoiced and set sail.
What brought you to our country?
They brought me here to promote [trade].
They loaded [my dhow] with camel loads.'
Youssef Omar Mohamed, captain from Obock, Djibouti.[1]

I have based the cultural history of the Red Sea dhow on a combination of pictorial, textual and oral accounts, with the addition of linguistic information where appropriate. There may be difficulties in interpreting data due to inconsistencies or lack of detail, but these sources help us to form a holistic picture of the unique dhow landscape.

EARLY MODERN PICTORIAL EVIDENCE

A striking Indian portolan chart, dated 1835 and acquired by Sir Alexander Burnes from a pilot in Gujarat, shows the route dhows took from Kutch to the Horn of Africa, through Bab el-Mandeb and into the southern Red Sea[2] (see Figure 7.1). It describes coastal features such as reefs and sandbanks in the Kutchi dialect of Gujarat,[3] but its true significance lies in its pictorial depiction of dhows sailing to and from the Gulf of Aden, Berbera on the Somali coast and Mocha and Jeddah on the Arabian coast. According to Burnes, Berbera was a

FIGURE 7.1 Indian long chart of the Gulf of Aden drawn by a native of Kutch and used by pilots, acquired by Sir Alexander Burnes on 2 June 1835 (courtesy of the Royal Geographical Society).[4]

'safe and good' anchorage, and it attracted around 100 vessels annually for a fair that took place on the shore, where people from the hinterland gathered to trade or exchange goods.[5]

The chart clearly depicts different types of dhow. According to Norbert Weismann, some of the vessels seem to have Indo-Arabian(-Persian) hulls, while others resemble sixteenth- and seventeenth-century Indian ships.[6] Weismann apparently did not consider the possibility that others may have Egyptian, Hijazi, Yemeni or Somali features. On the other hand, although distinctive features may have developed independently from one region to another, conjecturing as to types and shapes according to a region could be misleading as dhow-building technology was borrowed and features were adapted as necessary.

Iconographic representations may provide useful information when written and oral evidence is absent. In this instance the Indian chart is an important document in terms of what it reveals about dhow typology and the hull design features that are visible on some of the vessels.

FOUR EXTINCT DHOWS

Trying to access mariners' memories of dhows that have long-since disappeared was difficult, as I and the rest of the MARES team discovered. Informants either had a general mental picture of the dhow in question or they knew it by name but could not recall any specific details. We questioned them about four particular types that are mentioned frequently in travellers' texts and boat surveys: the *sā'iya*, the *dāw*, the *galba* and the *quyāsa*.

No interviewee was able to provide any details about the *sā'iya*; a number of Yemenis suggested that it was a large transom-stern vessel, but we were unable to verify this.[7] A local historian, Ṣāliḥ Bin 'Abd al-Laṭīf Al-Sayyid, from Yanbu al-Bahr, was no more successful at gleaning accurate information as his informants were just as vague as ours.[8] However, older Jeddawis recalled a coastal *sā'iya* that was used as a harbour launch, carrying cargo to and from large ships anchored offshore. Burckhardt mentions what seems to be a similar craft – 'the smallest vessel that navigates the Red Sea'[9] – before adding that the ship he boarded was 'dangerously overladen' with a total of 90 crew, merchants, pilgrims and slaves.[10] In a 1865 report, Antoine Guillain (d. 1915), a French engineer, described the *sā'iya* as 'long and narrow',[11] while Alan Moore, surveying vessels in the 1920s, suggested that at least one example of this 'swift sailer' was found in every Red Sea port.[12] Moore's description seems particularly apt, as the Arabic root-radicals of the word – √s.'.y. – carry the conceptual meaning 'to go along with vigorousness'.[13] Unfortunately, despite this textual, linguistic and oral data, we still do not have a full picture of the *sā'iya*; nor do the sketches of R. Morton Nance (d. 1959), a nautical archaeologist, clarify its features.[14] So, for the time being at least, it remains a mysterious craft.

The *dāw*, mentioned by some interviewees in the Hijaz, is an interesting craft that has long intrigued me. It seems to be a particular type of vessel, so *dāw* should not be confused with the generic nomenclature 'dhow' (see Chapter 1). According to Hornell, the word is of Swahili origin,[15] but there are many variants, including *dawh* (Per.), *tava* (Skt and Hin.) and *dāo* and *dāva* (Mar.), all signifying 'ship', which may have linguistic links with *dāw* as a result of the seasonal monsoonal trade network in the western Indian Ocean.[16] Therefore, it is possible that the East African nomenclature was borrowed from the East. The common morphological base for this Indo-European term shows its wide usage and adoption by seafarers and boat builders down the centuries. Its popularity seemed to increase in the nineteenth century, and the name, possibly due to East African maritime contact, became a byproduct of Anglo-Indian usage at a time when the British were patrolling the Arabian Sea and the Horn of Africa in search of slave traffickers and gun runners (see Chapter 16).

The search for the *dāw* outside of East African waters is complicated by the different graphemic representations in the Anglo-Indian records,[17] where the craft are generally presented as cargo–passenger and/or war vessels. Yanbu al-Bahr, strategically located between Suez and Jeddah, was known as the home of large *dāws*, and such craft certainly anchored there some 70 to 100 years ago,[18] but it is difficult to establish their precise dimensions or design.

Initially, when I set myself the task of compiling a more detailed picture of the *dāw*, the written evidence seemed promising. In the nineteenth century,

Burckhardt described it as the largest ship that sailed to India,[19] while Klunzinger pointed out that it had a 'long beak' and a 'large stern' – features that were also found in the *ghanja*.[20] However, Moore described the *dāw*'s stern as open-ended, in contrast to the *ghanja*'s transom stern.[21] The Catalan traveller Domènec Badia i Leblich, known as Ali Bey, provided some detailed measurements. He wrote that he sailed on a *dāw* that was 27.7 m long with a 13.1-m keel, while the elevated poop's projection was 4.8 m and the bow extended to 9.7 m.[22] Of course, we have to assume that all of these writers were referring to the same type of craft when they provided descriptions of *dāws*.

Neither the written nor the oral accounts suggest that these vessels were native to the Red Sea region. In the early decades of the nineteenth century, John Edye, a British colonial shipwright in Sri Lanka, mentioned a 'dow' that was built on the Malabar coast.[23] This term fitted his typology for a survey of boats he conducted in southern India and Sri Lanka, but we do not know whether Arabians used it in the same way.[24] Moreover, it was a vague term, because Edye's 'dow' was in fact a 'baggala' (Ar. *baghla*), with features that were similar to those of a *ghanja* (see above).

There is also no evidence that the *dāw* was of Indian provenance. Indeed, a vessel that was made in a Bombay shipyard and exhibited in London in 1851 was described as an 'Arab pirate "dhow"',[25] which seems to suggest more westerly origins. According to East India Company records, the vessel was associated with the Qawāsim pirates who operated mainly in the Arabian–Persian Gulf and Oman.[26] There are also occasional mentions of piratical *dāws*/ dhows (and other spellings) in the Red Sea, but it is impossible to know if this was an independent or generic coin term. For instance, four large pirate vessels were allegedly sent on a 'predatory excursion' from Ras al-Khaimah to the Red Sea,[27] while in the early 1830s 'some [were] [...] armed by the Arabs for cruising in the Red Sea'.[28] All of these craft seemed to start their voyages in the Arabian–Persian Gulf. However, the fact that they were described as 'Arab' does not necessarily rule out an Indian provenance, because until fairly recently Arabian vessels were built by Indians on the western coast of India.[29] But it gets even more complicated because skilled Hadhrami shipwrights migrated to Beypore, Kerala, in the late eighteenth century,[30] so it may have been their descendants who designed the craft that was known as the *dāw*/dhow.

Unfortunately, given all of the contradictory information, inconsistencies and gaps in the historical record, it seems that the search for the true origins of the *dāw* will remain a labyrinthine puzzle.

The name of the third type of vessel – *galba* – is still heard up and down the Yemeni coast. For instance, when I visited Fuqum, a fishing village near Aden, in 2010, a local fisherman used the term when pointing to an abandoned wooden boat on the beach. It was a double-ended vessel approximately 11 m in length with a pointed bow and a cut-off stern to fit an engine. There was an almost identical craft further along the beach.

In the medieval period, cargo–pilgrim boats were frequently described as *galba*s (or *jalba*s),[31] but it is difficult to establish a direct link in terms of form and function between such craft and more recent vessels of the same name. As far I know, the earliest drawing of a *galba* from the Early Modern period dates back to 1835. Robert Morton Nance found it in Captain R. Elliot's collection and reproduced it in a 1914 article. One of his sketches shows a transom-stern fishing vessel with a '"gooseneck" stern' that is raised with a slight curve at the bow. Another shows an unswept overhang.[32] A few years later, Alan Moore cited C.H.F. Jacob's 1918 account of a *galba* in Hodeidah with an 'upright' prow,[33] a 'curved' stem and a 'high raking stern', like a *sanbūk*.[34] According to the British Naval Intelligence survey of the Red Sea, *galba*s were used to transport commodities to Aden or Jeddah from India throughout the 1930s and 1940s, with some carrying goods as far north as Tur on the eastern bank of the Gulf of Suez.[35]

Collating the available data on the *galba* results in a patchy and incomplete understanding of the vessel's design features. The *galba*, featured by a small transom stern, I saw in Fuqum in 2010 was the only wooden dhow that the locals identified as such, and I did not hear the word or see a similar vessel anywhere else in the southern Red Sea region; nor did I find one further north. However, the Medieval and Modern Arabic name remains part of the Red Sea repertoire, as is indicated by the existence of Semitic cognates in Amharic ('small boat; ferry')[36] and Tigrigna (*ğālba* or *ğalba*; 'bark; launch; lighter').[37] But, of course, the word and the type of craft, then and now, are two different matters. We find from the Classical Arabic root √j.l.b. a verb form *jallaba*, meaning 'to transport [...] such as camels, sheep [...] slaves or any merchandise',[38] which suggests that the noun for ship-carrier derived from it. Morphologically, it is also related to the Egyptian/Sudanese Arabic root √j/g.l.b., which contains the dialectal verb *gallaba* ('to fish'),[39] and, by extension, *galba* (or *jalba*; a 'fishing craft'). The name survives, but it is now applied to the fibreglass boats that are found in great numbers in the region. This usage suggests that the old wooden *galba* was once similarly a common vessel, with the word either used to describe a particular craft or as a generic appellation for all dhows.

When I discussed *galba*s, *sā'iya*s and *dāw*s with fishermen, they understandably showed no interest in the historical-linguistic details, and I was unable to show them pictorial examples of the three vessels. However, our discussions of *quyāsa*s were even more frustrating because none of the

FIGURE 7.2 A *quyāsa* anchored not far from the Muhafaza, Suakin (photo courtesy of Mallinson Architects – Archaeological Projects).

FIGURE 7.3 *Quyāsa*s entering an inlet, Suakin (photo courtesy of Mallinson Architects – Archaeological Projects).

interviewees had ever heard the term before. Indeed, some wondered if I had made it up. This type of dhow is associated with Suakin, and examples were still sailing to and from the port in the 1930s (see Figures 7.2 and 7.3),[40] but I could not verify that fact with any written source. In his *Description de l'Égypte*, written in the Napoleonic period, J.-M. Le Père provides information about a Nile *qayyas* in Lower Egypt.[41] However, it is open to question whether the 1930s Suakin and early nineteenth-century Egyptian vessels are one and the same design.

Perhaps inevitably, the word *sanbūk* kept cropping up in conversation. Indeed, regardless of my descriptions of hull shape and the distinctive features of the stem and stern posts, most of the people I interviewed seemed to think of all extinct dhows as *sanbūk*s. On occasion, they might use the term *sā'iya*, *dāw* or *galba* – presumably having heard it during discussions with older generations of mariners – but they were never able to provide specific details.

In the next chapter I will look at the history of the *sanbūk* and try to establish whether this word is generally used to describe a specific type of craft or as a generic term for all traditional sailing vessels.

8

THE *SANBŪKS* OF THE RED SEA

السنابيك كانت زمان
حسن عبد القادر ، ريس البحر من القصير

'The *sanbūks* are long gone.'
Hasan Abd al-Qadir, sea captain, Quseir.[1]

As mentioned in the previous chapter, the word *sanbūk* is encountered all around the Red Sea, and many a travel and historical work have documented seeing or hearing of the craft. Unfortunately, though, they do not give details about this vessel's hull design. Hence, the information, including that provided by my informants, is incomplete. Ubiquitous as it seems to have been, the *sanbūk*'s origins and provenance are still shrouded in mystery.

TRACKING THE LINGUISTIC LINK

The thorny question as to where the name *sanbūk*[2] and other graphemic variants[3] originated has long thrown researchers into confusion. One possibility is that it has an Indo-European origin, coming from the Persian *sanbūk*, through Middle Persian **sambūk*[4] and ultimately from Sanskrit *çambūka*.[5] However, a second theory suggests an early north-eastern Semitic connection, possibly Akkadian *sanbuku* via Mesopotamia,[6] while a third advocates a Greek origin from *sambūke*, a '[triangular] musical instrument'[7] that supposedly resembles the shape of a ship.[8] The last of these theories seems particularly far-fetched, and there is no historical evidence for the Indo-European hypothesis. Hence, it is most likely that the term stems from a Red Sea Semitic base. This is because of its overwhelming lexical presence in Semitic cognates: Mehri, Hadhrami, Amharic and Tigré.[9] Arabic shares the word with these cognates, and it is listed in several Arabic lexica: al-Ṣaghānī's (d. 650/1252) *al-'Ubab al-zākhir* (*The Huge Flood*), al-Fīrūzābādī's (d. 816/1415) *al-Qāmūs* (*The Ocean*), al-Zabīdī's (d. 1205/1791) *Tāj al-'arūs* (*The Diadem of the Bride*)[10] and the Arabic Academy of Cairo's *al-Mu'jam al-wasīṭ* (*The Middle Dictionary*).[11] However, in his *Takmila* (*Supplement* [to the *Ṣiḥāḥ*])[12] al-Ṣaghānī questions whether the literary form – *sunbūq* – follows the Classical Arabic linguistic mould *fun'ūl*, the interfering 'n' being a fourth radical of a later development of the original tri-consonantal Arabic √s.b.q, with the conceptual meaning being 'to go ahead of something'[13] and, by extension, a 'fast sailer'.[14] This concept of 'fast-running' occurs in a pre-Islamic poetic verse by Sā'īda b. Ju'ayya (fl. first/seventh century).[15] Al-Ṣaghānī further claims that the nomenclature is dialectal Arabic used by the coastal people of the 'Sea of Yemen'[16] – that is, the southern Red Sea region. Given this linguistic background, it remains to be seen in what historical context *sanbūk* and its many variants exist in the Red Sea region.

THE HISTORICAL RECORD

The vessel is mentioned in an account of a sea battle fought by Ibn Ṭulūn's (r. 254–71/868–84) Red Sea war fleet.[17] This was a solitary event, but it does indicate that the *sanbūk* existed as far back as the ninth century CE, although we do not know if it operated with war machines or as a reconnaissance vessel. Several centuries later, the diaries of the Moroccan traveller Ibn Baṭṭūṭa (d. 779/1377) reveal that it was in use as a coastal vessel, as he says that he sailed on one from Aidhab on the Sudanese coast.[18] Sixteenth-century Portuguese accounts speak of 'Moorish' *sanbūk*s in the Red Sea and East Africa,[19] and one of these specifically mentions that both small and large *sanbūk*s[20] were used to guide *caravel*s through Bab el-Mandeb and into anchorages.[21] Importantly, the Egyptian historian Nuwayrī l-Iskandarānī (d. *c.*775/1372) asserts that the *sanbūk* was built solely on the Yemeni coast in his lifetime.[22] Clearly, then, the word *sanbūk* has been associated with the Red Sea region for many centuries, even if it has not always been used to describe a specific type of craft.

No medieval or Early Modern text provides a full description of the *sanbūk*'s (or indeed any other vessel's) hull design. However, a partial picture started to emerge in the sixteenth century. First, the Italian traveller Ludovico Di Varthema (d. 1517) stated that the *sanbūk* was 'flat-bottomed'[23] – that is, it had no keel – perhaps to enable it to manoeuvre through reefs. Of course, the indigenous to Di Varthema may have been using *sanbūk* as a generic term for any vessel in the Red Sea. On the other hand, his intention could have been to describe a specific boat that resembled a barge or a punt. Vessels without keels were certainly known as *sanbūk*s at Ma'alla in Aden in the 1940s. These ranged from 20 to 50 tons and were described as 'broad beam [and] shallow draft' craft.[24] As for construction, earlier Portuguese sources describe a stitch-planked *sanbūk*.[25] This should come as no surprise, as many boat builders used this technique long into the twentieth century. One report from the 1880s referred to the method,[26] as did several of my informants, who recalled that smaller vessels were often constructed in this way.[27]

Towards the latter part of the nineteenth century, records of business transactions, unearthed in the ruins of the Al-Rāḍī merchants' houses at Tur in the Gulf of Suez, revealed a busy Suez–Jeddah route plied by cargo *sanbūks*,[28] but once again they provided no information about the vessels' specific features. This was the route that Richard Burton followed. His 50-ton *sanbūk*, with two masts, carried 97 pilgrims in the hold[29] and had 'a sharp keel, narrow, wedge-like bows [and] a clean water-line'.[30] This gives some indication of its appearance, but little information about the overall design. Klunzinger, Burton's contemporary, who closely observed the comings and goings of ships at Quseir, similarly made no comment about the *sanbūk*'s hull design, except to say that it was 'somewhat smaller' than either the *ghanja* or the *baghla*.[31] Perhaps this enigmatic comment implies that the *sanbūk* was a smaller but otherwise identical version of the *ghanja* or the *baghla*, which would mean it was distinguished by a low, pointed prow, a high stern and a counter (see Figure 8.1).

THE TWENTIETH-CENTURY *SANBŪK*: PICTORIAL EVIDENCE

More detailed written and pictorial evidence from the start of the twentieth century starts to give a clearer impression of the appearance of the Red Sea *sanbūk*. In the 1910s N.F.J. Wilson described *sanbūks* arriving in Bombay from the Red Sea as 'the roughest kind of native craft' and insisted that they could not be 'compared either in finish or style with the Indian *kotias*, or the *baghlas* of the Persian Gulf'.[32] He did not go so far as to say they were unseaworthy, but his account certainly hints that they lacked finesse.

Cyril Crossland (d. 1943), director of the Sudan Pearl Fishery in the early part of the twentieth century, stated that a Sudanese *sanbūk* was 'both beamy and deep with long overhanging bow and square stern'.[33] (No doubt Crossland simply used the local boat builders' term for this type of craft.) On a journey from Alexandria to Quseir in the 1920s, Henri R. Maurer took a somewhat blurred photograph of what seems to be just such a vessel (Figure 8.2). Despite the similarities between the image and Crossland's description, however, it cannot be assumed that there was only one type of *sanbūk* in the early twentieth century.

FIGURE 8.1 A *sanbūk*-like vessel with no overhang near Massawa.[34]

Vice-Admiral Pâris's (d. 1893) 1880s drawing of a Red Sea double-ended vessel known as a *caboteur* (coaster), which he termed a *sanbūk*, is clearly defined by an upper curved bow, a raised aft deck and a poop (see Figure 8.3). Its hull design is akin to that of a *za'īma-sanbūk* I saw in Khor al-Ghureirah, and stands in stark contrast to Crossland's description of a square-stern vessel. So, as I have shown earlier and as I will discuss in the next chapter, people seem to apply the term *sanbūk* to a wide variety of vessel types. Clearly, Pâris's boat is far more elegant than is suggested by Wilson's description of *sanbūk*s as 'the roughest kind of native craft'.[35] But are we talking of one and the same vessel?

Some time after Maurer took his picture of a square-stern vessel on the beach at Quseir, Alan Moore described a craft on Kamaran Island, off the Yemeni coast, that was said to conform to the 1935 line drawings of Lieutenant J. Brett of the Royal Navy: 23.77 m long, 6.12 m wide, with a keel of 15.54 m (Figure 8.4).[36] Said to be 'a typical Red Sea *sanbūk*',[37] it resembles the *za'īma-sanbūk* described below: transom built with a raised stern and an upper curved bow.

The distinguishing features of the Adeni *sanbūk*, which similarly has a curved bow, are a scimitar-shaped upper stem piece and a transom stern with a slender overhang (see Figures 8.5 and 8.6). Hans Helfritz photographed a

FIGURE 8.2 A cargo *sanbūk* with a transom stern and slightly raised overhanging poop, Quseir, 1920s (photo from the Henri R. Maurer Collection, Archives of the Archaeological Society of Alexandria).

similar vessel with two masts in Ma'alla, Aden,[38] and reported that it carried cargoes of cotton from India, incense from Somaliland and coffee to Mocha.[39] This Adeni *sanbūk* was called *sakūna* in Yemen[40] although the name, not the design, is found in Egypt. The *sanbūk* on which Alan Villiers sailed in 1938, the *Sheikh Mansoor*, shared the same hull features (see Figure 8.7).

REMEMBERING THE TWENTIETH-CENTURY *SANBŪK*

Many of my informants confirmed that all merchant *sanbūks* were transom-sterned. However, during conversations with Farasanis, it emerged that pearling *sanbūks* in the early and mid-twentieth century were double-ended (20 to 40 m long and between 4 and 12 m wide), with either one or two masts. 'The finest of these' were constructed in Luheyya and Hodeidah, north of Yemen, according to 45-year-old Ala Allah Abdo Mujawir of Greater Farasan.[41] As to the question of these pearling *sanbūks* being double-ended, John P. Cooper suspects that the transom stern was shaped like a 'wineglass', with a

FIGURE 8.3 Vice-Admiral Pâris's portrait of a Red Sea double-ended *sanbūk*.[42]

small upper transom,[43] or what Hawkins, citing marine historians, described as 'escutcheon shaped', in the design of a 'shield'.[44] In other words, it was round in shape, as Jean-Marie Pujo observed in Djiboutian transom-stern dhows with large overhangs in the 1960s.[45]

Clifford Hawkins, writing about the dhows of the southern Red Sea region in the 1970s, pointed out that Adenis were replacing their transom-stern vessels with double-ended *sanbūks*.[46] We identified a variety of open-ended and

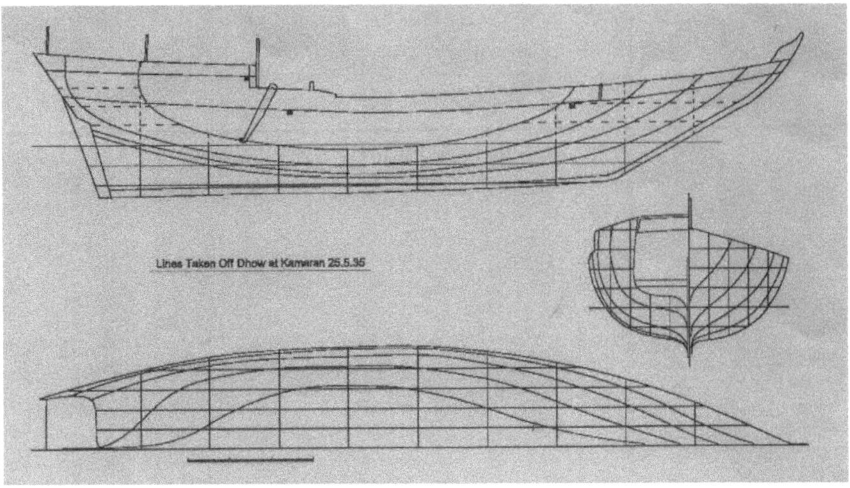

FIGURE 8.4 J. Brett's line drawings of a square-stern *sanbūk*, Kamaran Island, 1935.[47]

transom-stern designs in our survey of Yemeni *sanbūks* in 2009, so it is difficult to determine that one design preceded the other. One theory that has circulated for several decades argues that *sanbūks* with high overhanging transoms resemble sixteenth-century Portuguese *caravels*, and from there extrapolates that they were probably inspired by the European design.[48] For instance, Séan McGrail suggests that this is the most likely origin of the *sanbūk*.[49] However, he fails to consider the possibility that the transom stern could be an earlier design – an Arabian, Persian or Indian development that actually predated the *caravel*. I was often told that the square stern was chosen for practical reasons; it was a better option for cargo storage and the transportation of animals.

Wherever I went on the Red Sea coasts, the older generations' memories of this vessel were disappointingly vague. They spoke nostalgically, clearly recalled sailing on and/or owning *sanbūks*, and remembered what their fathers and grandfathers had said about them. Yet, they were unable to provide a complete picture of the hull design. To complicate matters, the word is often employed as a 'catch-all' term that is used to describe all types of merchant, fishing and pearling vessels. It was frustrating to know that plenty of valuable information was locked away in the memories of these old men, yet they could not tell us what we wanted to know, partly because there is so much confusion over the different types of vessel, the names that are applied to them and hull shapes.

FIGURE 8.5 The scimitar-shaped stem piece of an Adeni *sanbūk*, Aden, 1940s or 1950s (photo courtesy of Antonin Besse Jr).

A recurring topic of conversation was the ownership of *sanbūks*. The owner of a *sanbūk* was considered to be of high financial standing and therefore a man of importance in the hierarchy of maritime activity. One former pearl diver from the Farasan Islands, 74-year-old Mohammed Abdalla Ahmed Nasib, had worked for Hadi Bin Hasan, who owned five *sanbūks*,[50] while a 69-year-old shop owner from Yanbu al-Bahr, Abd al-Muhsin al-Khuwaishi, insisted that his father had owned nine *sanbūks*.[51] Finally, 41-year-old Siraj Muhammed Siraj from Massawa, Eritrea, remembered his grandfather owning 40 *sanbūks* and trading pearls and large shells containing mother of pearl (nacre) with the Hijaz.[52] Massawa is close to the Dahlak Islands, a centre of pearl diving for many centuries. Siraj's grandfather was obviously a very wealthy man, but there were many others like him.

FIGURE 8.6 The transom-stern overhang of an Adeni *sanbūk*, Aden, 1940s or 1950s (photo courtesy of Antonin Besse Jr).

The crucial point that emerged during these conversations was that all of these informants clearly associated the word *sanbūk* with high social status in the days of sail. They did not care if *sanbūk* referred to a specific type of vessel or if it was used as a generic term that encompassed many different designs.

OLDER SUB-TYPES OF THE RED SEA *SANBŪK*

The Egyptian gaṭīra

The Egyptian coast was the first place where I hoped to see an example of the famous *sanbūk*, which is mentioned so frequently in historical and travel literature. But I would leave disappointed. As one experienced sea captain in his 60s, Hasan Abd al-Qadir from Faradir, near Quseir, asked me in 2003: 'Why do you come to seek a *sanbūk* in Egypt? The *sanbūk*s are long gone' (*as-sanābīk kānat zamān*).[53] I later discovered that the true *sanbūk* had, indeed, long disappeared from Egypt. A smaller version, the *gaṭīra*, had survived up to some 20 or 30 years ago, but then it too had disappeared, leaving only the *falūka*, the traditional Egyptian Red Sea fishing vessel (not to be confused with the traditional Nile *falūka* or *felucca*).

FIGURE 8.7 The *Sheikh Mansoor*, 1938 (photo courtesy of the National Maritime Museum, London).[54]

The *gaṭīra* remembered by my Egyptian informants at Quseir and Mersa Alam featured an upper curved stem post and a transom stern. Hasan Abd al-Qadir claimed that nothing was 'more elegant' in the Red Sea. *Gaṭīras* varied in length from 12 to 30 m and in width from 3 to 6 m.[55] According to my informants, cargo *gaṭīras* ventured across the open sea to the Hijazi coast, carrying pilgrims and goods for trade. During my field visit in 2003, I saw some 20 of these vessels lying broken and abandoned on the shore at Idwa, south of Quseir. It seemed that some of their planks would be used to repair other vessels, but others were destined for firewood or simply left to rot.

Le Masson's 1879 line drawings of a 12-m Egyptian *gaṭīra* (labelled *khatira*) show a one-masted vessel (Figure 8.8). As part of the Red Sea governorate heritage programme, a reconstruction of this craft was built by master builder Atia Said Hussein Ali[56] and placed on exhibition in the fort at Quseir (Figure 8.9). The impressive vessel certainly attracted tourists to the fort, but I was left wondering what role it would play in reminding the Quseiris of their maritime past or, indeed, if any locals would even see it.

The Hijazi jurdī

The typical *sanbūk* of the north Arabian Red Sea coast, which Saudi and Egyptian mariners often mentioned, was the double-ended *jurdī-sanbūk* of the

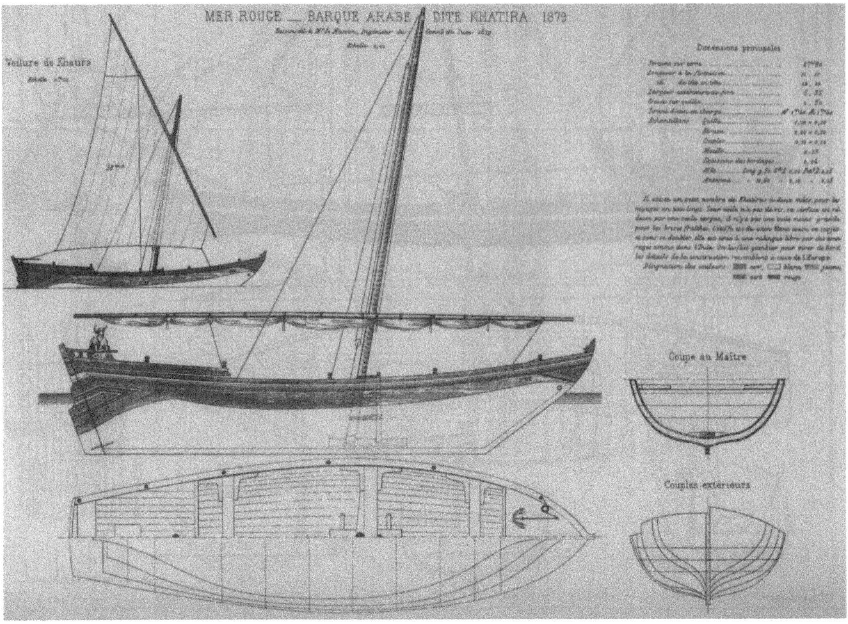

FIGURE 8.8 Line drawings of a *gaṭīra* by Le Masson, a Suez Canal engineer, 1879.[57]

Hijaz. Some informants claimed that this vessel had a transom stern. *Jurdī* is a very unusual word that stems from the Arabic root √j.r.d., and it could have its origins in either *injarad* ('to set out on a long journey') or *jarīd* ('an excellent, strong camel').[58] Both are possible, given that coastal people in the Hijaz have traditionally reared cattle and/or tilled the earth as well as ventured out to sea.

A *jurdī* was 7–15 m long and 3–4 m wide. In other words, it was almost as big as the Egyptian *gaṭīra*, but Quseiris often described the smaller vessel as 'finer' (*arfa'*). From the conversations I had with Hijazis, I concluded that the *jurdī* shared some features with a *za'īma* (i.e., an upper curved bow and a straight stern post; see below) and others with an *'obrī* (see Chapter 9). Both of these are also sister-types of perhaps an ancestral *sanbūk*. One unique feature of the *jurdī* was the crescent piece at the stem's head.

A replica of the double-ended *jurdī* may be found in Yanbu al-Bahr, next to the fish market. It was built by 40-year old Humaid Mani al-Muwallad, from Rabigh, and is owned by 60-year-old Ibrahim Abu Atayiq (see Figure 8.10).[59] Yanbu people are justly proud of their heritage and like to identify themselves with the *jurdī*, which they associate with their home town as well as the wider maritime history of the region.

FIGURE 8.9 Sketch of the *gaṭīra* in Quseir fort built by Atia Said Hussein Ali, 2002 (drawing by the author).

Trading *jurdīs* sailed from the Hijazi coast to Egypt and further south to Yemen. Arabians once sailed them to Quseir, as Shabhat Khaysa Hassan, a former assistant sea captain, and Ibrahim Ali Moosa, a dhow builder, both natives of the city, recalled.[60] Several years later, further enquiries led me to another former dhow builder in Yanbu al-Bahr, the 101-year-old Muawwid Abd al-Raheem Mirbas (see Plate 4). He told me that his father and grandfather had both built dhows too, and specifically *jurdīs*.[61] He recalled seeing transom-stern *jurdī-sanbūks*, as he correctly called them, entering the harbour, each with about 1,200 sacks of rice, equivalent to 132 tons. Yanbu al-Bahr had trading links with both Suez and Quseir, and its *jurdīs* shipped smaller cargoes than the larger *sanbūks*. Another informant, Fuad Ahmad Abdalla Bukhari, a 54-year-old fisherman from Jeddah and the son of a skipper, revealed that fishing *jurdīs* did not sail beyond Sudanese waters.[62]

The za'īma *– the pride of Aden*

Aden was known for the transom-stern *za'īma*, with its 'slightly raked aft'[63] and curve at the upper stem post.[64] Numerous informants mentioned the transom shape, but all of the *za'īmas* we saw during our fieldwork at Khor al-Ghureirah in Yemen, Ras Ali in Djibouti and Massawa in Eritrea were double-ended with a raised upper stern (see Figure 8.11).

FIGURE 8.10 A double-ended *jurdī* built by Humaid Mani al-Muwallad of Rabigh and now on display at Yanbu al-Bahr, 2007 (photo by the author).

The word *za'īma* comes from the Arabic root √z.'.m., seemingly from the Bedouin term for 'laden camel'.[65] Often remembered as the 'pride of Aden', these vessels ventured over great distances. I was already aware of journeys to East Africa and western India, but I was surprised to hear that 76-year-old Hasan Salih Shihab's father had 'sailed on a *za'īma* as far as Vietnam in 1948'.[66] On such long-distance voyages, the *za'īma* would lead a fleet of dhows, according to Siraj Muhammad Siraj of Massawa.[67]

Very few carpenters could recall *za'īma*s being built, but then I met the 90-year-old dhow builder Mohammed Ali Abdallah al-Najjar from Fuqum, near Aden, who told me: 'When I was twelve years old, working for my father, *za'īma*s were common. Hadhramis were employed to build them; they were the most skilled builders'.[68] He remembered that the largest *za'īma*s had 15–25-m keels and a weight capacity of 500 tons. When asked if this tonnage was unusual, he replied, 'Yes, as commonly they had a capacity of one hundred and fifty to two hundred tons, although I can remember my father saying that a few exceeded two hundred tons'. A *za'īma* with a capacity of more than 200 tons would have been as large as the Kuwaiti *baghla* or the Suri *ghanja*.[69]

Writing before 1920, Alan Moore recorded one *za'īma* in Hodeidah with a 'protracted' stern that 'slopes backwards' and another with a low stern.[70]

FIGURE 8.11 An open-ended *za'īma* with an upper curved bow and a raised stern, Ras Ali, Djibouti, 2009 (photo MARES by John P. Cooper).

James Hornell rightly points out that these descriptions are inherently contradictory,[71] and Moore provided no illustrations to support his written descriptions. In reality, the low-stern '*za'īma*' was probably a different type of vessel altogether (see Chapter 9), as none of my informants could confirm the construction of a *za'īma* without a raised stern. As Moore noted, these *za'īma*s had decorated transom sterns, a feature that is also visible on the *sanbūk* lying on the shore at Quseir in the 1920s (see Figure 8.2, above) and in the illustrations of Jean-Marie Pujo.[72] Moreover, we witnessed similar decoration on vessels in Yemen in 2009. John H.A. Jewell has correctly observed these *sanbūks*' sterns are 'painted far more extensively' than those of the Arabian–Persian Gulf and Omani *sanbūq*s.[73]

IN CONCLUSION

As this chapter has indicated, the word *sanbūk* probably has Semitic rather than Sanskrit or Persian linguistic origins.[74] Given this, and the vessel's historical connection with the Red Sea, it seems safe to assume that the *sanbūk* has its origins in the lower Red Sea region. However, other aspects of the history of this craft are much less certain. Over the centuries, while it retained the name, the vessel, large or small, may well have adopted the shape of similar or dissimilar hull designs, but these were never documented or captured iconographically. Some two or three centuries ago, under the Ottoman–Turkish–Egyptian administration of the Red Sea, it seems that a large vessel named the *sanbūk* with a pronounced stern overhang developed and then spread to the upper Red Sea, the southern Arabian coast and the Arabian–Persian Gulf. Such ships also boasted a prominent curved upper stem post and a transom-stern counter (see Figures 8.12 and 8.13), as is confirmed by travel writers and modern-day informants alike. Thereafter, the name was subsumed into sub-types with similar features. Although our interviewees knew these craft by their various names, they insisted on using the catch-all term *sanbūk*, which is so bound up with the Red Sea landscape and seascape.

The *gaṭīra*, *jurdī* and *za'īma* seem to be the most recent sister-types of the *sanbūk*, and all three were discussed at length by my informants, some of whom remembered them well. It is interesting to note that these interviewees occasionally applied the specific name followed by the word *sanbūk* (e.g., *jurdī-sanbūk* or *za'īma-sanbūk*). Two features that are common to all of these sister-types are the upper curved stem post and the elevated stern. The Adeni dhow had a scimitar curve at the upper stem post and a slender counter at the stern, characteristics that were also found in the now-extinct Arabian–Persian Gulf and Omani *sanbūq*s.

FIGURE 8.12 Sudanese *sanbūk*s at Flamingo Bay, north of Port Sudan, 1951 (photo courtesy of Palace Green Library, Durham).[75]

FIGURE 8.13 A Gulf *sanbūq* in the 1960s.[76]

Details about the older vessels gathered from written and oral sources can be scant or inconsistent, so line drawings, such as those of Pâris and Brett, are invaluable when attempting to establish the *sanbūk*'s hull shape. For instance, when I asked interviewees to explain the difference between a *sā'iya* (see Chapter 7) and a *sanbūk*, I was repeatedly told that there was no difference; they were one and the same vessel. However, the informants' perception of a hull shape is not necessarily how we view things. When I asked Farasanis about their pearling dhows, they answered that they were *abū samaka* (lit. 'fish-like') or *guddām wa warā wāḥid* (lit. 'fore and aft are one [shape]'). In other words, there was no square stern; they were 'open-ended'. By contrast, we would say that they featured a 'round' stern shaped at the upper part, because our 'Western' perception is different and more technical.

The *sanbūq* of the Arabian–Persian Gulf and Oman is the archetypal, romantic dhow that is so beloved of coffee-table books and nostalgic media articles. By contrast, the Red Sea *sanbūk* is a more prosaic vessel, notwithstanding its colourful decoration. The three principal variants, all of which may be descendants of a common ancestor, are still to be seen engaging in trade and fishing, just as they have for centuries.

9

THE DHOW LANDSCAPE: THE NORTHERN AND SOUTHERN RED SEA

الخشب يحمل الشمس الهوري ميزان
احمد قحطان من صيرة قرب عدن

'The traditional wooden boat can bear [the heat of] the sun and [at sea it] is like a balance.'

Ahmad Qahtan, fisherman, Seera, near Aden.[1]

As we have seen, some dhows are noticeably different from others in terms of their physical appearance. But irrespective of differences in hull design and other features, every dhow is a product of the coastal landscape and environment in which it is built. The word used for the vessel, the techniques that are employed to build it and the design may all take very different pathways over time. The first of these is enormously significant, because the name of each type of dhow connects it historically to a particular place and serves as a marker of cultural identity for the people who build and sail it.

DESIGNS AND PERCEPTIONS: A HISTORICAL OVERVIEW

Archival research of line drawings and sketches of dhows is essential before embarking on fieldwork along the coasts of Africa and Arabia. The line drawings of Red Sea craft produced by Vice-Admiral Pâris (see Chapter 8) are the earliest examples,[2] but they are not presented in a historical-cultural context. By contrast, images by his contemporary John Edye (d. 1873), surveyor for the Royal Navy's Office, though contextualized, are not technically detailed or satisfactorily reproduced.[3] In the early part of the twentieth century, James Hornell (d. 1949), director of fisheries for the Madras government, may be considered the first researcher to conduct a comprehensive and systematic survey of dhows, initially in the Indian Ocean, with a focus on the western and eastern coasts of India.[4] A little later, in the 1920s, Alan Moore (d. 1959), a temporary medical officer in the Royal Navy,[5] drew a number of sketches (not to scale) of dhows in Massawa, Port Sudan, Yanbu al-Bahr and Aden.[6] His work was paralleled or complemented some 20 years later by Hornell, who took on the task of surveying a number of Red Sea dhows.[7] There are classificatory issues with his work, but Hornell clearly shows variations in hull design that are still in evidence today. Richard LeBaron Bowen Jr, a nautical researcher, should also be mentioned, as he displayed a keen interest in both Arabian sea craft and primitive watercraft.[8] The contributions of these men, albeit sometimes lacking in adequate images or line drawings, have greatly enhanced our knowledge and understanding of the dhow's features, both technically and historically.

Of course, photographs of Red Sea dhows taken over the past 70 to 80 years were also invaluable in increasing our understanding of the similarities and differences between the various vessels we observed during our fieldwork. Those by the New Zealander Clifford W. Hawkins and the Australian Alan Villiers are perhaps the most iconic images of these craft.[9] Their mostly black-and-white pictures highlight the dhows' features with a clarity that earlier photography was unable to capture. In recent years, Henri Perrier[10] has adopted a more scientific approach, and his photographs and line drawings of Djiboutian Red Sea dhows display a much firmer grasp of the nuances of hull design. The late Ṣāliḥ Ḥasan Shihāb's (d. 2013) survey of Arabian dhows – the only Arabian study of the Red Sea region – is thorough but unfortunately marred by poor-quality sketches and photographs.[11]

THE FIELDWORK: IDENTIFYING DIFFERENT DHOWS

At the outset, the MARES team and I were under the impression that there would be specific names for different types of wooden craft that everyone we interviewed would recognize. However, in the course of our conversations, it became clear that the picture was more complicated than we had thought. First, we observed several types of wooden craft that could not be identified, as no reliable informant was in the vicinity. Second, we were given information about names and types of craft, but there were no examples with which to verify the data. Finally, there were regional variations, with different names for the same type of craft, or different craft with the same name, something I also experienced in the Arabian Gulf and Oman.

THE EGYPTIAN *FALŪKA*

The most common dhow on the Egyptian Red Sea coast today is the *falūka* – a fishing vessel that also sometimes serves as a ferry or pleasure boat. In the past it was used to ferry pilgrims to and from *sanbūks*, as it did at the entrance to Suakin harbour, Sudan. A *falūka* has a raked stem post with one straight mast and ranges from 4 to 9 m in length and 2 to 3 m in width, reaching a height of 1 to 1.5 m at the stem post. Its weight capacity is 6 to 7 tons. Sayyid Ahmed Musa Al-Barsi, a 58-year-old sea 'Ababda captain from Safaga, informed me that 'the double-ended *falūka* is sleek and faster', whereas, nowadays, to accommodate an outboard engine, the square-stern vessel has become 'wider-beamed but slower' in spite of the motor engine (see Figure 9.1).[12]

Some boatmen would use *falūka* and *bōt* seemingly interchangeably when discussing small fishing craft. When asked whether these were one and the same vessel, Sayyid Ahmed simply replied: 'There is no difference between one and the other, except that a *falūka* was always a double-ended boat. As soon as it is adapted with a transom stern, it becomes a *bōt*.'[13] I found this an interesting technical–linguistic nuance and it may indicate an identification

FIGURE 9.1 A square-stern fishing *falūka* at Quseir, 2004 (photo by the author).

with European 'boats' and '*bateaux*'; hence the name *bōt*. In any case, the name *falūka* is more commonly used. We also encountered the word *bōt* in Aden, where it is used to describe a square-stern vessel (see below).

The earliest reference to a *falūka* appears in al-Farāhīdī's (d. 174/791) lexicon.[14] Derived from the root √f.l.k., we find the term *fulk* in the Qur'ān in reference to Noah's ark,[15] which semantically denotes 'roundness', like the Mesopotamian *guffa*, a basket-shaped watercraft.[16] The lexicographer al-Zabīdī (d. 1204/1790) states that *falūka* is a dialectal diminutive for *fulayka*, meaning 'small boat'. Interestingly, modern Arabic dictionaries, such as *Muḥīṭ al-muḥīṭ* and *Mu'jam al-wasīṭ*, ignore the dialectal usage in favour of the standard written form.[17] The nomenclature has found its way into European languages. In English the vessel is known as the felucca, characterized by its protruding lateen sail,[18] which tourists visiting the Nile and the Red Sea in the nineteenth century and thereafter often described in travel literature. Comte De Landberg (d. 1924), who wrote a well-known lexicon of the Dathina region of Yemen, recorded the name in connection to Yemen and defined it as a 'small ship'.[19]

Craftsmen in Quseir and Safaga are still building *falūka*s. The oldest master builder I interviewed was Ibrahim Ali Moosa, who was in his 70s; another was 59-year-old Atiya Saad Sikiyan Guta.[20] Both were residents of Quseir. As we saw earlier, the increased demand for fibreglass fishing boats and metal trawlers (*lanch*) in the Red Sea has meant that dhow-building skills are gradually dying out. However, there was a young trainee in Atiya's dhow yard, Abd al-Basit Sugi Hamid, who was in his 20s. Moreover, over the last couple of decades, Mediterranean boat builders have been brought to Quseir and Safaga to build *falūka* pleasure boats, as both sea towns have experienced a boost in tourism.

Nevertheless, the Egyptian seascape continues to change, with ever more metal ferries and fishing vessels in Safaga and Hurghada. Just three decades ago, such launches were totally unknown to the Egyptians. Some now operate as pilgrim ferry boats to Jeddah, but many more carry workers back and forth between Hurghada and Dhuba on the Saudi coast.

THE HIJAZI BOATS LANDSCAPE

Ummlejj was well known for its dhow-building skills and the variety of craft built in the town. Today, though, traditional dhows are totally absent from the harbour, replaced by fibreglass boats. When I visited in May 2007, there was still talk of former sail makers and ironsmiths in the harbour area. All of that workmanship has now disappeared.

I witnessed some dhow-building activity at Yanbu al-Bahr in 2007; a square-stern boat with a slightly raked stem post, similar to a Suakini *zārūk* (see below), and a double-ended planked *hūrī* were both under construction. However, on my return to the town in 2013, I saw hardly any building activity; most of the work consisted of routine maintenance. There were still double-ended wooden dhows to be seen, some with a straight bow and others with a narrowed square piece added to the original stern. Also of note were a few one-masted square-stern dhows that had a curved upper bow with or without a crescent tip. I was unable to find anyone to identify these craft, and my impression was that many of them had been abandoned as there were signs of rot. Old dugout *hūrīs*, imported from the Malabar coast but no longer in use, were scattered all over the yard. Such vessels, which are generally hollowed out from the mango tree (Ar. *'anba*; Lat. *Mangifera indica*),[21] are ubiquitous in the western Indian Ocean[22] and I have seen a number of them in various places around the Red Sea coasts (see below for more information). The name is an old appellation with Indian origins (< Hin. *hōṛī* < Kan. *odi* < Dra. *odu* or *oru* < Skt *ḥoḍa*).[23] *Hūrīs* are also mentioned in Demotic and Hieratic writings, cognates of which are in Amharic, Somali and Southern Arabic dialects.[24]

The typical dhow of Yanbu al-Bahr and the Hijazi is said to be the double-ended *jurdī* (see Chapter 8). They are no longer being built (although I saw a replica of one in the Bangala, Yanbu's fish market), whereas fibreglass fishing boats are everywhere. Informants told me that a *nawrī*-type, flat-bottomed, wooden vessel is still used to transport cement, iron and other heavy goods in the harbour area, but I have not witnessed such a boat in operation myself.

SUAKIN'S TRADITIONAL DHOWS

Compared to Egyptian boats, Sudanese craft, except for the *hūrī*, are more colourful, often painted blue, green, yellow and white. On my visit to Suakin in 2004 two medium-sized dhows and three smaller vessels were under construction and a few were being repaired, but several lay abandoned on the beach. The *lansh-sanbūk* (8 to 12 m long and 2.5 to 4 m wide) is a smaller adaptation of what is generally called a *sanbūk* (see Chapter 8). It functions as a fishing vessel and a small trading boat for most of the year, but it also operates seasonally as a conch-collecting vessel. Transom-sterned with a low bow and prow, it has a projected straight stem post and an inboard engine, but many also carry a mast and a settee sail to economize on fuel.

The most commonly used dhows in Suakin are fishing boats – the transom-sterned *zārūk* and *shaṭṭiyya*. The *zārūk*'s stem post is straight, raked at 45°, while that of the *shaṭṭiyya* is curved at the upper bow. The former has two small 'fins' projecting at the stern, similar to those on the Yemeni 'winged' *hūrī* (see below), but much smaller. *Zārūks*, which measure 5 to 8.5 m in length and

1.3 to 2.5 m in width, are powered by a modest outboard engine (33 to 55 hp), but also carry sails and oars in case the engine runs into difficulties. *Shaṭṭiyya* comes from the Arabic root √sh.ṭ.ṭ., with *shaṭṭ* meaning 'seashore' or 'coast'.[25] Thus, a *shaṭṭiyya* is a boat that belongs to the coast, as opposed to deeper waters. The origin of the word *zārūk* will be discussed later.

Three types of double-ended Suakin *hūrī* were observed: log and planked *hūrī*s and a flat-bottomed type known as a *ramas*. The dugout *hūrī* – *hūrī lōḥ wāḥid* (lit. 'one piece of log') – is often used to ferry fishermen to and from dhows anchored in the Mina (harbour). Also called *hūrī ṣaddāfī*, some time ago this vessel was also used for collecting large shells. One example lying on the shore at El Geyf harbour measured 6 m long × 0.83 m wide × 0.43 m high and featured added ribs to strengthen the hull.

Informants at all the field sites I visited in the Arabian Gulf and Oman, as well as the north of the Red Sea, told me that dugout *hūrī*s were made from mango wood and imported from Malabar. To test the accuracy of this information, Lucy Semaan, a MARES member, sent wood samples from Yemeni and Suakini *hūrī*s to Rainer Gerisch for lab analysis and he confirmed that they were indeed made of mango wood.[26]

The plank-built *hūrī* (*hūrī māliki*) with raked stem and stern posts is round-bottomed and 4–5 m long × 0.8–1.25 m wide, while the *ramas*, slightly raked stem post and a straight aft post, is 4 m long × 1 m wide and flat-bottomed, although a batten is sometimes added to act as a keel. While it is designed for coastal fishing, a *ramas* will sometimes carry cargo as it is generally more stable than its sister-types. Both craft are powered by a single outboard engine, though sails, paddles or oars may be used to conserve fuel. They also seem to need constant plank repair.

THE YEMENI DHOWS: PACESETTERS OF THE SOUTHERN REGION

Historically, Yemeni dhows were pacesetters in terms of hull design because their owners and builders migrated to other Red Sea regions, and the area remains by far the best place to see a wide variety of dhows today, although of course these amount to no more than a tiny fraction of the number that once plied their trade off the coast of Yemen. Meeting Edward Prados in Sanaa, Yemen's capital, in February 2009, I was saddened to learn that the Socialist Republic (1967–90) destroyed many traditional dhows and repurposed much of the timber for road construction.[27] While devastating, this carnage failed to deal a death blow to the Yemeni dhow. Indeed, back in 1996, Prados himself pointed out that 'wooden boatbuilding continues to thrive in Yemen'.[28] Unfortunately, by the time of my visit, all building activity had ceased and the dhows I witnessed seemed to be at least 30 or 40 years old. Their survival is due to the fact that they can be easily repaired on account of the ready supply of old timber from obsolete boats. The Yemeni carpenters are unable to buy fresh teak for new planking from India (because of export restrictions) or south-east Asia (because of cost and the poor quality of the wood). Framing timbers could be obtained locally, but were limited in terms of quality and size.

In the past, Adeni dhow building took place mainly at a site called Dokkat al-Ghaz in Ma'alla. Some dhows are still repaired there, but much of the yard is now used as a lorry park. Muhammad Al-Ghaili, a retired 65-year-old Hadhrami dhow builder, recalled that there used to be seven dhow builders in Ma'alla, but 'the costs of building wooden vessels have become increasingly high, so there was no choice but to build fibreglass boats'.[29] His story is echoed in many other dhow-building yards, where unfinished wooden dhows are frequently left to rot.

One *bōt* in Ma'alla caught our eye because its square cross-section hull, the stern's box-like shape and its upright stem post are all atypical of Yemeni dhows. Such craft are far more common in Hodeidah and Djibouti.[30]

Khor al-Ghureirah turned out to be a haven for dhows. In terms of *sanbūk*s, we encountered *za'īma*s, *'obrī*s and *zārūk*s,[31] all of which shared similar features, although there were some differences in the stem and stern posts and overall hull size. They are powered by inboard engines and carry one mast. Alan Moore described these three types of vessel in the 1910s, but categorized all of them, simply, as *sanbūk*s.[32] As we saw in Chapter 8, many Yemenis use the same terminology today.

The now-rare oceangoing cargo vessel – the *za'īma* – is open-ended with an upper curved stem post and a raised poop. We saw only one example in Khor al-Ghureirah: 22.4 m in length with an inboard engine, lying in a state of decay in shallow water. The root of the word – √z.'.m. – is associated with a traveller to a country who 'mounts his camel, or beast, that serves to convey him, and journeys until he accomplishes the object of his want'.[33] The Bedouin reference to a 'camel, or beast' is semantically transposed to a watercraft that transports goods and people. A similar animal–ship word relationship exists in the names of two other dhows: the *jurdī*, possibly from *jarīd* ('an excellent, strong camel'; see Chapter 8); and *baghla*, from the term for 'mule'.[34]

Throughout the course of our fieldwork, we saw more *'obrī*s than any other type of dhow. This double-ended cargo and fishing vessel, which can be up to 22 m in length by 6 m wide, is characterized by a straight stem post and a stern post raking aft (see Figure 9.2). It is propelled by an inboard engine and generally has a single mast that is raked slightly forward. In a late nineteenth-century report at Mukalla, Captain F.M. Hunter referred to an *'abra* and described characteristics that resemble those of present-day *'obrīs*,[35] leading to the conclusion that they are one and the same vessel, especially as the two words share the same morphological radicals from the root √'.b.r. ('to cross over [the sea])').[36] However, perhaps unsurprisingly, neither word is documented in either Classical or Medieval Arabic sources.

Another double-ended cargo and fishing dhow, the open-hulled *zārūk*, sailed from the Red Sea to the Arabian–Persian Gulf and as far as the East African coast throughout the 1960s and 1970s, according to Clifford Hawkins.[37] We spotted a number of these vessels abandoned at Khor al-Ghureirah and one that was still operational. Interviewees confirmed that the *zārūk* was also used for slave trafficking and gun running (see Chapter 16). The hull shape is similar to that of the *'obrī*; it is narrow-hulled (*baṭnuhā ḍayyiq*) with straight stem (*hinnām seyf*) and stern posts. The outer stem post (the *seyf al-baḥr*, 'sword of the sea') rises to two-thirds of the height of the inner stem post.[38] *Zārūks* vary from 17 to 24 m in length and 4 to 6 m across the beam, and

FIGURE 9.2 A double-ended *'obrī*, Khor al-Ghureirah, 2009 (photo MARES by the author).

the keel is about two-thirds of the length of the craft (see Chapter 16 for further details). They have a 50–100-ton weight capacity.

I suspect that the word *zārūk* has ancient origins and Red Sea Semitic connections. The root –√ z.r.k. – is Arabic and follows the pattern of *fā'ūl.*[39] Semantically, it is related to objects that 'go fast', such as a *zarrāqa* ('javelin; spear').[40] But perhaps the closest term is *zurraq* (pl. *zarārīq*; 'a falcon').[41] The bird–boat relationship is not uncommon in the Islamic tradition: *ghurāb* ('crow') for 'a cargo or war ship'; *ḥamāma* ('dove') for a 'transport ship'; *ṭayra* ('a bird') for 'a swift boat'; and *būm* ('owl') for 'an ocean-going vessel'.[42] However, it should also be noted that *zarraq* is an intensive verb meaning 'to glide' in the Dathīna southern Arabian language.[43] The intensifying double 'r' indicates fast motion. Therefore, one may argue that this verb perfectly describes the motion of a vessel that was renowned for its swiftness and agility, as interviewees often emphasized. The morphological transition of *zurraq* or *zarraq* to *zārūk* is one of vowels but maintaining the radicals.

There was a sub-type of the *zārūk* called the *ghuweirī*, which the 90-year-old former master builder Mohammed Ali Abdallah mentioned when I interviewed him at Fuqum, near Aden.[44] He compared it to the *sanbūk* but was unable to recall its general design features. However, a photograph at the London Brass Foundry, Woolwich Arsenal, shows an Adeni native boat with the caption: '*Ghuweirī*: This vessel is a hybrid having a crescentic *sanbūk* and being in most respects a *zarūk*.'[45] The boat term is a diminutive of the place-name Ghureirah.

As mentioned earlier, another type of vessel we identified in the Khor al-Ghureirah lagoon was the craft we called a 'winged' *hūrī* (see Chapter 6). Edward Prados noted a similar dhow in the 1990s but did not give it a specific name.[46] Members of the MARES team spotted further examples in Aden, Kheesa, Fuqum, Umran, Mocha, Khokha, Hodeidah and Salif. It has a straight raked stem post and, as mentioned previously, two projecting fins at the square-shaped stern that form a quasi-triangular shape (hence the 'winged' appellation). It ranges from 14 to 20 m in length and 2.5 to 4.5 m in width (see Figure 9.3).[47] Like the other Yemeni dhows, it is deckless, with a tank to store fish and space to carry livestock to the western coast of the Red Sea.[48] It is powered by either one or two outboard engines.

The locals could not explain why they call this vessel a *hūrī*, given that this appellation usually refers to much smaller craft – dugout or planked beach canoes (see above). Similarly, there did not seem to be any good reason why they also now use it for fibreglass boats. However, Hornell reminds us that *hūrī* (or *hody*) is an Indian catch-all term for 'small craft [with] several distinct terms to distinguish varieties', although its usage is generally implied to mean

FIGURE 9.3 A square-stern 'winged' *hūrī*, Khokha, 2009 (photo MARES by John P. Cooper).

'fishing'.[49] Perhaps this helps to explain why the fishermen of the southern Red Sea routinely identify any fishing craft as a *hūrī*.[50]

Throughout the Red Sea, fibreglass (*faybir*) boats have largely replaced the traditional wooden (*khashab*) dhows because they are far easier to build and maintain. However, when asked whether wooden vessels held any advantages over fibreglass boats, Ahmed Qahtan, an experienced fisherman from Seera, Aden, told me:

> The timber can bear the heat of the sun better than the fibreglass because [the fibreglass] is susceptible to extremes of temperature. The wooden boat is like a balance; it is far more stable than the fibreglass boat. When water enters the fibreglass boat, there is a danger of it sinking [immediately], while a wooden boat would take a longer time to sink.[51]

Older fishermen, such as Ahmed, who was in his 60s, generally described the traditional wooden boats as safer, more secure and more economical, if slower, than the fibreglass equivalents. Nevertheless, a number of them were keen to embrace new technology and discussed encasing their wooden boats in glass-reinforced plastic.[52] However, this can be dangerous, as Aylin Orbaşlı, a conservationist, explained: 'Although the material is strong, the timber underneath is trapped and [this] creates an environment in which it corrodes or rots. Timber needs to breathe; it is organic and therefore needs to dry and expand'.[53]

THE SAUDI TIHAMA COAST: THE DHOWS OF JIZAN AND FARASAN ARCHIPELAGO

According to 55-year-old master builder Ibrahim Bilghaith from Al Hafa, Jizan, the dhow-building tradition on the upper Tihama coast closely followed that of Yemen.[54] Until about 15 years ago, he and the late Abdallah Mabruk Qammash built three types of large double-ended vessels – so-called *sanbūk*s, *'obrī*s and *za'īma*s – for Yemeni and Sudanese merchants. However, boat models in his workshop revealed that Ibrahim's *sanbūk*s and *za'īma*s were rather different from the vessels with those names in Yemen and Djibouti; they were transom-sterned, controlled by a rudder and carried a single mast and they had a raked stem post and two stern-quarter fins. The *sanbūk* was a sailing vessel while the *za'īma* was built to accommodate an inboard engine. Ibrahim also pointed out subtle differences in the hulls of the two models: 'The *sanbūk* is narrowly designed whereas the *za'īma*'s hull from the bottom is shaped wider.' This meant that the *sanbūk* sailed well into the wind, while the *za'īma* was slower but more stable.[55]

We saw no evidence of these designs outside of Ibrahim's workshop, aside from the large (16 × 5-m) *'obrī* that he built for the Heritage Village in Suais, near Jizan. He told me that Yemeni guest workers had built *'obrī*s in Al Hafa, but they were expelled for political reasons after the Iraqi invasion of Kuwait in 1990. Thereafter, he brought in Egyptian carpenters to build Mediterranean-style wooden trawlers. Meanwhile, the Red Sea experienced a boom in prawn fishing. This industry was initially dominated by metal Turkish trawlers, and Ibrahim switched to building similar vessels – which he calls *gārib*s – as demand increased. These large craft can be up to 17.5 m long by 5.5 m wide. The other main part of his business comprises smaller, fibreglass boats – *falūka*s – that are fitted with outboard motors.

However, as a sideline, Ibrahim also constructs wooden racing *hūrī*s (*hawārā lis-sibāq*), as dhow racing has recently become a popular pastime, especially during festivals. These boats are double-ended, wooden planked and stepped, with a single mast that measures 7.5–10.5 m. They are raced from the Mina to Ahbar Island, some 13 km away, west of Jizan, with each race lasting 60–90 minutes.[56] Each *hūrī* is sailed by a crew of three – one steers with the rudder; another sits astride a 3-m pole (*ma'dāl*) with an extended outboard, which is used to maintain the boat's balance during side-winds; and the third is in charge of the sail and occasionally sprinkles water on the wood to stop it drying out.

The only traditional wooden dhows we saw in the Farasan Archipelago had been left to rot on the road and the rocky beach. We were told that they were illegal Yemeni people-trafficking vessels that the Saudi water police had intercepted. As far as we could establish, the last of Greater Farasan's dhow builders, Abdo Hasan Mujawir, died some 45 years ago.

Muhammad Uthman Mahmud Hanas, a former pearl diver, now in his 70s, informed us that his uncle had built planked *hūrī*s (*hūrī bil-lawḥ*) in Saer village on Segid Island. Apparently these 9-m craft were used for fishing, carried six people and were propelled by either oars or a sail.[57] We stumbled across a number of abandoned dugout *hūrī*s, including one belonging to 100-year-old Mohammed Isa Aqili at Muharraq village, Greater Farasan. Someone had attempted to patch the cracks in the hull with metal strips, but in 2015 I heard that the boat was damaged beyond repair when a vehicle reversed over it.[58]

As in Jizan, small fibreglass fishing vessels known as *falūka*s now dominate the Farasan Archipelago. The transition from wood to fibreglass occurred abruptly towards the end of the last century, prompted, at least in part, by the soaring costs of timber.

THE AFRICAN DHOWS OF ERITREA AND DJIBOUTI

Threats to traditional dhow building

Yemen provided an excellent opportunity to examine dhows, but I later learned that Yemeni hull designs and other features were exported to the African coast of the southern zone of the Red Sea. Hence, John P. Cooper and I visited Massawa and the surrounding area in February 2011. We did not see any vessels under construction, so it is fair to say that dhow-building knowledge and practices are, to say the least, 'extremely threatened'.[59] However, we witnessed a number of working dhows as well as some 30–40-year-old dhows under repair in Tuwaled and Sigalat Lamba. Motors were introduced in 1967, but only richer owners could afford them. Poorer members of the trading and fishing communities, as in the rest of the Red Sea region, continued to use sails because they were obviously more economical.

At Tuwaled, we saw 35 wooden vessels either under repair or abandoned on the beach, including all four Yemeni designs: the *za'īma*, *'obrī*, *zārūk* and 'winged' *hūrī*. Siraj Muhammad Siraj recalled his father saying that these designs were copied from Khokha and Hodeidah and added, 'These Yemeni vessels could endure the waves' (*yatḥammal al-mawj*),[60] meaning they sailed well. Several of the dhows were decorated with bright colours at the waist, while the larger ones had been painted all over. We had seen similarly colourful vessels in Yemen. There were some 20 Eritrean 'winged' *hūrī*s at Tuwaled and others at Malkato, a fishing village on the Bay of Zula. In addition, we noticed some flat-transom vessels at Sigalat Lamba and Titr.

We met two of the last traditional dhow builders in Tuwaled: 50-year-old Hamid Suleiman Hamid and his 49-year-old brother Ali, who worked just to the north of the causeway.[61] Both had been apprenticed to their uncle, and much of their work comprised routine maintenance of fishing dhows. When we visited, they were in the process of repairing a battered 40-year-old vessel that had previously been repaired in 1996 and 2011. This entailed replacing many old planks with slightly better ones, recycled from other dhows, and a major overhaul of the keel (see Figure 9.4).

Such repairs may last many years, so they can be an economical option. Isa Muhammed, a 31-year-old fisherman from Sigalat Lamba, explained: 'Our *sanbūk* was built in 1980, fully repaired in 2000, and only recently have we changed some old planks'.[62] However, Muhammad-Nour Muhammad Al-Hasan, our guide and a government employee at the Department of Fisheries in Massawa, added, 'Maintenance is not as straightforward as it seems, and it can be really expensive'. Of course, he stuck to the government line and advocated replacing an old wooden dhow with a brand-new fibreglass boat (*faybar-sanbūk*, also known as a *jalba* in Eritrea). Yet, as in other areas, the local fishermen have been reluctant to accept grants that would enable them to make the switch amid concerns over the government's motives.

In addition to their repair work, the brothers claimed that they still built two small or medium-sized fishing dhows, three or four planked fishing *hūrī*s (*c.*10 m in length) and a number of small *ṣaddāfa*s (fishing and shell-collecting canoes) at Sigalat Lamba each year, although we saw no evidence of these dhows. However, they clearly had sufficient work, as Muhammad-Nour informed us that 'The local government offered both shipwrights working at

FIGURE 9.4 Hamid Suleiman Hamid and two of his workers replacing parts of the garboard strakes, Tuwaled, Massawa, 2011 (photo MARES by John P. Cooper).

Tuwaled a move to a new place called Mallahat Salina, but they refused as they preferred to stay where they are'.[63]

Ṣaddāfas are plank built, double-ended, about 4 m long and operate in coastal waters, propelled by oar or sail. They could be a recent adaptation of dugout *hūrīs*, which were brought to Eritrea from India until the early 1970s. We saw examples at Malkato on the Zula Gulf and at Titr on the Edana shoreline. There was also a *ṣaddāfa* boatyard near the Kubri, Tuwaled, where I interviewed a 32-year-old fisherman, Alam Bughri Bayri.[64] Nearby there were seven beach canoes, most of which were in a state of decay. These had raked or upright stems and stern posts that were either raised above the waist or reached to the waist. One was flat-bottomed, like the Suakini *ramas* (see above), and Alam commented that such vessels should only be used in coastal waters as they are liable to capsize in deeper water and/or rough conditions. We saw similar craft at Malkato, south-west of Massawa, on the Gulf of Zula.

The radical root √ṣ.d.f., a reference to which collectively means 'seashells', is well recorded by lexicographers, but they tend to overlook the derivative term *ṣaddāfa*. While these are often used as fishing canoes today, in the past they were specifically shell-collecting boats.[65] This typical Red Sea word, which is not found in the Gulf or Oman, has a long history of usage in Saudi, Eritrea, Sudan and Djibouti. Its morphological mould semantically marks 'frequency of usage' by doubling the middle radical 'd' – *ṣaddāf* ('shell collector') – and by analogy follows other maritime terms with the morphological pattern *fa''āl* (doubling the middle radical), such as *baḥḥār* (MSA–CA; 'sailor'), *ghawwāṣ* (MSA–CA; 'diver'), *mallāḥ* (CA; 'helmsman'), *saffān* (CA; 'shipbuilder, navigator or ship's master') and *ṣayyād* (MSA–CA; 'fisherman').[66]

Djiboutian dhows: A variety of traditional wooden dhows and fibreglass boats

In 2009, we saw a number of traditional cargo and fishing dhows in Port de Pêche and l'Escale, Djibouti City. The overwhelming majority of these craft were made of fibreglass, although, interestingly, some of these followed traditional designs. Wooden dhows still carried foodstuffs and passengers to and from Tadjourah and Obock, but there were no examples of these vessels in the Ancienne Pêcherie (the old fishing area); indeed, the whole area had been bulldozed to make way for a new French naval base. Some of the local fishermen were using old dugout *hūrīs* and we were told that others had moved with their wooden craft to Port de Pêche. However, further investigation revealed that those fishermen were now using fibreglass boats. The sheets of fibreglass were stamped with the name 'Masay'ad', the factory in Hadhramaut where they were made.

The few traditional wooden vessels in the harbour were in urgent need of repair. The Afars use *dhoonik* or *doonik* (Somali *dooni*) for such craft,[67] while the Djiboutian Yemenite Arabic speakers call them *hūrī-khashab*s (a catch-all term for all wooden dhows) or, sometimes, *za'īma*s. The Afars also use the word *būtī* (from the French *'boutre'*) when referring to watercraft in general. These terms reveal that ethnic groups can communicate in their own cultural–linguistic lexicons and yet mutually understand each other. One other term, the Arabic *merkeb*, is used infrequently in reference to a large deep-sea dhow.[68]

No traditional wooden dhows are being built in Djibouti today. The last to be constructed was completed in the 1990s, according to Perrier.[69] The hull designs of the *za'īma*, *'ibrī* (note that an 'i' replaces the Yemeni 'o' of *'obrī*) and *zārūk* were mostly imported from Aden and Hadhramaut. They measured between 25 and 40 m in length. Perrier mentions another type of dhow called a *mahadi*, which was apparently 'a hybrid of the [*za'īma-sanbūk*]'s prow and an *'ibrī*'s poop'.[70] Clifford Hawkins also seems to have encountered this vessel in Djibouti in the early 1970s,[71] but Perrier says that his predecessor did not bother to ask the locals for the name.[72] We did not come across either the name or a vessel that fitted the description in Djibouti, although Perrier suggests that *mahadi* is simply the Tihama people's term for what is known as a *jurdī* in Hodeidah and further south.[73] As we saw in Chapter 8, the *jurdī* does indeed have the curved upper stem post of a *za'īma* and the straight stern post of an *'obrī*. However, *mahadi* may not be a recent Djiboutian coin word for this hybrid craft, because a similar term for 'raft–boat', deriving from the root √'.d.w. ('to cross'), has been well established on the Nile for centuries. Similarly, in Jeddah, the locals call any ferryboat that transports passengers from ship to shore a *ma'diyya*.[74] This word was also known in the Mediterranean, and the Moroccan traveller Ibn Baṭṭūṭa used it in reference to any type of log, reed or bamboo raft in the Indian Ocean.[75] Therefore, the word that Perrier heard in Djibouti (possibly the plural form of *ma'diyya*) was probably used to describe various crafts' shared *function* – ferrying pasengers across the harbour – not to indicate a particular type of vessel.

In 2009, at Ras Ali, east of Tadjourah, 59-year-old master builder Ahmed Muhammad al-Gumaani, from Khokha, Yemen,[76] was commissioned to repair two Yemeni dhows – a *zārūk* and a *za'īma* – because no builder in Djibouti had the necessary skills. Ibrahim Abou Bakar, the owner, planned to use both vessels as pleasure craft for tourists and foreign residents in Djibouti.[77] The *zārūk*, with a weight capacity of 60 tons, was built in Khokha in 2000, while the *za'īma* hailed from Sheikh Said, opposite Mayyun Island (Perim) on the Bab el-Mandeb, where it was built in the 1980s. The latter vessel, which had a round transom stern, similar to the ubiquitous so-called *sanbūk* (see Chapter 8),

THE OVERSEER: THE SEA CAPTAIN

The sea captain, the highest position on board ship, is known as the *rayyes* in the north and the *nākhōda* in the south, indicating two distinct linguistic communities. *Rayyes* (< √r.'.s. 'to head; to lead'; pl. *rayyesīn*) is an Arabic dialectal usage that denotes someone who is in charge – 'a chief; manager'.[8] By contrast, *nākhōda* is of Hindī–Persian origin (Hin. *nāw* 'ship' + Per. *khudā* 'master'; pl. *nawākhid(a)*).[9] The *rayyes* or *nākhōda* is the 'master of the sea' (*ṣāḥib al-baḥr*), as one interviewee, Sadek Yakoub Abdalla of Obock, explained.[10] He knows the course (*majrā*) and the distance (*masāfa*) and understands how to use the compass (*dīra* or *būsola*), though mariners were traditionally guided by the stars (see below).

The captain is responsible for the ship's day-to-day management, from the moment it leaves the port to when it reaches its final destination. On fishing vessels, in addition to managing the ship and crew, he is in charge of the rudder and, of course, the fishing itself. In other words, as one mariner from Guweih, Egypt, said, 'He is responsible for all activities' (*mas'ūl li-kull ḥaraka*).[11] Five times a day, the captain will call the crew and passengers to prayer, and everyone will use a tin of seawater for their ritual ablutions. When in port, duties may include trading and supervising the loading and unloading of cargo, which means liaising with the harbour master, known as the *rayyes/nākhōda al-barr* (lit. 'the responsible on shore') to differentiate him from the *rayyes/nākhōda al-baḥr* (lit. 'the responsible on the sea'). Any skipper who carries passengers and pilgrims also has 'to account to the harbour-police and the sanitary authorities'.[12]

On board a trading or pearling ship, the skipper is assisted by a quartermaster or clerk (*kerrānī* of Skt origin < *karana*) who is in charge of recording the cargo and purchasing provisions at each anchorage but also keeps track of expenditure, notes the pearls found by divers and logs them in a register. He also assists the skipper with paying the mariners their final wages, with deductions made for money advanced during the voyage for clothing, cigarettes and so on[13] (see Chapter 15). On the return leg of a fishing trip, which in the days of sail could last two to three months, the skipper and/or owner record the catch and calculate the fishermen's wages on the basis of a share system.

Appropriately, literally the highest position on the ship – the quarter-deck or the poop – is reserved for the captain. From there, he issues instructions to the crew, passes judgement in disputes and deals with cases of serious misconduct. If the crew (or passengers) feel that the captain has behaved unethically, the 'traditional customary law of the sea' dictates that they should present their case to a high official once they have returned to port. In the past, this person was known as the *amīr al-baḥr* (admiral).[14]

A captain might apprentice his son or nephew from as young as 8 years old, although more commonly from 12 or 13, teaching him the basic principles of navigation, such as observing the stars, reading the compass, noting landmarks and weather changes, and monitoring the different wave patterns and the sounds of the sea.[15] The boy will also receive some elementary schooling (*kuttāb*), during which he learns rudimentary arithmetic and memorizes large sections of the Qur'ān.

Traditional dhows were rarely equipped with the navigational instruments that had aided European mariners for centuries. Indeed, the absence of these supposedly crucial pieces of equipment on long-distance voyages puzzled Western travellers. For instance, Richard Burton's *sanbūk*, which left Suez for Jeddah in 1853, had 'no compass, no log, no sounding lines [...] not even the suspicion of a chart'.[16] Earlier, John Ovington (d. 1731), a chaplain of the East India Company, had also noticed the absence of charts during his voyage through the Red Sea.[17] Moreover, matters had scarcely improved by the twentieth century. In 1938 Alan Villiers noted that his 20-ton *zārūk* from Ma'alla to Jizan had no charts or log, and the compass was faulty.[18]

I asked a number of old captains whether they had access to navigational instruments during their time at sea. They answered that a compass and sounding lines were both carried as a matter of course, but charts were unnecessary as they followed their 'instinct'. They claimed to have a mental map of the coastal landscape and said that experience taught them to calculate distances and the best time to depart from port. Ali AlGhabban recalled that his father and grandfather, both of whom were captains, insisted that an experienced mariner developed a sort of 'sea sense': 'The captain knew the sea very well; he was familiar with the routes [*masārāt*], the channels [*fasmāt*] through the coral reef, but most of all he knew the winds, the right time as to when to set off'.[19] (I will explore this subject further in Chapter 13.) Sailors with this 'sea sense' are also able to interpret the sounds and silence of sea. For example, when 50-year-old Idrees Daud Ali from Zula (see Plate 16), near Adulis, heard 'crashing waves', he could estimate the ship's distance from land with great accuracy.[20]

A skilled mariner has a good sense of the coastal topography as well as the depth and nature of the seabed. Mahmud Saad, a *rayyes* from Quseir, stressed the importance of memorizing landmarks (*'alāmāt*) because 'the accuracy of judging by the eye' is essential when sailing.[21] Burton noted that the *rayyes* on his journey 'knew the name of each hill, and had a legend for every nook and corner in sight'.[22] More remarkably, William Makin recalled a blind skipper who had lost his sight while pearl diving, but that had not dissuaded him from buying his own dhow after much scrimping and saving. When Makin asked him, 'How do you manage to navigate through these waters?' the captain replied: 'It is the boy whom you see here. He has my eyes.'[23]

Calculating distances and navigating through coral reefs are particularly important skills. As Alain Clouet stated: 'many shipwrecks were caused through errors of calculation made by the modern skipper'.[24] Ultimately, fellow mariners do not judge a Red Sea captain's competence on the basis of his familiarity with nautical instruments and charts; rather, it is his sailing experience that is of paramount importance. Skills are learned and experience is gained over many years. Indeed, as David Footman wrote: 'On every voyage it was the skill, the judgement and the integrity of the *nākhōda* that made all the difference between disaster and success.'[25]

Captains keep an eye out for landmarks. Boatswain Seif el Din Hasan Mahmud of Quseir told me: '[The *rayyes*] knew from the shape of the mountain which anchorage we were approaching.'[26] Ali Khalifa Ali Hammed, in his 90s, is a former pearl diver from Muharraq village on Greater Farasan Island. When we asked him to describe the voyage from his home to the Dahlak Islands, off the Eritrean coast, he recited poetic verses he had learned in his youth. These included details of the distance, the stars that were used to plot the course and the landmarks that were encountered en route.[27] This practice of memorizing landmarks dates back many centuries; the medieval navigators Aḥmad Ibn Mājid (d. *c.*906/1500) and Sulaymān al-Mahrī (d. 917/1511) documented several maritime verses. An illiterate mariner would memorize constellations, dangerous zones, depths, winds and currents, the colour of the sea in various areas, landmarks and local fish and birds in poetic verses and rhymes. The captain would also instruct a particular sailor to recite these verses to the rest of the crew each day. This was a useful exercise, as it forced the sailors to listen to each other's recitations and thus strengthened their mental retention of the crucial details. This meant that the crew could share important information with one another if the ship ran into difficulties during a gale or heavy rain, when they might lose sight of land and not know their exact position.

THE CAPTAIN'S SHIPMATES

The boatswain (*mugaddam* or *saranjī*) assists the captain by implementing his instructions with respect to the routine work on board ship. *Mugaddam* (which substitutes 'g' for the MSA 'q') comes from the root √q.d.m. ('to lead the way').[28] Like the skipper, he sits on the aft deck or stands at the foredeck or stem post. From this position, he can spot any obstacle close to the coast, and this is perhaps the origin of the word; that is, 'to place a person at the head'.[29]

In effect, the boatswain is the head sailor and he is in charge of the sails, the rigging (*rawājiḥ*) and the anchors. On a fishing vessel he is also responsible for the catch[30] and supervises the water rations. If the captain is indisposed, the boatswain will deal with any insubordination among the crew. Ibrahim Mousa Ahmed of Jizan, a former shell collector, recalled: 'It was not unusual for a boatswain to take charge of beating a sailor on board the ship as a lesson to the rest of the crew.'[31]

In the past, on the open sea, the boatswain was assisted by a lookout sailor (*munaddiḥ*), who sat where the yard crosses the mast. He would warn both the boatswain and the captain of any dangers or when land came into view, although this job was also sometimes performed by the *rayyes* himself. Ali Bey (d. 1818), writing in the nineteenth century, reported that the lookout played a crucial role on account of the many dangers of the coastal landscape. Disaster would befall the ship if the lookout did not see a coral reef or submerged rocks, or if the helmsman did not hear his call to change course in good time.[32]

Steering in and around reefs and rocks near the coast is a difficult skill to master, but the skipper and the boatswain are aided by their mental maps of landmarks (*'alāmāt*), anchorages and islands. There are other dangers far out to sea, of course. 'What can you do in the middle of the sea?' (*Fī wasṭ al-baḥr ta'mel 'ey?*) asked 64-year-old Duwi Toufiq Mahmud from Quseir, who had experienced many storms and high waves. He admitted that the waters in the middle of the Red Sea can be frightening and stated that 'the depths are immense' (*fil-baḥr a'māg*).[33]

The helmsman, known as *ṣāḥib ad-daffa* in the north and *sukkānī* or *sukūnī* in the south, is in charge of the wheel at the poop and takes instructions from the captain or his assistant. Said Mohammad Alaiwa, a helmsman from Mocha, told me that other sailors might be asked to take the wheel on occasion, but they were always kept under close supervision.[34]

Both *daffa* and *sukkān* are semantically related to 'rudder', the means of steering that is attached to the ship's wheel by a rope or a metal chain on larger vessels. Smaller boats are steered by a tiller and rudder, while even smaller dugout or planked *hūrīs* may have no rudder at all; instead, the fishermen use their paddles as quarter-rudders to steer the vessels. *Daffa*, from the root √d.f.f., means 'to move or flap the wings [of a bird]', so, by extension, to steer – hence the function of the board (i.e., the rudder) that is fixed to the stern.[35] Similarly, *sukkānī* (< √s.k.n.) derives from *sukkān* ('rudder'), which may have been Akkadian or Sanskrit in origin before entering Persian and then Arabic.

On a pearling dhow the boatswain or pilot (see below) would often take control of the rudder. The captain would sound the depths with a plumb line (*bild*) from his position on the poop and then inform the helmsman in which direction to steer the ship. Ninety-two-year-old Muhammad Bukhayyit Alsinani from Ummlejj recalled that 'the *rayyes* used to climb the mast and cry to the helmsman "*imlā*" [go right] and "*gam*" [go left]'.[36] The geographer al-Maqdisī heard similar commands during his journey across the Red Sea in the tenth century.[37] He reported that the captain's instructions were repeated by two cabin boys who would cry 'to the right' or 'to the left' to guide the helmsman.

THE DEEP-SEA AND COASTAL NAVIGATOR

For long-distance voyages, the skipper or dhow owner might hire a navigator called a *mu'allim* (pl. *mu'allimīn*). This word comes from the root √'.l.m. ('to know; to be familiar with').[38] Today, as in medieval times, *mu'allimīn* guide the large ships that sail across the middle of the Red Sea and/or into the open sea of the Indian Ocean.[39] In coastal waters the same role is played by the *rubbān* (pl. *rabābina*), who navigates the ship in and out of the canals and through the reefs and sandbanks. This word can be traced back to antiquity,[40] and the radicals of its root √r.b.b. ('to be master; to have command')[41] are found in Akkadian, Aramaic, Southern Arabian and so on. It is also documented in the medieval Islamic period, particularly in connection with the Red Sea and the Arabian Sea.[42] The distinction between *mu'allim* and *rubbān* is not always maintained; in the south, the latter term is often used for both open-sea and coastal navigators. Meanwhile, in the north, *rayyes* may be used in place of both terms.

According to my informants, Egyptian, Hijazi, Yemeni/Hadhrami and Somali deep-sea *mu'allimīn* – especially members of coastal tribes from Khokha, Mocha, Sheikh Said, Mukalla and Shihr – were renowned for their navigational skill. These men were particularly adept at dealing with the wind regimes in the Gulf of Aden and the Arabian Sea during voyages to the south-west coast of India.[43] One small town, Al-Hami, on the Hadhrami coast, produced many deep-sea *mu'allimīn*, but these brave men are now largely forgotten in the rest of Yemen and around the coasts of the Red Sea.[44]

Red Sea *mu'allimīn* have never kept logs of their ocean crossings, and this remains the case today. Interestingly, though, the *mu'allimīn* of the north-west coast of India have kept pilot manuals (*pothi*) for centuries. These contain day-to-day sailing instructions for the voyages from one port to the next and record trips into and out of the Red Sea, the Arabian–Persian Gulf, India and South-East Asia.[45]

Any ship entering the Red Sea from the Indian Ocean would not dare to travel along the coast without first hiring an indigenous navigator. Manoeuvring a vessel through the coastal channels demanded particularly skilful navigation, and getting it wrong could have disastrous consequences. I heard many stories of boats wrecked and/or lives lost due to poor navigation (see Chapter 12 for more details).

In 1513 Portuguese officers called upon a number of pilots (*rabābina*) to guide them through the more treacherous stretches of the Red Sea.[46] Three centuries later, Burckhardt was critical of Yemeni navigators, though he praised the bravery of the coastal pilots,[47] while Viscount Valentia was thankful for a knowledgeable local pilot with 40 years of 'sailing [experience] between Mocha and Suakin'.[48] Around the same time, according to Carsten Niebuhr, Egyptian mariners who lived near Tur in the Gulf of Suez were renowned for their skill. They received a stipend of 500 crowns and some extra money to train younger pilots.[49]

All *mu'allimīn* and *rabābina* had to master navigation by the stars, while captains and boatswains had more general knowledge of the major constellations. This traditional wisdom dates back to antiquity and it has persisted into modern times, as many interviewees in Egypt, Eritrea, Djibouti and Yemen confirmed. The navigator would observe the rising and setting of a number of stars to guide the vessel across the sea, to a safe anchorage through an inlet[50] or to a favourite pearling bed. He would also use the stars to calculate the distance travelled. The oldest technique, known as *aṣḥāb al-aṣābi'*,[51] which was practised for centuries by Chinese and Indian mariners alike, involved placing 'the palms of the hands on the eyebrows. The number of fingers covering stars indicated the [approximate] distance.'[52]

The navigator supplemented his observation of the stars with an important piece of equipment: the *dīra* (CA *dā'ira*) or *būsola* (< It. *bussola*) (see Figure 10.1). This was a circular nautical chart 'with stars written on it' (*yuktab 'alayhā an-nujūm*), as one fisherman explained, 45-year-old Muhsin Saud Muhsini from Massawa.[53] It showed the north–south–east–west directions and names of stars that were well known to the ancient Arabians. The western edge of the *dīra* was labelled *maghārib* ('setting') while the eastern edge was labelled *maṭāli'* ('rising'). Navigators continued to use such charts until roughly 70 years ago, although I was told that captains rarely kept them on board because they preferred to observe the stars in the sky.

Navigation by the stars is now a dying art, but we were able to gather some interesting information. For instance, we learned that the *jāh* (Polaris; the North Star) was widely used to plot the southerly route to Yemen. Egyptian interviewees frequently spoke of the *tureyya* (CA *thurayya*; the Pleiades), which

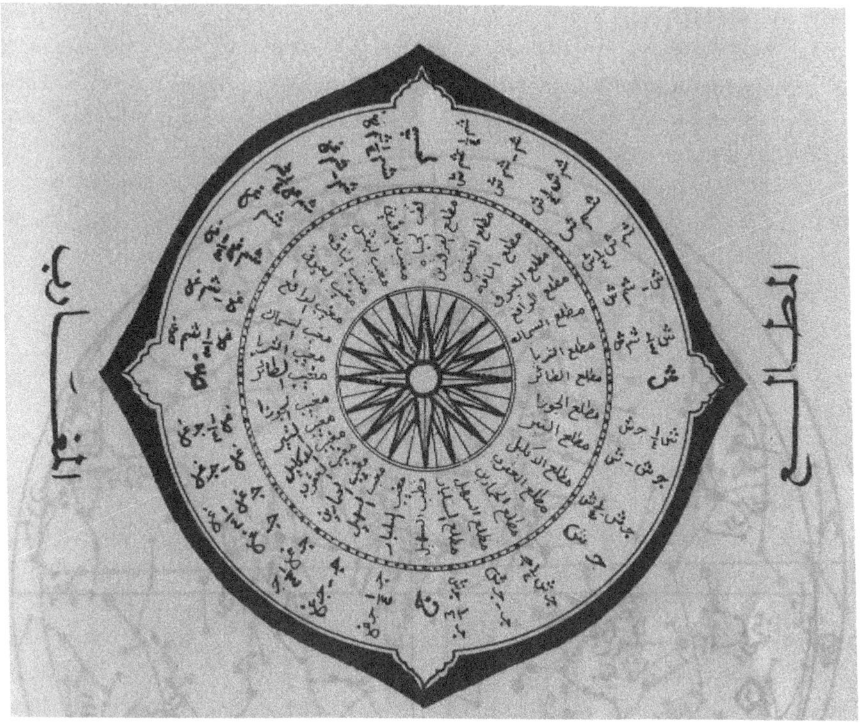

FIGURE 10.1 A navigator's chart or *dīra*.[54]

sets in the last days of April, along with the *gawza* (CA *jawzā'*, parts of Gemini and Orion). This marks the beginning of the forty days of summer (*arba'īnēt eṣ-seyf*). Egyptian navigators watch out for the *na'sh* (the Great Bear) which announces the coming of the north wind. Another star that several interviewees mentioned was the *nasr* or *an-nasr aṭ-ṭāyir* ('the Flying Eagle'; Altair), which heralds the start of winter and north-westerly winds.[55] (There is more on the winds of the Red Sea in Chapter 13.) One experienced 77-year-old captain, Youssef Omar Mohamed of Obock, explained, 'We watched the star Ḥimarayn as our guide to cross over from one point to another', when sailing from Aden to Berbera on the Horn of Africa in early October each year.[56] At Port de Pêche in Djibouti City, 80-year-old Muhammad Hummid Ali remembered the old days with pride: 'The sailor used his head ... unlike modern times [when he relies] on devices.'[57] Indeed he did. When piloting a dhow, the Italian adventurer Lorenzo Ricciardi found it 'easier to steer by picking one star than keeping [his] eyes glued to the quivering compass-needle'.[58]

According to Hasan Salih Shihab, his father and a Hadhrami shipmate, Ustādh Muhammad Abd Allah, had used a compass and the stars to find their way through difficult waters en route to Vietnam in the 1940s.[59] A number of older informants confirmed that they had used a similar technique in the past, although most of them found it difficult to remember the names of the stars. For instance, Mohammad Ahmed Zaid al-Anbari (see Plate 5), a *nākhōda* from Khor al-Ghureirah who was in his 60s, admitted: 'I recognize them but the names do not come to my head.'[60] Meanwhile, younger navigators were far less familiar with the stars. Even those who had a vague knowledge of the constellations and individual stars were unable to name them. Of course, the younger generation now rely on technology, and they are teaching the senior mariners, such as Mohammad, the basics of satellite navigation.[61]

THE SAILOR

In the Red Sea region, the most common term for a sailor is *baḥḥār* (pl. *baḥḥāra*), from the root √b.ḥ.r. ('to put to sea; set sail'),[62] with a collective use being *baḥriyya*. Intriguingly (or coincidentally), the radicals of this term may have an Indo-Aryan link, either directly or indirectly, to the Sanskrit and Pāli *bharu*.[63]

Sailors were hired either at the harbour or while the ship was at an anchorage. They were chosen by the captain, and no previous experience was needed. A sailor could be hired or fired as it pleased the skipper, but a good one might stay in service on one vessel for a long time if his workmanship was deemed exemplary. On the other hand, Norman Lewis states that mariners moved regularly from one dhow owner or captain to the next.[64] None of the sailors I interviewed confirmd this, although they did agree that it was rare for them to settle permanently in one place. Moreover, it was not unheard of for a sailor to relocate and marry a new wife, with or without the knowledge of the previous one.

It was a cosmopolitan world as sailors were recruited from a variety of countries. Antonin Besse Sr, who built dhows in Aden from the 1920s to the 1950s,[65] singled out Mocha, Khokha and Somaliland as particularly good recruiting grounds.[66] According to my informants, northern skippers frequently employed Hijazi Bedouins and Egyptian farmers for six months at a time on a seasonal basis: 'from the palm tree to the sea' (*min an-nakhal ilā l-baḥar*), as Awwad Bin Bakhit Al-Juhuni from Yanbu al-Bahr poetically explained. Awwad himself was a farmer–sailor for many years, so I asked him whether it was an easy transition to make. He replied: '[Riding] the sea is a passion. Not everyone who rides the sea is a sailor' (*al-baḥr gharām lā man ṭala' al-baḥr baḥḥār*).[67] While, at first sight, there seems to be no connection between the roles of farm labourer and sailor, Ali AlGhabban told me, 'What is common between them is that both are guided by the stars'.[68] The sowing and harvesting seasons are signalled by the first appearance of certain stars, while, as we have seen, mariners have traditionally used the stars for navigation, to predict seasonal shifts in the prevailing wind and as indicators of the start of the fishing season.

Sailors travelled for months on cargo vessels to the Red Sea ports and further afield, into the Indian Ocean. Although the majority were Arabic speakers, a significant number were not, so a common Red Sea pidgin Arabic was used to communicate with, for example, Swahili, Persian, Kutchi and Malayalam speakers. The Red Sea mariner's lexicon that grew out of this pidgin language was used by foreign traders, merchants, craftsmen, dhow builders and pilgrim settlers, and this has now developed into a wider Arabic pidgin that is spoken throughout the coastal western Indian Ocean. Meanwhile, a Red Sea Arabic *lingua franca* has developed over many years on both the African and Arabian coasts. As Alain Clouet noticed in the 1970s, this is 'a particular dialect composed of borrowed words' from wherever speakers of Arabic and other languages came into contact with one another.[69]

A number of sailors' tasks require a great deal of muscle power and good coordination. When describing East African sailors in Quseir, Carl Klunzinger wrote, 'with a spring or two they scamper up the mast, seizing a rope with their hands and pressing their feet against another near it', invariably with 'agility and ease'.[70] Some jobs were more important than others. According to 75-year-old Muhammad Abd Allah al-Abbadi, a former sailor from Qunfudha, the hold often filled with water,[71] especially if the dhow was heavily laden,[72] so it had to be bailed out at regular intervals. Every member of the crew was expected to help with this critical task, and, as William Makin noted, the bailing might continue for 'hour after hour, fighting to save the dhow'.[73] Meanwhile, as the Red Sea adventurer Henri De Monfreid observed, one or two good swimmers might have to dive down to repair the worst leaks with small bags of rice, which were placed in the holes and sealed the gaps as they expanded.[74] Makin wrote that rags could be used in a similar way.[75] Other jobs included making ropes, mending sails and diving to place the anchor on the seabed. Pearling dhow haulers, in addition to fulfilling their rigging and bailing duties, helped with cleaning and washing clothes.

Fishermen who sail on wooden vessels today have a work routine that includes all of the jobs described above, but the trips are shorter than they used to be because most of the vessels are motorized (although the captains still frequently deploy sails to save fuel). For centuries, mariners have careened their dhows every six months for cleaning and repair purposes, and this sort of routine maintenance is still practised up and down the African and Arabian coasts. When the tide is out, the sailors scrape off the barnacles from the waterline to the bottom of the hull, then smear the outer planks with animal fat (*shaḥam*), shark-liver oil or paint (*rang*) and lime or gypsum, the composition called *nūra*. They also replace any damaged planks and recaulk, then coat the internal planks with fat or shark-liver oil.

Sailors are expected to jump to their feet as soon as the skipper shouts '*Yallāh!*' ('Come on!'), but they do not always need to be told. One former mariner in his 80s, Abbas Muhammad from Quseir, recalled: 'They knew when sail rigging was needed, for as soon as there was a change in the waves they took that as a sign to put up a new sail.'[76] Rigging can seem chaotic at first, but then everything invariably comes together. 'Each sailor took charge of his [rigging] rope' (*kull wāḥid 'alā ḥablu*), explained 76-year-old Abou Bakar Habib, a former *nākhōda* from Tadjourah.[77] They all knew their specific roles and completed the process in perfect harmony.

Each watch (*zām*) lasts three hours, so the day is divided into eight *zām*s. Mohammad al-Anbari, a *nākhōda* from Khor al-Ghureirah, fishes along the southern Yemeni coast and combines this with some light trading at a few ports. In the past, when he did more trading, his dhow carried a crew of eight. At sea, four of the sailors would work while the other four rested, until Mohammad decided it was time for a new *zām* to begin: 'Those who slept were awoken by my voice: "Come on, get up!"'[78] I cannot imagine anyone disobeying the rather intimidating Mohammad, but a skipper's order is not always followed to the letter, as Alan Villiers discovered on a dhow in the 1950s.[79]

A carpenter (*najjār*) was usually hired to carry out major repairs on large vessels, but in his absence one or more of the sailors would do the job themselves. Mohammad Alaiwa, a 60-year-old sailor from Mocha, explained:

> If a plank or mast breaks, the sailors repair it temporarily by placing a piece of timber against the broken part and tying it with a rope. They do this until they arrive at an anchorage or port and have it replaced. They sometimes use gypsum as a temporary measure.[80]

Some sailors occupy themselves during the long, monotonous days at sea by carving scale models of dhows.

The *ṭabbākh* ('cook') – traditionally known as the *ṭahhān* ('bread-maker') on pearling dhows – prepares all of the food. Loaves are made simply from flour or ground corn, salt and water. If a pearling dhow carries a large number of divers and haulers, another cook, in addition to the *ṭahhān*, might be hired. *Taḥḥān* and *ṭabbākh* are genuinely Arabic terms, composed of the radicals √ṭ.ḥ.n. ('to grind') and √ṭ.b.kh. ('to cook'), respectively.[81]

Most meals consist of rice, fish and soup, while on feast days a goat or sheep will be slaughtered. Kettles, saucepans, pestle and mortar[82] and round grinding stones (*raḥā*) are stored near the foredeck. Water – which is now stored in an ice box on long voyages – is boiled in a copper kettle. William Makin claimed that an Arabian sailor could go for hours without drinking any water 'beneath a scorching sun [...] [not] even wetting his lips'.[83] However, if the water started to run out, the skipper would put in at an anchorage and replenish the ship's supply from the local wells. Villiers sailed on a *zārūk* with water that was 'warm, brackish and full of insects',[84] so passengers and crew alike were eager to reach port and refresh themselves with clean drinking water.

Each vessel usually has one or two cabin boys, known as *aṣ-ṣaghīrs* in the north and *aṣ-ṣghayyirs* in the south (or sometimes *walads*). On large dhows they often help out on deck and perform a number of other tasks, as required by the captain,[85] such as make the tea or coffee, pound the grain and prepare the flour for the *ṭahhān*, or grind spices and grill fish for the main meals.[86] Eventually, the cabin boy will be trained to become a sailor or a pearl diver. Soleiman Mohammad Ali Baloos from Greater Farasan, a pearl merchant, told me of a 97-year-old former diver by the name of Mohammad Ahmad Muzaffar who first went to sea at the age of seven as a cabin boy. Soleiman continued, 'These boys were taught manners and respect for their elders. Otherwise, they were beaten by the captain in front of their fathers'.[87]

SAILORS' WORKING CLOTHES

Crew members' sea chests are stored on the aft deck. These often contain items that they try to sell when they anchor at a port. Each sailor stores his single change of clothes in a bundle near his chest. In the past, the nature of these clothes depended on the region in which the vessel operated. In the 1950s, Alan Villiers reported that the captain of his dhow wore a 'chequered blue and white *sarong* [Mal. < *sārung*; 'a long kilt, tucked at the waist'[88]]. The money belt was tucked in a multi-coloured sash, and a golden turban wrapped around the cap. He carried amber prayer beads [*maṣbaḥa*] to pass the time'.[89] The following decade, Bob Serjeant met a southern Arabian captain who wore 'the *'imāma dabwānī*, a turban of Indian weave with a red stripe along the edges'.[90] In 1963 a Ugandan newspaper reported that Yemenis and Hadhramis wore 'large orange turbans', while Somalis had 'embroidered caps and multi-coloured turbans'.[91] According to Alain Clouet, writing in the early 1970s, the Yemeni al-Ḥakmīs wore a 'mat-woven' *ṭarbūsh* while the Hadhramis wore a turban fitted to their ears.[92]

Sailors' clothing is rather different today, but I did see some traditional working clothes in Egypt, Sudan and Yemen. Egyptian sailors wear a long shirt (*gamīṣ*) of *khām* (linen) or *damūrī* (a coarse, calico-like fabric)[93] down to their knees, a cloth belt (*maḥzam*) and a cotton turban (*'imāma*). In Sudan, mariners wrap themselves in a cloth called a *gingāb* made of Sudanese cotton that is folded around the waist; some wear turbans while others prefer hats made of palm-tree fibres. Some sport a distinctive waistcoat (*ṣidriyya*) over a collared gown (*jelabiyya*) and a long turban with a hanging tail on one side (see Figure 10.2). The vast majority of sailors and fishermen wear a flannel (*fanīla*) vest to absorb sweat, and when it gets chilly they put on a *kūt* (sweater). Matar Fikri Muhammed, a 48-year-old mariner from Mersa Alam, remembered a business in either his home town or Quseir that made and sold sailors' clothes some 30 or 40 years ago.[94] The Yemenis wear a similar style of clothing. Like their northern counterparts, they combine a *fūṭa* – a piece of cloth that is wrapped around the hips and reaches to the knees[95] – with a white or coloured cloth turban or a quilted skullcap (see Figure 10.3).

FIGURE 10.2 Sailors wearing the distinctive *ṣidriyya* and the long *'imāma*, Suakin, 2004 (photo by the author).

FIGURE 10.3 Said Mohammad Alaiwa, a helmsman from Mocha, Yemen, wearing a *fūṭa* and a golden turban, 2009 (photo MARES by the author).

IN CONCLUSION

My informants frequently mentioned the camaraderie that developed on board ship because everyone, from the captain to the cabin boy, worked together and shared the same confined space, sometimes for many months at a time. Today, on shore, that camaraderie is still evident in the cafés and evening gatherings (*umsiyyāt*) whenever old sailors meet to reminisce about the past. They remember colleagues who have passed away, the hard work they used to do, their departures and arrivals and their voyages to distant places. Younger Red Sea sailors still fish and trade on traditional wooden dhows. Life is faster now and technology increasingly controls their lives, but there is a timeless quality to dhow sailing on the Red Sea, and the rich terminology of this seascape still survives in the maritime lexicon.

In the next chapter, I will look at some of the social aspects of life at sea, such as the importance of communal mealtimes and how sailors keep themselves entertained during long voyages.

11

ON BOARD THE DHOW: EATING, RESTING AND ENTERTAINMENT

يا ناخودة لا تؤاخذنا
كثر الغياب ما تناسبنا
شوف الصغار يسألوا عنا
يم جا أبونا يفرحنا
ربي أدي الديون عني
عبد الله ابرهيم حسن، صداف من جزيرة فرسان

'Oh *nākhōda*, do not blame us;
We would like to return to our families;
You see the children are asking after us;
The day our father comes back we will be happy.
Oh God help us to pay our debts.'

Sea song recited by Abd Allah Ibrahim Hasan, former shell collector, Greater Farasan Island.[1]

The older mariners talk of their days at sea, the living conditions on board ship, sleeping arrangements and entertainment, while the younger fishermen's accounts of their working lives reveal a continuity of tradition and practice on wooden dhows, even though their journeys are considerably shorter than those of the past (see Plate 8). It is no surprise, then, that some of the information presented in the eyewitness accounts of old and young alike is also found in the written testimonies of Western travellers over the past 200 years.

DISCOMFORT ON-BOARD SHIP

According to my older informants, traditional wooden dhows provided little space for living and sleeping. Even when carrying passengers, coir mats and/or canvas tarpaulins that covered the cargo were usually the only bedding. An awning called a *sagīfa*, which covered an area from the poop to the foredeck, provided some shade during the day. On fishing vessels, then as now, fishermen slept under the fore- or aft deck, protected from the wind and rain. According to Seif el Din Hasan Mahmud, a boatswain from Quseir, if the weather was particularly hot, some members of the crew would sleep on shore (*bayāta*).[2]

On larger vessels, if a passenger paid for deck space, rather than a passage in the hold, he would be able to stretch his legs and place his luggage in a safe place. In the 1940s, Richard LeBaron Bowen learned from Antonin Besse Sr that the latter's company offered a variety of fares (in rupees) for voyages from Aden to Berbera, Djibouti, Massawa and Port Sudan.[3] Besse's passengers were unable to hire a cabin, but earlier merchants, pilgrims and European travellers were sometimes offered that (much more expensive) option. For instance, the Catalan Ali Bey paid for a cabin on his voyage from Suez to Jeddah. Meanwhile, his servants suffered the journey in the hold, where there were already some 50 pilgrims (see Figure 11.1).[4] Many of the pilgrims on Richard Burton's *sanbūk* similarly sailed in the hold as they had barely enough money for the passage. Burton paid for a cabin but was subsequently told it was taken, so he was forced to share a space on the poop with some wealthier pilgrims. Cabins on the

FIGURE 11.1 Pen-and-ink drawing of pilgrims in the hold of a dhow by F. George, 1875 (The Rodney Searight Collection, Victoria and Albert Museum).

poop were reserved for women and children, who were charged a special fee.[5] A large cabin on Carsten Niebuhr's ship bound for Jeddah accommodated 40 women, children and female slaves. Niebuhr and his Danish companions hired a somewhat smaller cabin.[6] None of these accounts provide measurements or details of the living conditions within the cabins, but it is reasonable to assume that the women's and children's cabin on Niebuhr's voyage would have been very cramped.

Over the years, many Western travellers have felt compelled to mention the overcrowding on-board ship. LeBaron Bowen saw dhows going from the Arabian Gulf to East Africa 'packed [with pilgrims] on the main deck like cattle'.[7] Although the former captains I interviewed frequently assured me they were very 'safety-conscious', in reality safety was never a primary concern for dhows carrying large numbers of passengers. Burton commented that his ship carried 97 pilgrims – far more than it could safely accommodate – as well as all manner of bales and luggage.[8] Similarly, Johann Ludwig Burckhardt reported that his dhow was overburdened with pilgrims when he set off from Yanbu al-Bahr to Quseir.[9] This was nothing new; cramming passengers on board had been standard practice since medieval times. Consider the heavily overcrowded ships that ferried pilgrims from Aidhab on the Sudanese coast to Jeddah. The accounts of the Andalusian traveller Ibn Jubayr (d. 614/1217) and the Egyptian historian al-Maqrīzī (d. 846/1442) both tell of fatal accidents.[10] Obviously, overladen dhows would lie lower at sea and were in danger of being swamped by a large swell, which would cause them to lose stability and capsize, but dhow owners usually prioritized profit over safety.

Seafarers were exposed to the elements throughout the day and night. On calm nights, the heat could be unbearable and the buzzing of mosquitoes would render sleep impossible. Burckhardt recalled a particularly 'fiery July day' in 1814, when his ship was anchored at Suakin, waiting for 'water supply'. The passengers' mood and the atmosphere on board were unpleasant; 'In remorseless heat', Burckhardt wrote, the Africans 'fought among themselves and were punched by the enraged [Suakini] sailors who, quite inefficiently, tried to restore some sort of order to the brawling chaos of the scene. They did not sail when at last the fierce red ball of the sun sank into the western hills.'[11] There was no comfort – '[not] enough room to stretch [one's] legs', according to Katharine Sim, who wrote about Burckhardt's adventures. Everyone was 'irritable, tormented by cramp and by the sun's scorching rays',[12] not to mention the mental stress of sharing very limited space with dozens of fellow seafarers. Niebuhr observed that women could be particularly 'troublesome' and 'indiscreet' on dhows.[13] Some 200 years later, LeBaron Bowen reported that female passengers were often louder than the men, and he noted that they could be quarrelsome.[14] It should be said that this was hardly surprising when one considers that they would have been confined to their hot, stifling and cramped cabin for the whole journey.

Alan Villiers mentioned that the smell of the bilge water could be horrible,[15] and the voyage could become insufferable when this merged with the stench of vomit, especially in the heat of the day. Seafarers also had to endure the reek of rotting fish, while the smell of opened oyster shells on pearling dhows was even worse. Thankfully, the toilet boxes generated little or no odour, as they were hung on the side of the prow. There was a hole in the seat and one would defecate while facing the sea before cleaning oneself with seawater. Neither the written accounts nor my informants mentioned the use of these toilet boxes by women. In general, sailors would wash themselves by bathing in the sea, but few passengers followed suit, and many wore the same clothes throughout the voyage. The smell of their stale sweat must have been unpleasant and irksome, to say the least.

Oceangoing vessels were equipped with one or two lifeboats, but there may have been none on medium-sized dhows. Hence, in an emergency, the only option might have been to jump into the sea and try to swim to shore. However, many passengers had never even seen the sea before, let alone learned how to swim. According to 64-year-old Duwi Toufiq Mahmud of Quseir (see Plate 6), if someone died on-board, 'the body would have to be buried as soon as the ship reached an anchorage'.[16] Otherwise, if the ship was far from land, the corpse (or corpses) would have to be thrown overboard. Burckhardt reported a spate of deaths on his journey from Yanbu al-Bahr to Quseir in 1814.[17]

MEALS

Dhows would carry sacks of dates, rice, lentils, corn and flour, packets of sesame seeds and sugar as well as wooden containers or metal cans containing black honey, cooking oil and/or butter. Further provisions might include sheep and goats, which, as we have seen, were slaughtered on festive occasions. The meat was then distributed among passengers and crew, who would eat it with rice. Some sailors fished by line or, on the western coast, by spear,[18] so there was usually a steady supply of fish for everyone on board.

All meals were cooked in either a fire box (*sarēdān* or *sureydān*), which was lined with a metal sheet, or an oven (*tannūr* or *kānūn*), an earthenware stove in which coal was heated and kept alight to boil water for coffee and tea. Traditionally, bread was baked in a *mīfa*, a tall, cylindrical clay vessel that was covered with dried palm leaves (*sa'af an-nakhīl*). This technique is still used in

Djibouti. The *mīfa* is placed in a metal barrel with sticks (*ḥaṭab*) and charcoal at the bottom, stones are put around the barrel to keep it steady and protect it from cracking, then the dough is baked on the hot sides of the *mīfa*.

Mealtimes brought people together. Everyone sat in a circle and ate from a huge straw-matting or metal platter, so the passengers shared their meals with the crew. The *rayyes* or *nākhōda* would occasionally participate in this communal meal, but otherwise he would sit on a bench on the poop deck. Sometimes on a trading voyage he would invite merchants and European travellers to join him. Passengers were expected to pay for their meals on top of their fare. For example, they might come to some arrangement to buy fish caught during the voyage and have it cooked for them, though it is unclear whether this was done on a day-to-day basis or if a lump sum was levied to cover the whole journey. They might also bring their own flour and other ingredients on board, and pay a fee for their preparation.

On pearling and fishing trips, everyone on board shared the same food. There were three meals each day – two small and one more substantial.[19] In general, *lubba* was served after the *fajr* (dawn) prayers. This was a very light breakfast comprising little more than coffee and dates. The first proper meal of the day, *fuṭūr*, was eaten a few hours later. It consisted of either bread (*faṭīr*) or unleavened bread (*rugāg*), sorghum or cereals and, when milk was available, very strong, milky tea. Otherwise, pure red tea was often served without milk. The custom was to have three glasses. Coffee in the morning was especially relished. It was made from freshly ground coffee beans (*bunn*) or from the husks of coffee beans (*qishr or gishr*). In Eritrea the sailors still make coffee in the traditional way in a *jabāna* (coffee pot), with the whole process taking half-an-hour or more. They seem to prefer *qishr*, which is heavily spiced and greenish in colour, to the more expensive *bunn*. As Daniel Van Der Meulen observed in the course of many voyages, the crew always looked forward to their first sip of the 'bitter Beduin coffee of Arabia, mixed with yellow cardamun'.[20] The Red Sea sailors I interviewed rarely mentioned ship's biscuit, that staple of European mariners.[21] One exception was Othman Humuq, a folklorist, of Segid Island, who recalled that Farasani sailors ate a biscuit known as *kurmush* on their pearling trips to Dahlak Islands and trading voyages to Yemen, Djibouti and Somalia.[22]

The evening meal, known as the *'ashā*, was more substantial than the earlier two, consisting of soup (*salūna*), boiled rice flavoured with spices, boiled or baked fish served on a palm-leaf mat (or oyster or turtle meat in the southern Red Sea) and bread. During Ramadan, the cook would usually prepare fish soup. In addition, Farasani pearling crews often enjoyed a delicacy known as *ẓufur* – a fingernail-shaped piece of hard meat extracted from oyster shells that was pounded and mixed with dates. Oyster meat was usually flavoured with cumin, pepper, oil and *shaṭṭa* (a specific type of pepper – *Capsicum conicum Mey*)[23] then mixed with sorghum. Ali AlGhabban, whose information came from his father, an experienced *rayyes*, told me:

> There are several eating habits in the Red Sea that are not practised in the Arabian Gulf and Oman. Oyster meat, for example, is eaten in the Red Sea but not in the Gulf, while prawns are liked very much by the Gulf people, but [historically were] not [eaten] in the Red Sea region.[24]

In the past, prawns were known rather disparagingly as 'sea locusts' (*jurād al-baḥr*), whereas today they are called *gambarī* (< It. *gambero*)[25] in the north and *rubyān* in the south. The boom in the prawn industry (see Chapter 9) has been fuelled by European tourists ordering them in Egyptian restaurants and the European fish markets' seemingly insatiable appetite for the shellfish. According to my informants, the fishermen themselves tend to live on a diet of fish, rice and bread, known as *ṣayyādiyya*. They fish with lines at night, weather-permitting. Rice or flour is rationed to just half a cup per person per day. Salt is usually avoided as this leaves the sailors feeling thirsty in hot weather. The evening meal is often cooked at an anchorage after firewood has been gathered on shore.

WATER

Passengers on long-distance voyages would often carry their own waterskins because the ship's water supply would soon turn brackish,[26] although this was less of a problem if the dhow was equipped with wooden rather than iron storage tanks. In 1701 Charles Jacques Poncet, a French physician, noted that ships built in Surat for the Ottoman Turks had tanks that could store 'five months provision of water for a hundred and fifty men'. They were 'varnished on the inside' and, remarkably, kept 'the water much more pure and clear than [the] casks which were used in Europe'.[27] There is no reason to disbelieve Poncet's account, but no other source – either written or oral – has ever described such large water tanks on Red Sea vessels. My informants told me that water is now usually stored in a glass container (*dabajana*), often imported from India, or an earthenware *mā'ūn*. The latter, which has a capacity of approximately 12 litres, is made of clay mixed with sheep or goat hair, as John P. Cooper and I learned in Afta, a village near Adulis, Eritrea. The pot is then left to dry in the sun for two days before use.

Water rationing has always been an essential feature of life on-board Red Sea ships. A pearling vessel may carry 24 *mā'ūn*s for 120 divers and haulers, each of whom will be limited to just four or five cups (s. *mughrāf*) a day. One former pearl diver, 76-year-old Sheikh Muhammad Isa Muhammad Aqili of Greater Farasan, remembered, 'The ration was tough on hot and sweaty days',[28] but the crew survived as they were strong and used to it. Cheating was not unheard of, however, especially as desperation set in during very hot trips, and quarrels might break out among crew and/or passengers. At such moments the captain would often search for an anchorage and instruct the crew to fetch water from wells, though these were not easy to find along the coast so longer trips inland might have had to be organized. Sometimes the captain was forced to barter some of his cargo for water with local Bedouin tribesmen. However, Burckhardt commented that the Bedouins were liable to rob the passengers of their possessions while the sailors were away from the dhow, collecting the water.[29] Similarly, Niebuhr reported that Bedouins looted a corn ship while the mariners were on shore.[30] Bedouins were notorious for their pillaging, usually of caravans between Cairo and Suez or when travellers ventured across the desert from the Nile to Quseir.

A 71-year-old fisherman, Hammuda Abdalla Baghit of Massawa, explained that the crew used 'to commission a donkey boy to fetch water for us' on fishing trips to the Dankalya coast. 'He brought water in a *turbāl* [...] that was hung across the donkey's back.'[31] The 60–80 litres of water in the *turbāl* were poured into *ṣafīḥas* (4-litre cans) when the donkey reached the coast. I saw a donkey carrying water in this way in Massawa in 2011. Some wells are quite a long way inland, so a dhow might have to remain at anchor for several hours before it can fill its tanks or containers. And the water may be far from fresh when it finally arrives as some wells contain distinctly brackish water. When I asked Seif el Din Hasan Mahmud of Quseir whether anyone suffered health problems from drinking salty water, he replied, 'None that I remember', but then added that they routinely diluted brackish water with fresh water, which may have mitigated any harmful effects.[32]

ENTERTAINMENT: SEA SHANTIES

The captain and other sailors would take turns to recite stories to the rest of the crew. Favourite topics were holy men, their miracles and their triumphs over evil forces, all of which appealed to pilgrims, of course.[33] Games such as *dāma* – a popular form of draughts that is played throughout the Middle East – were played both on-board and on shore.[34]

Singing and dancing were other common pastimes. Sea shanties (s. *mawwāl*; pl. *mawāwīl*) were sung on long trading and pearling voyages, during fishing trips and while the dhow was anchored at the port. Antonin Besse Jr recalled that sailors anchored at Aden would entertain themselves by banging big drums, singing and dancing throughout the night.[35] Youssef Omar Mohamed, a *nākhōda* from Obock, Djibouti, has spent most of his life at sea. He recalled that sea songs were often sung in the early evening.[36] The crew would wait for the captain's signal, then begin to sing and dance to the rhythms of the *ṭabla* (open-ended drum) or *mirwāṣ* (double-sided drum), the *naqrazān* (a tambourine with cymbals) and hand-clapping (see Figure 11.2). The singing was usually led by a *naḥḥām* (singer), with or without a chorus of other singers. The drummer would beat the drum a few times to set the rhythm, then the *naḥḥām*, with a deep-throated voice, initiated the singing with a single word or a couple of short verses. The rest of the crew then either repeated his words or chanted a response.

Some shanties were accompanied by a *simsimiyya*, a wooden or tin stringed instrument that resembles a lyre. Its haunting tunes can still be heard up and down coasts of the Saudi Hijaz and the Tihama. In May 2010 the governor of the Farasan Islands invited the MARES team to attend a performance by Abd Allah Ibrahim Hasan (see Plate 7), a local fisherman and an accomplished *simsimiyya* player, at Harat al-Rifa'i village.[37] Many of his fellow villagers attended the event and clearly enjoyed hearing the music of their forefathers. The clapping and singing continued long into the night as the *simsimiyya* repeated the same refrains over and over again. It has a beautiful, hypnotic, timeless timbre when played correctly; Henri De Monfreid rightly declared that

FIGURE 11.2 Singing and dancing to the rhythm of the drums and tambourines with cymbals on board the *sanbūk* in Farasan, 1950s (photo credit Ibrahim Muftah).

'these notes have been the same for thousands of years, and are changeless as tradition'.[38]

Another stringed instrument that former divers and fishermen mentioned was the lute (*'ūd*), which was played on long-distance voyages and pearling trips. It has five pairs of strings and the player extemporizes in a method called *taqāsīm* while singing sea songs. These songs have a variety of themes: expressions of love for wives and family, God, friends or one's homeland; laments for the past, the loss of a diver or a crew member; ballads for a dear friend or a relative and so on. Broadly speaking, the happy songs (*rāgiṣ*) have a lively rhythm that encourages dancing, while the sad songs (*ḥazīn*) are slower in tempo. They may have poetic lyrics written by well-known marine poets or simple, extempore verses composed by the sailors themselves. In general, they are sung by a solo voice.

Muhammad Alhazmi recorded the following well-known lyrics in 2015:

Words in the night
are spoken in the candlelight;
the candle burns
without the heat of the day.

Kalām al-laylī
makhdūm bish-sham'a
yadūb ash-sham'a
bilā ḥarr an-nahār.[39]

Clearly, the burning candle is a metaphor for the sorrow that lies deep within the singer's heart.

Naji Ruwaysi, the head of fishermen, recited another popular song:

My resting place is the sea
and the waves built my house.
Seven waterwheels rotate but
do not extinguish my fire;
the fire of the wood is extinguishable
while my love is burning with fire

Marāqidī fil-buḥūr
wa-l-mawj banā lī dār
sab'a swāqī btijrī
wa-lā inṭafat lī nār
nār al-ḥaṭab tinṭafī
w-nār al-maḥabba nār.[40]

So, while the wood on a fire eventually burns out, the singer's love will never die. Even seven waterwheels – a number long associated with mysticism and the occult in the Middle East – would be unable to extinguish the flame.

Sea songs were frequently sung after a day's pearl diving. Former shell collector Ibrahim Mousa Ahmed, in his 60s, is now a well-known singer in Jizan.[41] He recalled one particular song that he and the other divers sung while opening shells and looking for the precious *dāna* – the most beautiful pearl, which symbolized love. One of the stanzas links the pearl's beauty to Allāh's love for the shell collector and the whole of mankind:

> Oh night – oh *dāna*; oh night – oh *dāna*;
> he who says that love has beset me
> as though it entered my body and clung to me;
> you are on my mind; who will restore my strength
> except my God who created me and knows everything about me?
>
> *Yā layl dāna yā layl dāna;*
> *illī yiqūl al-ḥubb jāblī 'aṣra*
> *kinnu dakhal fī baṭnī nashshabnī*
> *w-inta 'aqlī min yirudd al-qudra*
> *siwa ilāhī khāliqī hū adrā bī?*

Singing, music and dancing were – and remain – very much part of the cultural landscape of the Red Sea. The return of a fleet of sailing dhows from distant trading ports or pearling sites was a joyous occasion for the sailors themselves as well as their family and friends. They expressed their happiness and excitement by beating drums, clapping their hands and singing at the tops of their voices. Women and children would run down to the beach to greet the sailors as their dhows entered the harbour. My guide in Quseir, Muhammad El Wafaa Hasan, remembered people climbing onto the rooftops and cheering loudly while the women ululated,[42] although he said this custom died out with the introduction of the mechanized dhow. The 32-year-old folklorist Muhammad Al-Mahdi, from Khutub on Segid Island, told me that elders still spoke wistfully of pearling *sanbūk*s returning to the village after three-month trips to Eritrea. There would be great commotion on the beach at Ayqat al-Arayis (Brides' Point), where the sailors were welcomed by their wives and children or sweethearts, who would ululate, sing and clap their hands.[43]

IN CONCLUSION

Life on board a dhow may not have been the most comfortable mode of transport for passengers, but the sea was and remains a passion for many mariners. Sailors share a life of hard work, communal meals and prayers, song and dance and storytelling, and develop unbreakable camaraderie as a result.

During interviews, the elders spoke nostalgically of the joy they experienced whenever their dhows returned to shore and they could finally put the fatigue and exhaustion of the voyage behind them, for a time at least. Their songs remain a vibrant part of the cultural landscape of the Red Sea – an uplifting mental and physical counterpoint to the hazards of a dangerous sea.

12

THIS DANGEROUS SEA

ازا السفينة انكسرت – خلاص – دا قدر الله
دوي توفيق، مقدم من القصير

'If the dhow breaks, it is over – it is the will of Allāh.'
Duwi Toufiq Mahmud, boatswain from Quseir.[1]

On his *roteiro* (nautical chart), João de Castro (d. 1548) stated: 'I do not believe that any rules or experience could make [Red Sea] navigation safe.'[2] Alan Villiers called it 'one of the worst seas in the world [. . .] full of reefs and sets and maritime dangers [. . .] [that] still, upon occasion, prove the undoing of great steamers'[3] as well as dhows. It is no wonder that Bab el-Mandeb, through which ships enter this perilous sea, is known to locals as the 'Gate of Tears'.[4] Moreover, the wind in both the Red Sea and the Gulf of Aden, though seasonally regular, has unpredictable patterns and can sometimes run wild (see Chapter 13).

Nevertheless, almost all of my informants insisted that the Red Sea is no more dangerous than any other large body of water, as long as you familiarize yourself with the environment, the coastal landscape and the underwater hazards. '[T]he only answer is to keep a sharp lookout', warned Elaine Morgan and Stephen Davies.[5] My interviewees agreed, but added that the secret of Red Sea navigation lay in developing a good sense of when and where to sail. Of course, it takes many years to develop the nautical skills that a good Red Sea skipper or navigator requires. Experienced mariners eventually become familiar with the reefs and learn that sailing too close to the coast in poor visibility can lead to fatal accidents, but they face other hazards, too. Not the least of these is the constant threat of piracy.

RED SEA PIRATES

Although communiqués and reports in the India Office in Aden reveal a long history of piracy in the Red Sea,[6] my interviewees had very little to say on the matter. Indeed, they became hesitant and uncomfortable whenever I raised the subject, possibly because there were almost weekly reports of Somali pirates seizing European hostages in the Arabian Sea at the time.[7]

Piratical activity has always been a feature of the Red Sea and the Indian Ocean, as I have discussed previously.[8] However, in the absence of information from contemporary interviewees, we are forced to rely on written records, especially travellers' accounts of their journeys. In the nineteenth century, the Arabian–Persian Gulf and the Red Sea were rife with pirates, all of whom used similar tactics, though they differed in their goals.[9] Slavers coordinated their trafficking with the pirates and also participated in the looting and ransacking of cargo–pilgrim dhows. As David Howarth explains, this meant that they eventually 'ran foul of the British navy' (see Chapter 16 for more on the Royal Navy's activities in the Red Sea).[10]

Both pirates and slave traders hid on islands or in coastal creeks, from where 'they watch for some richly-laden dhow and then sally forth'.[11] The pirates would attack local cargo ships as well as European vessels, as two nineteenth-century reports attest. Joseph B.F. Osgood (d. after 1854), an American lawyer and traveller, recorded the activities of a certain Mohammad Akil, formerly the ruler of Dhofar, Oman, who became a pirate. In June 1806 Akil looted 6,000 dollars from the American ship *Essex*, which was en route to Mocha to buy coffee. He ordered the captain, Joseph Orne, to steer the ship towards Hodeidah while he followed in an armed vessel. Before long, though, Akil and his men 'seized the vessel [...] and slaughtered all on board except a Dutch boy',[12] who was subsequently brought up as a slave in Dhofar. In 1848, another Western traveller, an indigo trader by the name of Thomas Machell (d. after 1856), was sailing on a *baghla* from India to the Red Sea via Muscat when Yemenite Bedouins launched an assault north of Loheia. They used a common tactic: 'to swim off at night and cut the cable then when the vessel drifts on shore they will wade aft' and board the ship.[13] Fortunately, the crew had been keeping watch and spotted the assailants, so they and the passengers managed to avoid certain death.

For many years, the Banī Zarānik tribe, from south of Hodeidah, were notorious for their piracy in the Red Sea and the Horn of Africa.[14] However, in the 1930s, Yaḥyā Muḥammad Ḥāmid al-Dīn (also known as Imām Yaḥyā; r. 1904–48) of Yemen launched a brutal crackdown against the tribe and put an end to their activities. Around that time, William Makin reported that 'many a dhow with hacked bodies has been found floating about in the Red Sea'[15] – perhaps a reference to the victims of Yaḥyā's repression.

For safety, dhow captains preferred to sail in convoys of at least three or four vessels, while a fleet of dhows would 'join to defend themselves'.[16] Given that piracy was endemic in the southern region, the ships' crews invariably carried firearms, and they were prepared to fight to save their belongings, as both Bob Serjeant (d. 1993)[17] and a number of my interviewees testified. 'Whether a lawful or unlawful trader', the crew of a dhow would carry 'muskets, swords, spears and shields', according to Captain Philip H. Colomb of the Royal Navy (d. 1899).[18] Any attacks were reported to the British Colonial Protectorate in Aden until the 1960s.

Pilgrim ships were often prime targets. One of my interviewees, a 75-year-old camel driver named Muhammed Khalifeh from Al-Awayna near Quseir, recalled his grandfather saying that 'the Zubayda and Rashayda notoriously attacked pilgrims [...] The Saudis drove them out of Arabia and into Sudan in the nineteenth century'.[19] Moreover, as we have seen, the desert route was just as dangerous as the sea crossing, as Bedouin raids on pilgrims' caravans were common occurrences.

An infamous base for coastal pirates was on Cape Guardafui (Ar. Ras Asir), at the tip of the promontory at the western entrance to the Horn of Africa in Puntland, Somalia. Henri De Monfreid reported that the Warsangali tribe would simply wait for ships to founder on Guardafui, a headland that is notorious for its fierce winds and dangerous swells. Whenever a foreign ship ran aground, the tribesmen would help the stranded passengers and offer them food, but then demand the ship's cargo. So, 'the entire wreck becomes their property'. According to De Monfreid, this was why the Warsangalis refused to build a lighthouse on the headland, as doing so would have reduced 'the risk of shipwreck'.[20] In July 1905, the French steamer *Chodoc* ran aground on Cape Guardafui, whereupon Somali dhows rescued some 500 passengers and crew but then 'stripped the vessel of everything moveable, and conveyed their plunder to a village'.[21]

Norman Lewis described piracy as an 'ancient evil'.[22] However, as noted earlier, it has re-emerged with a vengeance in the twenty-first century. Many contemporary Somali pirates launch attacks simply in the hope of enriching themselves with ransom money or booty, but others have a more political goal – financing terrorist organizations such as Al Qaeda and Al Shabaab. They 'prey on merchant ships' off the Somali coast, posing as fishermen and seizing foreign hostages, which might prompt a response from the Royal Marines, but the pirates are happy to 'play cat and mouse with the world's most powerful navies'.[23] The pirates operate in a highly sensitive region, a crossroads of 'one of the world's most important trade routes with 25,000 ships' each year.[24] Interestingly, their vessel of choice is the *zārūk* or *'obrī*, the craft their ancestors used in the days of slave trading and gun running (see Figure 12.1).

THE NATURAL HAZARDS OF THE RED SEA

Throughout history, many dhows have failed to complete their journeys. Countless lives have been lost, not to mention personal belongings and merchandise. Of course, fellow sailors always mourn such losses, but they see no point in taking out insurance. As Duwi Toufiq Mahmud explained, 'There is no insurance! What can the dhow owner do? If the dhow breaks, it is over – it is the will of Allāh' (*Mā fī ta'mīn! Ṣāḥib el-markab, ha-ya'mel 'ey, yā rājil? Izā es-safīna nkasarat, khalāṣ – da qadar Allāh*).[25] This firm belief in fate or predestination – *qadar* – is one of the six articles of faith in Islam.[26] Theologically, this is a complex concept,[28] but for maritime communities it is manifested most vividly in the sailors' phlegmatic acceptance of the fact that some things lie beyond their control.[29] However, as Sheikh Abd al-Hamid Bukhari of Jeddah explained, this deference to the will of Allāh has never equated to reckless fatalism:

> We were not worried [. . .] [W]e raised our white sails, racing on the waves, the wind blowing with force; no motors to operate, no navigational equipment to guide us,

FIGURE 12.1 A pirate *'obrī* off the coast of Somalia (courtesy of *The Times*).[27]

> no radio to contact anyone on land; there was nothing but Allāh's omnipotence and the eyes [of the skipper] that remained awake.[30]

In other words, while the will of Allāh is paramount, sailors should still do their utmost to protect themselves. This includes looking out for coral reefs and sandbanks, some of which 'are much bigger than others; some look like little islands, others just appear above water, and some are to be seen a little under water', according to Joseph Pitts (d. *c.*1739),[31] an Englishman who was enslaved on the Barbary (North African) coast and then crossed the Red Sea with his master to perform the *ḥajj*.

Winter in the northern region can be stormy, and extra care and skill are required to sail in strong winds. Richard Burton's *rayyes*, whom he praised as a 'weather-wise man', predicted that a gale on 9 July 1853 was about to blow in when their *sanbūk* was moored at Tur. He was soon proved correct: 'When morning broke', Burton wrote, 'we found the wind strong, and the sea white with foam'. He added that he and his pilgrim companions were largely unaware of the damage such a storm could wreak. However, while their captain was 'valorous [...] he dared not for his life cross [...] the mouth of ill-omened Akabah'.[32]

Large vessels that attempted to sail down the coast from Suez to Jeddah relied on exact calculations of their distance from the reefs. During my interviews, Egyptian and Hijazi captains often mentioned that they might instruct sailors to observe the sea closely and look out for submerged rocks. Travellers have documented this technique throughout the centuries, but of course it is only feasible in the hours of daylight. The Catalan spy Domènec Badia i Leblich (Ali Bey) warned of the disaster that may ensue if a sandbank were spotted 'too late', if the helmsman failed to 'keep far enough off' the rocks or a coral reef, or if he failed to hear or heed the lookout's warning cry.[33]

On 9 December 1805, Viscount Valentia noted that his ship finally reached Jeddah's harbour 'after [being] baffled by adverse winds and currents'.[34] Strong winds frequently roar across the whole Red Sea region, generating unruly waves. In his survey of the Gulf of Aqaba, James R. Wellsted (d. 1842), an Indian Navy officer, highlighted 'the effects of its boisterous winds in the dangerous swell they create'.[35] And when he passed Muweilah on the Hijazi coast in a native *baghla*, he remarked, 'in the middle of the night the gale returned with all its former fury'.[36] Bound for Mocha on 16 January 1848, Thomas Machell's ship was exposed to 'a wind [that] blew so stiff' that they had to head for Hodeidah instead. As the evening progressed, 'the unfortunate crew [...] [were] drenched and shivering shipmates [...] all huddled like a pack of sheep'.[37] On one of Henri De Monfreid's voyages, 'the waves were enormous' and he admitted, 'I was afraid [...] as the ship fell into the trough of the waves [...] I heard shrieks and cries in the blackness of this abyss'.[38]

Sometimes the wind and waves could smash a dhow to pieces or leave it drifting and helpless in the middle of the sea. Ali Bey described the perils of navigating through a storm, 'almost continually between banks and rocks, above and under water'. Therefore, it was no surprise to him that 'there are so many ship wrecks every year in this sea'.[39] Having anchored at one of the Hamra Islands, just off the Arabian coast,[40] the crew and passengers were terrified when a storm arose in the middle of the night:

> We all thought we were lost, and uttered cries of desolation and despair [...] I perceived the ship abandoned to its wretched fate, and it continued to beat in the most horrible manner against the rocks [...] At length, after a whole hour passed in this frightful agony, the clouds cleared a little: a ray of light from the moon served to point out the east to me, and to bring joy to my heart.[41]

Ali Bey described this as the greatest moment of his life. However, the relief of surviving a violent storm was often tempered by the realization that the ship had run out of food or water, and fresh supplies might be hard to find.

Several interviewees provided equally vivid accounts of the dangers of life at sea. For instance, Abou Bakar Habib, a 76-year-old mariner from Tadjourah, described one occasion when he sailed against strong winds in the Gulf of Tadjourah: 'We raised a small sail when the wind was strong but often we had to return [to port] after sailing for some distance because [we were afraid] the wind might break the yard.'[42] Setting the sails in the correct configuration is crucial to keeping the ship on an even keel and sailing in the right direction, as we will see in Chapter 13.

At Yanbu al-Bahr, 69-year-old Abd al-Muhsin al-Khuwaishi, a former merchant whose father owned nine *sanbūk*s, explained that navigators frequently lost control of their vessels in the strong winds and currents of the Saudi coast in the 1940s and 1950s. He remembered one particular *sanbūk* foundered and lost 'sacks of money and another named *Al-Sa'īdī* went down with a huge cargo'.[43] He did not elaborate on how much cash was lost, but merchants frequently crossed the sea with large sums of money as there were few banks on either shore.

Other old sailors have described their own near-death experiences. Ahmed Imam of Jeddah, known as Sheikh Ahmed, claimed to have survived 'drowning twice' and said: 'I saw death in front of my eyes.'[44] Understandably, he and his fellow sailors especially feared the sea's unpredictability:

> I was on a cargo ship heading north [of Jeddah]; the waves suddenly became threatening and we would have been lost had it not been for the mercy of Allāh [...]

> [W]e sway[ed] day and night, struggling with the waves and the waves pushing us and we did not know what was above or below us, except Allāh [...] until we reached the coast, almost dead. No one drowned![45]

The sailors who relate such tales tend to display a combination of relief, solemnity and joy, because they invariably attribute their survival to God's mercy. A similar story concerned a blind merchant who set off from Yanbu al-Bahr to trade goods in Sudan. Halfway across the sea, a storm blew up and the merchant heard the *nākhōda* issuing orders to the crew to lower the sails, but the sailors could not hear him above the strong wind and crashing waves, and the mast snapped. The crew continued to struggle with the ship's gear but there seemed no hope as the planks started to splinter and the dhow started to sink. Everyone, including the blind merchant, jumped overboard, and he managed to hold on to a plank until another ship passed by and hauled him out of the water.[46]

There are very few newspaper reports of such incidents, so it is hard to verify the accuracy of these oral accounts. On the other hand, there is little doubt that the Red Sea is still a very dangerous place, as a number of official reports indicate. For instance, one PERSGA report lists 22 vessels lost at sea in Port Sudan and the surrounding area in 2008 alone.[47] Although this report concluded that 'human error in navigation is nearly always the reason for the accident', it also suggested that severe weather conditions contributed to 'boat grounding accidents', especially when the wind was from the north-west.[48] Many of my informants similarly cited 'human error' as one of the main reasons for accidents at sea.

MAINTAINING STABILITY ON THE WATER

Dhows are sometimes overladen with huge cargoes and consequently lose their balance and sink. In Djibouti several interviewees accused dhow owners or *nākhōda*s of not checking their vessels' balance or seaworthiness, resulting in a number of disasters. One *zārūk* owner, Ibrahim Abou Bakar, told me about a dhow that used to ferry passengers from Djibouti City to Tadjourah: 'The *nākhōda* did not bother to examine the [weight of the dhow] with its merchandise in the hold [before setting off] and the dhow was carrying five hundred people. It capsized in the rough weather and one hundred and thirty people died.'[49]

Sand or rocks were traditionally used as ballast to maintain stability in rough seas, but some skippers insisted that merchandise and/or passengers do the job just as well. Naturally, I asked: 'So, what happens if you have no cargo and no passengers on the return journey?' I rarely received a straight answer, so

I presume risks are taken. In principle, the harbour master – the *rayyes/nākhōda al-barr* – should always check the balance before a dhow leaves port (see Chapter 10). However, is unclear whether this procedure is always carried out, and many skippers seem to believe it is unnecessary, as they are confident that they have sufficient expertise to balance their vessels by eye. Yet,

> too little weight and the vessel would ride high, increasing the danger of capsizing; too much and the vessel would ride low and be in danger of being swamped by a swell. [Hence,] the balance between the cargo supplies and the extra weight of ballast [must] be adjusted at every port of call.[50]

A report dating back to the 1920s describes a dhow laden with 100 bags of sorghum, some sheep and 13 passengers that set sail from Berbera to Zeilah. It capsized not far from the Somali coast and four of the passengers drowned, but most of the others held on to the mast and were rescued three days later. Another, a young boy, saved himself by grabbing the tail of one of the sheep, which then swam safely to shore.[51]

Animals have always been notoriously difficult to transport. On the beach at Godoria, Djibouti, there is the hulk of a *za'īma* that was wrecked in the early 1990s. Ahmed Jaber, from nearby Obock, remembered that the vessel hit a rock while en route to Yemen after encountering the strong summer *khamsīn* wind (see Table 13.3). The *nākhōda* survived, but he lost his entire cargo of cattle and, 'tragically, all his crew too'. According to Ahmed, transporting cattle by sea is particularly dangerous, because they 'tend not to stand still when the boat is rocking and tossing; they sway here and there, causing the ship to capsize'.[52] However, cattle command higher prices in Yemen than they do in Djibouti, so the dhow's owner was prepared to risk a sea crossing in the hope of securing a bumper profit.

It is difficult to establish how many dhows are lost at sea each year, especially as many of those that founder are involved in the illegal business of smuggling Somali and Eritrean migrants to the Arabian coast. One large Somali dhow (19.8 × 4.93 m with a 15.5-m keel) ran aground on a beach at Amran, near Khor al-Ghureirah, Yemen, some time before 2010. The local police told us that it was carrying about 100 Somali refugees, 20 of whom lost their lives.[53] Such hulks now litter the coasts of the Red Sea. For instance, we spotted examples in Yemen, Eritrea and the Farasan islands, although it is impossible to know what they were carrying or what caused them to founder.

Of course, it is not only wooden dhows that come to grief in the waters of the Red Sea; many steamers have been lost, too. Consider the Egyptian ferry *Al Salam Boccaccio*, which was carrying 1,310 passengers, mostly workers returning to Safaga from Dhuba on the northern Saudi coast, when it sank some 64 km off the Egyptian coast on 3 February 2006. The disaster claimed more than 1,000 lives. According to the *New York Times*, 'high winds and a sandstorm' on the Saudi littoral may have contributed to the accident,[54] whereas the official Egyptian Government inquiry concluded, 'water that had pooled on the deck as a result of blocked drains destabilized the ship'.[55] A BBC report added,

> Even a small amount of water sloshing about below decks can seriously affect a ship's stability. As the vessel rolls, the water pours to one side which moves the ship's centre of gravity. If this moves beyond a critical point, the ship cannot right itself and will capsize.[56]

Therefore, this terrible tragedy highlighted the importance of ensuring that the whole ship – and every part of it – is balanced before it is allowed to venture into the perilous waters of the Red Sea.

THE 'ADMIRABLE SKILL' OF THE NATIVE PILOT

In January 1806 Viscount Valentia and his secretary Mr Henry Salt admitted that they were surprised by the strong northerly winds they encountered on the Red Sea: 'Had we not considered ourselves as certain of a fair wind at this season of the year, we should have hired a pilot from Jidda [Jeddah], who would have taken us into some harbour during these heavy gales.'[57]

As we saw in Chapter 10, *rubbāns* (pilots) have played a crucial role in Red Sea navigation for centuries. The *rubbān* knows the channels between the coral reefs and keeps a sharp eye out for any submerged rocks. Valentia belatedly concluded that 'it would have been madness to attempt to enter even the sea of Akaba, which looked free from all danger', without one.[58] For example, the narrow channels that lead to Jeddah are almost impassable in the absence of an experienced pilot. A chart simply does not suffice, as James Wellsted noted:

> A chart can avail the mariner no further than in marking the outer boundary, to which our attention was therefore especially directed; within this, the navigator must be directed by the eye [...] [which] enables him to distinguish the dangers, and also to estimate from the various shades the changes in the depth of the water.[59]

The charts that appeared in Commanders R. Moresby and T. Elwon's *Sailing Directions for the Red Sea* and even those in E. Morgan and S. Davies's much more recent *Red Sea Pilot*, while undeniably helpful to the captains of Red Sea steamers (if not the *nākhōdas* of Red Sea dhows), cannot compare with the trained eye of a native pilot who is well acquainted with the reefs and corals of a particular area: 'However extensively charted and profoundly surveyed', Alexis Wick accurately observes, 'the Red Sea remains as hazardous, and the navigator can still rely only on the age-old power of the ocular'.[60] The contribution of nautical science is indisputable, but the human eye has proven to be more effective and reliable over the centuries. As Wick points out: 'Needless to say [...] elaborate and ground-breaking the *Sailing Directions* may have been, [but] they did not succeed in preventing shipwrecks from occurring in the Red Sea.'[61]

IN CONCLUSION

Numerous written accounts highlight the inherent and exceptional dangers of the Red Sea, yet most of my informants assured me that hundreds of thousands of dhows have sailed safely across this stretch of water over the centuries. Indeed, the number of successful voyages far outweighs the number of shipwrecks, and this should be kept in mind when assessing whether the Red Sea truly is 'inhospitable', as many commentators suggest.

It is beyond dispute that the Red Sea can be dangerous, but this is true of most seas. As long as a skipper possesses the right skills and, of course, the right vessel and the right configuration of sails (see Chapter 13), he is more than likely to reach his destination. With their knowledge, experience and determination, the mariners of the past masterered the Red Sea, and their descendants do the same today.

13

'YOU ONLY RIDE THE SEA IF YOU KNOW THE SEA': WINDS AND SAILS

الناس قديم انقرضوا وانقرضوا معهم الشراع
حمدان عبد المرواني ، حواط من املج الحجاز

'The old people are gone and with them the sails have disappeared.'
Hamdan Abd al-Marwani, fisherman from Ummlejj, the Hijaz.[1]

John Sabini, reporting on the trials and tribulations of four Englishmen of the East India Company during their passage across the Red Sea in 1777, wrote, 'the breeze was constantly against them, forcing them to lay up for many hours and sometimes to run back several miles to find a safe berth for the night'.[2]

The Red Sea is notorious for its dangerous headwinds. Sailing on this body of water is all about understanding and mastering the seasonal wind patterns. 'You ride the sea only if you know the sea' (*taṭla' al-baḥar man ya'raf al-baḥar*), insisted Ahmed Jaber Ali, a fisherman from Obock;[3] in other words, a skilled navigator learns to 'decipher the patterns of winds and currents'.[4] As we saw in Chapter 12, Red Sea navigators are guided by their eyes rather than charts, 'trust[ing] only to their outward senses', as John Ovington noted in his diary in the final decade of the seventeenth century.[5] Indeed, as William Makin observed, 'to navigate a dhow [...] in the teeth of a storm demands a sea sense', which, in his opinion, 'only a few of the Arabs possess'.[6] However, my interviewees told a different story, one in which Hijazi, Yemeni and Hadhrami skippers tackle the winds and waves with extraordinary skill and impeccable seamanship.[7]

The often-cited Aḥmad Ibn Mājid (d. *c.*906/1500), who was himself an Indian Ocean navigator, documented the art of navigation in the Arabian Sea and the southern Red Sea. His nautical treatise was based on the knowledge and experience of his grandfather and father, and he informs his readers that he spent 40 years 'collat[ing] and study[ing] the knowledge of these exceptional men' before finally transcribing it, lest it were 'scattered in the minds of various persons'.[8] His father, Mājid Bin Muḥammad, who was known as the *rubbān al-barrayn* ('navigator of the two [African and Arabian] coasts'), wrote a 1,000-verse *rajaz*-metre poem titled *al-Ḥijāziyya* (*Concerning the Hijaz*), which provided a wealth of information relating to navigation on the southern Red Sea. Aḥmad then updated it.[9]

Over the years, large vessels have sailed to every corner of the Red Sea. No part of the sea is unreachable. In Ibn Mājid's words: 'He who reaches Yemen will reach the Ḥijāz for the sea of Qulzum al-'Arab [the Red Sea] is not closed especially with reliable ships when you have the goodwill of the crew and can rely on the equipment.'[10]

Rather than taking 'an overly environmental determinist approach' to the study of sailing activity in the Red Sea, Julian Whitewright explored dhows' 'capabilities' and 'their abilities to navigate most areas of the Red Sea'.[11] I believe it is useful to supplement his findings with the oral accounts of Red Sea skippers, whose knowledge and skills have guided countless vessels through difficult waters. Speaking to a number of captains up and down the Red Sea coasts, it soon became clear that 'indigenous knowledge systems' play a far more important role than the theories prescribed in books.[12] Certainly, individual skill and experience are pivotal to handling a ship in a gale and steering it to a safe anchorage. I did not come across any modern Red Sea nautical treatise that was comparable to those compiled by Kuwaiti and Omani navigators, but the material in the latter is not original anyway, as they follow John William Norie's *Nautical Tables*.[13]

My ethnographic work raised various questions relating to how different vessels sail in different wind patterns. The captains I interviewed were unaware of any nautical theories, let alone those written by Aḥmad Ibn Mājid and Sulaymān al-Mahrī in the early sixteenth century. Bob Serjeant also noted this lack of knowledge in the 1960s when talking to Indian Ocean navigators at al-Hami in Hadhramaut.[14] The nautical instructions credited to Aḥmad Ibn Mājid have rarely been used.[15] Instead, skippers and navigators have long relied on the traditional method of memorizing nautical poems containing information about winds and currents, sailing distances and landmarks. However, while members of the older generation are still able to recite some of the verses, it seems certain that the poems will die with them.

THE SQUARE AND LATEEN OR SETTEE SAILS

Large merchant vessels generally have two masts while smaller fishing craft have just one. The main mast always leans forward, while the second – or mizzen – mast, if fitted, is shorter and sits vertically. Most of the fishermen I interviewed now use lateen or settee sails (s. *shirāʿ*; pl. *ashriʿa*) as this is a cheaper option than renting or buying an engine and burning diesel. However, contrary to popular belief, most dhows were equipped with square sails, rather than lateen or settee sails, until relatively recently. Indeed, the latter remained uncommon in the Red Sea for centuries, despite their prevalence in the eastern Mediterranean since at least the second century CE and perhaps earlier.[16] Nevertheless, a portolan chart does show the simultaneous use of square and lateen or settee sails in the Gulf of Aden prior to 1835 (see Figure 7.1 in Chapter 7).[17]

It is open to question whether the idea of a triangular sail eventually entered the Red Sea from the Mediterranean, perhaps via Egypt. Efforts to identify lateen sails on images in medieval Islamic sources are pure guesswork, as none describes or depicts their features distinctly. Indeed, aside from a few references to what may have been triangular-shaped sails in literary Arabic sources, there is no evidence of the use of lateen sails or rigging in the Red Sea or the Indian Ocean in the Middle Ages. Instead, the vast majority of the written and iconographic sources suggest that the square sail was predominantly used.[18]

Dhow sails vary in size and their function depends on the air pressure 'across and upwind',[19] although square and lateen sails perform at 'very similar levels on a range of different courses'.[20] Lincoln Paine makes the interesting point that a lateen sail works better than a square sail on small and medium-sized vessels (30–60 tons weight capacity).[21] However, Julian Whitewright believes that fewer sailors are needed to manage the latter type of sail on such craft.[22]

In 1763 James Bruce wondered how the square sail of a vessel 'drew up like a curtain, but did not lower with a yard, like a sail'. Moreover, in rough weather, 'if the sail was furled, it was so top-heavy that the ship [would] founder'.[23] By contrast, when Bruce boarded a ship from Quseir bound for the Indian Ocean, he was relieved to see that it was 'well rigged'.[24] His concerns about the first vessel seemed to be based on the rigging and consequently the sail's potential performance. He need not have worried, however, because it was the sailcloth that determined the performance, not 'the shape of the sail' (see below).[25]

One of my informants, Ibrahim Muhammad al-Anbari, from Khokha, recalled using a combination of lateen and square sails on long voyages: 'We used to raise a lateen sail on the main mast but a square sail on the mizzen.'[26] The square sail sits 'square to the centreline of the vessel', while the lateen or settee sail 'lies along the centreline (fore and aft line) of the ship'.[27] Hung from the 'head', all sails are tied to a yard (*farmān* or *thurmān*) and secured to the main or mizzen mast by a large coir rope in the following configuration (see Appendix I): at the mast head, two ropes (*fīshas*) that are attached to the yard pass through sheaves; then, tied to a hanging pulley block, these are stretched to a fixed block on deck, from where the crew heave to raise the yard while singing in chorus. The yard is made of bamboo (*bashkīl*) and has two extensions on each hollow end.[28] The sailmaker reinforces the yard with *dūm*-palm-fibre rope, which supposedly ensures that it will hold firm even if the bamboo cracks. The top part of the sail is then strung to the yard (see Appendix II). Today, nylon or metal string is used. Raising a huge single yard requires a great deal of effort: 'Just hoisting the lateen yard with the sail secured lightly with fine cord took at least an hour.'[29]

On a two-masted ship, *wāṣṭī* (big) and *galamī* (small) sails are hoisted in favourable winds, while *fteyni* (small) and *farkh* (very small) sails are used in strong winds. Single-masted vessels hoist a *wāṣṭī* or *galamī* in fair winds and a *farkh* when a gale is blowing (see Table 13.1). One of the big sails – about 600 square metres – looks enormous, even on a 400-ton dhow.[30] Such sails 'are cut to belly slightly in the direction away from the wind'.[31]

In theory, these configurations worked for many of the mariners I interviewed, but 'the force of the wind can prevent the handling of the sail', according to Antonin Besse Jr. 'The sail could get torn and the yard could snap against the mast.'[32] For example, turning head-on to the wind carried a risk of tearing the sails, in which case the captain might give instructions to enter the nearest port, find an anchorage or even return home. Spare sails were stored in the foredeck and the sailors would mend torn sails when they put into harbour.

In particularly strong winds the sails were lowered to reduce the risk of capsizing. This had to be done carefully as there was a danger of the sail tearing to pieces. To avoid this, captains 'preferred coasting, where the winds were gentler [...] and the tides and currents weaker'.[33]

SAILCLOTH

Square sails were made from the leaves of date (*Phoenix dactylifera*) or *dūm* (*Hyphaene thebaica*) palms, as Charles Poncet noted on a journey to Ethiopia as far back as 1699.[34] These leaves were not particularly strong, but they were long and wide. Around the same time, Joseph Pitts described the sails on Ethiopian ships as 'being made of matting'[35] or 'pleated together'.[36] A century later, according to Niebuhr, matting sails may have been responsible for Red Sea ships'

TABLE 13.1 Dhow sails.

Name	Size	Wind force
Wāsṭī	Big	Light (*hawā khafīf*)
Fteyni	Small	Strong (*hawā gawwī*)
Galamī	Small	Light (*hawā khafīf*)
Farkh	Very small	Very strong (*hawā shadīd*)

slow pace, since they 'receive so little wind'.[37] Sails were also made of 'coarse canvas',[38] although this was expensive, as it was imported from India. Coarse cotton (*guṭn jāff*) was more commonly used, for instance in Lahej and Aden, Yemen.[39] A type of white woollen linen (*gumāsh abyaḍ kattān*) called *ḥōk* or *ḥūk*[40] was imported from Bahrain, according to 56-year-old Ahmed Mohammed Shahhar, a fisherman from Jizan.[41] Similarly, F.M. Hunter reported that Persia exported cotton sailcloth to the Arabian ports of the Red Sea in the 1870s.[42] Some sailmakers in Jizan remembered another type of linen – *mabrad* – which was used for curtains (*burdāya*).[43] Today, Quseiris make sails out of *khayṭ tīl* (linen) and a stronger material called *khārj*. Abd al-Karim Khalil Khayaya from Ummlejj told me that Egyptian 'firm coarse linen' (*khām matīn*) is high quality,[44] but it is expensive, so Hijazi, Jizani and Yemeni sailmakers often import a similar but cheaper material from Malaysia.[45]

SAILMAKING

Making and repairing sails remains a local activity,[46] as I observed in Suakin in 2004. Several workmen, mostly sailors, often work together to manufacture the larger sails. In Jizan the local fishermen make the sails for the annual Al-Hafa *hūrī* races (see Chapter 9).[47]

Every sail is a patchwork of a number of pieces (*fitgas* or *ḥadfas*) that are sewn together. Abd al-Hamid Hasan Hassan, a 67-year-old *rayyes* from Quseir, told me: 'The captain and workmen decide on the size of the sail and its strength with or against the wind.'[48] On an Egyptian *gaṭīra* (8 × 4 m), the *wāsṭī* consists of either 8–10 or 13–14 pieces, while the smaller *galamī* is made of about 6 pieces.[49] Sheikh Yahya Ibrahim Al-Najdi of Greater Farasan Island suggested that a 35-metre *sanbūk* would usually have 'a *wāsṭī* of 27 *fitgas* and a *fteyni* of 15 *fitgas*'.[50]

ROPES AND ANCHORS

Sailors with some free time on board ship might occupy themselves making ropes (s. *ḥabl*; pl. *ḥibāl*),[51] although only professional rope makers were entrusted with the task of manufacturing rigging rope. The latter are now few and far between on the Red Sea, although I met one, Ata Bishar Mhammed, a farmer from Quft on the Nile, who still makes ropes out of fibre from the date palm (*līf*).[52] However, such ropes are considered inferior to those that are made out of *dūm*-palm fibre, so they are generally not used for rigging hawsers or anchors.[53] Rope making involves fraying the fibres by hand and then twisting them into a cord. One rope maker in Suakin's souq dipped the fibres in water to soften them before beating them with a stone to make them pliable and then plaiting them to form the rope.[54] This would be too weak to serve as rigging rope; Indian coconut fibre is much sturdier.[55] Coir rope has been imported from Zanzibar, Malabar and Bombay for centuries.[56] Hornell saw 'quantities' of it loaded on to ships at Malabar ports in the 1970s[57] and the trade continues to this day; in 2013 I saw several shops in Calicut selling coir for export around the world. However, a much more common import in the Red Sea region is *dūm*-palm fibre, which is widely available on both coasts, despite its relatively poor quality. One or two craftsmen refuse to use it, though. For instance, the master dhow builder Ibrahim Ahmed Bilghaith told me: 'We tend to import a type made from *benj*' (Eng. sisal; jute).[58]

Metal anchors (s. *marsā*; pl. *marāsī*) are now in widespread use, in contrast to the stone anchors that were once commonly used along the south-east Omani coast.[59] There are two basic types: the *barūsī*, with three to six pronged grapnels, which weighs some 80 kg and is laid on a sandy (*ramlī*) or clay (*tīnī*) seabed; and the *bū shlayla*, with four pronged grapnels, or *killāb*, with one to four grapnels, which is laid on a coral reef base (*sha'ābī*). A two-masted Egyptian *gaṭīra* (14 × 7 m) will generally carry five *barūsī*s and one *killāb* on a Red Sea trading voyage. All of the anchors are stowed on the foredeck and the aft deck. Just the foredeck anchors are deployed during fair winds, while two anchors are dropped from the foredeck and another two from the aft deck in strong winds. Of course, strong ropes are used for the hawsers, but the effects of friction when the anchor is raised and lowered and repeated immersion in saltwater can weaken them. Hence, some hawsers are coated in lime in an effort to increase their longevity.

SEASONAL WIND PATTERNS

In the northern region of the Red Sea, the prevailing northerly wind blows for nine months of the year (roughly May to January) from the Gulf of Suez. This wind reaches the southern region from May to September, 'coinciding with the westerly wind in the Gulf of Aden'.[60] The main factor in the northern region is the 'North African anticyclone which produces [...] northerly airflow [...] directed towards the Red Sea low pressure trough [...] [Hence, the] predominantly north-west to north winds'.[61] The north-westerly is known as the *shamāl*, or *turābī* ('dusty') in Egypt, because it frequently carries burning-hot sand from the desert (see Table 13.2). Storms from the north-west may last for 15 days, so, understandably, this is the wind that Red Sea mariners fear the most. Although 'typhoons, hurricanes and cyclones [...] are rare', they are 'not unknown'.[62] For instance, Viscount Valentia described winds blowing 'with irresistible force',[63] while James Wellsted reported that winds on the Arabian coast blow 'with the greatest violence' in the summer months (June to August).[64] He observed that 'the water [was] then so low, that the reefs, which at other times are covered, appear 3 and 4 feet above the surface'.[65] According to Aḥmad Ibn Mājid, navigators 'kept clear of the reefs off the Arab[ian] coast [...] [and] preferred to sail nearer to the coast of Sudan', because land and sea breezes (*sawram*) along that coast could be 'used to advantage'.[66]

The Gulf of Suez and the northern Red Sea are exposed to a hot and dry south-westerly wind known as the *khamsīn* between February and May each year (see Table 13.2). This can reach 'gale force'.[67] John Edward Conant (d. 1848), a midshipman who sailed across the Red Sea in February 1795, described fine particles of sand rising in the air that 'are driven in mists [...] resembling at a distance an immense cloud of dust'.[68] I saw similar clouds of sand near Quseir in March 2003 as they whirled through the distant desert like columns of dust. South-easterly and easterly winds, on the other hand, reach the Gulf of Suez in the winter months. Henri De Monfreid reported that they are rare, but 'when they do blow it is with the violence of a tempest'.[69] The strong prevailing northerly or north-easterly wind of summer in the Gulf of Aqaba, known as the *rudūd*, blows all morning but calms down by late afternoon.[70]

The winds in the southern region of the Red Sea and the Gulf of Aden are varied but consistent. A north-north-easterly called *rīḥ azyab* blows throughout the months of winter and spring up to the beginning of summer

TABLE 13.2 Winds of the northern Red Sea.

Wind	Description	Period
Shamāl	Northerly/north-westerly that reaches the northern Red Sea	May–January
Khamsīn	Southerly/south-westerly that reaches the Gulf of Suez and the northern Red Sea	February–May

and the appearance of the star known as al-Aklīl.[71] It is strongest from February to April, according to Ibrahim Muhammad Abduh al-Anbari, a former dhow builder from Khokha.[72] Usman Ali Ahmed, a 62-year-old fisherman from Diese Island in the Dahlak Archipelago, informed me that the 'the water is plentiful and the nights are long' (*yakthur al-mā' wa yaṭūl al-layl*) in the winter season (*mōsem esh-shitā*).[73] The *azyab* coincides with the north-east monsoon from October to March. The latter reaches as far as Ras Asir (Cape Guardafui) at the easternmost edge of the Gulf of Aden, against which it 'throws itself with extreme violence'.[74]

In the southern region, a south-south-easterly wind known as the *janūbiyya*[75] 'blows regularly and violently' (*rīḥ shadīd min al-janūb*) from November to June, as Idrees Daud Ali of Zula, near Massawa, told me (see Table 13.3).[76] When

FIGURE 13.1 An Adeni dhow under sail in the 1930s (photo courtesy of Antonin Besse Jr).

TABLE 13.3 Winds of the southern Red Sea.

Winds	Description	Period
Azyab	North-north-easterly	October–March/April
Khamsīn or *miṣriyya*	North-north-westerly	June–September
Janūbī or *janūbiyya*	South-south-easterly	November–May/June
Aṣ-ṣabā	South-west monsoon in the Gulf of Aden	June–September

Viscount Valentia was heading south towards Massawa on 24 November 1805, he wrote: 'At night it came to blow so heavy a gale from the S.E. with a violent swell, that we were obliged to lay to [an anchorage]'.[77] (Valentia's account of navigating through the Indian Ocean and the Red Sea is one of the best on record; certainly, his comments on the winds and currents are well worth noting.) Similarly, William Makin, who travelled through the region in the 1920s, described the southerly winds as 'a nightmare experience [...] [with] waves [...] mountainous high'.[78]

The summer season (*mōsem eṣ-ṣeyf*) in the southern region is characterized by the aforementioned violent, hot and dry north-north-westerly known as the *khamsīn* (sometimes called the *miṣriyya* in the southern regions because it comes from the Sahara via Egypt; see Table 13.3). It starts blowing around 7 June, when the star known as aṣ-Ṣabā rises, and continues throughout the summer until the end of September. Meanwhile, in the Gulf of Aden, the same period is marked by the *aṣ-ṣabā*, the term that is used throughout the Horn of Africa for the south-west monsoon's 'boisterous and stormy' winds (see Table 13.3).[79] The Hijazis and Hadhramis call these winds the *kōws*,[80] and the latter close their ports until they cease: 'No country craft put to sea during the gales.'[81]

HOW RED SEA NAVIGATORS USE THE PREVAILING WIND

Matar Fikri Muhammed Mustafa, a 48-year-old sailor from Mersa Alam, told me: 'We sail south [*mgabblīn*] with the *azyab*. We spread the sail from Sudan to Yemen. It takes fourteen days.'[82] Both Matar Fikri and another interviewee, Ali Hussein Ahmed Ibrahim, suggested that a typical trading trip from Quseir via the coast of Sudan to Yemen and back home takes three to four months in total but this includes stops for unloading and loading and waiting for fair winds.[83] Ali Hussein is a *rayyes*, like his father and grandfather before him, so he knows the north and south of the Red Sea very well. However, I was curious about the Egypt–Sudan–Yemen route he described, because many other Quseiri and Hijazi captains had told me they preferred to head due east from Quseir to El

Wejh, then hug the Saudi coast all the way to Yemen. I shall return to this topic in the section on sailing techniques, below.

Inexperienced mariners may view the relatively short hop across the Gulf of Tadjourah as a fairly routine voyage, but this is rarely the case as the winds and currents can have a significant bearing on both time of departure and length of journey (see Map 1). Abu Bakar Habib, a 76-year-old *nākhōda* from Tadjourah, made the trip to and from Djibouti for over half-a-century:

> We set sail from Tadjourah to Djibouti between October and April with the north-easterly *azyab* against us [*ar-rīḥ guddāmnā*]. It would take six to nine hours. Coming back, with the wind behind us [*ar-rīḥ warānā*], it would take about four hours to reach Tadjourah from Djibouti.[84]

Another 76-year-old *nākhōda*, Houmed-Gaba, told me he travelled from Tadjourah to Mocha and back three times a year: 'We sailed with the southern *aṣ-ṣabā* from Tadjourah at 6 a.m. to Obock and from there across to Mocha in Yemen, arriving at 12 p.m.' The return leg was much more of a battle: 'From Mocha, we stopped at Sheikh Said then crossed over to Obock. The [*aṣ-ṣabā*] winds were so strong that we could not hear ourselves.'[85]

It was crucial for inbound and outbound cargo vessels in the northern and southern regions to avoid sailing headlong into the monsoon winds. Dozens of dhows would leave Suez, Quseir, Suakin and Jeddah in June to catch the *shamāl* to Bab el-Mandeb and then benefit from the south-westerly *aṣ-ṣabā* in the Gulf of Aden.[86] All being well, they would arrive in Aden in late June or early July, then travel on to Sur before reaching Basra in time for the date harvest in September. After loading the dates, the dhows would time their departure from Basra to coincide with the start of the north-east monsoon in October. This would propel them to Aden and through Bab el-Mandeb, at which point they would catch the *azyab* or *janūbiyya* back to their home ports.[87]

The *shamāl* 'was always uppermost in the minds of the Red Sea navigators for its strength varied at all times [...] when sailing northwards towards [Jeddah from Yemen] it had to be encroached at some time or other'.[88] In a survey of the wind regime in the Gulf of Aden, D.N. McMaster stated: 'October and April [i.e., the months of the *azyab*] exhibit less decided wind patterns' during the seasonal monsoonal winds, which are 'sufficiently decisive to be accompanied by a reversal of currents'.[89] In these months, pilots 'shun the Gulf of Aden because of the winds that cannot be trusted'.[90] The sailing season eastwards, known as *futūḥ* ('open'), occurred during the south-west monsoonal winds, while the reverse, sailing westwards, was undertaken with the north-east monsoon.[91] However, dhows bound for India from the Gulf of Aden *could* sail with the north-east monsoon in October and November; otherwise, they would be stuck in Yemen for months, as no sailing craft could leave the Red Sea when the north-east monsoon was at its height in the *ghalq* ('closed') season, between December and February. In these months, fishermen maintain and repair their dhows, as I witnessed at Khor al-Ghureirah in February 2009. The vessels are careened on the beach and readied for March, when they set out for fishing grounds in Djiboutian, Somali and Adeni waters.

SAILING TECHNIQUES

As stated earlier, no native pilot has compiled an up-to-date nautical guide for sailing in the Red Sea region in recent years; the only example of such a work from the medieval and Early Modern periods is Aḥmad Ibn Mājid's text, which goes no further north than Jeddah. The UK Hydrographic Office's *Admiralty Sailing Directions* is still consulted by 'Western' mariners in the region, and it has been updated numerous times over the past 150 years on the basis of increasingly comprehensive surveys. However, there are still significant gaps in the information it provides, with several sectors uncharted.

In the course of my fieldwork, I asked many mariners about the sailing techniques they employed in various parts of the Red Sea. 'Quite apart from navigational hazards like fog and unmarked rocks', noted Brian Fagan, 'headwinds could delay a passage for weeks'.[92] Historically, as we have seen, Red Sea dhows would use the *shamāl* to head south and then sail back with the *azyab*, and a number of my informants in Egypt, Sudan and the Hijaz confirmed that they did the same.

The north–south leg was far more straightforward than the return trip. Dhows would follow the Arabian coast from Suez or El Wejh to Jeddah from the end of January to the beginning of May, a journey of 10 to 20 days with favourable winds. From Quseir to Jeddah would have taken, depending on fair winds, 6 to 12 days. The peak season for the return journey from Jeddah to Suez was June to November. On average, this took twice as long as the outward journey. However, it is worth mentioning that Henri De Monfreid claimed to have sailed all the way from Djibouti to Suez in just a month in mid-summer.[93] As Julian Whitewright commented, 'The timing, speed and season of his voyage go totally against all of the accepted understanding of things. But [it] proves what could be done with seamanship and determination'.[94] Stops were inevitable because of the strong winds, 'quite apart from navigational hazards like fog and unmarked rocks',[95] and progress was 'intolerably slow', as Richard Burton lamented.[96] Unavoidable headwinds[97] and the frequent summer storms could add days if not weeks to journey times.[98]

The middle channel was the safest route from Bab el-Mandeb to Suez, as the Portuguese Jesuit missionary Jerónimo Lobo (d. 1678) reported.[99] This was also the course described in *Periplus of the Erythraean Sea*, a manual for mariners and merchants written in Greek by an anonymous author in the middle of the first century CE.[100] However, sailing mid-channel became progressively more difficult for large vessels if the wind was 'head-on' (*mu'ākis*). Hence, medium-sized and larger dhows would try to keep their time in the centre of the sea to a minimum (see below).

My informants stressed that navigating a few kilometres from the coastal coral reefs was common practice. Henri De Monfreid, who had extensive knowledge of the waters, winds and tides of the Red Sea, said that this was done 'in order to benefit by the cross-currents and eddies', but added,

> [I]t can only be practised by very small ships, and even for them it is often fatal. One can never be sure how such a struggle will end; one always enters upon it with apprehension, each time one swears never again, and each time as soon as one has come safely through, all is forgotten in the joy of victory.[101]

He struggled with the sea for 12 hours[102] before finally deciding to enter the channels of the Assab Archipelago near Ras Bir. Undoubtedly the saftest option for large ships was to sail on the open sea, and most skippers would not run the risk of approaching the coast without the help of a local pilot. Moreover, coastal sailing by night was impossible even under a bright full moon, as moonlight can cast misleading shadows on the water.

It is good practice to sail from one island to the next while the pilot keeps 'constant track of his position' and steers away from the coastal reef.[103] Aḥmad Ibn Mājid advised pilots heading south from Jeddah to look out for Saiban Island, near the Yemeni coast – 'the most important landmark in the whole of the Red Sea' – before setting a course for Zubair Island, which lies south-south-east of Saiban and 'the last important landmark [...] the island of al-Zuqar'.[104] If there is no island in the vicinity, the pilot should look out for a cape or promontory. The Portuguese nobleman João de Castro (d. 1548)[105] and his contemporary Sulaymān al-Mahrī (d. 956/1550), a Hadhrami pilot, both mention Ras Dawair (now known as Ras Shagara on the northern coast of Sudan), which Samuel Purchas (d. 1626) terms 'the most famous and named point of all this coast'.[106] Apparently, this was because vessels sailing north from Massawa and Suakin 'must of force fetch this point',[107] which lies at roughly the 'same latitude as Jeddah'.[108] Therefore, it could be said that Ras Dawair 'marks the end of one wind regime, and the beginning of another'.[109] However, I have found no definitive evidence that this is the case, and none of my Egyptian, Sudanese and Saudi informants mentioned the promontory by name. By contrast, a number of them recalled islands with safe anchorages: Gezirat Wadi Gimal, Greater Mahabis Island, Gezirat Siyul, the El-Akhaiwein Islands and the Giftan Islands on the Egyptian coast; plus several near Dhuba and many between El Wejh and Ummlejj on the Saudi coast.[110] As we saw in Chapter 10, skippers and navigators routinely used celestial navigation to find these moorings, and this could be far more precise than merely pointing the ship in the general direction of a particular island. For instance, the pilot might sail directly towards a rising or setting star in order to locate the narrow channel through a coral reef, as Ali AlGhabban recalled his father and grandfather telling him.[111]

As mentioned earlier, a number of Egyptian sailors told me that they never attempted to sail a direct course from Quseir to Jeddah with the *shamāl* wind in a medium-sized vessel. Instead, they sailed due east to El Wejh and then down the Arabian coast (see Map 5).[112] This was also the route that pilgrim ships and other vessels took in the nineteenth century, as John Budgin and Carl Klunzinger both documented.[113] With a reliable wind, the Red Sea crossing could be completed in less than 24 hours, holding a course with no compass. From El Wejh, ships would head south to Yanbu al-Bahr and then on to Jeddah, with fairly long stops scheduled to load and unload goods at various ports along the way and shorter ones to allow for the disembarkation of pilgrims, who continued their journeys to Mecca and Medina in camel caravans.

Similarly, there was no attempt to make a direct diagonal crossing from Jeddah back to Quseir into the teeth of the prevailing wind (*ar-rīḥ mu'ākis*). Indeed, it would have been impossible to cross from Yanbu al-Bahr to Quseir. Hence, dhows travelled from Jeddah to Yanbu al-Bahr and then continued on to El Wejh. From there, the captain would guide his vessel even further north, to Dhuba, Muweilah or Ras Muhammad, on the southern edge of the Sinai Peninsula (see Map 5), although the latter could be dangerous because of 'the meeting of winds from the Gulfs of Suez and Aqaba'.[114] Finally, the dhow would catch a northerly wind and head down the Egyptian coast, back to Quseir.[115] In total, the return trip from Jeddah usually took from a fortnight to a month. However, if it was attempted either early (March) or late (November/December) in the year, it might be several weeks before a ship finally arrived back in Quseir.[116] It should be noted that during the summer months the prevailing north-westerly wind dies down in the afternoon, and in winter it is 'often interrupted' by south-easterly winds.[117]

'A good *rayyes* would know when a gale was approaching', said 81-year-old Abbas Muhammed Ali Daud, himself a former captain from Quseir, whereupon he would 'take the ship to a nearby anchorage and save the ship from wrecking'.[118] Abbas's father and grandfather were sailors, too. Speaking to AlGhabban, he recalled that his father used to sail from Khuraiba or Dhuba to Ras Muhammad and from there south to Hurghada, Safaga or Quseir: 'He knew exactly the right wind, when to set off, because if, in the middle of the sea, the wind grew stronger, it might end in disaster.'[119]

Encountering a gale is the stuff of nightmares for dhow captains. Some of the strongest winds are seasonal, so an experienced skipper might be able to predict changes in the general wind pattern by observing the rising and setting of certain stars. In turn, this might enable him to steer his ship away from the most blustery winds and the strongest currents. However, it must be emphasized that familiarity with the winds and sophisticated celestial navigation skills cannot guarantee a ship's safety. Sometimes, a *rayyes* is best advised simply to remain in harbour until a gale abates.

Ever since navigation began on the Red Sea, captains have had a dual responsibility to ensure the safety of all those on board and to protect their cargoes. However, if a heavily laden dhow is caught in the middle of a wild sea, the skipper might have no option but to jettison the cargo. Hashim Muhammad, a 54-year-old former captain from Suakin, recalled sailing on a small dhow that encountered problems in a strong wind. They approached land and threw the cargo overboard, but it was too late to save the dhow because the keel had already broken on the reef. Fortunately, no one was killed as all the passengers and crew were able to swim to shore.[120]

Another former captain from Suakin, 56-year-old Ali Said, remembered:

> We were sailing on a *sanbūk* against a strong wind in the direction of the Saudi coast when the ship lost control and headed straight into the coral reef. The *sanbūk* broke into pieces, but only one of the six people on board lost his life.[121]

Of course, as smaller and medium-sized ships hugged the coast to take advantage of the land breezes, they always ran the risk of being dashed to pieces on rocks or reefs. On the other hand, the captain of a seriously damaged ship might steer deliberately onto a reef as this would allow the passengers to wade safely to shore through shallow water.[122]

In Quseir, Abbas Muhammed Ali Daud, mentioned above, remarked that: 'A good, experienced *rayyes* senses when a gale is coming.'[123] Countless experienced navigators have called on this sea sense over the centuries. Heading east to Jeddah, either from the middle channel or from the Sudanese islands, has always been 'a hit and miss affair'.[124] Noting this, João de Castro (d. 1548) suggested that 'The expert like the stranger must pass at a venture and escape by chance'.[125] A good mariner takes calculated risks, but there is always

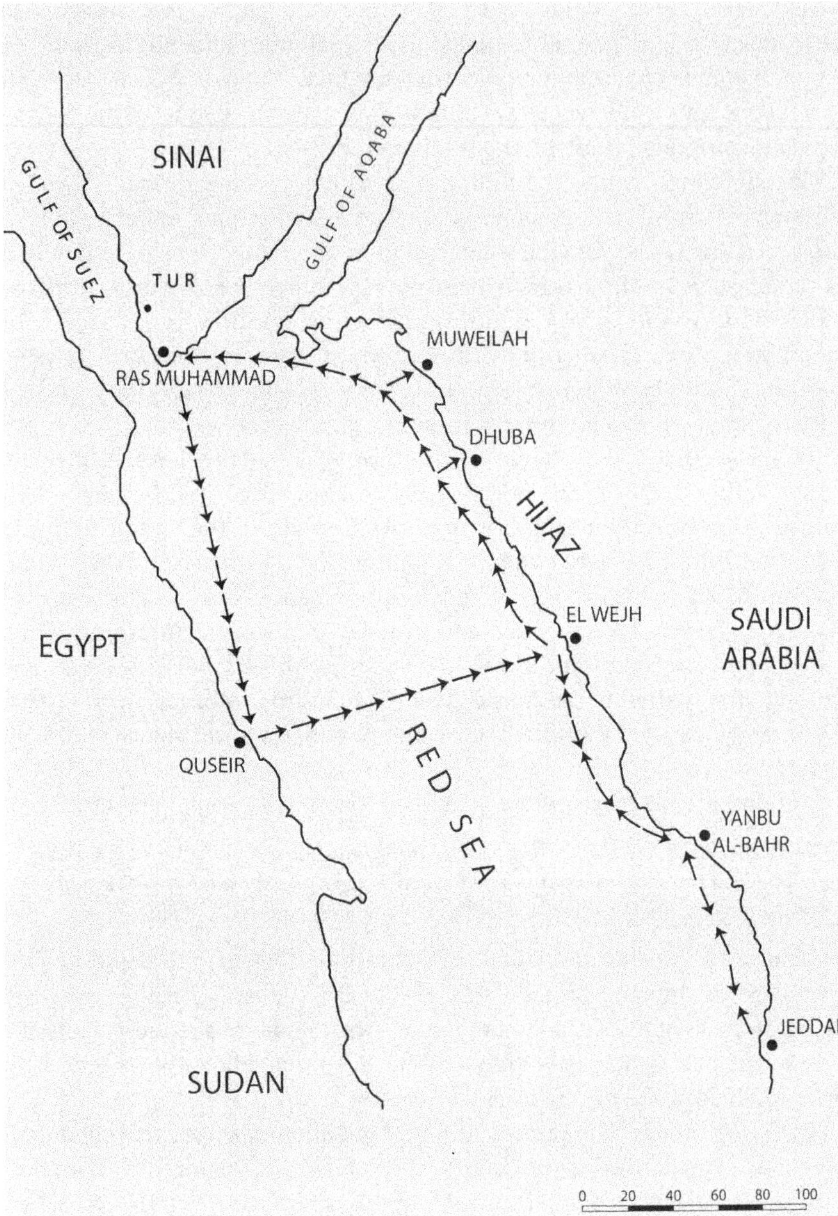

MAP 5 The sea route from Quseir to Jeddah, then returning north to Ras Muhammad and back to Quseir (cartography by Anna Sirica).

the danger of being unable to find a creek (*sherm* or *mersā*) before nightfall. A captain may wisely wait for a fair wind before setting out from port, but thereafter his judgement may betray him as the weather can change in an instant, at which point it may be too late to reverse his decision.

WEARING

Alain Clouet observed that dhows were 'bad in manoeuvrability and tacking', but concluded that they were 'good in wearing'.[126] Many of the captains I interviewed agreed. According to *The Oxford Companion to Ships and the Sea*, tacking involves 'bringing a sailing vessel head to wind and across it so as to bring the wind on the opposite side of the vessel'.[127] On dhows, instead of tacking straight across the wind, the technique is to apply wearing around – stern to the wind, carrying the sail 'round before the mast'.[128] For instance,

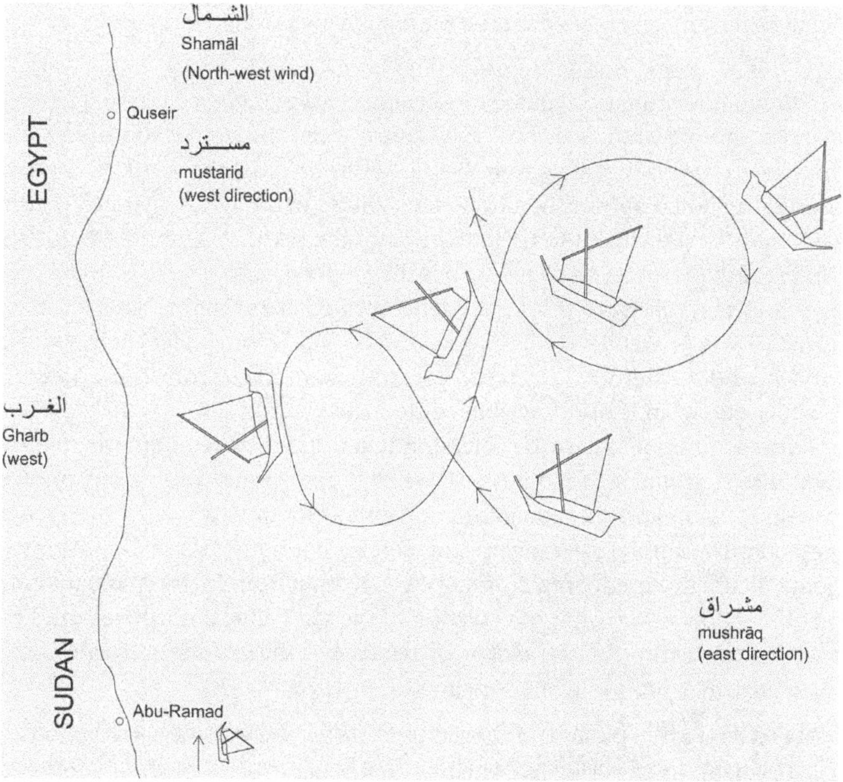

FIGURE 13.2 Circular wearing, the preferred method of the Red Sea mariner (drawing by Lilli Haar).

wearing may involve sailing in an easterly direction (*mushrāg*) and then, via a circular manoeuvre, steering in a westerly direction (*mustarid*) (see Figure 13.2). An experienced *rayyes* from Mersa Alam, 63-year-old Saad Ali Hasan, mentioned only wearing, not tacking, when describing the techniques that skippers employ on the Red Sea. He suggested that a *falūka* travelling from Abu Ramad, near the Egyptian–Sudanese border, to Quseir would usually achieve a speed of only 15–20 km per day into the *shamāl*[129] because of the relentless wearing. (By contrast, a *falūka* sailing in the opposite direction with a *shamāl* tailwind would expect to cover about 100 km in a day.) As Abdo Suleiman, a 60-year-old captain from Obock, told me, when sailing into the wind, 'You need to allow the wind to come to the side of the boat [*ar-rīḥ ikūn jānibnā*] in order to cover some distance'.[130] On reading Abdo's comment, Julian Whitewright explained:

> In essence, [he is] saying that the wind needs to be on the beam(ish) rather than ahead if any kind of speed over the ground is to be [achieved. This illustrates] the inherent trade-off between making a better angle to the wind, but losing forward speed.[131]

For centuries, mariners on square-rigged vessels have employed wearing to steer a course into the wind. Specifically, it is used 'when the wind is too strong and the waves prevent the ships from being driven through the wind'.[132] During wearing, as noted above, the dhow manoeuvres in a circular manner, so the yard 'must be transferred to the other side of the mast'.[133] During a tack, 'the wind is brought round the bow',[134] but this method cannot be used to wear as the wind may obstruct the yard. Hence, when manoeuvring lateen/settee-rigged vessels, as well as square-rigged vessels, the skipper prefers 'to bring the wind around the stern';[135] or, in simple terms, he steers the ship into a position in which the wind is blowing from behind (see Figure 13.3).

Running the sail astern by releasing it and tying it requires two tightly coordinated groups of sailors (see Plate 9). They spring into action on the captain's command in apparently chaotic spontaneity, but then work methodically through the rigging in perfect harmony. Hasan Mohammed Hamd Allah, an experienced 55-year-old boatswain from Mersa Alam, told me that the sailors would alter the position of the sail before a northerly wind by grabbing the two ends – the *gōsh* or *jōsh* (tack) and the *daymān* or *damān* – and switching them around while wearing. He recalled:

> We set off at five in the morning from the Sudanese border with the sail facing east [i.e. towards the Arabian coast] and the mast facing west [towards the African coast]. Around midday we changed the position of the sail, so the sail faced the Egyptian coast while the mast looked towards the east.[136]

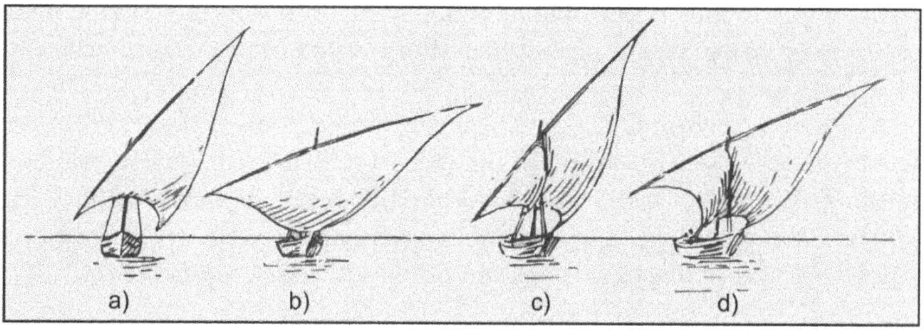

FIGURE 13.3 Tacking technique: lateen/settee yard positions when sailing downwind: a) yard and sail before the mast with the yard peaked; b) yard and sail before the mast and the tack eased until the yard is nearly horizontal; c) yard and sail abaft the mast with the yard peaked; d) yard and sail abaft the mast and the tack eased.[137]

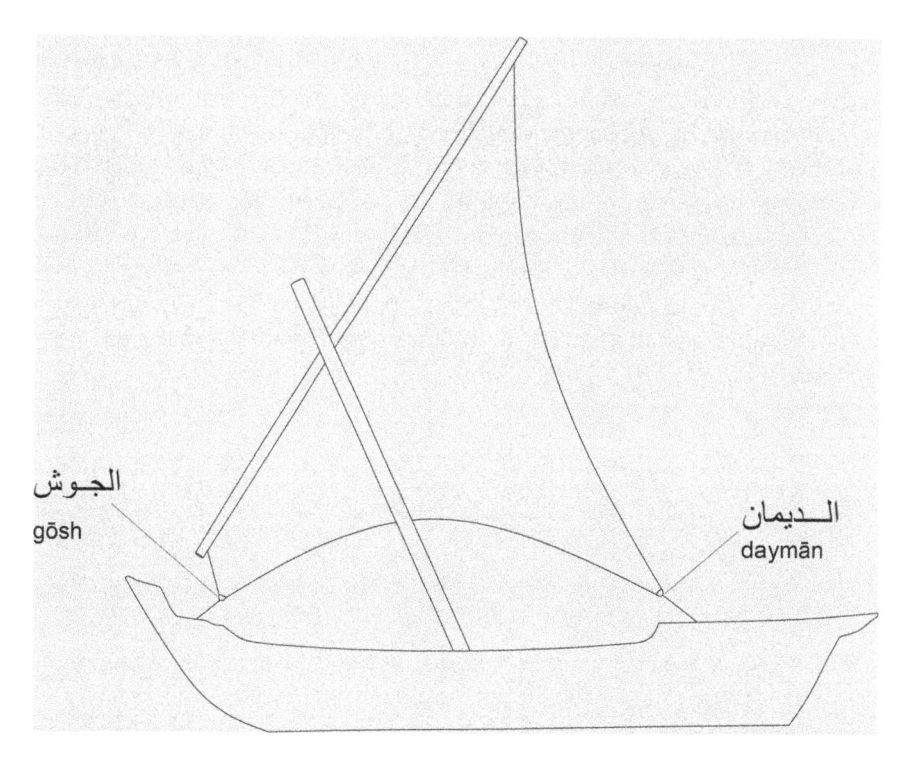

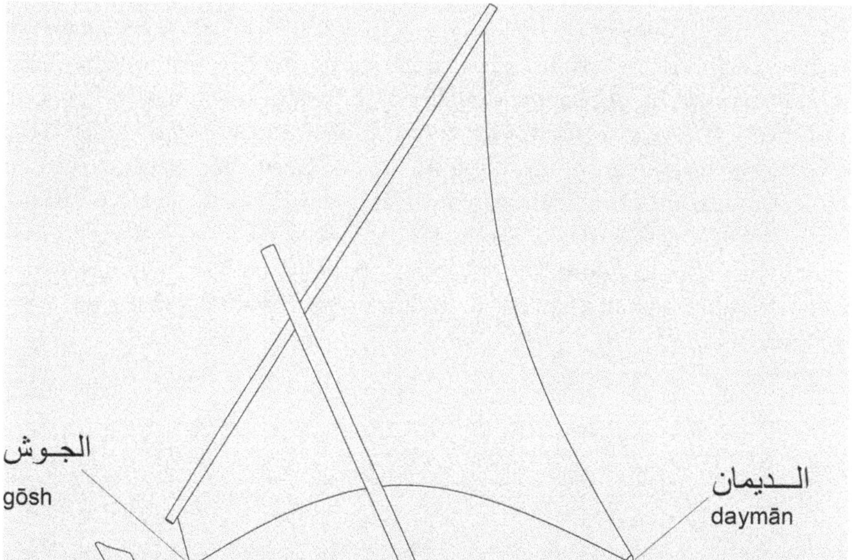

FIGURE 13.4 Sailing with a *shamāl* tailwind (drawing by Lilli Haar).

In other words, the vessel would head north-east with the sail on the Arabian side throughout the morning, but then they would wear and head north-west all afternoon.

As Ahmed Jaber from Obock explained, when a dhow is heading into the wind, 'You use the *daymān* end of the rope to turn the sail.' By contrast, in a tailwind, 'You untie the *gōsh* rope to sail with the wind' (*yahomm – tamshī li-'and ar-rīḥ*).[138] Ibrahim Mousa Ahmed, a Jizani fisherman in his 60s, recalled that the *nākhōda* of his pearling dhow would sit on the aft deck, holding the tiller:

> We listened to his instructions. He used to say '*ḥajjib*' when the wind was aft, and we would untie the *gōsh* to loosen the sail slightly, until there was a fair wind, when he would say, '*kassib*', which meant we had to tie the luff rope.[139] (see Figure 13.4.)

IN CONCLUSION

Today, very few sailors have the skill and experience to handle sail ends, loosen and tie the *gōsh* and *daymān*, or sail astern, into the wind and with a tailwind, because most of them rely on engines. Hence, much of the traditional sailing craft is simply fading away. That is a tragedy because, while the introduction of engines in the 1970s revolutionized seafaring on the Red Sea, today's diesel-powered vessels 'do not have the quality of those ancestral dhows'.[140] Indeed, their performance is inferior to that of the old sailing craft, as Saad Ali Hasan, a 63-year-old sea captain from Mersa Alam, explained: 'Big waves slow their progress; sails, unlike engines, help the boat to sail smoothly up and down the waves.'[141] The sailing dhows also had longer lifespans. Nevertheless, the vast majority of mariners now opt for motorized dhows because they mean they can set out to sea in all weathers, regardless of the vicissitudes of the infamous Red Sea winds.[142]

14

'WE SET FORTH WITH A FAVOURABLE WIND': THE RED SEA DHOW TRADE

Damba mrnisso bda damba
Mraisso damba mraiso
'I voyage across the seas
I don't know if I will return.'
Aphorism recited by Somali-Issa-speaking sailors.[1]

One of the main incentives for travel or seaborne exploration is trade. In this chapter we will explore the dhow trade networks from the north to the south of the Red Sea and the Horn of Africa, venturing into the ports that the mariners visited at regular intervals, as dictated by the winds. What is presented here is by no means an exhaustive account of trade on the Red Sea, but it offers some important highlights of how dhows were and still are used to transport goods from one place to another. It includes accounts from European travellers of the eighteenth, nineteenth and twentieth centuries as well as old sailors' memories of life on trading dhows in the age of sail.

CONNECTIONS AND DESTINATIONS

The Red Sea trading dhows shuttled up and down the African and Arabian shores, criss-crossed the sea itself, and connected with the lucrative Indian and African trade. They often sailed in a convoy (*sanjār*) of several vessels, with one of them enjoying the privilege of leading the rest. In the lower Red Sea region it was customary for a dhow's captain to greet a passing vessel with the cry: *'Sanjarnā bis-salāma'* (We in company salute you), followed by *'Salām'* (Safe journey).

In response, the captain of the other vessel would shout, '*Salām*'.[2] This exchange of greetings demonstrated an unwritten code of respect, collegiality and the captain's pledge to help fellow skippers who ran into difficulties in bad weather, ran aground or, as often happened, suffered an attack by pirates.

As we saw in Chapter 13, the cargo dhows of the northern Red Sea would depart in June or July to take advantage of the prevailing northerly winds. Suez was the point of departure for numerous dhows bound for Jeddah, and these craft would often also make stops at Tur, Dhuba and Yanbu al-Bahr. Many of the older sea captains I spoke to on the Hijazi coast remembered sailing this route. They recalled their *sanbūks* arriving at the harbours laden with cargo from Cairo or Jeddah, and carrying hundreds of pilgrims. Other routes from the north followed by merchants and pilgrims from North Africa and the sub-Sahara region reached Yanbu al-Bahr and Jeddah from the ports of Quseir, Suakin and Massawa. After a long stop at Jeddah, some long-distance dhows would continue on to Aden before the south-west monsoon ended in August. They and the Adeni oceangoing dhows would then set sail for Sur, Oman and Basra to catch the date harvest, and perhaps even the west coast of India, where they would trade their goods for Indian clothes, foodstuffs and other commodities[3] prior to setting sail for home before the wet monsoon set in.

The south-west coast of India was exposed to the monsoon in June while the more northerly shores experienced it in July. Indian ships left Kutch bound for Aden and Jeddah in November and returned in June or a little earlier with the south-west monsoon. Those from Surat and Bombay left at the beginning of May and returned in June or July.[4] These Indian vessels carried large cargoes of foodstuffs and other commodities. Their journeys ended in Aden and the goods were then trans-shipped to the Red Sea ports. Similarly, many Arabian–Persian Gulf dhows that arrived in Aden loaded their cargoes of dates onto smaller Red Sea vessels, while others continued on to Jeddah or some of the southern Red Sea ports.

The commercial route between Aden and the East African ports was always busy. Seagoing vessels picked up passengers at Aden and then, with a new consignment of goods also loaded on board, embarked on their outward journeys. Thousands of people made this trip each year in the 1960s.[5] On the return journey, deep-sea dhows could reach either Arabia or India 'within a relatively short time'.[6]

THE CAMEL CARAVAN AND THE DHOW

The port was a centre of activity where goods were received and distributed throughout the town and hinterland or sent further up or down the coast with outgoing dhows. The port of Jizan that the dhow builder Ibrahim Ahmed Bilghaith remembered from his childhood was 'bustling with harbour activity: dhows entering and leaving the harbour and the porters and sailors unloading and loading goods'.[7] Every approaching cargo dhow would create a stir of activity. With the ship anchored out at sea, a customs officer would demand the unfolding of sails, which were then stored on shore. Next, he would board the ship to inspect the water tanks or barrels and the sea chests, because mariners and passengers routinely hid items in the hope of dodging customs duties and taxes.[8] Health inspectors then examined the pilgrims and quarantined any sick passengers until a doctor issued an assurance that they could be discharged. Once all of the inspections had been completed, rope ladders were attached to the side of the dhow and passengers and crew climbed down into waiting *hūrīs*, which ferried everyone to shore.

A camel caravan was usually already assembled just outside of town, as the arrival times of oceangoing dhows was quite predictable, especially in the peak sailing season. A signal would be sent, and the caravan would make its way to the quayside. Ibrahim Ahmed Bilghaith recalled, 'Some fifty to sixty camels would approach the shore line, each carrying four loads [*akyās*], about ninety kilograms'.[9] Meanwhile, the dhow's cargo was carried by porters and deposited in the port's storehouses. Everything – the ship's cargo and the goods from the caravan – was sorted, weighed and baled, with samples left out for inspection by the market authorities and potential buyers. A few days later, negotiations would begin between an agent (*dallāl*), the dhow owner and/or captain and the camel drivers (*jammāla*) to establish prices for the incoming and outgoing merchandise.[10] In general, all of the trading (*mugāyada*) was done verbally and sealed with a handshake. Only one of my informants mentioned paper contracts; Ali Said, a 56-year-old former *rayyes*, told me that captains sometimes carried proof of purchase documents and agreements signed by the seller and the buyer.[11] However, when I asked to see one of these contracts, Ali told me they had not been kept, and anyway a man was as good as his word. As Djiboutians often put it, '*La force de la parole*'. That said, Mutsuo Kawatoko and his team of archaeologists have recently discovered 290 letters, accounts and memoranda belonging to the Al-Rāḍī mercantile family from Tur, with the earliest dating back to 1848.[12] In addition, Ulrike Freitag has found a series of business letters sent to the Jeddawi merchant Muḥammad Bin Aḥmad Bin Ḥimd between 1919 and 1946.[13] Both of these collections, which are awaiting detailed study, may provide unprecedented insights into the trade of grain, foodstuffs and other merchandise in the days of sail.

There were no commercial registers, no permits, but merchants knew and trusted each other, forming a close-knit community. One of them, Sheikh

Muhammad Said Matbuli, recalled, 'If a merchant was broke, his fellow merchants would get together to support him, offer him an interest-free loan and any security he needed, or any aid to ensure he got back on his feet'.[14] He insisted that 'the cargo [usually] reached the port; we rarely heard of any losses or damaged articles'. When asked what happened if goods *were* damaged, he answered, 'Merchants would discharge the cargo at a lower price'.[15]

As we saw in Chapter 13, a dhow's departure depended on the arrival of a favourable wind, while unexpected gales or calm spells could cause lengthy delays, with some long-distance trading voyages stretching to 9 or even 12 months if the vessel was particularly unfortunate. In this respect, the traditional trading dhow had no option but to work in harmony with the natural world.

THE TRADING DHOW'S WEIGHT CAPACITY

Each dhow had a specific weight capacity *(ḥumūla)*, calculated in terms of the number of sacks (s. *kīs*; pl. *akyās*) it could carry in the hold. The sacks might contain rice, pearl millet (*dukhn*), dates or sugar, all of which provided essential ballast (although see Chapter 12 for the risks that some captains took when sailing with little or no ballast after selling their merchandise). Muhammad Bukhayyit Alsinani (see Plate 10), a 92-year-old former sailor from Ummlejj, worked for his uncle, the *rayyes* of a 13-m *sanbūk* that carried up to 1,000 sacks of pearl millet or rice, with each sack weighing in *kayla*s (1 *kayla* = 4 kg). There could be about 3 to 4 *kayla*s in one sack.[16] In the Hijaz, a dhow's weight capacity was sometimes calculated in terms of sacks of coal (*faḥam*). According to 61-year-old Abd Allah Dahi, who worked as a border inspector for the Saudi Government at Yanbu al-Bahr,[17] a *sanbūk* could carry up to 1,000 *kīs* of coal (about 50 tons), while a *nawrī*, a ferry launch, had a capacity of 300 *kīs* (about 15 tons). Meanwhile, the unit of measurement on the Saudi Tihama coast for sacks of rice was the *farāṣila*. Ibrahim Ahmed Bilghaith and Ibrahim Muftah, a local folk historian of the Farasan Islands, told me there were 9 *farāṣila*s in 1 *kīs*, so a *farāṣila* was equivalent to about 10 kg.[18]

There were two terms for tonnage in the southern Red Sea region. The first of these, *gūnya* (or *jūniyya*), a Dathīna term for 'a sack of rice', was equivalent to 100 kg.[19] In the 1980s Alain Rouaud documented a Djiboutian *za'īma* and a 13-m *zārūk*, both of which could carry 200 *gūnya*s (about 22 tons). The second term was *qūṣayra* – 'a palm-leaf basket bag of dates'[20] – which equated to about 70 kg. A *za'īma* could carry anything between 100 and 700 *qūṣayra*s and a *sanbūk* 500 to 2,000, as Michel Lesourd noted in the 1950s.[21] These figures more or less accorded with the information I received from Djiboutians in 2009 for dhows ranging from 40 to 400 *gūnyas* (roughly 4.5 to 45 tons).[22]

However, much larger, oceangoing *sanbūks*, known as *ḥammālas*, plied the waters of the Indian Ocean. Antonin Besse Sr owned a number of dhows at Aden, ranging from 50 to 400 tons,[23] but they were minnows in comparison with some of the vessels that sailed out of that port. Mohamed Salem Omar, a 79-year-old sailor from Tadjourah, recalled a large (25–40-m) Yemenite *sanbūk* that could carry 5,000–6,000 *gūnyas* of rice (552–662 tons).[24] There is also documentary evidence of a 30–40-m Kuwaiti *baghla* with a capacity of 400 tons in the 1940s, while Hawkins recorded a 34-m, 516-ton vessel sailing from Lingeh and a 32-m, 413-ton ship in Bahrain at the end of the nineteenth century.[25] However, there were probably very few dhows of this scale, and in any case Hornell suggests that there was a general decline in weight capacity in the 1940s.[26] This occurred as the era of large sailing dhows neared its end because of the escalating price of timber and the spread of motorized vessels. By the 1960s, most of the Red Sea merchandise was distributed on smaller vessels and some was even airlifted.

THE NORTHERN DHOW TRADE

The northern Red Sea trade between Egypt, Sudan and the Arabian coast was steady for most of the months of the year. Egyptian grain was in great demand in Arabia, while other commodities traded by land and sea sustained the coastal communities in the northern sectors of the African and the Arabian littorals. The Quseir–El Wejh–Muweilah triangular route complemented the longer Suez–Yanbu al-Bahr–Jeddah route, a network that probably dates back to the Ptolemaic and Roman periods (300 BCE to 400 CE). However, the Hijazi coastal towns became thriving commercial hubs only in the Islamic period, when they started to receive thousands of pilgrims each year. The captain of each dhow would choose a particular port or ports on the basis of the goods he had to trade and the nature of the wind.

Suez: the corn and pilgrim port

The desert route from Cairo to Suez was well established in antiquity. Nevertheless, Ali Bey, who visited the port in 1806, described it as small,[27] while Viscount Valentia, who had passed through the year before, called it 'wretched' on account of French 'hostility' towards the Egyptian elite: '[It] was formerly a place of considerable splendour', he wrote, 'each Bey having a house there, in which his factor resided'.[28] Neither of these diarists recorded Suez's trading activity, but the Scottish traveller James Bruce (d. 1794), the German cartographer and explorer Carsten Niebuhr (d. 1815) and the German physician Carl Klunzinger (d. 1914)[29] all noted that corn arrived on the backs of camels from Cairo and was then regularly shipped to the northern Arabian sea towns and on to Jeddah.[30]

Indian goods reached Suez for distribution on the Egyptian market and throughout the Mediterranean countries. The British explorer Richard Burton mentioned vessels arriving with bales of Yemeni coffee, gum-arabic, wax and mother-of-pearl from the Red Sea.[31] Several decades earlier, the Swiss geographer Johann Ludwig Burckhardt had noted that Sudanese 'water-skins, leathern sacks, and leather in hides' were all much in demand in Suez because of their 'well-tanned leather and the excellence of the sewing'.[32] When Burton arrived in the town in 1852, he counted 92 vessels, ranging in size from 25 to 250 tons, at the port. In all likelihood, a number of them would have been cargo–pilgrim vessels, such as the one he took to Jeddah. Burton wrote that these ships departed from Suez twice a week,[33] although just five years earlier the Finnish explorer Georg August Wallin (d. 1852) had complained that 'several weeks might elapse before one would leave'.[34]

As the Al-Rāḍī mercantile correspondence shows, many corn ships from Suez stopped at Tur en route to and from Jeddah in the nineteenth and early twentieth centuries.[35] Countless Egyptian, Hijazi and Jeddawi merchants plied this route over the centuries, but there was an alternative – south from Suez to the Egyptian coastal town of Quseir and then across the sea to El Wejh and on to Jeddah from there.

The Quseiri dhows

The French diplomat and archaeologist Vivant Denon (d. 1825) described Quseir as 'the point of contact between Asia and Africa'. He first visited the town around the turn of the nineteenth century and accused the Egyptian Government of leaving it 'without a custom house, without warehouses, without even a single [water] cistern' while demanding unreasonable taxes that inhibited trade.[36] In the latter half of the century, Klunzinger painted a rather more complimentary picture of the town and its administration between 1863 and 1875 (see Figure 14.1),[37] although the water supply remained an issue; it was fetched from Wadi Hammamat and was invariably brackish. This was still a favourite topic of conversation for the Quseiris I interviewed in 2003 and 2004. They informed me that the wadi is now a dry river bed.

Quseir's prosperity was based on the steady flow of pilgrims from North Africa and the Nile region. The port also benefited greatly from the transport of corn to the Hijaz: 'Hundreds of vessels entered the harbour every month', reported Klunzinger.[38] Corn was such an important product for Quseir's

FIGURE 14.1 A view of the busy port of Quseir in the nineteenth century (Wilkinson Collection at Bodleian Library, Oxford; courtesy of the National Trust).[39]

economy that James Bruce observed, 'every merchant has a shop or magazine for corn'.[40] All of the corn from farms along the Nile was stored in the official government grain store (*shūna*) in Quseir. The corn trade and the pilgrim activity tempted numerous traders and merchants from the Hijaz and the Nile Valley to settle in Quseir,[41] and many of them established successful businesses in the town. There were grain stores on the Arabian littoral, too, to supply the pilgrims and the people of Mecca and Medina. The ruined *shūna* at Yanbu al-Bahr once stored grain that had crossed the sea from Quseir.

The Egyptian skippers I interviewed in Quseir all lamented the recent decline in the grain trade, which had sustained the town's economy from the 1940s to the 1960s. Some said they had spent all their working lives sailing to the Arabian coast on ships laden with grain. For instance, 81-year-old *rayyes* and trader Abbas Muhammed Ali Daud recalled: 'For many years, I traded grain [*ghalla*] on trips to Yanbu al-Bahr, Muweilah and Dhuba in return for *samn ḥijāzī* [Hijazi clarified butter] and camels.'[42]

Many other foodstuffs were exported from Suez and Quseir to the Hijaz, such as sorghum, wheat, flour, beans, chickpeas, lentils, rice, tahini, molasses, coffee beans, pickled vegetables, potatoes, olives and cheese, as well as soap, tin, copper utensils, earthenware crockery, fabric, paper and ink.[43] According to 61-year-old former *jammāl* Jumaa Hamdan, vegetable and olive oils were traded in Dhuba and Yanbu al-Bahr.[44] In addition, Sudan and the Hijaz both produced charcoal, extracted from *samr* or *sumur* (*Acacia mellifera*) and *sayāl* (*Acacia tortillis*) trees. My guides Ibrahim Khalil Al-Sharif and Rashid al-Balaw of Yanbu al-Bahr recalled that this was shipped to Quseir and Suez.[45]

Another former *jammāl*, 40-year-old Saad Abdallah Jouma, a member of the 'Ababda tribe from Tandura, south of Mersa Alam, recalled that his father's generation eked a meagre living from the trade between the desert and the shore: 'I remember old people talking about coal being transported on camels across the desert to Edfu [Upper Egypt], and from there the caravan traders brought sorghum, flour, sugar, *bunn* [coffee beans] and clothes.'[46] Sudanese caravans must have transported the *bunn* from Ethiopia to Edfu. The 66-year-old boatswain Seif el Din Hasan Mahmud, from Quseir, recalled that his captain primarily traded oil, rice and cloth, but he also sailed to Sudan with rice, vinegar and tahini, then returned with *baṭṭāniyyāt* (blankets).[47] A few dhow owners transported camels and cattle from El Wejh to Quseir, including 67-year-old Mahmud Saad Ibrahim, a *rayyes* from the 'Ababda tribe who owned a *sanbūk*.[48]

The Hijazi dhow trade

Egypt established a strong political and military presence in the Hijaz and Sudan as it controlled the sea lanes from Suez, Quseir and Suakin as well as the overland caravan routes. Muweilah and Dhuba, both in the north of the Hijaz, were important trading ports. Georg August Wallin, who visited the former in 1847, reported that there was a garrison of Egyptian troops in a fort in the town.[49] Similar forts were built up and down the coast to guard the ports, their citizens and pilgrims from attacks by marauding Bedouin bandits. Dhuba was about a two-day sail from Muweilah. About 735 km north of Jeddah, it has a good anchorage, as a painting by Samuel Austin from the first half of the nineteenth century indicates (see Figure 14.2). Indeed, Burckhardt claimed that it was 'one of the best harbours on this coast'.[50] Today, the harbour is lined with fibreglass fishing boats (see Figure 14.3), while larger vessels depart for Hurghada, directly opposite Muweilah on the Egyptian coast. Many Saudis spend their weekends or long vacation there.

Further south, El Wejh was much frequented by Egyptian skippers. As we saw in Chapter 13, Quseiri dhows routinely sailed due east across the Red Sea to reach this port, a journey of about one day with a fair wind. El Wejh relied 'largely on the caravan trade to Mecca'.[51] In the first half of the nineteenth century, Lieutenant James Wellsted reported 'the constant flow of pilgrims', with some 'four thousand people assembled here, mostly from Constantinople [Ottoman Turks] and the Barbary States [North Africans]'.[52] A number of Quseiri interviewees recalled their fathers and grandfathers talking of North African pilgrims who preferred the Quseir–El Wejh route, which linked with the Nile through the desert, to the Suez–Jeddah route, probably because they felt it was safer as it meant less time at sea. They also suggested

FIGURE 14.2 The port of Dhuba with cargo dhows, painting by Samuel Austin, nineteenth century (unknown source, author's private collection).

FIGURE 14.3 A view of Dhuba from the restored fort overlooking the harbour, 2007 (photo by the author).

that the pilgrims usually chose to disembark at El Wejh and continue their journeys to Mecca or Medina by camel caravan, rather than sail all the way to Jeddah and meet a caravan there. El Wejh eventually developed into a commercial hub on the back of the pilgrim trade and traded goods all year round, as can be seen from the rows of merchants' houses that still line the seafront.

Another port with a long maritime tradition is Ummlejj, roughly halfway between El Wejh and Yanbu al-Bahr. Today, it is primarily a fishing harbour, but it was once a busy hub for cargo dhows and pilgrims en route to Medina – a journey of two to three days by camel caravan. In 2013, I spoke to the head of fisheries in Ummlejj and Amin Alsanousi, a 65-year-old *rayyes* who had spent much of his career sailing a cargo ship to Egypt, Sudan and Somalia.[53] I also met 92-year-old Muhammad Bukhayyit Alsinani, who first went to sea at the age of six under the tutelage of his uncle, a *rayyes*.[54] And he is still working to this day, selling charcoal from a shop in the harbour. Another interviewee, 52-year-old Abd al-Karim Khalil Khayaya, had also spent a long time at sea, often sailing on a *sanbūk* to Hurghada, Suakin and Massawa and returning with oil and sugar cane.[55]

In the 1930s Yanbu al-Bahr, 296 km north of Jeddah, was described as 'the second port of Saudi Arabia in importance',[56] and that is still the case today. In 1814 Burckhardt counted between 40 and 50 ships moored in the harbour.[57] At the time, there was a great deal of trade between the town and Egypt; so much so, said Burckhardt, that many natives of Yanbu had moved to Suez, Quseir, Cairo and Qena on the Nile in order to set up businesses.[58] Fifteen years later, Lieutenant Wellsted conducted a survey and found that Yanbu imported 'mostly grain, coffee, and articles of dress', with the latter coming from India via Jeddah.[59] By the twentieth century, dhows from India and Yemen were carrying cargoes of salt, *nahīd* (seashells), dates, cooking butter, honey, hide, goats and camels, while rice, wheat, flour, coffee beans, sugar, tea, oil, barley, cloth, perfume, soap and timber were also imported.[60] This extensive list gives a fair idea of the social and dietary habits of Yanbu itself and the villages that lie in its hinterland. Naji Muhammad Abdallah al-Humi, a 61-year-old native of the town, recalled his father sailing to Egypt and Sudan, shipping phosphate from Quseir and importing cattle and oil from Sudan. Cattle had to be imported to the Hijaz as there was a shortage of good grazing land on the Arabian shore. Lentils, sugar, seeds and fruit such as *ḥabḥab* (watermelon) also arrived from Quseir. Naji himself worked on a dhow that imported cement, iron and lime from India via Yemen.[61]

Around the middle of the twentieth century, in addition to camels and sheep, the Hijazi ports exported a vast array of goods,[62] including:

'wild cooking fat' (*al-saman al-barrī*; presumably extracted from sheep's milk), honey, butter (*maslī*), dried and salted fish, *sinamāka* (a medicinal herb that is used to treat diarrhoea), oil extracted from the fruit of the *ben* (moringa) tree, gum (*samgh*) extracted from the *samar* tree, *ṭalḥ*[63] and *sayyāl* (both from the Acacia tree),[64] *qilw* (alkaline solution used to clean clothes), *'irn* wood (used in the tanning industry) and conch and trocas shells, which were fashioned into buttons or used as inlays in wooden furniture.[65]

The cargo dhows of Suakin

Many of my conversations with captains in Suakin revolved around the subject of trade. This should come as no surprise, as the island town (now in ruins) has catered to countless merchants and pilgrims from inland Sudan and as far afield as Central and West Africa for centuries. Of course, the Sudanese *sanbūk* was mentioned frequently because it has provided employment for thousands of Sudanese and migrants alike.[66] Throughout history, every vessel that has entered or left the harbour has had to negotiate a passage through the narrow inlet that leads to the open sea.

As with so many other ports in the northern Red Sea region, much of Suakin's success was built on the fact that it was a convenient disembarkation point for pilgrims bound for Mecca and Medina. In this respect it superseded Aidhab after the latter's harbour fell into disrepair in the thirteenth century. Occupied by the Ottoman Turks in 1517, by the end of the seventeenth century Suakin was a thriving commercial centre where silk and spices from India were exchanged for local luxury products,[67] including gold and ivory, according to Charles-Jacques Poncet (d. 1706).[68] However, shortly thereafter, both trade and the fishing industry fell into a steep decline. James Bruce laid the blame squarely at Ottoman mismanagement,[69] but the establishment of a new sea route to India and the East Indies around the Cape of Good Hope was probably a more important factor in the port's fall from grace.[70] By 1804, Viscount Valentia could 'only perceive a few miserable d[h]ows anchored alongside a few wretched houses'.[71] Yet the town subsequently staged a remarkable recovery to become one of the most prosperous ports on the Red Sea in the latter part of the nineteenth century.

In Valentia's day, merchandise was transported on caravans of 'five hundred and a thousand camels'. The two main hubs of this caravan trade were Berber and Kassala, with the goods then traded on by agents to inland Ethiopia and Sudan.[72] Meanwhile, many European products made their way to Suakin, including 'sugar, candles, soap, rice, cloth from Manchester, cutlery and metal goods from Birmingham'.[73] The fact that these goods were classified as 'European' may indicate that they were not only made in Europe but also destined for European clients. This is not as far-fetched as it might seem, as a large proportion of Suakin's population in the nineteenth and early twentieth centuries was European in origin. They lived alongside Egyptians, Arabians from the Hijaz and Hadhramaut, and even a number of Indian merchants (*banians*) who had settled on the island. Indeed, Suakin was uniquely cosmopolitan until many of its long-established mercantile families decided to relocate to Port Sudan in the first few decades of the twentieth century as the latter became the British Empire's second-most important port in the region, after Aden (see Figures 14.4 and 14.5).

When visiting Suakin in 2004, I spoke to a very old former *rayyes*, Hussein Abd al-Hamid Abd Allah (see Plate 12), who was said to be 112 years old. He told me he had spent many years captaining a *sanbūk* to and from Jeddah and Aden, then recited the names of a number of merchants: Umar as-Safi, Muhammad Said Buzara from Hadhramaut, Abd al-Aziz al-Duruni from Yemen, Muhammad as-Siyan from Egypt and Umar Uthman Ubayd from the Hijaz. Hussein continued:

> In those days, goods came from India via Yemen: rice, lentils, sugar, tea, perfume and timber as well as well as various types of material and clothes, mainly *fūṭas*

FIGURE 14.4 A Royal Air Force photograph of the island town of Suakin, 1930 (photo courtesy of Palace Green Library, Durham).[74]

FIGURE 14.5 The ruins of the island town of Suakin, 2004 (photo by the author).

> [aprons], *surati* [thick cloth from Surat], *gamāṣīṣ* [women's gowns] and *thawb Abdallah Khans* [women's dresses].[75]

I also spoke to 50-year-old Muhammad Hasan Mahmud, who recalled earlier generations of traders talking of dhows carrying Chinese porcelain, timber for windows and doors, long beams from Java and mangrove poles from East Africa.[76] Another *rayyes*, 52-year-old Hashim Abd Salim Garmushi, added that sorghum, oil, sesame, sumac, various seeds, watermelons, peanuts, tobacco, ostrich feathers, ivory and cattle were all exported from Suakin to Yemen.[77]

Suakin's cargo *sanbūks* also traded along the western coast of the Red Sea, sailing with the *shamāl* to Agig in Sudan, Massawa and the Dafran Islands in Eritrea, Djibouti and even as far as Berbera in Somalia. Agig, which lies 165 km south of Port Sudan and 54 km south-east of Tokar, was a bustling port and a popular anchorage for pilgrim ships. Muhammad Hasan Mahmud recalled his father sailing to Massawa with cargoes of sorghum, butter and cotton (which is cultivated in Tokar) and returning with cloth, sugar, coffee, rice and timber.[78] Others shipped sesame, gum and ivory as far north as Suez. Live animals were also routinely transported from Sudan to the Saudi coast, with each vessel carrying perhaps 30 camels or 100 sheep.[79]

THE SOUTHERN RED SEA TRADE

Trading dhows at Aden

Aden has a long history of seafaring from the days of the Southern Arabian kingdoms to modern times. Its natural harbour, 170 km east of Bab el-Mandeb, controlled 'the entry and exit of the Straits of the Red Sea'.[80] The Portuguese were eager to occupy both Aden and Jeddah after their reconnaissance vessels reported the economic advantages of controlling these ports. However, they suffered a disastrous defeat against the Ottomans in their attempt to seize both towns, and thereafter they were prevented from setting foot in any Red Sea port. The Ottoman administration established firmer control over the various imports and exports at Aden and thus the whole Indian Ocean trade by blocking Portuguese access to the Red Sea corridor. Only in the eighteenth century did international trade resume in the Red Sea, when Mocha on the Yemeni coast started to export coffee to the Mediterranean, Europe and the Middle East. Nevertheless, in 1804 Viscount Valentia described Aden as 'the only good sea-port in Arabia Felix [...] [it] has the great advantage over every harbour',[81] even though it was overshadowed by Mocha's coffee trade.

A flourishing sea trade between India and Europe began in earnest with the opening of the Suez Canal in 1869 (see Chapter 4). By then, Aden had already been a protectorate of the British Empire for 30 years, and any attempt at piracy, slave trafficking or gun running was rigorously suppressed by the Royal Navy (see Chapter 16 for more details).

Western travellers to Aden in the first half of the twentieth century noted the hectic commercial activity as dozens of cargo ships entered and left the harbour.[82] Dhows from various ports arrived in the harbour with the north-east monsoon, bringing dates from the Arabian–Persian Gulf, rice from Bombay, flour from Karachi, goats and sheep from Somaliland as well as Japanese cloth and US oil.[83] Indeed, in the 1920s, the Adeni businessman Antonin Besse Sr insisted that the port 'controlled 72 per cent of the Red Sea oil trade'.[84] In addition, my informants recalled the arrival of traditional Indian clothing, such as shirts, waistcoats, aprons, sandals and shoes. The importation of Indian fabrics meant that Arabian women's attire on festive occasions was heavily influenced by Indian clothing, although the outfits were decorated in more traditional, local styles, according to Ibrahim Abdalla Muftah, a folklorist.[85]

By the 1940s, imports to Aden included 'salt, sugar [from Java], rice [from Rangoon], canned goods, hardware, kerosene, [and] cotton goods', while from Hadhramaut there were cargoes of 'dried shark or other dried fish, ghee, honey, tobacco, grinding stones and straw work [fans, mats and baskets]', all destined for the Red Sea or East Africa.[86] Visiting Arabian–Persian dhows at Aden transported dried fish all the way to Zanzibar, while a number of Adeni and Hodeidah (north Yemen) dhows were still sailing to Mombasa with 'salt and fish' as late as the 1970s.[87] However, thereafter the dried fish trade started to decline on account of the imposition of higher duties by the Kenyan and Tanzanian governments.[88] Mangrove poles were collected on the Rufiji Delta and transported, with other East African timber, to Aden and the Somali ports.[89]

In addition to the Indian and African goods that were trans-shipped from Aden to the smaller ports of the Red Sea, dhows laden with sharks' fins departed for China, while wild honey was exported to Java.[90] Freya Stark noted cargoes of hides, frankincense and coffee from Ethiopia, Somaliland, Yemen and Hadhramaut bound for the Mediterranean, India and the Malay Peninsula.[91]

There is more to be said about this important port. Strangely, though, despite the wealth of information we have about Aden's commercial activity, a comprehensive study of its trade network, which connected the Red Sea with the Indian Ocean for thousands of years, has yet to be written.

The coffee ships of Mocha

Mocha and the minor ports of Khokha, Hodeidah and al-Salif were strongly connected with Aden and Jeddah. An Ottoman port in the Early Modern period,[92] Mocha gradually superseded Aden as the coffee trade with Europe and the Middle East increased, and by the eighteenth century it was a key anchorage for coffee dhows and vessels of the European East India Companies. A report on the total number of ships that visited Mocha between 1614 and 1640 recorded 21 ships of the English and Dutch East India Companies, 36 Arabian and East African dhows, and between 155 and 169 vessels from the west coast of India. A significant number of the dhows and most of the Indian ships also called on Jeddah and other ports. Yet, as C.G. Brouwer argued, these figures are not as 'impressive' as they look because many coffee ships set off from neighbouring Yemeni ports, rather than Mocha.[93] Hence, more figures are needed if we are to gain an accurate impression of Mocha's significance as an international trading port before 1650 and over the subsequent century.

Interestingly, Viscount Valentia claimed that the East India Company exported a total of 3,816 bales of coffee 'round the Cape of Good Hope' between 1795 and 1801, clearly to avoid the swingeing Egyptian trade tax. Compare this with 16,000 bales of coffee that were 'carried from Loheia [on the Tihama coast], by d[h]ows, to [Jeddah]', whence the bales were then exported 'by caravan of pilgrims to Constantinople, or, in large Turkish vessels by sea, to Suez, and across Egypt to Alexandria; where it found its way to every port to Europe'[94] (see Figure 14.6). All of this trade was taxed by the Egyptian–Turkish authorities. Mocha's port declined in the nineteenth century as the British East India Company vessels dwindled in number and the colonial government selected Aden as its main base in the region and its principal gateway to both the Indian Ocean and the Red Sea. Jeddah, however, continued to thrive as the Red Sea corridor was a safe route for merchant and pilgrim dhows.

COFFEE MERCHANTS.
THE CUSTOM OF EXTRACTING A DRINK FROM COFFEE BERRIES IS LOST IN ANTIQUITY— THE
BEST COFFEE IN THE WORLD IS PRODUCED ON THE MOUNTAINS OF YEMEN, FROM BEING EXPORTED
FROM MOCHA IT IS CALLED MOCHA COFFEE, THE ENGRAVING SHOWS A PARTY OF MERCHANTS
ON THEIR WAY TO THE COAST WITH THE PRODUCE OF THEIR COFFEE PLANTATIONS.

FIGURE 14.6 Coffee merchants at Mocha.[95]

Jeddah

Jeddah's development into an important port was inevitable, as it is conveniently located just 87 km west of Mecca. For centuries, it has been a 'transit point for Eastern trade'[96] and a cosmopolitan city, with Muslim pilgrims arriving in their thousands from east and west each year. The Portuguese noted its strategic importance in the early sixteenth century, but their attempt to capture it failed disastrously in 1517, as we saw earlier.[97] At the time, Jeddah was an Ottoman stronghold, and it remained so even as the Portuguese established control over the Indian Ocean. Indeed, it prospered and became an economic powerhouse in the Red Sea region. The Jesuit missionary Jerónimo Lobo (d. 1678) summed up the city's growth and success when he wrote that 'the ships which sailed to [Jeddah] made excellent business profits, because of the great wealth of the universal market of people and merchandise carried in that city'.[98] It was indeed a bustling place in the early nineteenth century. When Johann Ludwig Burckhardt entered the port in 1814, he saw a crowd of people from the Red Sea region, the wider Middle East and the Indian Ocean, as well as a number of Bedouin Arabs from the hinterland who had settled there. In the harbour he counted 250 trading vessels,[99] a remarkable number that demonstrates the city's commercial importance even before the opening of the Suez Canal.

The French traveller Théophile Lefebvre kept exhaustive records of the imports from Suez to Jeddah and the exports from Jeddah to Suez in the early 1840s, while his countrymen Ferret and Galinier did the same for imports a few years later.[100] These accounts aid our understanding of the economy and sustainability of the port in the middle of the nineteenth century and give some idea of the prices that were paid for various items, usually in Maria Theresa thalers. The thaler, a silver bullion coin that was first minted in 1741, was the main currency of international trade throughout Arabia, the Red Sea and the Horn of Africa, not to mention in the Americas and China.[101]

In the late 1990s, Khalid Muhammad Bāṭarfī asked a number of merchant elders for their recollections of Jeddah harbour in the early part of the twentieth century. They remembered dhows and steamships arriving at Jeddah, whereupon *lanch*es would transport the merchants, pilgrims and their belongings to the quayside. Each *lanch* would ferry between 20 and 50 passengers before returning to the ship for the cargo. It should be mentioned that many of the pilgrims were merchants who combined the *ḥajj* with trade. This was a financial necessity, as the once-in-a-lifetime pilgrimage could take six months or more, especially if it began in South-East Asia. The boatmen (*rijāl al-ma'ādī*) were an organized group who worked from sunrise to sunset before returning to their homes in Harat al-Bahr, Harat al-Yaman or Harat al-Mazlum. Their leader, the sheikh of the ferrymen, was in charge of recruitment and work distribution; he also collected the merchants' and agents' fees and the pilgrims' fares. In addition, he would sit in judgement over any disputes or fights between the boatmen.[102]

The residents of the old city were informed of the arrival of fleets and even individual cargo dhows by 'the town crier', according to Sheikh Mahmud Matbuli, a Jeddawi merchant. The crier 'went around the squares and souqs of the city to announce [the news] and he would call upon anyone who had a consignment of cargo, letters or a distinguished guest to get in touch with the agent'.[103] The agent also received applications for bills of lading.[104]

The nineteenth-century explorer Richard Burton observed that spices (such as coriander), rice, aloes, sugar, perfume, Kashmiri shawls and carpets all arrived from India, along with pepper from Malabar, cloves from Java, Borneo and Singapore, pipes from Persia and Basra and tobacco from Persia and Surat.[105] Meanwhile, vegetable oil, sugar, aloes, carnelian-red stones and precious stones and Javanese timber (which was renowned for its strength and so was often used for ceilings) were imported from South-East Asia. Japanese cloth, Egyptian *'ushārī* cloth and muslin were other popular cargoes. Indian goods purchased by Suakini merchants, including 'dresses and ornaments for women, household utensils, and several kinds of provision for the table' were in great demand in 'the African markets', wrote Burckhardt in the early nineteenth century.[106] Many of my Jeddawi informants mentioned similar merchandise, indicating considerable continuity in the port's commercial activity over many years (see Figure 14.7). LeBaron Bowen captured the hustle and bustle of this trade in the 1940s, noting that the dhows carried 'teak timber, teak dugout *hūrīs*, coir rope and coir mats, bamboo, cotton material, coconuts, spices, tea, chests and chains [...] cement, tiles and bricks [from Malabar]'.[107]

These trading voyages to and from India and Africa continued long into the 1980s, while peanuts, pearl millet, sesame seeds, sorghum, almonds, oil, oranges and tangerines arrived in Jeddah from Sudan, along with Yemenite coffee beans and tobacco. A number of my informants also mentioned the trade in frankincense from Dhofar and Hadhramaut, which was shipped to Suez for the Egyptian and European markets.

The trade network on the African coast of the southern Red Sea

Eritrea, Djibouti and the Horn of Africa were connected to the Indian trade, and some Indian goods were shipped directly to the ports of Massawa, Tadjourah, Djibouti City, Zeila and Berbera, while others arrived via Aden, Mocha or Hodeidah.

James Bruce visited Massawa (a small island that is now linked to the mainland by a causeway) in 1769 and saw that it was 'once a place of great

FIGURE 14.7 The *baghla Fatḥ al-Khayr* setting off on a voyage from Lingeh, Iran, to Jeddah on 30 December 1847 (watercolour by Thomas Machell; courtesy of the British Library).[108]

commerce, possessing a share of the India trade'.[109] When Viscount Valentia arrived some 50 years later, he remarked that there was 'a great deal of trade' among Massawa, Suakin and Mocha.[110] In the 1860s the camel caravans brought 'slaves, ivory, gums, civet musk, honey, hides and grain' from the northern Ethiopian mountains. The slaves were shipped to Mocha and Jeddah, where they were sold (see Chapter 16); the ivory was exported to India, where it was traded for 'cottons, silks, rice, sugar and so on'.[111]

The Eritrean *sanbūk* trade with Yemen, the Hijaz, Egypt and Assab thrived under Italian colonial rule (1885–1932) and continued to do well under British (1941–50) and Ethiopian (1952–90) occupation, although it suffered somewhat under military control. Ahmed Zabib Usman, a 65-year-old porter from Zula village who worked on the quayside for 25 years, told me: 'I was young then; there used to be about a thousand porters serving the many large dhows calling at Massawa from Yemen and Egypt.'[112] He worked for captains who shipped sesame seeds, lentils, animal skins, sugar, oil, cloth and iron throughout his working life.

Massawa was an important port for the export of pearls collected from the nearby Dahlak Islands. Pearling was a lucrative industry for many centuries, with the trade stretching from the Red Sea to India and on to South-East Asia and even Japan. Much has been written about the Arabian–Persian Gulf pearl industry over the past six decades. By contrast, inexplicably, there has been little interest in Red Sea pearling, even though 35-year-old Suleiman Mohammad Ali Baloos and Sheikh Muhammad Hadi Al Rajhi, in his 50s, pearl merchants from Greater Farasan, insist that their pearls are among the finest in the world.[113] (I will provide an overview of oyster and shell collecting in the next chapter.)

A number of informants mentioned the importance of Eritrean–Hijazi trade for Massawa's economy. For instance, 41-year-old Siraj Muhammed Siraj, who lives in the town, spoke of the days when his grandfather traded with the Hijaz.[114] Much of this trade was conducted via Suakin and Jeddah. Our guide, Muhammad-Nour Muhammad Al Hasan, told us that the Eritrean *sanbūks* of that era carried ghee, sesame seeds, honey, lentils, animal skins and goats to the Hijaz, then returned with dates, flour, clothes and a variety of domestic items.[115] Some of the goods, such as the flour and the clothes, were offloaded by Suez and Quseiri dhows at El Wejh and Yanbu al-Bahr and then trans-shipped to Massawa. High-quality Egyptian cotton came from Upper Egypt.

Eritrea also traded with the Tihama coast. Abdallah Yasin Othman, 69 years old from Afta village, near old Adulis, remembered: 'Dhows from Massawa transported small cattle to Mocha, then returned laden with flour and oil.' He added, 'We brought from the Yemeni ports of al-Salif, Hodeidah and

Khokha iron, oil, flour, sugar, rice, biscuits. It took two days to sail to Mocha in fair winds.'[116]

Muhammad-Nour Muhammad Al Hasan suggested there was also significant trade between Massawa and Jeddah before the 1960s, with large dhows stopping at Massawa to collect pilgrims during the *ḥajj* season. However, this traffic started to dwindle with the departure of the Italians and the Yemenis after 1962, and many residents, merchants in particular, left Massawa to pursue better prospects in Saudi Arabia. The Suez Crisis of 1956–7 and the Arab–Israeli wars of 1967 and 1973 also had 'a tremendous effect on the Massawa trade', according to Muhammad-Nour.[117] Indeed, by the time that Eritrea gained independence from Ethiopia in 1991, much of the dhow industry and infrastructure had already been destroyed.

There is still a little trading activity – some of it involving traditional wooden vessels – among Djibouti City, Tadjourah and Obock. Cargoes of barley, rice and flour, juice and carbonated drinks are loaded onto dhows at Port de Pêche. In 2009, I met the skipper of a dhow named the *Al-Baraka*, 48-year-old Ziyad Ahmed Khizari, who was in the process of loading a cargo of sugar and tea.[118] 'In the past such dhows sailed to Yemen and Assab in Eritrea, smuggling guns', Ziyad confided. I also saw an *'ibrī* ferrying passengers between Djibouti City and Tadjourah or Obock. Meanwhile, goods are still shipped to Djibouti from Yemen.[119]

In the medieval period, the geographer al-Idrīsī (d. 548/1154) mentioned that the sea town of Tadjourah had an oasis with water cisterns, which meant it became a haven for merchants and slave traders.[120] Today, the firewood (*ḥaṭab*) trade comprises one of the important parts of the local economy. One experienced *nākhōda* from the town, 75-year-old Hadjdj Idrees Habawita, told me: 'Tadjourah was well known for supplying firewood, which was gathered from a place called Heija and then transported on camels. The firewood was mainly shipped to Djibouti City and in return the *za'īma* carried rice, sugar and flour', all of which would have been shipped from Aden.[121] This was the typical trade pattern for most of the year; firewood in exchange for foodstuffs. The 36-km journey from Tadjourah to Djibouti took about 24 hours, with one or more stops at an anchorage to load and unload cargo. Mohamed Salem Omar, a 79-year-old former sailor from Tadjourah, worked for a *nākhōda* who made hundreds of these short trips around the Djiboutian coast. He explained: 'The firewood trade was all year round [...] The firewood we carried was measured by the square metre, and we transported five to twenty square metres' to Djibouti City.[122] Firewood is still shipped to the city in great quantities. During my stay at Tadjourah in 2009, I saw huge heaps of it stacked on the quayside.

PLATE 1 Dhow builder Mudassir Mousa Othman Mohammed of Nigerian origin, Suakin 2004 (photo by the author).

PLATE 2 Former pearl diver Munawwar Aqili, Farasan Island 2010 (photo MARES by the author).

PLATE 3 Fishermen from the Dahlak Islands at Sigalat Lamba, Massawa 2011 (photo MARES by the author).

PLATE 4 Former dhow builder Muawwid Abd al-Raheem Mirbas with director of heritage, Awad al Subhi (standing) Yanbu al-Bahr 2007 (photo by the author).

PLATE 5 Sea captain Mohammad Ahmed Zaid al-Anbari Khor al-Ghureirah 2009 (photo MARES by the author).

PLATE 6 Boatswain Duwi Toufiq Mahmud, Quseir 2004 (photo by the author).

PLATE 7 Singer Abd Allah Ibrahim Hasan playing the *simsimiyya*, Farasan Island 2010 (photo MARES by the author).

PLATE 8 Sailors resting on board the dhow at Khor al-Ghureirah 2009 (photo MARES by the author).

PLATE 9 Tying the sail to the yard on an Adeni *sanbūk* in the 1950s (photo courtesy Antonin Besse Jr).

PLATE 10 Former sailor Muhammad Bukhayyit Alsinani, Ummlejj 2013 (photo by the author).

PLATE 11 Former sea captain Abu Bakar Habib, Tadjourah 2009 (photo MARES by the author).

PLATE 12 Former sea captain Hussein Abd al-Hamid Abd Allah, Suakin 2004 (photo by the author).

PLATE 13 *Kukyān* diver Salim Salman Salim, Suakin 2004 (photo by the author).

PLATE 14 Master dhow builder Ibrahim Ali Moosa, Quseir 2004 (photo by the author).

PLATE 15 The fishing village people at Khor al-Ghureirah 2009 (photo MARES by the author).

PLATE 16 Fisherman Idrees Daud Ali, Zula 2011 (photo MARES by the author).

There was a sense of loss among the Tadjourian skippers, now that the long-distance trade to Aden and the Indian Ocean is just a memory. Hadjdj Idrees recalled some 30 working dhows in the town in the 1950s,[123] while 76-year-old Houmed-Gaba Maki Ibrahim remembered 20 merchant dhows operating in the Red Sea and the Indian Ocean in 1958 alone.[124] The Tadjourians exhibit great nostalgia for some of these dhows, such as *Taalibballa*, a transom-sterned *sanbūk* that 76-year-old former *nākhōda* Abu Bakar Habib (see Plate 11) skippered for many years.[125] Today, he runs a grocery shop.

Many of my informants recalled Djibouti's busy trade with the southern Red Sea and the Horn of Africa in the 1950s and 1960s, prior to the country's independence in 1977. Dhows would arrive in the country from the ports of Assab (Eritrea), Hodeidah, Mocha and Sheikh Said (Yemen), while others sailed from Ras al-Arah, Mukalla and Shihr in Hadhramaut or even as far as Basra.[126] Wheat was imported from Assab and Hodeidah as well as from Somali Zeila and Berbera, with the latter also supplying hides and sheep. Sugar, soap, cloves and charcoal came from Doubab, and coffee from Mocha,[127] although Ethiopian coffee also must have reached Djibouti via Harar, not far from the border between the two countries. Dhows sailed from Tadjourah and Obock to the Yemeni coast via Sheikh Said, west of Mayyun (Perim Island), and from there to Khor Angar, Ras Siyan and other anchorages. Ethiopian mules, cattle, camels and butter were all exported, while the dhows returned with large cattle, spices, lentils, dates, white and black cloth, sorghum, water jars, other pottery, copper chains and guns. Mohamed Salem Omar recalled that 'the cloth came in rolls [pl. *ṭākāt*; each *ṭāka* was a hundred metres in length]; our craft carried about twelve *ṭākāt*; these were then carried on camel back and up the mountain tracks to Ethiopia on mules'.[128] The former police commissioner of Tadjourah, Ibrahim Ishak, told me that Ethiopian horses, animal skins, myrrh and incense were also transported down the mountain tracks to Tadjourah.[129] Another local official, Houmed Maki, added that the horses were then exported to Yemen,[130] as they were well equipped for life on the steppes and in the mountains.

The traditional Djibouti–Yemeni–Eritrean trade, while smaller than it used to be, continues to the present day. Mohammed Ali Humaidan, a 45-year-old *nākhōda* from Khor al-Ghureirah, Yemen, told me that he and his crew still export rice, sorghum, wild flour, tobacco and charcoal to Djibouti, although they travel back with no cargo as they prefer to catch fish on the return journey.[131] Other dhows head north to Massawa. For instance, Muhammad Ahmed Zaid al-Anbari, in his 60s, makes regular trips with cargoes of reeds and butter; again, however, he carries no cargo back to Khor al-Ghureirah.[132]

IN CONCLUSION

Our information on trading vessels and shipping in the Red Sea often comes from travellers' accounts or official government surveys. Western travellers have contributed to a wealth of data on imports and exports by compiling extensive lists of merchandise, from which we can draw a general picture of the trade networks that existed throughout the nineteenth and twentieth centuries. Consider the old port of Jeddah, which 'underwent explosive changes with the demolition of the confining wall in 1947', according to Angelo Pesce, writing in 1976.[133] Just three years later, Shirley Kay wrote, 'the dhows already look like the relics from the past, dwarfed by the huge ships and cranes of the modern harbour'.[134] So, by the 1970s, some of the traditional wooden dhow trade had passed to skippers of much larger diesel-powered vessels that could operate in all wind conditions, while the bulk of it was already being airlifted and delivered in hours, rather than days, weeks or months.

As a result, the quayside workers – the dhow builders, the blacksmiths, the sailmakers, the boatmen – are much less visible than they once were. But they have not yet disappeared entirely, as a stroll along the seafront of many of the old Red Sea ports soon reveals.

15

'WE SAIL WITH THE HOPE OF A GOOD CATCH': FISHING AND SHELL COLLECTING

عاشق النبي يصلي
هي حول هي حول
عاشق النبي يصلي
شذلي احمد عطاء الله، مقدم، القصير

'For the love of the prophet
Heave pull, heave pull
For the love of the prophet.'

Fishermen's song sung by Shadhli Ahmed Atallah, boatswain, Quseir.[1]

This chapter describes fishing and shell-collecting activities on the eastern and western coasts of the Red Sea both today and in the past. Red Sea mariners follow the maritime solar calendar, which begins on 10 August, the Nayrūz (< Per. *naw-roz*; 'new year') each year.[2]

In the northern Red Sea region, the fishing season (*mōsem eṣ-ṣīd*) is divided from September to January and from April to June. Very little fishing takes place in January, February and part of March 'due to predominant north-westerly winds which are persistently strong'.[3] For the southern Red Sea, oral communication was more specific about the days for the fishing season (*mōsem es-sijān*): summer – 2 April to 1 July; autumn – 2 July to 1 October; winter – 2 October to 1 January; spring – 2 January to 1 April. The rising (*maṭla'*) and setting (*maghīb*) of certain stars indicate when the fishing season (*mōsem es-sijān*) begins and ends, and inform the fishermen when they should move to new fishing grounds and shell-collecting areas. Al-Ḥarbī of Thuwal, Saudi Arabia, geographer and environmentalist, lists a total of 28 fishing-star periods each year.[4]

Fishing activity in the south is strongly linked to the monsoonal winds, and for centuries celestial navigation played an important role in helping the fishermen predict when these would arrive. It is still practised today, albeit on a much smaller scale than in the past. The Sāhil (or Suhayl) star appears on the horizon on or around 10 August, in the inter-monsoonal season, and this signals the official start of the fishing season (*futūḥ al-baḥr*). In particular, this is when the shark (*lukhum*; Carcharhinidae Sp.) season begins. *Nākhōda* Sadek Yakoub Abdallah of Obock, Djibouti, told me the shark-fishing industry is a crucial element in the southern Red Sea economy.[5] The end of the fishing season (*taghlīq al-baḥr*) is signalled by the first appearance of the Sewfra star, on or around 20 March. The pearling season (*mōsem el-ghoṣ*) officially begins when the Zaban star rises on 11 May.

Importantly, 'the appearance of a star or constellation tells us the winds to expect in each season', explained Abu Hilal, a member of the Juhayna tribe from Yanbu al-Bahr.[6] According to 66-year-old Mahmood Rahmat Allah of Qrijab on the Egyptian coast, two clusters are observed in the northern region: Thurayya, between 15 May and 10 June, and Miḥaymir, in November, both of which signal strong winds.[7] On the Arabian coast, Abu Hilal suggested that Bethīn (or Baṭnayn), which appears in early November, announces the high and fair winds.[8] A few weeks later, the rise of Berkān heralds winter gales at the start of December, while Hena, Dra and Netra are all harbingers of the very strong *azyab* in January. The skies need to be watched closely throughout these months because 'it is life or death' (*amma al-mawt aw al-ḥayāt*), claimed 43-year-old Muhsin Said Muhsini of Massawa.[9]

However, while observation of the stars and knowledge of the Red Sea's wind regime help captains to decide when to embark on a fishing trip and when to remain safely in port, all over the Red Sea fishermen emphasized that the quality and quantity of the catch rested much more 'on luck' (*ḥasab ẓurūf er-rizq*).

THE FISHING DHOW

The Arabic term for fisherman is *ṣayyād* (pl. *ṣayyādīn*) from √ṣ.y.d. or *ḥawwāt* (pl. *ḥawwātīn*), a word originating from *ḥūt* ('fish'), with the radicals √ḥ.w.t. Today, a fishing trip (*'azba*) usually lasts for two to three weeks, whereas in the past a fishing dhow could have been away from home for three months or longer, due to the time it took to reach the fishing grounds, unfavourable winds and the necessity to stop for fresh water. Numerous Quseiri fishermen told me that sailing southwards, with the prevailing north-westerly wind, was far easier than sailing north, into the wind (see Chapter 13).

In the southern region in the days of sail, a shark-fishing trip might drag on for six months because the dhow would sail to a number of favoured sites and wait at each one until sharks were spotted. If the catch was good, the captain would try to sell it to agents in several harbours before setting out to sea again. The agents then auctioned the fish to fishmongers, who either sold their purchases in the market or dried and salted the meat and transported it on camels to neighbouring villages.

Today, all fish are placed in ice containers (s. *tallāja*) as soon as they are hauled on board; on larger vessels, one or two 'ice men' (s. *mutallij*; pl. *mutallijīn*) are employed to freeze the fish. Other essential pieces of equipment are reed traps (*'idad*) and nets (*shawārāt*), and three to four *hūrī*s are usually carried on board the Egyptian *falūka*. As soon as the *rayyes* gives the signal to stop at what looks like a promising site, the *dannāy* (his deputy) sets out on one of the *hūrī*s to look for fish. The reed traps are then floated in the reef area and the fishermen chase the fish by beating the water with rods. The idea is that the noise and turbulence cause panic among the fish, which flee towards the traps.

The *hūrī*s are usually basic dugouts (*hūrī maḥfūr*), but some are plank-built (*hūrī bil-lawḥ*), for use in shallow water. The open-ended, plank-built *hūrī*s I saw in Safaga were flat-bottomed, measured roughly 4 m by 1.5 m, and could carry two fishermen as well as the reed traps and other equipment. In the Hijaz, the flat-bottomed (*bidūn nahr*) fishing dugout is called a *ṣaddāfa* or *ṣaddāfī*. In the past, these vessels were also used for shell collecting (see Chapter 9). The planked *hūrī* in this region has a more rounded bottom (*bin-nahr*) and a keel. Another common fishing vessel on both the Egyptian and the Hijazi coasts is the *dangī*. There are two types: a square-sterned, frequently decked, wide-beam boat with a keel that is used for line fishing; and a double-ended craft that is used for net fishing. Both the *hūrī* and the *dangī* are paddled, although a sail may be raised when fishing along the coast in a fair wind. Sayyid al-Barsi, a 58-year-old captain from Safaga, told me that the *dangī* is designed 'to go faster while the *hūrī* is slower',[10] and added that the *dangī* is more stable than a dugout, which is prone to capsize and so demands the skills of an experienced boatman.

Until a few decades ago, the Sudanese authorities issued permits to Egyptian and Hijazi captains who wanted to fish along the Sudanese coast, but this practice ceased when Sudan descended into anarchy and the coastal waters became far too dangerous for fishing trips. Some of the older Egyptian fishermen expressed regret that they could no longer fish there as it was a particularly good area for *būrī* (Mugilidae Sp.; grey mullet). Nevertheless, their home waters are rich in many other species. The peak of the Egyptain season is between April and July, although *kushrān* (Epinephalinae Sp.; small grouper) is caught all year round, while *bāgha* (Scombridae Sp.; mackerel) and *shirwī* (Scombridae Sp.; tuna) are mostly landed in the winter months. April is an especially good month for *kharmāya* or *khumkhuma* (Lutjanidae Sp.; snapper), *barākūdā* (Sphraenidae Sp.; barracuda) and *murjān* (Sparidae Sp. *Polysteganus coeruleopunctatus*; blueskin seabream). In May and June *sha'ūr* (Lethrinidae Sp.; emperor), *nājil* (Epinephalinae Sp. *Plectropomus pessuliferus*; roving coral grouper), *twayna* (Epinephalinae Sp. *Epinephelus lanceolatus*; giant grouper) and *fāris* or *ṣar'a* (Lutjanidae Sp. *Aphareus rutilans*; rusty jobfish) are all widely caught.[11]

Like the Egyptians and the Hijazis, the Sudanese do a lot of reef (*shu'āb*) fishing from February to July and from mid-September to November. The fishermen search for pelagic species (*asmāk as-saṭḥ*) away from the shore and demersal fish (*asmāk al-gā'*) close to the bottom of the sea. In Suakin alone there were some 600 fishermen when I visited the town in 2004.[12] They caught a wide variety of reef fish: *nājil* (roving coral grouper), *sha'ūr* (emperor or redspot emperor), *ismūt* (Lutjanidae Sp. *Lutjanus gibbus*; humpback red snapper), *quṭṭ ar-rubbān* (Epinephalinae Sp. *Aethaloperca rogaa*; redmouth grouper), *sulamānī* (Chanidae Sp. *Chanos chanos*; milkfish), *buhār* (Lutjanidae Sp. *Lutjanus bohar*; two-spot snapper) and *kusharān* (Epinephalinae Sp.; hexagonal-spotted grouper). The pelagic fish they caught mostly comprised: *bayāḍ* (Carangidae Sp. *Gnathanodon speciosus*; golden trevally), *darāk* (Scombridae Sp. *Scomberomorus commerson*; narrow-barred Spanish mackerel), *tūna* (Scombridae Sp. *Grammatorcynus bicarnatus*; shark mackerel) and *'arabī* (Mugilidae Sp.; grey mullet). Among the demarsel fish were: *fārisī* (Lutjanidae Sp. *Aprion virescens*; green jobfish), *ghurayb* (Carangidae Sp. *Elagatis bipinnulata*; rainbow runner) and *ḥamūr* (Epinephalinae Sp.; grouper).[13]

Interviewees in Egypt, Sudan and the Hijaz confirmed that seasonal workers were hired as mariners on trading vessels but even more so as fishermen. They spent half of the year as farmers in the hinterland and the other half as fishermen. Thus, the Hijazi Bedu often participated in fishing and pearling trips. Abu Hilal explained that his father and grandfather had been seasonal workers, but he and both of his sons are full-time fishermen. Like many others, Abu Hilal had left his inland home town of Yanbu al-Nakhl (lit. Yanbu of the Palm Trees) to settle in Yanbu al-Bahr (lit. Yanbu of the Sea).[14]

Jeddah is renowned as the unrivalled epicentre of fishing activity in the Red Sea. However, it was only when I visited the fish market for the first time in 2013 that I fully understood the scale of that activity. The vast variety of fish on sale each day is truly astonishing. Most of the fish are caught some three or four days before they reach the market, but they are fresh because they are put into ice boxes almost as soon as they come out of the water (see above).

The vast majority are caught in the Red Sea, of course, although some are imported from the Nile, the Arabian Gulf and Oman.

An auction (*ḥarāj*), led by an auctioneer (*dallāl*) and supervised by the Sheikh ad-Dallālīn ('Head of Auctioneers'), is held at around six o'clock each morning. This is where the market's fishmongers buy their stock for the day. The fishermen place each fish, known as a *ḥabba*, in a plastic basket called a *zanbīl* or a more traditional *quffa*, made of palm branches. Some of the daily catch is strung in twos, fives or tens, called a *shikka*, depending on their size. Fish sold in a *shikka* are relatively expensive. Other fish are put in plastic crates and weighed by the *mann* measure depending on the size of the crate.

SOUTHERN RED SEA FISHING

Fishing for sharks (*lukhum*) is the principal occupation in southern Yemen today, just as it has been for centuries, according to 60-year-old Mohammad Ahmed Zaid al-Anbari, a *nākhōda* from Khor al-Ghureirah.[15] Like his father and grandfather before him, Ahmad Qahtan, another 60-year-old fisherman from Seera, near Aden, sails to Somalia, Djibouti, Eritrea and Hadhramaut to fish for them.[16] Shark fishing is also common among Djiboutians. Sadek Yakoub Abdalla, a captain in his 60s, reported: 'We set off at the start of winter in late September and return in April.'[17] Youssef Omar Mohamed, a 77-year-old *nākhōda* from Obock, explained: 'We use an anchor [*borōsī*] with the two ends of a net tied to it at the bottom of the sea.'[18] All of the fishing is done at night.

There are 44 species of Red Sea sharks (Carcharhinidae Sp.),[19] although the most common are the 'requiem sharks' – the *girsh sulmānī* (*Triaenodon obesus*; whitetip reef shark) and the *girsh buḥānī* (*Carcharhinus melanopterus*; blacktip reef shark).[20] Some species, such as the above, attack humans, as Suleiman Muhammad Ali Baloos, a pearl merchant from Greater Farasan, explained. He said his father, a pearl diver, had a number of narrow escapes.[21] In the early twentieth century the director of pearl fisheries in Sudan reported that 'a man's feet were taken off [by a shark] and he bled to death'.[22] And as recently as 2010 the *Guardian* reported 'unusual and shocking' shark attacks in the Egyptian tourist resort of Sharm el-Sheikh; two swimmers suffered injuries, with one losing 'her right hand and left leg'.[23] Similarly, the Saudi daily newspaper *Al-Riyāḍ* reported a shark attack on a pearl diver near Greater Farasan Island in 1990. The diver, Ahmed al-Awaini, lost an arm after struggling with the shark for several minutes.[24] According to 85-year-old Ahmed Muhammad Saad, former pearl merchant of Massawa, 'When the sharks saw many pearl divers diving, they would swim away. But they attacked if there were only a few.'[25]

Fish are routinely caught by net (*saḥwa*), line (*jalab*) or hook (*sunnāra*), but sometimes less-conventional methods are used. For instance, on one day each year, at some point from the end of March to the middle of April, the inhabitants of the Farasan Islands gather at Sahil Hasis to trap the *ḥarīd*, the longnose parrotfish (*Scaridae Hipposcarus harid*), which congregate in huge numbers close to the shore. This species of parrotfish usually hides from predators – such as sharks and humans – on coral reefs. The day before it comes out of hiding, the Farasanis hold a celebration from late afternoon into the evening, with sea songs and dancing, while newly wedded couples dress in full festive attire and parade on the shore, accompanied by music.[26] The following morning, a huge crowd of islanders run into the sea to catch the fish (see Figure 15.1). Ibrahim Muftah, a local historian, explained that the Farasanis know when the fish will head to the shore

> by the smell of the sea; the odour only comes when the parrotfish is in the area. When it appears, fishermen from the various islands work together to cordon off the schools of fish and direct them into the netted-off areas.[27]

Many of the caught fish are simply eaten at home, but some Farasanis take the opportunity to sell their hauls at the markets in Jazan and elsewhere.

Farih Gaas Mu'min, a 63-year-old former fisherman from the Dankala region of Eritrea, mostly went net fishing 'on an open-ended *zārūk* with two sails to Aden. That took ten days in fair winds but six to seven days with strong

FIGURE 15.1 Fishing festival at Greater Farasan Island, 13 April 2012 (photo courtesy of *Jazan Arab News*).[28]

winds. It would take about two days to reach al-Salif [on the Yemeni coast from Dankala]'.[29] The nets were made of palm-tree branches (*'asaf an-nakhīl*). Smaller *sanbūk*s that fished by net mostly operated along the Eritrean coast, but some sailed as far as the Saudi and Yemeni coasts.

There is fishing for sardines around Obock, Djibouti, throughout the year. Ali Ahmed Jaber, a 24-year-old fisherman from the town, told me that his boat usually fishes for 12 hours at night with nets that are 8 *bā'* (10–12 m) wide. As for other fish, he said 'the best season is between February and April', when they catch *zaynub* (Scombridae Sp. *Thunnus tonggol*; longtail tuna) and *darāk* (mackerel).[30] *Bayāḍ* (golden trevally), *nājil* (roving coral grouper), *sha'ūr* (emperor) and *ḥāmūr* (grouper) are also frequently caught by net. When fishing for small fish, dugout or planked *hūrī*s (4–10 m in length) are used. These carry three to four fishermen who fish by hook. Some hooks are dropped to a depth of 100 m, according to 60-year-old Ahmed Youssef Mohamed from Tadjourah.[31] These beach canoes are punted with poles or paddled with round- or spoon-bladed oars, which are also used as quarter rudders when the sail is raised. Ahmed Jaber Ali, father of Ali Ahmed Jaber (above), said they can sail as far as Mayyun (Bab el-Mandeb) and even Yemen.[32]

Fishing today in Massawa, Eritrea, as in the past, is by net (*shabaka*) and line (*jalab*). Net fishing trips can last 8, 14 or even 20 days in the main November–March season. Among the fish caught are: *bayāḍ, darāk, turnat, durab* (Chirocentridae Sp. *Chirocentrus dorab*; wolf-herring) and *girsh* (any species of shark). Plenty of fish are also caught by trailing lines from the deck. Experienced fishermen know which fish is on the end of the line by the way it pulls. *Jaḥsh* (Latin and English names not known), *sha'ūr, 'anta* and *kusharān* are all caught in the principal line-fishing months – April to November.

Usman Ali Ahmed, a 62-year-old fisherman from Dese Island, said that fishing for anchovies (Engraulidae Sp. *Stolephorus indicus*) and *balam* (Engraulidae Sp. *Thyrssa baelam*)[33] was very popular until a few decades ago; the season was from November to February.[34] In Massawa, 71-year-old retired fisherman Hammuda Abdalla Baghit recalled one- to three-month fishing trips on a *sanbūk* to the Dankala region. They mostly fished for anchovies, which were stored on board in *zanbīl*s made of palm (*dūm*) branches (1 *zanbīl* = 15 kg).[35] In the days of the Ethiopian Emperor Haile Selassie (r. 1930–74), the fish were then processed at Campo Marta, packaged in *akyās* (s. *kīs*) and exported to Europe. Anchovies make very good fertilizer and animal fodder. Idrees Iribi Idrees, a 65-year-old former sailor who worked on a British steamer (*bābūr*) for some 30 years, also fished for anchovies in the Haile Selassie era, although his catches were exported to Latin America (Costa Rica, Panama and Honduras): '[Before 1960], the catch was some one thousand to two thousand kilos a month, and from 1960 to 1968 fifteen to twenty thousand tons were caught each year'.[36] The fishermen cast a net as far as possible out to sea, then formed a semicircle and pulled the net ashore. Other informants remembered fishing for *hidra* (Holothuridae Sp.; sea cucumbers), known as *zubb al-baḥr* ('the sea's penis') in Eritrea. These were exported to the Far East, but the Eritrean Government banned the practice some time ago.

Alan Moore described a raft called a *ramas* that was used for fishing in Massawa in the early twentieth century. These were simple craft: three to four main logs and two cross-timbers lashed together and paddled with round-bladed oars.[37] This technique has now died out in Eritrea, but rafts are still used for inshore fishing in Khokha, Yemen.[38] The Arabic term *ramas* occurs as *ramath* in pre-Islamic poetry; also documented in the Ḥadīth (sayings and deeds of the Prophet Muḥammad) and in more recent travel literature, it is of Hamito-Semitic origin, with cognates in Demotic, Ethiopic, Kebra-Nagast, Somali and Socotri, all indicating that the word is indigenous, in particular to the southern Red Sea and the Horn of Africa.[39]

SHELL COLLECTING IN SUAKIN

Seashells are collected on the southern African and Arabian coasts of the Red Sea. The general term for shells is *qawāqi'* (s. *qawqa'*), but the larger ones are known collectively as *ṣadaf*. Suakin, in Sudan, is a well-known centre for the collection of both conch and trocas. This thriving industry provides significant revenue for the regional government and steady incomes for the divers, many of whom are members of the Beja (Hadandawa) tribe who are employed by the government on a seasonal, part-time basis. The spider conch (RSA *kukyān*; Strombidae Sp. *Lambis truncate sebae*)[40] is collected for its mother of pearl, while the spiral shells[41] of the trocas (*Trochus dentatus*),[42] which the locals also term *kukyān*,[43] are made into shirt buttons, beads and pendants. Both of these shells are exported to Europe and the Far East (Indonesia, Korea and Japan). The trocas are weighed by the kilo on the quayside at Suakin and placed in *tanaka*s (metal buckets), which the *nākhōda* then sells for export via Port Sudan.[44]

Trocas and conch collecting has now largely superseded the local pearl diving, which was far more prevalent in Suakin until neighbouring states imposed restrictions on Sudanese vessels that attempted to operate outside of home waters in the 1950s.[45] Consequently, many pearl divers lost their jobs and turned to shell collecting or fishing (see Plate 13). Of course, this led to increasingly fierce competition among the fishing vessels.

The trocas-collecting season runs from November to March, all along the Sudanese coast. Most shell-collecting trips, which last three to four weeks, are undertaken on a *lansh-sanbūk* that carries two or three dugout *hūrīs*. The crew usually consists of the captain and eight to ten divers and haulers. When some shells are spotted by the *hūrī*-man, the diver (s. *ghawwāṣ*; pl. *ghawwāṣīn*) dives to a depth of 3–4 m holding a basket and a stone to help his descent. Each of these is attached to a cord, with the other ends held by a hauler (*jarrār* or *barrāḥ*) in one of the *hūrīs*. The diver releases the stone when he reaches the bottom and the hauler immediately pulls it up. Next the diver collects shells in a palm-leaf basket (*danjīl* or *dangīl*), then signals to the hauler by tugging on the basket's rope, whereupon the hauler pulls both the diver and the basket to the surface. Muhammed Idrees and Hamid Hammad Jubouri, both trocas divers, estimated that they could collect some 60 to 70 *shawāls* (sacks) of shells on a single trip,[46] equivalent to 6 or 7 tons. The Sudanese do not eat trocas meat, so it is left to rot on the deck and creates a 'horrible stench [...] [A] ship laden with trocas can be scented six miles away', according to Henri De Monfreid.[47] However, Eltayeb notes that these mollusc species make good animal protein for local farmers.[48]

Djiboutians also collected trocas and other shells in the waters around Sudan, Eritrea, the Dahlak Islands and Ras Hafun in Puntland until the late 1970s. A trip could last anywhere between one and five months. Abdou Suleiman, a 60-year-old *nākhōda* from Obock, told me that Somaliland also had rich trocas beds, especially from February to April. It is not entirely clear why Djiboutians stopped collecting these shells, and Abdou believes 'the younger fishermen' are now keen to resume the practice.[49]

Other informants in Suakin mentioned collecting dark red sea cucumbers (Holothuriidae Sp. *Actinopyga mauritania*),[50] known locally as *izīrī*, which fetch high prices in East Asia.[51] They are collected from shallow water with 'sea grass meadows and on sand close to coral reefs'.[52] So-called 'white' sea cucumbers (*Bohadschia graeffei*)[53] are also collected for export to South Asia.

FISHING COOPERATIVES

Until a few decades ago, Red Sea fishermen received no government protection or support. There was an unofficial code of conduct and the camaraderie of the fishing fleet got many mariners through difficult times, but ultimately, as Hamdan Abd al-Marwani, a fisherman in his 40s from Ummlejj, recalled, 'Everyone worked in his own interests' (*Kull wāḥid yamshī 'alā maṣlaḥtu*).[54] Recently, however, governments throughout the Red Sea region have established fishermen's cooperatives, each of which is headed by a local sheikh. At Massawa, the government loans fibreglass boats to all of the dhow owners and fishermen who join the cooperative, and they also benefit from subsidized fuel, equipment and training.[55] Muhammad-Nour Muhammad

Al Hasan, our guide but also an official in Eritrea's Department of Fisheries, told us: 'Fish that are sold in the market today have to pass government control quality. [The fishermen] sell their fish to the government agency, which then sells them on at a higher price.'[56] Thus, the fishermen make a profit of some 15 per cent, whereas the agency can make anything up to 30 per cent. Similar schemes operate throughout the region. During the People's Democratic Republic of Yemen period (1972–90), government incentives almost certainly accelerated the fishermen's abandonment of their old wooden sailing dhows and the switch to diesel-powered, fibreglass vessels.[57] This scheme was funded in part by the Soviet Union, and it contributed to significant growth in the Yemeni economy in the final quarter fo the twentieth century.[58] Similarly, when the Centre de Pêche was formed in Djibouti in the 1980s, many fishermen accepted the financial assistance it offered to buy fibreglass fishing boats and equipment. Tadjourah benefited significantly from this scheme as the town's ailing fishing fleet was given a considerable boost.

Elsewhere, however, government schemes have had less-positive effects. Egyptian fishermen are offered assistance to rent or buy fibreglass boats, but this is still a costly process. Moreover, as Abu Al-Hamd Ahmed Khalil, a 65-year-old fisherman from Trombi, near Quseir, explained: 'Fishermen need money for a fishing permit [...] and motors are very expensive.'[59] In addition, engines tend to break down, and there is a shortage of mechanics to fix them, which can lead to long waits and high bills. For these reasons, a number of Egyptians, Sudanese, Eritreans and Yemenites have refused to participate in the government schemes. Instead, they have kept their traditional (albeit motorized) wooden boats and continue to operate independently of the cooperatives. If the engine fails, they simply hoist a sail; and if the sail rips or the mast breaks, they handle the repair themselves.[60]

In Sudan, government subsidies are available for hiring and repairing fishing boats, and compensation is provided for vessels that are lost at sea, as Hammad Tokulia Augan, Suakin's head of fisheries, informed me.[61] Yet this apparently generous scheme has proved unpopular among local dhow owners because they do not like the idea of entering into a partnership that would oblige them to abide by the government's regulations and pay taxes.[62] Several informants insisted that the scheme was in fact a scam that allowed the government to take the lion's share of any profits, leaving little income for the dhows' owners, builders and crews. Hussein Ibrahim Muhammad, a 72-year-old master builder from Suakin, explained the situation bluntly: 'We prefer no money rather than paying taxes. We have plodded along on our own for a long time and we will continue to do so.'[63]

FARASANIS' MEMORIES OF PEARL DIVING

This section is an updated account of the MARES team's 2010 ethnographic survey of small-scale pearl diving in the Farasan Islands, which was published in 2016.[64] We learned that oyster pearl shells (Far. *bilbīl*, *maḥār* or *gumāsh*; Pteriidae Sp. *Pinctada radiata*)[65] were highly prized because of the beauty of their pearls and the income they yielded. Today, these are found in small quantities around the islands of Qummah, Saluba and Dumsuq and in the Khor Ma'adi (see Map 3). Farasanis still believe that a pearl is formed after a drop of rainwater falls into the open shell of a female oyster. Hence, if it does not rain, no pearl will form. This is one of many medieval folk beliefs recorded by the geographer and historian al-Mas'ūdī (d. 345/956).[66]

In addition to pearl oysters, a number of other seashells are collected in the Farasan Islands: the pen shell (Pinnidae Sp. *Atrina vexillum*), a large black bivalve that is found on the seabed (it is every diver's dream to chance upon a black shell that contains a black pearl);[67] *bisir* or *busur* (Fasciolariidae Sp. *Pleuroploca trapezium*; tulip shell), which is much prized for its mother of pearl;[68] *likiz* (Murcidae Sp. *Murex tribulus*), a type of comb shell;[69] *luḥam* or *liḥam* (Murex tribulus L.),[70] a venus comb shell with two pointed ends; and *lakhu* (Strombidae Sp. *Strombus bulla*), a large conch shell. *Likiz*, *luḥam* and *lakhu* are all collected for their mother of pearl and opercula.[71] The tough operculum (*ẓufur*) is ground up with flowers and mixed with perfume to make a paste that women rub into their hair on festive occasions, such as weddings. Several informants also remembered collecting large quantities of *ḥawṭa* (Trochidae Sp. *Tectus dentatus*; topshells), another source of mother of pearl,[72] but this practice has long since ceased. At one time, conchs were collected in British Somaliland, and Farasani *sanbūk*s also sailed to Sudan and Djibouti in search of trocas shells.

Women still collect small, 'fragile-egg shells with sunken spines', known as *rukhum* (Far. *wada'*; Atyidae Sp. *Atys cylindricus*[73]), on Qummah today. Wooden planks are placed in shallow water and these soon attract colonies of tiny molluscs. The women then gather the shells from the wood, place them in buckets and pour hot water over them. The hot water kills the molluscs and the women then string the dried shells into necklaces or use them as decoration on boxes or cushions.[74]

In the Farasan Islands, diving (*ghōṣ*)[75] for the large spider conch (*ṣadaf*) took place in relatively shallow water – to a depth of between 3 and 9 m. *Ṣadaf*s were also collected further north – in the sea off Rabigh, Yanbu al-Bahr and El Wejh. These shells were usually transported to Sudan, where they were sold to agents for export.[76] Each dive lasted between 30 and 40 seconds, at which point the diver would return to the surface and rest on a plank of wood known as a *ramas* (a word that derives from the local term for a log raft; see above). The search for a large *ṣadaf* could take many hours, and only one or two could be hauled to the surface at a time. A number of dugout *ṣaddāfa*s (shell-collecting boats) were carried on board the main vessel and lowered into the sea whenever the shells were spotted. Each *ṣaddāfa* had a crew of three; one man looked through a metal box with a sealed glass bottom called a *nāẓūr* or *magwām*; the second rowed; and the third dived. The fisherman who peered through the *nāẓūr* would guide the diver by means of a *sabra* (a lump of lead or a stone) attached to a rope that he moved towards the shells. Abdou Suleiman, a sea captain of Obock, explained that this could be a risky business:

> The [diver] must know what he is doing, because a large open shell, if not handled correctly, can shut abruptly on both sides and will not let go. I knew some guys who lost their lives as the shock of the pain made them lose their breath.[77]

The Farasan Archipelago was renowned for its pearl divers for centuries. Ali Khalifa Ali Hammed Damri, a former diver in his 90s, recalled that the best pearling beds in the islands were about a kilometre south of Dumsuq, at a place called Al-Ayn.[78] Muhammad Abd Allah Said Al-Hussayyal, aged 69, from Khutub on Segid Island,[79] started diving when he was just ten years old. He remembered nine good pearling beds and explained that a typical trip would involve setting out on a *hūrī* for some 20 days at a time and camping overnight on various islands. He was almost the last of his kind; all but one of his fellow divers had passed away when we met him in 2010.

Interestingly, over the course of the last century, the Farasani pearling fleet probably spent more time in the Dahlak Archipelago, off the coast of Eritrea, than it did in home waters. This was because the Dahlaki beds were highly productive and their pearls were of superior quality, as Soleiman Baloos, a Farasani pearl merchant explained.[80] Farasani *sanbūk*s usually sailed across the Red Sea in convoys of 12. However, Farasanis also hired Dahlaki *sanbūk*s 'as pearling dhows during the season. The larger ones, with two masts [...] carried six to eight canoes on board', recalled Usman Ali Ahmed, a 62-year-old fisherman from Diese Island in the Dahlak Archipelago.[81] Sheikh Muhammad Isa Muhammad Aqili, a 76-year-old former pearl diver from Greater Farasan[82] who spent 60 years in the pearling industry, identified ten good locations in the Dahlak Archipelago. Asked about the relationship between Farasanis and the local Dahlakis, Ali Khalifa Ali Hammed Damri (mentioned above) said: 'The Farasanis and Dahlakis agreed to work together. In general, there were amicable relations with each other.' He added that several Dahlakis settled on the Farasan Islands, while some Farasanis sought employment on the Dahlak Islands or in Massawa. However, stricter immigration rules were imposed during the Italian occupation (1890–1941) and especially after the formation of the Saudi kingdom in 1932.[83]

Each Farasani pearling trip (*jawsh*) could last two or even three months, with each dhow carrying up to nine *hūrī*s. The *hūrī*s had a dual purpose: searching for pearling beds (*ma'ādin* or *mazāri' al-lu'lu'*) and, as noted earlier, diving for conch or trocas shells in shallow waters. Sometimes the search for pearling beds proved fruitless. Indeed, it was not uncommon for long trips to the Dahlak Islands to yield no pearls at all. Ali Hasan Hammud Sharif, a 49-year-old part-time pearl diver from Khutub, recalled: 'Once I spent sixteen days collecting shells. Not one pearl was found'.[84]

The number of divers and haulers varied according to the size of the *sanbūk*. Smaller vessels had crews of between 20 and 40, while the larger ones sometimes carried as many as 120. In fair weather it took about 24 hours to cross from the Farasan Islands to the Dahlak Islands, but the crew would have to row if there was no wind, which made the journeys much longer. When the dhow finally arrived at a pearling bed, work could begin as early as 7 a.m. and continue until 2 p.m. – a punishing schedule.[85] The divers often wore goat-skin finger protectors (*khabaṭ*) and nose-clips (*kharṭūm*), and they could dive to depths of 27 m. This required perfect coordination between the diver and his hauler. Similar to the technique used in Suakin, the diver went down to the seabed with a rope basket (*dangīl*) hanging around his neck and a weight (*jalīla*, *jawla* or *thaqqāla*) in his hand. Each of these items was attached to a cord (*'īda*), with the other end held by the hauler. As soon as the diver reached the bottom, he released the *jalīla* and the hauler pulled it up to the surface. About two minutes later, when he had finished collecting shells in the basket, he tugged on the second cord to signal to the hauler to pull both himself and the basket up to the dhow or *hūrī*. However, some divers could stay down for longer; one Farasani, Muhammad Ahmed Muzaffar, claimed he could dive for four minutes at a time.[86]

Sharks near the pearling beds usually struck fear into the hearts of the divers, but they were reassured when they saw dolphins, because they believed that these drove away the sharks. There were other threats, though. For instance, William Makin, writing in the 1930s, remarked that 'the devil fish was feared much more than sharks'.[87] He was probably referring to the spinetail mobula (Myliobatidae Sp. *Mobula mobular*), which has a poisonous sting.[88] Makin also mentions giant clams (Tridacnidae Sp.), which can grow to 1.21 m in length and have been known 'to seize a naked foot with crushing force',[89] and *dawl*s, which can leave a burn mark as if the victim has been struck by a red-hot iron.[90] Unsurprisingly, the diver would usually recite a solemn prayer before plunging into the water. (There is more on religious devotion and divine assistance in Chapter 17.)

'The life of the pearl diver is short', remarked Makin, and they were especially susceptible to 'heart disease or phthisis [pulmonary tuberculosis]'[91] as well as blindness or deafness. A number of interviewees also mentioned that divers suffered from vitamin deficiency (*gishāsh*) during the pearling season. In a bid to combat this, they would eat the stalks and leaves of a plant called *kumthir*. The leaves of the guava shrub were also said to be beneficial, and indeed they are 'packed with antioxidants, antibacterial and anti-inflammatory agents [...] [so they act] as a natural pain reliever'.[92] The preferred remedy for another common problem, chest infections, was the liver of the swordfish (Far. *abū munshār*; Xiphidae Sp. *Xiphias gladius*).[93] Meanwhile, jellyfish stings were treated by rubbing on 'chewed tobacco'.[94]

MARINERS' PAY

The northern Red Sea

Fishermen were paid for their labour – and received a proportion of the profits – of a fishing trip on the basis of a 'share system' (s. *sahm*; pl. *ashima*)[95] that varied according to the skills and experience of each mariner. Each *sahm* was established by the owner or captain of the dhow.

Recently, the discovery of the Al-Rāḍī family accounts in Tur has provided some useful details on how this system worked in the nineteenth century.[96] I have used these records to supplement the information provided by two Egyptian fishermen in 2003–4: Shadhli Ahmed Atalla, a 51-year-old fisherman from Quseir who formerly worked as a sailor on a trading vessel that sailed to Sudan and Yemen;[97] and Matar Fikri Muhammed Mustafa, a 41-year-old sailor from Mersa Alam.[98] Other interviewees in both the northern and southern regions generally confirmed their testimonies, albeit with a few slight variations.

Consider a crew of 12 fishermen under the command of a *rayyes*. The *sahm* was calculated after the *rayyes* sold the dhow's catch to an agent (*dallāl*). See Table 15.1 for the first stage of a typical Red Sea *sahm*.

Next, the dhow owner might distribute the net figure of 1,359 Egyptian pounds as follows: the *rayyes* received 3 shares; the boatswain (*mugaddam*) received 2 shares; each sailor (*baḥḥār*) received either 1 or 1.5 shares; and the cook (*tabbākh*) received 1.5 shares. In addition, a sailor might receive a bonus of a quarter of a share if he climbed the mast to watch for coral reefs or dived beneath the hull to mend leaks.[99]

TABLE 15.1 Sample *sahm* for an Egyptian Red Sea fishing trip.

Item	Egyptian pounds
Income (*maḥṣūl*) from salted fish sold at market	3,000
Advance payment (*tagdima* or *sulfa*) to buy cigarettes: *rayyes* 5; crew (12 sailors) 36	41
Provision for food, water, diesel etc. (*zawāda*)	100
Total of advance payment	141
Dhow owner's profit (50 per cent of income)	−1,500
Advance and provision payments	−141
Grand total for distribution among the crew	1,359

There were many variations on this basic model. For instance, Shadhli Ahmed Atalla told me that the owner of a *gaṭīra* or *falūka* might receive 3 shares plus another 3 shares for his provision of the fishing equipment (*'idad*) and 2 shares for the dhow's *hūrīs*: that is, 8 shares in total. However, 'The share system had no fixed rules' (*mā kān fī niẓām mu'ayyin*), Shadhli Ahmed continued, so the share each fisherman received varied from one owner and/or skipper to the next. The most important point was that the fishermen frequently ended up in debt (*madyūn*) to the owner once the advance and provision payments had been subtracted from their share of the profits. Tragically, the system ensured that many of them remained in debt all their lives. Moreover, a fisherman's children were expected to pay off any outstanding debt after his death.

Pearling in the southern Red Sea

Divers opened oyster shells with a knife (*maflaka*), probed inside the flesh for a pearl, then, if they were lucky enough to find one, placed it in a piece of red cotton cloth (*maṣarr*). Next, the pearls were sorted by dropping them on a tower of different-sized sieves, with the largest holes at the top and the narrowest at the bottom. Finally, they were weighed by a pearl merchant using a highly sensitive brass balance (*mīzān*; see Figure 15.2). Formerly, the main unit of measurement was the *shaw* (< Port. *chao*)[100]: 1 *mithgāl* = 330 *shaw* (5 g), so 1 g = 82.2 *shaw*.[101]

A number of Farasani pearl divers explained the industry's payment system to the MARES team.[102] As with the *sahm*, a dhow's *nākhōda* would first arrange a loan (*salāf*) or advance payment that covered the crew's food, clothes, cigarettes and sometimes family assistance. However, thereafter the two systems were rather different. For instance, the divers had to hire their own haulers and negotiate their wages. Typically, a hauler would receive half of a diver's income (*naṣfa*).

FIGURE 15.2 Sheikh Muhammad Hadi Al Rajhi weighing pearls with a *mīzān*, 2010 (photo MARES by the author).

The whole Farasani pearling fleet practised the *khumsī* system – a five-day working week. Each diver's pay was calculated on the basis of the number, size and quality of pearls he collected during the first four days of the week – from Sunday to Wednesday. On the fifth day, Thursday, all of the pearls were sent to the captain or owner for valuation; hence the term *khumsī*, which means a fifth. The amount he had loaned in advance for clothing, cigarettes and so on was then subtracted from the value of the pearls, as determined by the captain/owner himself. Of course, when the ship arrived back in port, he would sell the pearls to a merchant at a much higher price.

One or two informants maintained that the divers were not forced to sell their pearls to the ship's captain or owner while on board; they could sell them directly to a broker (*dallāl*) on shore if they so desired. However, 'either way, [the diver] had to pay the debt he owed to his *nākhōda*, and that could accumulate to a lot of money over the years', according to former pearl diver

Sheikh Muhammad Isa Muhammad Aqili.[103] Once again, after his death, any outstanding debt was passed on to his heirs. Fortunately, 74-year-old Mohammed Abdalla Ahmed Nasib's father did not leave him in that position; he worked very hard for two years and managed to pay off all the money he owed. In general, though, as Mohammed lamented, '[The diver] was poor, and died poor' (*'āsh faqīr wa-māt faqīr*).[104]

LeBaron Bowen rightly argued that this system was totally unjust. In effect, it was a 'debt pyramid' because whenever a money-lender advanced a payment to a *nākhōda*, as a 'nominal owner' of the dhow he expected to receive his lump sum *plus* a share of the boat's income in return. This placed immense pressure on the skipper/owner because he often had previous debts to service, too. As a result, most of the money he received from the sale of pearls went straight to the financiers, which meant he frequently did not have a float to pay for the next trip. Hence, he would be forced to negotiate yet another loan. Similarly, the divers became increasingly impoverished because the skipper advanced more money than they could afford to pay back in the first year, then did the same in subsequent years.[105] LeBaron Bowen summed up the situation as follows: 'Get a man in debt and then never pay him enough to get out of debt.'[106] It was almost impossible for a sailor or a diver to work for another captain/owner if he was in debt to someone else, as LeBaron Bowen[107] and some of the older Farasani interviewees explained.

Fortunately, the share system started to disappear in the 1950s and 1960s when the oil boom in Saudi Arabia, the Gulf and Oman finally provided alternative employment opportunities for the workers of the Red Sea.

IN CONCLUSION

Large wooden fishing dhows are now almost completely absent from the coastal landscape of the Red Sea, although smaller vessels and *hūrīs* are still used for short-distance fishing trips. Moreover, traditional fishing techniques have not changed significantly, despite the prevalence of fast, motorized, fibreglass vessels in the region today. As William J. Donaldson noted, 'Fish[ermen] over the ages have found the same similar solutions to the same ubiquitous problems'.[108] As in the past, men from inland towns still make their way to the coast each year to work as fishermen during the fishing season. However, most of the younger residents of the cities of Jeddah and Yanbu al-Bahr show no inclination to follow their fathers and grandfathers into the fishing industry. As a result, Saudi Arabia's fishing fleet has recruited thousands of Bangladeshi (known as Bangala) sailors. Similarly, in Obock, Djibouti, the members of the younger generation have looked for alternative sources of income from the sea over the last couple of decades, including smuggling Ethiopians and Eritreans by boat to Yemen and Saudi Arabia. Of course, this trade in 'undocumented migrants'[109] generates significant profits, and it has weakened the country's ties to fishing. Therefore, it seems doubtful that the traffickers will ever return to Djibouti's traditional industry, even if there is a crackdown on their illegal activities. They are much more likely to move to the cities or seek new lives abroad.

Festivals associated with the sea are common sights in Europe and the Mediterranean, but rare in the Red Sea region. This makes the Farasanis' parrotfish festival a particularly fascinating and joyful occasion. The whole community comes together to reaffirm their maritime heritage and their centuries-old relationship with the sea. However, some observers have expressed concerns about sustainability and marine conservation. As Linda Pappagallo stated in 2012, the Red Sea was once 'a healthy ecosystem and able to recover from such "shocks"; nowadays we can no longer afford these practices – with all due respect to culture and tradition'.[110] This is a valid point and there are signs that the Saudi authorities are starting to take such concerns seriously, so it will be interesting to see if the festival will be adapted – or even banned – in the future.

Large-scale commercial pearl fishing in the Red Sea is now a relic of the past, although a handful of amateurs in the Farasan Islands still dive for pearls (and shell collecting remains a thriving industry both within the archipelago and in Suakin). At least two Farasani pearl merchants (Suleiman Baloos and Sheikh Muhammad Hadi Al Rajhi)[111] still sell the amateur divers' finds to traders in Bahrain, the last remaining Gulf state to deal in natural pearls, as opposed to the cultured pearls that are sold in the rest.[112]

Shell collecting, pearl diving and fishing were traditionally viewed as low-status occupations even among the coastal communities of the Red Sea, and the workers who entered those industries had to resign themselves to lives of hard labour and perpetual debt. The work is probably just as tough today, although the fishermen are unlikely to be as indebted as their grandfathers were.

The share system had a profound effect on the whole community; the indebted sailor/diver/ fisherman in effect became his skipper's slave (*mamlūk*), but in turn the skipper was at the mercy of the financiers, because he could only survive by negotiating ever more loans.[113] LeBaron Bowen has argued convincingly that the trading dhows of the Red Sea would not have survived as long as they did if the sailors had received a monthly wage, as their Indian counterparts did,[114] and the same could certainly be said of the shell-collecting, pearling and fishing industries. The share system meant that crews were forced to work for very little (or even no) pay, and it was this that made the sailing dhow economically viable for so many centuries.

16

THE DHOW HUNT: THE SLAVE TRADE AND GUN RUNNING IN THE SOUTHERN RED SEA

فكفارته اطعام عشرة مسكين
من اوسط ما تطعمون
اهليكم او كسوتهم او تحرير رقبة

'For expiation, feed ten poor people
on a scale that you feed your families;
or clothe them; or give a slave his freedom.'
Sūrat al-Mā'ida ('The Table Spread'), 5.92.[1]

The southern Red Sea and the Horn of Africa have a long and complicated history of slavery; as such, it is beyond the scope of this book to provide a comprehensive discussion of the subject.[2] Nevertheless, I shall attempt to present a brief but informative overview of slavery in the southern Red Sea, with a specific focus on Djibouti.

What follows is based primarily on ethnographic fieldwork conducted in that country in 2009, supplemented with the testimonies of some Early Modern and more recent travellers to the region. Of course, this is a sensitive subject, and I have encountered significant reticence to discuss it in most places. However, Djibouti is something of an exception, as both young and older people are generally willing to offer their views and experiences of slavery both in the past and today.

Understandably, given the secrecy that surrounds it, 'the documentary record on slavery [...] is incomplete'.[3] Indeed, in 1868, at the height of the Indian Ocean slave trade, Captain Philip Howard Colomb (d. 1899), an officer on HMS *Dryad*, suspected that he had gained only a tiny glimpse of the problem, despite his and the rest of the Royal Navy's best efforts to stamp it out.[4]

Moreover, the subject is clouded by a host of inaccurate, contradictory and biased reports. 'Anecdotal travellers' observations' should be treated as especially flimsy evidence, according to Jonathan Miran.[5] I tend to agree, although in my experience the subjects of ethnographic inquiries almost always try to give an accurate impression of their experiences. Similarly, as an eyewitness to slave trafficking, Captain Colomb justifiably regarded himself as 'bound to try to state what seem[ed] to him the truth, however much it might leave him open to misconception'.[6]

THE BACKGROUND TO SLAVERY

It has been said that combating the slave trade was 'a justification [for] colonialism'. In other words, it legitimized the British presence in the Red Sea and the Horn of Africa, as many Europeans believed that 'the best way to stamp [...] out [slavery] was via the exercising of western control'.[7] In spite of their position as the dominant colonial power in the Red Sea region, the British found that they still had to cooperate with both the Ottoman Empire and Khedive Egypt if they were to have any impact on the slavers. France also played a role in denting the trade, but the British certainly led the patrols in the Red and Arabian seas after claiming full power to clamp down 'on the slave boats while in transit'.[8]

First, we need to establish why slave trafficking was rife in the southern region of the Red Sea and the Horn of Africa from the 1850s to the 1940s. One contributory factor was that the profits from slavery could be used to buy guns, and guns were needed to fight wars. By the mid-nineteenth century there was considerable tension and conflict between the recently arrived Europeans and local governments, in addition to the perpetual internecine warfare among various tribes that vied for supremacy in particular regions. Slave trafficking also provided opulent lifestyles for rulers and merchants who traded openly in human cargo as well as those who operated covertly to avoid the taxes that were levied by local governments. They established highly efficient trafficking networks that included the traders who captured the slaves from their villages, dhow owners, skippers and sailors.

While slavery is now condemned around the world, it is important to stress that the version that was practised in the Red Sea region was very different from the brutal trade that transported millions of Africans to the Americas.[9] The Qur'ān acknowledges the reality of slavery,[10] but insists that all slaves must be treated with kindness: 'Alms are [...] for those in bondage.'[11] It also suggests, 'Give a slave his freedom'[12] either through manumission or after receipt of an appropriate fee. I heard several accounts of masters treating their slaves well. Indeed, one resident of Jeddah told me that many slaves chose to remain with their masters even after manumission.[13] Similarly, a resident of Medina spoke with fondness of his grandfather and the two slaves he owned and subsequently freed. He recalled that the ex-slaves always visited the old man during the annual *'īd* festivities, bringing him gifts and wishing him well for the coming year. Such displays of affection between slaves and their masters were quite common throughout the Middle East.[14] Many Omani owners 'prided themselves on the care they took of [their slaves] and the mutual affection which existed between so many of them', according to Genesta Hamilton (d. 1990).[15] This 'paternal relationship' was unique to Islam, and the institution of slavery in Islamic countries was certainly 'much more benevolent than its western counterpart', wrote the Dutch scholar Christiaan Snouck Hurgronje (d. 1936).[16] Joseph B.F. Osgood (d. 1913), an American lawyer and judge from Salem, Massachusetts, reported that Ethiopian slaves who were shipped to Mocha were generally treated well, 'often taught to read and write, and seldom worked severely'.[17] Similarly, Viscount Valentia insisted that 'a slave in Arabia is by no means an object of compassion'. Indeed, those in Jeddah were considered members of the master's extended family; each slave 'lives well, is comfortably lodged, and splendidly cloathed'. Valentia added that a slave could even ask a *qāḍī* (judge) to authorize his resale at a public auction if he was unhappy with his master.[18] All of these travellers' comments are worthy of note, as none of them had any reason to misrepresent the facts.

Nevertheless, obviously it would be naive to think that everything was rosy for a Red Sea slave. As late as the 1960s, John and Irene Tunstall heard that pilgrim parents often sold their children into slavery 'to provide the fare for the family to cross from Suakin to Jeddah',[19] although none of my interviewees was able to verify this story. Similarly, I heard of a Saudi master in the 1960s who regularly beat his two slaves until they finally escaped to Yemen in a dugout *hūrī* after suffering years of abuse.[20] Another elderly Saudi informant expressed his dislike of slavery but was quickly silenced by his younger relative before he could elaborate.[21]

Female slaves fetched higher prices than either men or boys. The slave trader (*dallāl ar-ragīg*) divided them into two categories: kitchen domestics (*jāriya al-maṭbakh*) and concubines (*jāriya as-sarīr*; lit. 'slave for bed').[22] If one of the latter bore a child to her owner, the child was raised as a free citizen and the mother became the master's wife. Male slaves might work as pearl divers, farm labourers, shepherds, camel drivers, servants, doorkeepers or grooms, but equally they might learn a trade and become blacksmiths, carpenters, weavers or rope makers.[23] Finally, there were the boy eunuchs, who were trained to become the 'owner's responsible servants; managers of his household, and property; keepers of his treasure'.[24] Albert Londres (d. 1932), a French journalist who was based in the region in the 1920s, wrote that the Hijaz and Najd absorbed a significant proportion of this human cargo,[25] and 80 years later my informants corroborated his account. Indeed, they told me that almost every wealthy Hijazi family had house slaves until at least the 1960s.

It is difficult to assess the number of slaves who were transported and traded between Africa and Arabia. Janet Ewald suggests that between 1,500 and 30,000 slaves were imported into Arabia each year,[26] with the latter figure based on a British report of 1877.[27] Although Cairo and Khartoum attempted to suppress the trade during the reign of the Egyptian Khedive Ismail (r. 1863–79), it continued in both cities and up and down the Red Sea coasts until at least the 1930s. One report suggested that about 4,000 slaves were traded each year in the early part of the twentieth century,[28] whereas another report put the figure at 5,000, most of whom were Ethiopian.[29] These figures seem surprisingly high considering that the colonial authorities had devoted significant resources to the suppression of slavery for more than half-a-century.

In addition, the British Consulate in Jeddah had strongly encouraged manumission from the 1870s onwards, but the Hijazis were none too pleased about this consular activity.[30] Slave owners and traders saw nothing wrong with the practice[31] and insisted that it was legitimized by both religious law and local custom. Moreover, tradition dictated that all slaves were freed eventually, so no one was condemned to a lifetime of bondage. The British also encountered opposition from the Egyptian administration in the last decades of the nineteenth century as they attempted to suppress the activities of the the coastal 'Ababda and Bisharīn tribes, who controlled the transportation of slaves to the Hijaz. I met several members of the 'Ababda tribe, but none of them wished to discuss their ancestors' role in the slave trade.

Throughout the Red Sea region, some of my informants felt that slavery was unethical, but far more insisted that it was 'an honourable profession'. Many of those on the Arabian coast suggested that the slave trade was no different from the legalized servitude of Indians under the British Raj.

THE SLAVING DHOWS

At the end of the 1870s, Royal Navy officers received authorization to confiscate any slaving dhow and mete out summary punishment to the traders.[32] However, their operations were limited to waters that were officially under the jurisdiction of the British crown,[33] so they could do nothing about slaving dhows from Eritrea and French Somalia that flew French flags. (The French had a far more laissez-faire attitude towards the slave trade.)

The British also reached an agreement with the Ottoman Empire with respect to searching dhows and steamers, but the Turkish authorities were hardly enthusiastic partners in the fight against slavery.[34] Isabel Burton (d. 1896), the wife of the explorer Richard Burton, remarked:

> I will only state that the traffic still flourishes at Jeddah; that the market, till lately, was under the eyes of the British Consulate; that on representation it was removed a few yards off; that the Turkish authorities, even if they wished, are unable to stop or even to hinder it.[35]

In addition, an official British report of 1884 criticized the Ottoman patrol boats for their seeming reluctance to intercept any dhows in the Jeddah region.[36]

Ingeniously, Arabian dhow owners in the southern Red Sea sometimes bought land in Djibouti, which enabled them to sail under the French flag and almost guaranteed that they would not be stopped by the Royal Navy.[37] However, the ruse did not always work; in 1916 a British gunboat intercepted the *Fateh-el-Rahman*, which was 'lightly armed' and flying a French flag, not far from Mocha, a 'chief landing place for contraband'.[38] The British authorities in Aden detained the skipper, Henri De Monfreid, and his crew for a number of months on suspicion of smuggling slaves and guns until they finally agreed to the Government of Djibouti's request to release them the following year.[39]

Slaving dhows that did not attempt to hide under French protection tended to fly no flag at all in the British zone, according to Captain Colomb. He also noted that the typical slave trader 'carries no papers, belongs to nowhere, and claims nobody's protection'.[40] For instance, in 1902, two slaving dhows were intercepted off the coast of Berenice, north of Suakin; 'by law they should have had a passenger list [but] to no surprise, they did not'[41] (see Figure 16.1). Of course, the lack of paperwork, in itself, usually raised the authorities' suspicions.

According to Reginald Coupland (d. 1952), there were countless reports of slaves suffering filthy conditions on-board ship and even being thrown overboard when skippers tried 'to escape the penalties of capture'[42] (see Figure 16.2). Later, Irene and John Tunstall reported that pilgrims might be left to their fate as 'unscrupulous ships' captains would land on an isolated part of the Arabian coast where, without any documents, the [pilgrims] would be a prey to the slave traders'.[43]

Newspapers published lurid stories of slave catching (often illustrated with equally sensational pictures, such as Figure 16.2) in the hope of increasing their readerships, but these exaggerated tales caused considerable embarrassment to

FIGURE 16.1 The suppression of piracy and slave trading in the Red Sea, 1902 (drawing by Frank Dadd based on a sketch by C.E. Eldred).[44]

the colonial authorities, who were presented as almost powerless against the slave traders. In response, the civil servants in Aden set about painting a more accurate picture of the fight against slavery. They invited journalists onto British cruisers in the Arabian–Persian Gulf, the Indian Ocean and the Red Sea on condition that they reported the facts. William Makin was assigned the Red Sea region and went on to publish his (somewhat sensational) memoirs under the title *Red Sea Nights* in 1933. He reported that some European readers remained 'sceptical of the existence of slave trafficking', because 'the trails of the slavers [were] [...] secret and hidden'.[45]

The British gunboats usually hired an interpreter because the officers rarely spoke Arabic. Recruiting someone who could speak, read and write Arabic posed no problem, but it was more of a challenge to find a trustworthy interpreter, as most of the locals sympathized with the skippers and slave dealers. Moreover, the interpreter could be fed false information about land and sea routes and the slavers' hideouts. In a bid to solve these problems, interpreters were offered a share of the prize money for the capture of a slaving dhow.

FIGURE 16.2 An Arab slave ship in the Red Sea with a British cruiser in sight, 1874 (drawing by H. Harrell).[46]

According to De Monfreid, local people were hired to keep constant vigil along the length of the western coast of the Red Sea. If they saw anything suspicious, they would send a signal by means of a bonfire on the beach or one of the coastal hills.[47] But Arabian and African skippers were adept at playing hide-and-seek with the Royal Navy's anti-slavery patrols; they would lower their sails and hide in bays or mangrove swamps until the danger had passed. Étienne-Félix Berlioux (d. 1910) claimed there were 'countless hiding places'.[48] Moreover, a Royal Navy report of 1855 suggested that the patrols were hindered by their own charts, which omitted many dangerous sandbanks and submerged rocks.[49]

If a gunboat did manage to close in on a slaving dhow, the crew sometimes took the extreme step of jumping overboard to escape capture. Obviously this was extremely hazardous, given the prevalence of sharks in the Red Sea and the fact that crew members were often poor swimmers, but the life of a sailor on a slaving dhow was perilous even at the best of times. The crossing from Africa to Arabia was always made at night to minimize the risk of being spotted by the patrol boats, and catching a favourable wind – the *shamāl* from the north or the *azyab* from the south – often proved difficult.[50] As was noted in Chapter 13, the winds in this part of the southern Red Sea are unpredictable, and dhows often capsized because they carried insufficient ballast. Of course, in such circumstances the slaves were almost certain to drown because they (some, if not many) were chained on deck or in the hold.[51]

THE SWIFT AND AGILE *ZĀRŪK*

As the Royal Navy's pursuit of slaving dhows intensified in the latter half of the nineteenth century, Yemeni shipbuilders were in the process of perfecting a much faster and more manoeuvrable dhow. The British officers were truly 'fascinated by the strange sea-craft, so apparently ungainly and yet swift and agile'.[52] This was the *zārūk*, the vessel that Western commentators often termed, simply, 'the dhow'.[53] Before long, dhow yards on both shores of the southern Red Sea were producing *zārūk*s in tremendous numbers (see Chapter 9). These craft were 'fast sailers in any wind', Hornell observed, and 'better at beating to windward' than other *sanbūk*s.[54] They were 'sharp at each end and light of draft',[55] which meant they could be manoeuvred easily through inlets and coral reefs and slid over most submerged rocks.[56] As they lay low in the water, they could 'glide rapidly out of the anchorage'[57] and escape the attentions of any approaching gunboat. Henri De Monfreid observed that 'the sail could be unfurled in a second', the anchor raised and the *zārūk* would be on its way.[58] As Devereux noted, to the Royal Navy, 'the dhows were game to be hunted' and it was 'joy of joys' if they ever managed to catch one.[59]

Charles Doughty (d. 1926) called Jeddah the 'staple town of the African slavery',[60] but Ethiopians were highly prized in all of the Arabian markets and usually fetched large sums of money.[61] Massawa exported many of these slaves to Hodeidah, Lith and Mocha in addition to Jeddah and further north on the Hijazi coast.[62] Meanwhile, Djiboutian *zārūk*s from Tadjourah and Obock made the crossing to Perim (Mayyun) Island or headed further north to Sheikh Said. From there, they might sail to Mocha, Hodeidah or Jeddah, while other slaves were transported via the Hijazi route and ended up in Transjordania.[63] Mocha was an important slave-trading centre, with 'cargoes of slaves often brought to this port from Abyssinia', according to the American traveller Joseph Osgood, writing in the 1850s.[64] Several decades later, De Monfreid noted: 'Many slaves taken into the heart of Arabia don't even remember having seen the sea, so swift was their nocturnal crossing.'[65]

The *zārūk* was indeed the 'king of the Red Sea', so it was 'favoured for most of the nefarious occupations of the Arab: slaving, smuggling, gun running and the like'.[66] They not only outperformed other dhows but 'were so fast that the

English frigates and brigs [...] could seldom catch them', claimed naval historian David Howarth.[67] However, as a Foreign Office report of 1890 admitted, British cruisers were not designed to chase fast-moving slavers on the Red Sea.[68] They were too slow, their boilers generated so much heat that conditions on board could become intolerable when they went full steam ahead for any length of time[69] and they could not venture too far from a coaling station for fear of running out of fuel. Moreover, they belched out smoke that was visible from miles away[70] and so alerted the slavers to their presence. At one point the British Admiralty suggested supplementing the steamers with a 'special class of fast-sailing small craft',[71] but these would have required skilled Red Sea pilots who were familiar with the coastal landscape (see Chapter 10). Recruitment would have been quite a challenge, given the local ambivalence towards the slavers coupled with the local antipathy towards colonial rule. There was another concern, too: after the Suez Canal opened in 1869, Egyptian and Ottoman steamers started to play an active role in the slave trade,[72] which made the Royal Navy's patrols even less effective. Before long, the Red Sea had become, in the words of Étienne-Félix Berlioux, 'a great warehouse' of black slaves.[73] Eventually, the British were forced to accept that they were fighting a losing battle.

GUNS FOR SLAVES

Gun running ran in parallel with slave trafficking throughout the latter half of the nineteenth century and well into the twentieth. It became 'so rife in the Gulf of Aden that the British Government redoubled its vigilance'.[74] The Royal Navy 'hunted the dhows in pinnaces and cutters',[75] chasing them throughout the night. William Makin reported: 'I have been on the deck of a British sloop in the Red Sea at night when the searchlight [...] suddenly cut the darkness and revealed the dhow with dreadful clarity.' In those days, 'every dhow was suspect',[76] and if the suspicions proved justified, the penalty was confiscation (and possibly destruction) of the dhow and sometimes imprisonment for the skipper and his crew.

Africans, Arabians and Europeans all made lucrative livings from gun running in the Red Sea, with Henri De Monfreid supplementing his income from the arms trade with hashish smuggling. The French poet Arthur Rimbaud (d. 1891) shipped rifles to King Menelik II (r. 1889–1913) of Shewa in the 1880s,[77] while a former member of the British armed forces, Francis Waterhouse, openly admitted that he was involved in the gun trade in Aden. In the 1930s Waterhouse reported that 'large supplies of arms' from America 'were being brought through British Somalia, concealed in elephants' tusks'.[78]

The weapons were exchanged for slaves or shipped to Oman. As the British civil servant Bertram Thomas (d. 1950) observed, 'arms and ammunition and the health of the camel [were] the primary necessities of life' at the time.[79] Another European, Antonin Besse Sr, the famous French Adeni dhow owner, was accused of 'smuggling, gun running and drug traffic', though this was never proven.[80]

TADJOURAH, THE DANKALI CAPITAL OF SLAVE TRADE

For many years, the main source of income for the twin sea towns of Tadjourah and Zeilah was the illegal trade in slaves, guns and armaments, cattle and horses. The former is now in the Republic of Djibouti (formerly French Somaliland), while the latter is in the self-declared Republic of Somaliland (formerly British Somalia and at the time of writing still officially an autonomous region of the Federal Republic of Somalia).

Ibrahim Ishak, a former police officer from Tadjourah, and other Djiboutian interviewees told me that the Afar and Issa tribes bartered salt, butter and cattle, as well as slaves, in exchange for guns, while Ethiopian horses were exchanged for Yemeni guns and armaments.[81] A local fisherman confirmed this in a 2014 BBC documentary: 'My father was a fisherman, and my grandfather was a boat builder. He also worked with pirates, taking Ethiopian slaves to Yemen and trading them for guns.'[82] Ziyad Ahmed Khizari, from Djibouti City, told me that he traded guns and smuggled drugs on *zārūk*s for some 30 years, travelling back and forth between Yemen and Assab. When asked if he ever exchanged slaves for guns, he merely smiled.[83]

Tadjourah town is the capital of Djibouti's Tadjourah Region, which was once known as 'Dankali country' because most of the population are members of the Afar (or Dankali) tribe. The region came under French protection in the nineteenth century because it is strategically well placed on the northernmost tip of the Horn of Africa. The ancient port was probably built on the site of Malaō, a well-known slaving centre in the first century CE.[84] William Cornwallis Harris (d. 1848), who visited the town in the 1840s, called it 'the city of the slave merchants'.[85]

In the fourteenth century CE, Ibn Baṭṭūṭa recorded a visit to Zeilah, which now lies close to Somaliland's border with Djibouti.[86] Five centuries later, slaves were marched from Harar, in the Ethiopian foothills, to the port – a route that was also followed by the British explorer Richard Burton in 1854.[87] Many of the Ethiopian slaves were then transported to southern Arabia or the Gulf,[88] especially Oman, which also received slaves from Tadjourah. Houmed Barkat Siradj, a 55-year-old local historian, told me that this trade continued until the 1930s, and 'Tadjourah's contacts with Oman led to Afar settling there'.[89]

The caravan traders who marched slaves in chains from the southern Ethiopian highlands to Tadjourah would halt at the town's oasis (which has long since dried up) and wait for a *zārūk* to transport their human cargo to Arabia. Salt, ivory or grain were often shipped at the same time.[90] Mohamed Salem Omar, a 79-year-old former *nākhōda*, said that '*sanbūk*s picked slaves from the Songo-boda community and sailed to Yemen' from Sagalou, on the Gulf of Tadjourah.[91] De Monfreid, who was known to the Afar as Abd El Hai, described a mountain trail through the Mabla foothills that he followed many times, although always disguised as a Dankali, because Europeans were 'not welcome' in the area in the 1920s.[92] He continued that the headmen of three Ethiopian tribes – 'the Chancallas, Wallamos and Gouragays' – bought slaves from their families and then sold them to Aragouba slave dealers, who also paid taxes to the chieftains. Once in Tadjourah, these dealers met Arabian traders and exchanged the slaves for 'cotton goods and copper leaf'.[93]

By the 1920s, the sultan of Tadjourah was 'one of the richest slavers of the Red Sea coast',[94] and some Europeans certainly profited from the slave trade, too. Yet, it is difficult to link specific individuals definitively to slaving, irrespective of their other nefarious activities. Consider Arthur Rimbaud and Henri De Monfreid. Rimbaud lived in Tadjourah between 1880 and 1891 and there is irrefutable documentary evidence that he was an active gun runner. However, Charles Nicholl disputes the widely held assumption that he was also a slave trader. According to Nicholl, Rimbaud's references to '*esclavage*' in his letters to relatives should not be taken literally; rather, they merely 'describe his own conditions of employment'.[95] I asked Houmed Barkat Siradj what the local elders thought of Rimbaud's alleged involvement in the slave trade, and he said that the general belief is that he was not a slaver. On the other hand, when I asked if De Monfreid ever participated in the trade, the answer was a categorical 'yes'.[96]

De Monfreid certainly did not seem to disapprove of slavery, and he was quite open about his friendship with Sheikh Makki, a well-known slave trader in Tadjourah. One day in the 1920s or 1930s, seeing that Makki was nervous about an upcoming voyage, De Monfreid reassured him, saying: 'You need fear nothing.' Makki raised his sail in the moonless night 'and discreetly, silently [...] [his *zārūk*] slid past us towards the mouth of the inlet'. De Monfreid added that the vessel 'seemed empty, save for three or four dark figures silhouetted against the canvas. Another slaver had left for Arabia.'[97] While this does not confirm the Frenchman's active involvement in the trade, it does seem to imply tacit approval.

Slavers often tried to trick the British patrols into believing that their human cargoes were crew members, fishermen or pearl divers.[98] Alastair Hazell claimed that 'Slaves were terrified into masquerading as crew, or as domestics belonging to the [*nākhōda*]'.[99] Clearly, for this tactic to work, the dhows had to carry only a few slaves at a time.[100] Ruqayya Hassan Mahalla, the 83-year-old widow of a former *nākhōda* from Obock, was unusually forthcoming on this subject. Her late husband Abdalla had owned two *sanbūk*s, but both 'were seized by the British and were taken away to Zeilah. He was trafficking slaves bought from Ethiopia in exchange for guns and ammunition.' I asked if this put an end to his involvement in the slave trade. She replied immediately: 'No. He continued to buy slaves and transported them to Yemen.' When I asked if these voyages were risky, Ruqayya answered:

> Except for that one incident, he was never caught. He placed the slaves in the hold of the vessel together with goats that he was transporting to the Yemeni coast. When the British patrol intercepted his *sanbūk* they would open the hatch that led to the lower deck and could only see the goats, not the slaves, as it was dark. Their skin was too black to see in the dark of the night.[101]

She attributed the success of this ruse to *seḥer* ('magic'). Similar techniques were employed in the 1920s. William Makin told of a Red Sea skipper who instructed his crew to cover the slaves in the hold with a tarpaulin. If a patrol boat approached, the sailors would simply step on the tarpaulin to distract the searchers.[102]

The dhows that transported human cargoes from the African to the Arabian shore certainly took risks, but the rewards were great, and such trips were only ever made on an occasional basis. Even those who were more deeply involved in the slave and arms trades returned to their ordinary occupations once a run had been completed; no *nākhōda* worked full-time as a slaver.

IN CONCLUSION

The European colonial powers, particularly the British, saw it as their moral duty to stamp out the slave trade. Basking in the warm after-glow of the 1807 Slave Trade Act and the 1833 Abolition Act, which abolished slavery throughout the British Empire, they were determined to impose their moral superiority over their 'backward' colonial subjects.[103]

This chapter has drawn extensively on the reliable records of the British India Office at Aden and the National Archives, supplemented (and I feel enhanced) by the oral accounts of a small number of interviewees who were willing to discuss the subject of slavery. The short case study on

Tadjourah serves as an example of how this more holistic approach might be taken further in the future.

Slave trafficking and arms dealing were co-dependent, with the traders often turning to piracy to loot guns and even human cargoes. In the early days, the British authorities found it almost impossible to hinder the transport of arms from Belgium to Djibouti and America to Aden. However, as Henri De Monfreid wrote in 1914, gun running eventually 'grew difficult' and 'buyers became rare'.[104] Nevertheless, slave trading continued in Lahej and two other Hadhrami states into the 1940s[105] and in Saudi Arabia until the early 1960s. Ibn Saud's (r. 1932–53) self-proclaimed opposition to slavery was half-hearted, at best, because he never banned the sale of slaves in public places.[106] It was only in 1962 that the Saudi Government finally abolished the trade and ordered the manumission all of the country's remaining slaves.

Yet, the economic conditions that engendered slavery still exist today. Two days before leaving Djibouti in 2009, the MARES team arranged a visit to Godoria, to the north of Obock. En route, we came across 12 Eritreans walking along a desert trail. They were heading for the coast and explained that they had already paid large sums of money to fishermen to smuggle them across Bab el-Mandeb to Yemen. In other words, while they were not in chains, they were following one of the well-trodden slave routes that have been used in this region for thousands of years.

17

THE DHOW, THE COAST AND THE SEA: INTERACTING WITH NATURE, THE SPIRITS AND THE SUPERNATURAL

'Abū Zulayma, the patron saint of the [Red Sea] [...] sits watching over the safety of pious mariners in a cave among the neighbouring rocks.'

Rayyes of a pilgrim *sanbūk*, Suez to Jeddah, July 1853.[1]

Any attempt to define what is meant by 'the spirit' or 'the divine' must, of necessity, touch on theological and psychological issues. However, it is not my intention to delve deeply into these matters here. Rather, my aim is simply to present what the people of the African and Arabian coasts of the Red Sea have to say about their interactions with nature, the spirit world and the supernatural, and to explain why the dhow and its culture sit at the heart of those relationships. I will explore how these people connect with nature and the supernatural in an environment that is often hostile, using examples from European travellers' accounts, colonial officials' and ethnographers' reports and the testimonies of the local population themselves.

In earlier chapters, we saw that coastal reefs, the turbulent wind regime and many other perils pose significant threats to the lives of seafarers on the Red Sea. Now, we shall see that the region's mariners still routinely turn to the supernatural and the divine for protection against these dangers.

In the past, many pilgrims and merchants chose to travel by sea in preference to the alternative overland routes, not least because the desert trails were rich hunting grounds for marauding Bedouin bandits, who looted money and goods from travellers with impunity. There was also the matter of the scorching sun, from which there was no escape in the desert. Whether journeying by sea or land, though, all travellers sought talismanic protection against the dangers they were likely to face. As a result, a rich material culture associated with folk beliefs developed over the centuries. This subject has attracted the attention of a number of researchers – Hornell, Myers, LeBaron Bowen, Serjeant, Johnstone, Naumkin and Smith, to name but a few – who have written many excellent articles on both maritime and terrestrial folk beliefs in the southern region of the Red Sea.[2]

THE MATERIAL CULTURE OF MARITIME FOLK BELIEFS

Travel to unknown and distant lands must have been a daunting prospect for medieval and Early Modern seafarers, given that their journeys could last a year or more. Hence, it is hardly surprising that they turned to a number of talismanic objects to keep malign forces at bay. Examples include strings of cowrie shells worn around the neck[3] and charms and amulets bearing Qur'ānic verses or religious aphorisms. In the middle of the nineteenth century, E.W. Lane quoted one of the latter, which read: 'God is the best protector; and He is the most merciful of those who show mercy'.[4]

The need for protection extended to the means of travel itself. Dhows were decorated at both the bow and the stern with long tassels, ostrich eggs and feathers, as William Daniel noted in 1700.[5] Camels were (and still are) decorated in the same way for the same reason. All of these items are meant to provide talismanic protection against the evil eye (*al-'ayn*)[6] – a superstitious belief that is both ancient and still widespread throughout the Middle East and North Africa. It is believed that a single glance from a human eye with evil intent can harm or kill the targeted person, or summon up powerful natural forces such as gales that could wreck a ship. The Old Testament warns, 'Eat thou not the bread of him that hath an evil eye, neither desire thou his dainty meats',[7] while the Qur'ān equates the evil eye with unbelievers who 'would almost trip thee up with their eyes'.[8] In order to keep these evil forces at bay, both public places and personal amulets were frequently decorated with vivid depictions of eyes.

For centuries, it was also customary for a dhow to boast a striking painted eye – the *oculus*[9] – which was considered crucial for the safety of the seafarers themselves, their cargo and their belongings. Hornell argued that this tradition dates back to pre-Islamic times and pointed out that almost identical emblems were painted on seacraft from the Mediterranean to China.[10] Indeed, they are still seen on Mediterranean vessels today. The practice remained widespread in the Red Sea and East Africa until the late 1970s, but it started to wane with the emergence of a more austere form of Islam that prohibits the depiction of any part of the human body. I was fortunate to spot one of the few survivors in Djibouti's fishing harbour in 2009 (see Figure 17.1). However, while the *oculus* has almost disappeared from Red Sea dhows, the ships' owners still seek talismanic protection by painting them in vivid colours and inscribing reassuring and inspiring texts on the hulls.

The dhows of Yemen, Sudan, Eritrea, Djibouti and the Hijazi coast are painted in particularly vibrant colours, while their Egyptian counterparts are rather more drab. It is possible that this tradition arrived in Yemen when boat builders returned to the Middle East from South-East Asia and brought with them that region's long-established custom of painting vessels in bright colours. The Yemenis and Hadhramis then probably exported the practice to the African and Arabian littorals when they migrated in search of work in the nineteenth century. Ettinghausen has pointed out that the dhows' vivid colours contrast well with 'the barren coastal landscape and the desert',[11] which is certainly a romantic explanation for why the tradition was adopted so widely, but I think there might be more to it than that. Blue and turquoise are the dominant

FIGURE 17.1 An *oculus* on the bow of a *mahadi*, Port de Pêche, Djibouti City, 2009 (photo MARES by the author).

colours for ships' decoration, and these were also the colours that featured prominently in most depictions of the evil eye, including the *oculus*. Hence, I believe that the intention is still to guard against evil spirits; it's just that the colour itself, rather than the image of an eye, now provides the protection.

Dhows are also decorated with Arabic text as well as stylized flower designs and geometrical motifs[12] that comprise 'the quintessence of the abstract form' in Islamic art.[13] Interviewees in Suakin, Djibouti and Yemen repeatedly stressed the talismanic power of this maritime folk art. The text frequently includes positive abstract nouns, such as *al-rajā'* ('hope'), *al-majd* ('praise') or *al-karam* ('nobility'), but references to *al-raḥḥāl* (traveller), *al-dabbāgh* (tanner), *janāḥ as-ṣaqr* (the falcon's wing) and *al-ra'd* (thunder) are also common. Such words and phrases are inscribed on the sides of the vessel to ward off evil. Sometimes Qur'ānic or poetic verses are engraved or painted on the stern.[14] The most evocative lines refer to travel and adventure as well as recollections of the past, such as: *'alā ash-shawāṭi' tursā as-sufun wa-'alā al-qulūb tursā adh-dhikriyyāt* ('off the coast the boats drop anchor and in the hearts lie memories'). Both the calligraphy and the abstract designs are often beautifully executed and the end result can have powerful emotional resonance. The underlying messages of positivity and protection help to connect the maritime communities of the Red Sea to the region's spiritscape.

SPIRIT–HUMAN INTERACTIONS

There are countless folk tales on the subject of spirits' relations with the coast, the local people and the sea. The spirits are known as *jinns*, and a large proportion of the people I interviewed on the coasts of the Red Sea still believe in them. However, while several informants were keen to chat about them, others were far more cautious and refrained from providing details about the nature of their belief. Indeed, the latter group seemed rather embarrassed to discuss such matters – which they laughingly termed '*Arabian Nights* thinking' – with a Westerner. But these were the educated few: local government officials in the Farasan Islands, for instance, who were well aware that most Westerners know little about the human–*jinn* relationship beyond what they have read in stories such as 'Aladdin and the Magic Lamp' and 'The Merchant and the Genie'.[15] Nevertheless, I found that belief in *jinns* was much more pervasive than they would like to admit. Customs such as burning incense in the home or on-board ships to keep the mischievous spirits away are not confined to simple fishermen and sailors; sophisticated, wealthy families and skippers still practise them, too.

The Qur'ān mentions *jinn*s in a number of verses[16] and suggests that they are created 'from fire free of smoke'.[17] The Qur'ānic commentator Yusuf Ali describes them as 'subtle like a flame of fire'.[18] The word *jinn* comes from the root √ *janna – yajunnu* ('to cover, hide, etc.' but also 'to descend, to become dark (night)').[19] The spirits are interdimensional beings that take different shapes and forms (i.e., a black cat, a dog or a black fig) and they can be any age, gender, religion, free or slaves. The Qur'ān identifies a relationship between the divine and *jinn*s in pre-Islamic Arabia that clearly delineates the spirits' role in early Arabian spirituality.[20] They are also described as a 'hidden force',[21] and in folk tales humans call upon their services, for instance to guard the tomb of a sheikh or to visit an ailing holy man and keep him company.[22] Afreets (*'afrīts*) are a sub-category of *jinn*s: 'They are Allāh's worst afflictions.'[23] In Quseir 68-year-old Kamil Muhammad Abu Lubb al-Burri and 81-year-old Abbas Muhammed Ali Daud described afreets as creatures of the mountains, which neither man dared to visit on his own. In the past, they said, the Bedouin often acted as mountain guides for the camel drivers and desert travellers.[24]

There is widespread belief in *jinn*s in the Farasan Islands, where many of the locals are convinced that they live among the spirits. Abdo Mohammed Isa Aqili, a 46-year-old fisherman from Muharraq, insisted: 'They are everywhere [...] they enter houses and [live in] caves.'[25] Apparently, they come and go in seconds and travel vast distances in no time at all. On Greater Farasan, Abdo took me to the caves of Shida, on a hill close to the shore. The first cave was spacious, but there was a second chamber that we could access only through a small hole. Abdo explained that a one-eyed creature appears there at night, then added that the cave swarms with bats and hissing serpents. These creatures are closely associated with the *jinn* world, as Bertram Thomas, a British civil servant, observed in the 1920s after visiting the Qara Mountains in Dhofar. He was told that snakes and scorpions abide either inside or with the spirits.[26] At Shida, Abdo continued that there is a third chamber, but it should be 'avoided at all costs' because of its blood-sucking bats. His story chimes perfectly with Thomas's desciption of *jinn*s that 'share a dark existence' with other frightening creatures.[27] In Abdo's words, 'offering loyalty to the master *jinn* would be fatal'.

Deserted settlements are said to be haunted by *jinn*s. A number of informants mentioned Qusar on Greater Farasan, which was a thriving summer resort until about 50 years ago. However, tales of mischievous *jinn*s started to circulate, which frightened off first the tourists, then the residents. Farasanis do not holiday in Qusar today, and certainly never visit at night. Similar stories of haunted villages abound throughout the Arab world.

For instance, in the 1940s, Oliver Myers reported that the population of Little Aden had been left terrified by stories of *jinn*s snatching people away.[28]

If possible, people are even more fearful of *jinns*' malicious activities at sea, where they are said to stir up the waves and summon gales. Burton reported the prevalence of this belief on his voyage from Suez to Jeddah.[29] Members of the Hadandawa clan of coastal Sudan claim that 'the sea is infested with immortal deceitful spirits'.[30] On the other hand, some sailors are terrified by land *jinn*s. In the 1930s De Monfreid wrote of sailors near Assab, Eritrea, who were so afraid of *jinn*s that they refused to go ashore.[31] This is not to say that sea *jinn*s are viewed as benevolent, though; Sadek Yakoub Abdalla, a 55-year-old former *nākhōda* from Obock, Djibouti, told me that they 'surround us at sea and on board our dhow' (*ginn ma'nā fil-baḥar ma'nā fis-sufun*). He believes that they play tricks with the sailors' minds and can 'cause a mirage to happen'.[32] Of course, there are more scientific explanations; a sailor's vision might be compromised through exhaustion (a common issue for fishermen and pearl divers) and he might think he sees all sorts of things that are not really there, especially when staring into heat hazes and rippling waves. Similarly, phosphorescence on the sea's surface at night may well explain why sailors usually describe *jinn*s as brightly coloured, shimmering, dancing spirits.

Nevertheless, belief in the spirits remains as strong as ever. Muhammad Abd Allah Abbas, a fisherman in his 70s from Qummah Island, told me: 'Some fishermen in a dugout *hūrī* were fishing not far from where I was. Then, all of a sudden, they were whisked away by some *jinn*, never to return'.[33] Similarly, Youssef Omar Mohamed, a 77-year-old former *nākhōda* from Obock, claimed that 'people were disappearing from the dhow'.[34] Both of these accounts might be linked to the fact that there is evidence of mariners being taken prisoner (and possibly never released), especially in times of political upheaval. For instance, Oliver Myers heard that the British authorities routinely imprisoned fishermen in the 1940s.[35] Given the prevalence of folk beliefs in the region, it is easy to see why *jinn*s were subsequently blamed for these mysterious disappearances. Moreover, the locals were afraid of the *jinns*' retribution, so they usually failed to report the incidents to the police or the municipal government and consequently never heard a more rational explanation. Instead, the stories were told, retold and embellished at evening gatherings, which left the local community even more convinced that *jinn*s were respsonsible for the kidnappings.

*Jinn*s are not viewed as entirely malevolent, however. Myers reported that fishermen in Little Aden thanked sea *jinn*s for guiding them towards good catches,[36] while other accounts suggest that the spirits could be appeased with offers of food. This practice probably dates back to pre-Islamic Arabia. Bob Serjeant reported that sailors on dhows approaching Ras Hafun on the eastern tip of the Horn of Africa would place pieces of coconut in model boats and float them out to sea 'for the *jinn* to pacify them'[37] and neutralize their power.[38] A similar custom was practised on the coast of western India and in the Arabian–Persian Gulf. According to Burckhardt, it was believed that *jinn*s 'would impede the vessel's course' if the crew failed to offer them food.[39] This is a perfect example of the intimate relationship between man, nature and spirit in the Red Sea region.

Many of the coastal communities' old, superstitious traditions have shamanistic roots, with origins in Arabia and north-eastern Africa. Burckhardt observed passengers and crew on a dhow off Yanbu al-Bahr who viewed 'certain passages in great horror; not because they are more dangerous than others but because they believe that evil spirits dwell among the coral rocks, and might possibly attract the ship towards the shoal, and cause her to founder'.[40] This relationship between rocks and spirits is a recurring theme in the region's folk tales. The belief that certain rocks are magnetic dates back to Roman times,[41] when mariners feared that the invisible force could pull nail-planked boats inexorably to their doom. However, it is unclear whether the sailors attributed the magnetism to *jinn*s who dwelt within the rocks.

COMMUNICATING WITH THE SUPERNATURAL

Running alongside these shamanistic beliefs, the seafarers and coastal communities found spiritual solace in the petitionary act of prayer. Spilka and Ladd suggest that people turn to prayer in times of 'turmoil' in the belief that it 'eradicates problems'.[42] Praying, therefore, is a psychological need and an expression of humankind's dependence on divine mercy. This deep need for 'communication' with the divine has various facets, including petition, praise and thanksgiving, so prayer is 'typically [an] intentional expression of one's self in an attempt to establish or enhance connectivity with the divine, with others in a religious or spiritual framework, and with the self'.[43] Devout Muslims ask Allāh for protection on a daily basis by reciting the *fātiḥa* (the first Qur'ānic verses)[44] and invoking Allāh's name in prayers and sea songs. Thus, while the 'need' to pray might be viewed as a manifestation of personal insecurity and helplessness, the act of praying itself is a solemn recognition of Allāh's goodness and kindness.

Sheikh Abū l-Ḥasan al-Shādhilī (d. 656/1258) initiated the custom of chanting the Litany of the Sea (*Ḥizb al-Baḥr*), which includes petitionary invocations and expressions of thanks to Allāh. Sailors still chant these verses today. Of North African origin, al-Shādhilī lived in Egypt and wrote a number of protective litanies,[45] such as this appeal to Allāh: 'Subject to us this sea as Thou didst subject the sea unto Moses [...] Subject to us every sea [...] the sea of the life to come. Subject to us everything.'[46]

There are many psychological and spiritual benefits of prayer for the devout believer. The litany quoted above is a plea for deliverance not only from the dangers of the sea but also from the tribulations of life. Just as Noah and his family were saved by 'the grace of God and infinite bounty', the lives of a dhow's crew will be saved as long as they maintain their faith in Allāh.[47] Once the danger is over, however, the crew's commitment to the divine may start to wane. Abou Bakar Habib, an experienced captain from Tadjourah, candidly told me:

> Each of us prays to Allāh out of fear because anything can happen at sea – the mast breaks or the sail tears. But that sincerity may wear off [...] When the sailor returns home and goes to the *souq*, he forgets his God.[48]

This is a good example of petitionary prayer theory.[49] The seafarer feels the need to pray when he believes that Allāh will protect him in his hour of need; but once the crisis has passed, the sailor may no longer think of – or feel the need to communicate with – the divine, so 'any response is heavily dependent on how the individual perceives the surrounding environment'.[50] By contrast, the truly pious pilgrim communicates with Allāh irrespective of the environment and their own personal circumstances. According to al-Shādhilī, such pilgrims never cease to praise and thank Allāh for His mercy. When at sea, prayer is often a 'specified response'[51] to the perceived presence or threat of evil spirits, which, as we have seen, are kept at bay with talismanic objects and appeals to Allāh.

THE SAINT'S TOMB: BLESSING AND PROTECTION

Legends from Arabia's hinterland reflect the ancient Semites' belief that thickets, groves, forests and stones were sacred.[52] The cult of stones, in particular, is well known and is still seen today in a practice that developed in Islam over hundreds of years: visiting (*ziyāra*) rocks or stone-built holy men's tombs. In Ptolemaic and Roman times (third century BCE to third century CE) seafarers would visit holy sites after seeking refuge on islands close to the Hijazi coast, where they would dedicate prayers to the goddess 'Isis as their protection'.[53] These rock monuments were 'potential dwelling places for spirits [...] some of which were believed to house very powerful spirits',[54] so the mariners felt the need to perform rituals in order to pacify the spirits and/or protect themselves from evil forces. It is worth considering whether the same rock–spirit relationship is still evident today in the practice of burying holy people (*murābiṭs*) under cairns or within stone tombs, and then reverentially visiting these sites.

The tombs (s. *maqbara*), which are whitewashed with lime extracted from burnt seashells, are often cubically built, with domes. They are found all along the western and eastern Red Sea coasts, and their connection with the sea is crucial, both geographically and spiritually. The tombs tend to stand in isolation in quite barren environments, so seafarers use them as landmarks when sailing close to the coast. Hence, they perform a very valuable, practical function. But there is a spiritual aspect to the protection they provide, too. Burckhardt mentioned Sheikh Ḥasan al-Murābiṭ, patron saint of the Red Sea, whose tomb lies on an island off El Wejh,[55] while Richard Burton reported the local sailors' belief that the sheikh's spirit, Abū Zulayma, resided in a cave. The *rayyes* of Burton's *sanbūk* told him that Abū Zulayma ensured 'the safety of pious mariners'.[56]

Hence, the tombs commemorate holy men whose souls supposedly provide protection to the coastal communities and seafarers. They are said to guard against both malevolent forces of nature and creatures of ill omen, such as *jinns*, which may manifest either as spirits or in animal form. It is also thought that animals, especially birds and cats, may contain the souls of dead people. When De Monfreid was sailing between the Yemen and Djibouti he reported

> a mysterious night bird that used to perch on the dhows and [was not] afraid of the mariners [. . .] [N]obody dared to touch it [as the mariners believed] that the soul of a dead man who had not been buried was incarnated in the bird.[57]

Similarly, in Yemen 'a cat is almost sacred [. . .] on the ship it is the mysterious guardian of [the sailors'] fortune at sea'.[58]

Visits to tombs usually include an offering of food, prayers and a blessing (*baraka*). Occasionally, other objects, such as ostrich eggs, might be presented as gifts. According to Carl Klunzinger, these were hung from the ceilings of mausoleums in nineteenth-century Egypt,[59] and fragments of ostrich eggs have been found on the site of a mausoleum on the beach at Quseir al-Qadim.[60] Presumably, the worshippers believed that these objects provided magical protection against evil.

As noted earlier, the pre-Islamic practice of offering food to nature has continued into modern times in the Red Sea region as well as along the coasts of north-east Africa and western India.[61] In Carolyn Merchant's analysis: 'People accepted fate while propitiating nature with gifts, sacrifices and prayer.'[62] De Monfreid mentioned a cult surrounding the tomb of Shaykh Isḥāq, close to

Mait (Maydh) Island, off the Somali coast, which involved the dhow's crew throwing food on the tomb.[63] I saw a tomb dedicated to another holy man, Sheikh Muḥammad, near Tadjourah, where devotees leave offerings of food that are then distributed to the poor. Meanwhile, Tihama fishermen lay sawfish snouts at holy sites to signal their 'gratitude' for their safe delivery from danger.[64]

The seventeenth-century English slave Joseph Pitts was struck by pilgrims' and mariners' devotion towards their holy men and recorded the ritual that the sailors performed when they passed the tomb of one *murābiṭ*. A crew member made a model boat, then the sailors

> took some wax candles, with a little bottle of oil, and put them into the [boat], together with the money they had received [from the travellers] [...] This being done they all held up their hands, begging the [*murābiṭ*'s] blessing, and praying that they might have a good voyage.[65]

Obviously, this practice closely resembles the ritual of placing food in model boats to placate *jinns* (see above). However, there is a subtle difference between the two customs. In the latter, the ceremony revolves around the model boat's mystical, magical power to appease the *jinns*. By contrast, while there are some talismanic elements when respect is paid to a holy man's tomb, the ritual also has powerful spiritual overtones of blessing and prayer.

Cyril Crossland told of a holy man, Sheikh Barūd of Port Sudan, who sailed a canoe across the sea to Jeddah, but died of thirst just as he approached the Arabian coast. His body was subsequently returned to Port Sudan, where he was buried. The tomb became a place of pilgrimage and was reputed to have magical powers. In addition, though, whenever a dhow sailed past the spot where he died on the opposite coast, the crew would pour 'a little fresh water into the sea' in the hope of receiving a blessing, on account of the fact that the sheikh had died of thirst.[66] Another story concerns a holy man called Aibat who lived on an island off Zeilah (now in the Republic of Somaliland). The island was named after him and a tomb was built there by 'the men of the sea', even though Aibat died somewhere else. Visitors 'place offerings of shells and other beautiful marine products in the old saint's honour' at the tomb.[67] There are also annual gatherings of devotees at the tomb of Sheikh 'Alī Ibn 'Umar al-Shādhilī (d. 820/1418)[68] in Mocha (see Figure 17.2).[69] One legend has it that an Indian ship anchored at the port and the sheikh brewed coffee for the skipper that cured him of a serious illness. The holy man's fame grew over the years and, to this day, Indian pilgrims en route to Jeddah believe that he can cure the sick, so they stop at Mocha and ask for his blessing.

FIGURE 17.2 Sheikh 'Alī Ibn 'Umar al-Shādhilī's tomb, Mocha, 2009 (photo MARES by the author).

Coastal Yemenis still firmly believe that Allāh entrusts mortals with the power to perform miracles. Myers mentions 'Aydarūs, a legendary figure, renowned for his piety and miracles, who lived in Aden in the fifteenth century.[70] One day, a merchant arrived in the port from Basra on a dhow laden with dates. His return home to Sur, in Oman, was delayed because he had not been paid and he started to fear that he would miss the upcoming *'īd* celebrations with his family. He was finally paid just two days before *'īd* was due to begin, at which point 'Aydarūs told him not to worry – he would arrive home in time. The merchant set sail at 6 p.m. and arrived in Sur just three hours later – a truly miraculous journey time. He was accompanied on the dhow by Sheikh Aḥmad Bin Aḥmad al-Za'īliyya, who was famous for his good deeds. After arriving at Sur, the sheikh died in nearby Gabal Ihsan. Meanwhile, back in Aden, 'Aydarūs had a premonition of the sheikh's demise and sent six sailors to Gabal Ihsan to take care of the funeral arrangements. He also gave each one a basket of dates and a pot of ghee to distribute to the poor, then elevated the sheikh to the status of sainthood. Devotees soon started visiting al-Za'īliyya's tomb in the hope of receiving his blessing.[71]

Many similar stories demonstrate that the people of the Red Sea firmly believe that prayers and offerings to holy men have the power to rectify difficult situations and alleviate hardship. Indeed, this is an important and recurring theme in the *Arabian Nights*, tales that are deeply rooted in the rich folk traditions of this part of the world.

IN CONCLUSION

Over many centuries, the people who live and work on and around the Red Sea developed intimate relationships with the natural environment, the spirit world and the supernatural. Islam is now the major unifying factor on both coasts, but there has long been a strong tradition of superstition and magic on the Red Sea, whether it is manifested through solemn prayer, talismanic objects or propitiatory rituals. However, the relationship between the landscape/seascape and the spiritscape was far stronger in the days of sail than it is today. Life was harsh and full of danger for seafarers before they had the benefits of modern technology, so the need to interact with spirits and the divine seemed much more urgent. The sea, its perilous passages, the seasonal winds and the unpredictable gales could all 'reduce people to madness', so it was no wonder they turned to the supernatural in the hope of counteracting the natural.[72] Now that these dangers are greatly mitigated, many of the old practices and rituals have either disappeared completely or live on only in the memories of ancient seafarers. And yet, the folk beliefs and superstitions that have existed since pre-Islamic times have persisted to the modern day, including the general belief in *jinns*. As recently as 1973, there was a report of sacrifices to 'the genies of the sea [*baddi maskin*]' in Tadjourah.[73] Moreover, many people still maintain that some material objects possess magical powers. Although the *oculus* is now rarely seen on dhows, goatskins and tassels are still nailed to the stem head in the belief that they will provide talismanic protection against the evil eye. Another important belief that has its origins in the pre-Islamic age is the notion that 'spirits [have] to be propitiated'; hence, rocks (and the spirits that dwelt within them) were offered bread, coconut and other foodstuffs.[74] Gradually, that traditional evolved into the Islamic practice of praying and leaving offerings at the stone tombs of holy men in return for blessings, a ritual that continues to flourish in an environment that remains hard and demanding. Nature and people are connected through the visitors' material offerings and prayers, and the sailors, passengers and pilgrims draw spiritual benefits in the form of mental comfort and renewed faith in Allāh.

18

CULTURAL IDENTITIES OF A RED SEA LANDSCAPE: RECOLLECTIONS AND REFLECTIONS

ا لم تران الفلك تجري في البحر بنعمت الله ليريكم
من اياته ان في ذلك لايات لكل صبار شكور

'Seest thou not that the ships sail through the ocean by the Grace of God? – that He may show you of His Signs? Verily in this are Signs for all who constantly persevere and give thanks.'

Sūrat Luqmān ('Luqmān [the Wise]'), 31: 31.[1]

It was a privilege to meet the older people of the Red Sea before they depart from this world. The waters the old mariners mastered are no longer a part of their daily lives: 'The sea fades away as we age', one old Jeddawi remarked, 'but its stories, surprises and secrets remain'.[2] The seascape is evoked in the recollections of earlier generations as well as those of younger mariners who continue to pursue a life by and on the Red Sea. Notwithstanding the many diverse communities that live on its shores, the African and Arabian coasts of the Red Sea share common cultural and linguistic features that are not found in either the Mediterranean or the western Indian Ocean.

The maritime identity of a sea people is a composite of many factors related to their daily lives, language and ethnicity, their spirituality, their perception of the landscape and the seascape, their material culture and, in Assmann's words, their 'active working memory [. . .] that defines and supports the cultural identity of a group'.[3] I hope that this book has clearly demonstrated the prominent role that ethnographic fieldwork can play in uncovering cultural identities and the value of adopting a qualitative approach that combines empirical evidence with theoretical analysis and corroborates oral testimonies with travellers' accounts and official reports.

Within the maritime cultural landscape in which my fieldwork was conducted, study of physical and cognitive elements, as well as the interplay between human and non-human elements, is vital to enhance our understanding of the social dynamics of the Red Sea people and their perceptions of their environment (see below). I developed a relationship with the informants as they spoke about their former or current maritime activities, always with an awareness of and pride in the past, because they felt that they shared a maritime cultural landscape with their ancestors. Many of our conversations centred on the dhow itself, along with the shipwrights, mariners and other coastal people who comprise such a large part of the cognitive (the 'mental process of perception, memory, [and] judgement')[4] maritime landscape and seascape, and their interconnectivity with nature and culture.

Consider the coral reefs that fringe the western and eastern coasts; dhow builders designed their craft to navigate smoothly through the narrow channels. Shipbuilders ensured the hulls of large dhows could resist the waves and swells of the open sea. The winds dictated when and where the dhows could sail. The rising and setting of stars heralded the start and end of long-distance trade and the fishing seasons. Camel caravans crossed the desert and timed their arrival on the coast to coincide with the dhows' appearance in the harbours. The beliefs and ritual practices of the Red Sea people formed an important aspect of their relationship with nature as they struggled with the ever-present threat of storms and disasters. In moments of despair, they frequently turned to the supernatural world, as we saw in Chapter 17. And their descendants still ask for Allāh's protection today.

TERRITORIALITY

The concept of an open sea emerged as an important topic in the interviews. There were no borders on the Red Sea 80 years ago; they were only defined after the coastal countries gained their independence. This meant that fishermen from Egypt, Sudan and the Saudi territories needed no fishing permits, the Yemenis were free to fish in the waters of the north-east African coast, and the Eritreans and Djiboutians could sail over to the Tihama coast. No specific areas were delineated for pearl diving, although there were mutual oral (or sometimes unspoken) agreements between the Farasani and Dahlaki dhow owners and *nākhōda*s as to where they could dive. These loosely defined but well-observed rights had a long history, and any dispute was resolved by the local port's harbour master or the region's sheikh of fishermen.

A number of older interviewees remembered that people could travel from one coast to the other with ease before the countries of the Red Sea gained independence. Many recalled dhow owners, captains and merchants from the Hijaz settling on the Egyptian coast and vice-versa. They also related their fathers' and grandfathers' stories of the Rashayda tribe fleeing from political and economic turmoil in nineteenth-century Arabia and arriving in Sudan to make new lives for themselves, sometimes as cattle herders but also as traders and dhow builders. Similarly, many Yemeni and Hadhrami dhow builders and captains migrated to Eritrea and Djibouti around the same time, while Yemenis and Farasanis settled on the Dahlak Islands to gain easy access to the archipelago's rich pearling beds. Meanwhile, some Dahlakis went in the opposite direction and set up home on Greater Farasan. This merging of coastal communities – as well as significant immigration from other countries – typifies the Red Sea and has given the region a decidedly cosmopolitan ethno-linguistic character.

THE ETHNO-LINGUISTIC CHARACTER OF THE RED SEA

The coasts of the Red Sea have been settled by ethnically, linguistically and culturally diverse communities who, over time, have merged with the indigenous populations. The ease of mobility and migration 'shaped the development of many Red Sea towns [...] [and] moulded [the region's] specific social, cultural and urban make-up'.[5] Interestingly, the coastal communities have developed independently from the region's inland capital cities, and, as a result, they have markedly different characteristics. Compare Jeddah with Riyadh; Quseir with Cairo; Suakin with Khartoum; Massawa with Asmara; Aden with Sana'a. By contrast, all of the Arabian Gulf's capitals are located on the coast, and their respective sheikhs, kings and sultans all share a maritime past that revolved around trading, pearling and fishing.

The port cities of the Red Sea are still thronged with dhows, both wooden and fibreglass, loaded with fish, merchandise or pilgrims en route to Jeddah and Mecca. These ports' long histories and today's fast-paced urbanization have created a unique, ethnically and linguistically diverse Red Sea tapestry. Hadhramis are perhaps the most widely travelled of all the Arabian communities on the southern Red Sea coast, and their descendants are found as far afield as Indonesia, East Africa, western India, the Arabian–Persian Gulf and Oman. Next come the Hijazis, who for centuries were actively involved in the transport of pilgrims from Suez or Quseir to Jeddah and in trade between Aden and India. Today, the Hijazi ports boast a variety of ethnic communities who crossed the Red Sea from the African coast and then intermingled with the tribal Arabs, many of whom eventually settled on the coast after finding seasonal work at sea. Jeddah is the largest, most cosmopolitan harbour town for one obvious reason – it is the principal port of arrival for *ḥajj* pilgrims. Moreover, small but significant communities of Bangladeshis, Pakistanis and South-East Asians are actively involved in the town's fishing industry.

Jonathan Miran has argued that 'it is essential to move away from perceptions of seemingly monolithic so called "Indians" of Massawa, or "Africans" of Hodeidah, Zabid, or Jeddah'.[6] There is a long history of people of African and Indian origin settling on the Arabian coast during the Ottoman, Egyptian and European colonial eras, while *banian* (Indian) merchants established themselves on both the eastern and western shores of the Red Sea. Miran maintains that those who settled on the African coast 'negotiated new social categories and identities (cultural, ethnic and racial) in the specific contexts of local realities and conditions'.[7] The same may be said of indigenous ethnic groups who mixed with coastal communities after migrating from inland.

One common denominator right across the Red Sea is the use of Arabic, while a powerful cohesive factor is the predominant adherence to Islam. The religious vocabulary is Classical Arabic, which is known to all Muslims, but this is not a spoken language. Nevertheless, irrespective of the wide ethnolinguistic origins of the various coastal communities, they can communicate with one another in a maritime Arabic *lingua franca*; the 'Ababda of Egypt, the Beja and Hadandawa of Suakin in Sudan, the Tigre of Massawa, Zula and Afta of Eritrea, the Afar of Tadjourah and Obock in Djibouti and the Somali of Somaliland and Puntland have all adopted Red Sea Arabic as either their first or their second language, or in a mixed register with Arabic, as have Iranian, Uzbek, Afghan, Baluchi, Indian, Bengali, Malaysian, Indonesian and Swahili immigrants. Hence, the maritime terminology of the Red Sea is lexically influenced by Tu-Bedawie from Sudan, Tigrinya from Eritrea, Afari from Djibouti, Isa from Somaliland, Hindī and Urdu from the Indian sub-continent, Afghani and Swahili.[8] Moreover, intermarriage between Arabians and Somalis, Zaraniq Arabians from Yemen and

Djiboutian–Eritrean Dankalis and countless other individuals helped to stir the pot of this complex lexical stew.[9]

Consequently, the Red Sea has a rich maritime vocabulary, although many words are starting to disappear from day-to-day conversation as the local idiom increasingly reflects the modern world and new technology rather than ancient traditions. Unfortunately, Arabic material cultural terms, such as those that are used in a maritime context, have generally been left undocumented because both medieval and modern Arabic lexicographers have felt that they represent an inferior society whose language should not be recorded in dictionaries that contain Classical Arabic words. This purist philosophy has remained entrenched for many centuries. The argument is that the language of the masses has been corrupted by foreign terms that do not fit the linguistic moulds of a literary language.[10] Terms for boats, such as *sanbūk*, *ṣaddāf* and *ṣayyādī*, are familiar right along both coasts of the Red Sea, as are words for parts of those vessels, such as *dagal* (mast), *sukkān* (rudder) and *shalmān* (frame). All of these words and many others belong to the coastal people's common maritime register,[11] yet they have not been included in dictionaries because the lexicographers insist that only terms relating to significant literary or scientific knowledge, religious or not, should be listed. Recently, Muhammad Alhazmi has attempted to redress the balance by taking the bold step of studying these previously undocumented terms in a book that delves into the complex lexical development of Hijazi maritime terminology.[12]

HEREDITARY CRAFTSMANSHIP

In the Arabian Gulf and Oman the members of the younger generation shun wooden dhow building. Instead, they search for alternative occupations in the capitals and major towns. It is a way of life that has almost disappeared as fibreglass boats have taken over. And the same process is now well under way in the Red Sea region. The vestiges of wooden dhow building are already few and far between, as 45-year-old Ahmed Jaber Ali from Obock explained: 'My children view these [wooden] craft as old and economically unsustainable [...] [T]here is nothing left of this old craftsmanship except myself to talk of what was once part of our life.'[13] Yet, the indigenous heritage of dhow building in the Red Sea is still alive in Egypt, Sudan and, to some extent, Saudi Arabia; and the boats are at least still repaired and maintained in Yemen and Eritrea. Egypt and Sudan's long tradition of craftsmanship is unique, and the old, primitive tools are still used in Suakin as the El Geyf area is not yet connected to the national electricity network. Across the sea in Saudi Arabia, master builder

Ibrahim Bilghaith of Jizan believes that building wooden dhows is a hereditary tradition that should be maintained, so he has taught his two sons the skills they need to keep it alive.[14] However, in recent years, like many Egyptians, even Ibrahim has started building metal trawlers. Now his only link with the past is his sideline of building wooden *hūrīs* that are raced at an annual festival. The transition from wooden craft to metal and fibreglass vessels has been remarkably swift throughout the region.

COMMUNAL MEMORIES

Interviews with local people often rekindle their socio-cultural links with the past, and those I met around the Red Sea were more than happy to relive bygone days and share their memories with me. It was interesting to see how the past has survived into the present, for instance in Khutub on Segid Island in Farasan, where the villagers told me that sailors used to eat a biscuit called *kurmush*. Muhammad Al-Mahdi, a 32-year-old secondary-school teacher, explained that this biscuit was special to the mariners as it 'reminded them of their wives and fiancées when they were away on three-month pearling trips'.[15] Today, *kurmush* is served at village festivals or family gatherings, so it remains a tangible reminder of the community's maritime identity.

The decaying buildings on both coasts are other tangible reminders of the past, standing as emblems of a former way of life. In a few old merchants' houses it is still possible to identify ship's timbers that were repurposed as lintels or window frames. Similarly, the ceiling of an Obock café was clearly fashioned out of a ship's planks, while the rudder was turned into a bench. Facing the sea in towns like Mocha, El Wejh, Yanbu al-Bahr, Quseir, Suakin and Massawa, former storehouses as well as carpenters', blacksmiths', rope makers', tanners' and sail makers' workshops are now little more than ruins. At El Wejh, what is left of a boatyard contains some abandoned coastal vessels. It is a poignant site – a relic of the town's maritime past.

At Yanbu al-Bahr many buildings in the old Sur district are crumbling. Back in 2007, the local heritage superintendent, 60-year-old Awad al-Subhi, explained that there were plans to restore the buildings to their former glory,[16] but progress has been slow and some of the merchants' houses are now even more decayed.[17] It is a similar story in Suakin, where many of the once flourishing port's buildings are now just heaps of rubble. Many rich Yanbawi and Egyptian merchants used to live in the island town, but it started to decay when they left a number of decades ago. Today, to the south of what has become a ghost town, poorly paid fishermen, shell collectors and boat builders still ply their trades in the modest local economy.

The region's forts are still imposing buildings, and ubiquitous on both shorelines. They were built to protect the ports and trading dhows from attacks by pirate ships and marauding desert nomads. The El Geyf quarter in Suakin is surrounded by a fortified wall and no fewer than six forts because its wells provided fresh water for all of the dhows that moored in the harbour as well as the town's inhabitants (see Figure 18.1). Quseir was not so fortunate; its water had to be fetched from inland wells in Wadi Hammamat – an area that stretched all the way from Quft on the Nile to the Red Sea. However, as we have seen, the water was always rather brackish. The remains of an old cistern owned by the Alsadiq family are still just about standing in Dhuba on the northern Arabian coast;[18] for many years, it stored water for pilgrims en route to Mecca.

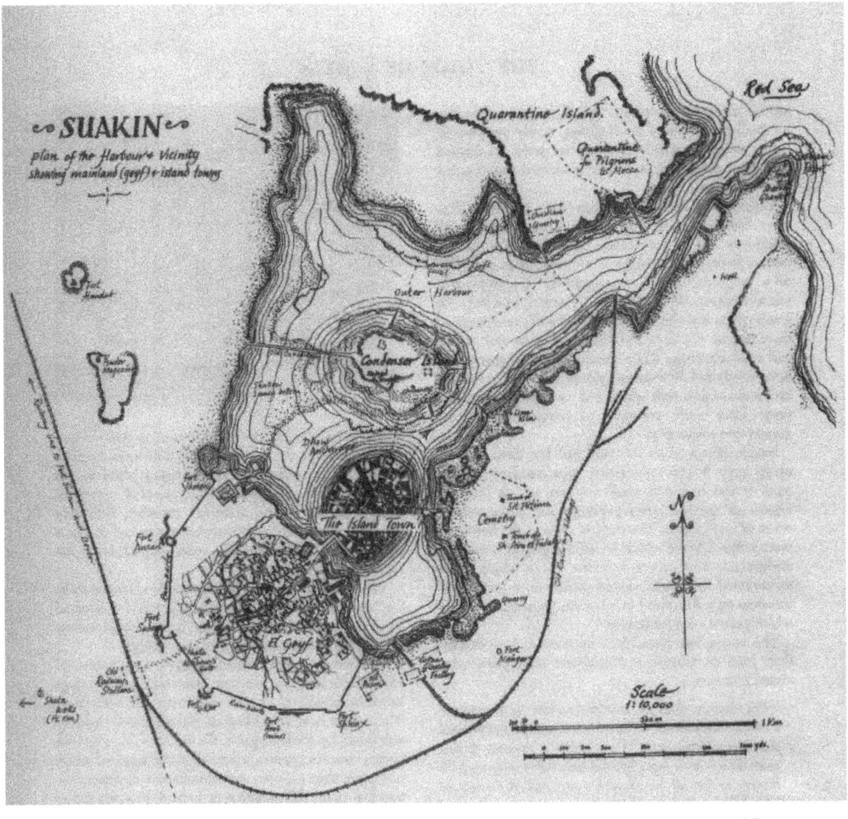

FIGURE 18.1 Plan of Suakin's El Geyf district showing its six forts.[19]

In the late eighteenth century James Bruce commented on Quseir's mud walls, which were protected by a square fortress erected by Sultan Selim II (r. 1524–74) in 1571.[20] Similar forts were built in Muweilah[21] and Mocha. The authorities in these buildings tracked vessels' movements at sea, provided protection for coastal settlements, pilgrims and the fishing fleet, and administered tax collection and other commercial business from the hinterland to the coast. They also served as useful landmarks for mariners, as did those other characteristic features of the coastal landscape – whitewashed mausoleums and holy men's tombs[22] (see Chapter 17).

Many of my informants highlighted Quseir's importance as a pilgrim port. Several recalled the port's grain silo (*shūna*), which was converted into a quarantine station in the nineteenth century. Such stations performed a vital function at the time because of recurring cholera epidemics (see Chapter 4). Others were established in Tur and El Wejh, while hospitals were founded in Jeddah and Yanbu al-Bahr.[23] Another significant building in Quseir is the *mibkhara*, which was erected close to the shore to the south of the port and still stands to this day. The name of the building comes from the radicals √b.kh.r 'to fumigate';[24] here the pilgrims fumigated and perfumed with incense their clothes, then donned the *iḥrām* (pilgrimage garments) and waited for a dhow to the Arabian shore.

MEMORY LANDSCAPE

Place names in the Red Sea region were often inspired by the maritime cultural landscape. Consider Bir as-Sawa'i ('Well of Dhows') in the fishing village of Khutub on Segid Island in the Farasan Archipelago. Sailors on passing ships (*sawā'ī* [see Chapter 7]) knew this as a place where they could 'refresh themselves'. As 41-year-old local government employee Othman Humuq explained, 'There was good, sweet water in this well'.[25] Another place name in Khutub that is closely connected with the local cultural landscape is a small promontory called Ayqat al-Arayes ('Brides' Barrier'). Sailors' fiancées would gather here to wave goodbye to their future husbands as they set off on their seasonal voyages and to welcome them home again. In light of this history, most of the locals now believe that the first part of the place name – Ayqat (lit. 'obstacle') – is a reference to the couples' enforced separation as the ships sailed away, but in fact it was coined because the promontory is unsuitable for anchorage. Ibn Jubayr (d. 614/1217–18) mentions an island not far from Jeddah – Ayqat al-Sufun ('Obstacle for Ships') – that was similarly named as a warning to seafarers.[26]

The place-name Kamaran, off the north Tihama coast, signifies 'two moons'. A legendary belief among the Yemenis is that the moon reflects itself in the sea on both sides of the island, thus ending up with 'two moons', hence the place-name. However, the Semitic Arabian suffix /-ān/ is unrelated to the Southern Arabic grammatical concept of 'two' which appears in several place-names such as Farasan, Jizan, Sharm Habban and Sharm Naman on the Hijazi coast.

When I visited Quseir in 2004, I asked the locals for their views on their town's name. The overwhelming majority believed that it referred to the short crossing from the port to El Wejh on the Arabian coast, whereas a few thought it simply meant 'lookout post' or 'fortress'. The two theories are almost equally valid. Morphologically, Quseir may well derive from *qaṣara* ('to be short'),[27] with the adjective *qaṣīr* ('short') giving the diminutive form *quṣayr*, thus assuming a dialectal usage meaning 'a very short distance'. On the other hand, it could stem from the noun *qaṣr* ('a well-known kind of edifice'),[28] from the Latin *castrum*, which took an indigenous application in a diminutive form: hence, Quseir ('small fortress'). The town's current fort was built in the eighteenth century, whereas the place name dates back to at least the thirteenth century,[29] which might seem to disprove the second theory. However, a much earlier fort is marked on a map from 1486,[30] so I believe the latter is still plausible. Indeed, overall, I think it is more likely than the alternative explanation. Nevertheless, as mentioned, the locals overwhelmingly identified with the first theory, probably because of its close association with Quseir's heyday, when the town was an important port precisely because of that 'short crossing' to the Arabian shore. This is just one of many examples of Quseiris' fierce pride in their maritime heritage.

Perhaps because the old way of life has not yet entirely disappeared, it is rarely commemorated pictorially. A restaurant in Massawa is decorated with a picture of the sea and an anchor; a poster showing a dhow from the 1960s or 1970s hangs on the wall of the mayor's office, Obock (see Figure 18.2); and the Abdul Raouf Khalil Museum in Jeddah displays paintings by local artists that evoke their ancestors' fishing and boat-building enterprises (see Figure 18.3). Otherwise, though, such images are few and far between.

EVOCATIONS

However, this should not be interpreted as indifference to the region's cultural identity. Indeed, numerous monuments have been erected on roundabouts and roadsides to evoke memories of the Red Sea's maritime past. These displays

FIGURE 18.2 Poster in the mayor's office, Obock, Djibouti, 2009 (photo MARES by the author).

FIGURE 18.3 A fisherman with his catch, Jeddah (courtesy of the Abdul Raouf Khalil Museum, Jeddah).

often feature dhows and oyster shells. For instance, in Crater Square, Aden, a model of a *sanbūk* stands on a column in the middle of a roundabout. Moreover, the column is engraved with maritime scenes, including the Aidarus lighthouse and the cisterns that made Aden a crucial stopping point at the crossroads of the Red Sea and the Indian Ocean. In Quseir, the letters of the word 'Allāh' form a dhow's sail to mark the intimate relationship between seafarers and the divine (see Figure 18.4), while at Ummlejj on the Hijazi coast a monument depicts a sailing boat, palm trees, seabirds and a fish (see Figure 18.5).

Folk museums are now attempting to preserve both individual and collective memories of the region's maritime rituals and symbolic practices. I have visited two particularly fine, non-municipal examples; the first is curated by the headmaster of a boys' primary school on Greater Farasan Island, while the second is in a private house at Hedab Tourist Village owned by Muhammad-Nour Hedab, *omda* (chief) of the Ortega tribe in Suakin, Sudan. Both of these museums demonstrate the important role that private collectors have to play in conserving their local heritage, especially in the absence of significant state support. The artefacts they exhibit are indeed 'cultural messages that are addressed to posterity'.[31] Similarly, the display of traditional

FIGURE 18.4 Maritime sculpture, Quseir, 2004 (photo by the author).

FIGURE 18.5 Monument at Ummlejj, Saudi Arabia, 2013 (photo by the author).

musical instruments in a museum at Yanbu al-Bahr suggests that members of the local community wish to preserve their cultural memories of the town's maritime past by conserving items that they associate with that past. This practice is likely to grow as the traditional lifestyle recedes further from the modern world.

One way to understand the culture and heritage of a group of people is to observe how they celebrate. Two festivals in Jazan Province, Saudi Arabia, strongly reflect the region's maritime cultural identity. As we saw in Chapter 15, almost all of the islanders of the Farasan Archipelago attend the parrotfish festival each April to give thanks to both nature and Allāh.[32] Then, a few weeks later, the mango harvest festival in Jizan attracts visitors from throughout Jazan and other provinces.[33] Mangoes were originally imported from India, but then it was discovered that the tree thrived in Jazan's hot, humid climate, so the region started to grow its own fruit. As a result, many Jazani sailors and pearl divers spent some of the year working in the mango orchards. Then, when the days of sail came to an end, a number of them became full-time mango-growers. The Ministry of Agriculture introduced the festival to promote the local fruit industry in 1982 and it has since become a joyful nine-day annual event during which proud farmers exhibit their produce and, importantly, commemorate their maritime heritage with songs of the sea and traditional dances.[34]

DIETARY HABITS

The food that the people of the Red Sea eat constitutes a significant part of their cultural landscape. Of course, the coastal diet is based on fish: 'Lawful to you is the pursuit of water-game and its use for food – for the benefit of yourselves and those who travel',[35] as the Qur'ān states. Perhaps surprisingly, the Qur'ān is far less definitive on whether shellfish are *ḥarām* (forbidden) or *ḥalāl* (permitted).[36] Hence, the subject is open to interpretation and rulings tend to differ from region to region and among the various schools of thought: Sunnī Ḥanafī, Mālikī, Shāfi'ī and Shī'ite Zaydiyya. Some communities, such as the Hadandawa clan, view all seafood as *ḥarām* because they associate the sea with 'immortal deceptive spirits'. Hence, they believe that the shells themselves provide protection against evil forces.[37] Generally, though, the Red Sea's fishing communities eat the adductor muscle of the pearl oyster but do not eat prawns. By contrast, the residents of the Arabian Gulf are happy to eat prawns but do not eat oysters. Similarly, many Red Sea people enjoy the unique taste of grilled parrotfish, yet it is rarely consumed in the Arabian Gulf (perhaps because the local species taste rather different).

A NATURAL ENVIRONMENT

With the exception of a few fishing villages, most of the Red Sea's coastal communities, all of which were once intimately connected to the sea, are gradually distancing themselves from the natural environment. However, unlike the Arabian Gulf and Oman, the Red Sea has not yet been spoiled by 'petroleum culture'.[38] Oil has not 'colonized the environment', as it did on the eastern coast of Arabia in the latter half of the twentieth century.[39] On the other hand, the tourist industry has had a significant impact on both the seascape and the sea itself through the pollution it generates. The beautiful seaside resorts that were created for the general public are now full of exclusive, luxurious holiday homes, while a few stretches of the Egyptian and Hijazi coasts have developed as resort towns. Nevertheless, many local communities have survived on both the African and Arabian coasts, in marked contrast to the Gulf states, which have suffered severe coastal depopulation over the past 50 years as a result of unprecedented migration to the urban centres. The past becomes more precious as it fades into the distance, and these Gulf residents are now eager to learn about their heritage; in other words, the more divorced they feel from the natural coastal landscape, the more they want to reconnect with it. The people of the Red Sea have not yet gone through this process, as significant numbers of them still live a traditional way of life. Indeed, some interviewees could not understand why I wanted to ask them about the past, given that their present is a living heritage. And the traditional wooden dhow in many ways is still very much part of that Red Sea heritage. But for how much longer? Neither the state nor the local communities themselves have much interest in preserving these vessels, so they are abandoned to rot on the beach or left unfinished in boatyards.

As these dhows and other material objects of the maritime past continue to disappear, the local people are starting to forget them. Moreover, both coasts suffer from a regrettable lack of photographs, logbooks, maritime manuals and harbour registers, all of which have been lost (or were never kept) over the years. This absence of well-stocked archives has certainly contributed to the decline in 'maritimity' that is evident among the coastal communities.[40] Then there is the parallel loss of intangible heritage, such as the art of celestial navigation, which only a few aged mariners can barely remember. Other communal memories are fading and links to the past are fraying as 'intergenerational mechanisms of maritime memory transmission' continue to decay.[41] Of course, private and state museums' preservation of maritime artefacts should be welcomed, but they rarely restore those crucial links to the past or contribute to memory transmission, because the objects are generally displayed in isolation, out of their original historical context.

I adopted a different approach by visiting the coastal communities and talking with the residents. As a result, this book has managed to salvage some important memories by documenting the voices of Red Sea people who were willing to share their knowledge, skills and material culture. One example is Munawwar Aqili (see Plate 2), a 75-year-old former diver from Greater Farasan, who produced a pearl wrapped in a handkerchief that he kept under his bed.[42] That tiny object would have been meaningless on display in a glass case in a museum. But in Harat as-Sulm it triggered a torrent of emotional memories that brought history to life. Such encounters made it a joy and a privilege to undertake this study.

GLOSSARY

Note the uvular fricative 'q' and velar fricative 'k' are sometimes interchangeable due to regional or tribal phonetic differences; and, in some instances, 'q' is rendered 'g' (palatal affricate), while 'j' (palatal fricative) becomes 'g'.

'abbāra (pl. *'abbārāt*)	Hijazi term for a pilgrim transport vessel; a ferryboat
'abra	general term for ferryboat
abū munshār	swordfish
abū samaka	double-ended dhow
(al-)Aklīl or *Aklīl al-'Aqrab*	Scorpio ('Crown of the Scorpion')
'alāma (pl. *'alāmāt*)	landmark
amīr al-baḥr	admiral
'arabī	grey mullet
arba'īnēt eṣ-ṣeyf	the traditional 40 days of summer in Egypt
(aṣ-)Ṣabā	star sign for the south-west monsoon (*kōws*)
'aṣaf an-nakhīl	palm-tree branch
'ashā	the crew's evening meal
asmāk al-gā'	demersal fish
asmāk as-saṭḥ	pelagic fish
(al-)'ayn	the evil eye
azyab	winter and spring north-north-east winds
bābūr	steamer
bāgha	mackerel
baghla (pl. *bghāla*)	deep-sea vessel characterized by its low bow, square, galleon-type stern, high, unswept quarter deck with

	rear windows and quarter galleries and two or three masts; often associated with Kuwaiti dhows
baḥar or *baḥr* (pl. *biḥār*)	sea
baḥḥār (pl. *baḥḥāra*) or *baḥriyya*	sailor
balam	type of anchovy
banian	Indian merchant
barākūdā	barracuda
barrāḥ (pl. *barrāḥīn*) or *jarrāḥ* (pl. *jarrāḥīn*)	hauler
barūsī or *borōsī*	a three- to six-pronged grapnel
bashkīl	bamboo
baṭn dayyiq	narrow hull
baṭṭāniyya (pl. *baṭṭāniyyāt*)	blanket, cover
bayāḍ	golden trevally
bayāta	sleeping on shore
bilbīl or *maḥār* or *gumāsh*	oyster (pearl) shells
bild	plumb line
bisir or *busur*	tulip shell
biṭān	green area before reaching the deep sea
bōt (pl. *abwāt* or *bwāt*)	Egyptian term for a transom-stern boat; a square-sterned (box-shaped) Yemeni vessel; also a bolt
boutre	Djiboutian French term for a square-stern dhow
bōya or *būya*	see *rang*
bū shlayla	a four-pronged grapnel
buhār	two-spot snapper
buhya	see *rang*
bunn	coffee beans
būrī	mullet
būṣola	compass
būtī	generic Djiboutian Afar term for a boat
caravel	Portuguese or Spanish vessel with a broad bow and a high, narrow stern, lateen-rigged, with two or three masts
dabajana	a demijohn – a large glass water container
daffa	see *sukkān*

dagal (pl. *adgāl*)	mast
dallāl (pl. *dallālīn*)	agent; commission merchant; auctioneer
dallāl ar-ragīg	slave trader
dalū	bucket made of skin, wood or metal
dāma	type of game using stones as counters
damūrī	brightly coloured fabric
dangī (pl. *danāgī*)	Egyptian and Hijazi double-ended or square-stern vessel; the latter, powered by a motor, has more sheer and a wider beam; both paddled by oar and stepped with a sail
dangīl or *danjīl*	palm-leaf basket
darāk	mackerel; narrow-barred Spanish mackerel
dāw	double-ended vessel with a long bow, a large stern and an elevated poop, rigged with one or two masts
daymān or *damān*	one end of the sail
dayn (pl. *duyūn*)	debt; liability
dhirā' (pl. *adhru'*)	unit of measurement – the length of a forearm
dhoonik or *doonik*	generic Djiboutian Afar term for a dhow
dīra (pl. *diyar*)	star compass
dooni	generic Somali term for a dhow
dukhn	pearl millet
dūm	type of palm tree; doum
dunnāy	captain's deputy
durab	wolf herring
faḥam	coal; charcoal
fajr	dawn prayers
falūka (pl. *falāyik*)	Egyptian fishing and pilgrim ferryboat, double-ended or square-sterned to accommodate an outboard motor, with a raked stem post and a single straight mast
fanīla	flannel
farāṣila	a dry measure
fāris or *ṣar'a*	rusty jobfish
fārisī	green jobfish
farkh	a very small sail
farmān (pl. *farmānāt*) or *thurmān*	mast's yard
fasma (pl. *fasmāt*)	channel through a coral reef
fātiḥa	the first Qur'ānic verses

faṭīr	bread
faybar-sanbūk	Eritrean fibreglass boat
faybir	generic term for a fibreglass boat
fīsha	ropes passed through pulleys attached to the mast's head
fitga or *ḥadfa*	a piece of sail cloth
fteynī	a small sail
fūṭa	item of clothing consisting of a piece of cloth wrapped around the hips that reaches to the knees
futūḥ al-baḥr	start of the sailing season
fuṭūr	crew's second breakfast
(bil-)gadaḥ	square-sterned dhow
galamī	a small sail
galba (pl. *galbāt* or *gilab*)	single-masted, double-ended Yemeni fishing and cargo vessel with a slightly curved bow and a short elevated raking stern, operated by an outboard motor
gam	command to 'go left'
gambarī	term for prawns in the northern Red Sea
gamīṣ (pl. *gamāṣīṣ*)	sailor's long shirt; woman's gown
gandal	a mangrove tree species
gārib (pl. *gawārib*)	medium-sized metal vessel
gaṭīra (pl. *gaṭāyir*)	double-masted Egyptian fishing, cargo and pilgrim vessel, double-ended or square-sterned with an upper curved bow
gawza	stars of Gemini and Orion
ghalla	grain
ghalq al-baḥr or *taghlīq al-baḥr*	end of the sailing season
ghanja (pl. *ghanjāt*)	double-masted deep-sea vessel characterized by a curved bow with a parrot's beak on the stem head, square galleon stern and high poop; associated with Oman
ghawwāṣ (pl. *ghawwāṣīn*)	diver; pearl diver
ghishāsh	vitamin deficiency
ghōṣ	diving; pearl diving
ghurayb	rainbow runner
ghuweiri	Yemeni fishing vessel with a crescent-shaped bow and straight stern post

gingāb	fabric made of Sudanese cotton
ginn	see *jinn*
girsh	shark
girsh buḥānī	blacktip reef shark
girsh sulmānī	whitetip reef shark
gishr	see *qishr*
gōsh or *jōsh* or *jowsh*	tack; tacking one end of the sail
guffa	see *quffa*
gumāsh	see *bilbīl*
gūnya or *jūnya* or *jūniyya* (pl. *gūnyāt* or *jūnyāt* or *jūniyyāt)*	a dry measure
guṭn	cotton
guṭn jāff	coarse cotton
ḥabba (pl. *ḥabbāt*)	term used for a single fish
ḥabḥab	watermelon
ḥabl (pl. *ḥibāl*)	rope
ḥadfa	see *fitga*
ḥājj (pl. *ḥujjāj*)	pilgrim
ḥajj	pilgrimage
ḥajjib	command to untie the *gōsh*
ḥammāl (pl. *ḥammāla*)	generic term for a cargo vessel
ḥamūr	grouper
ḥaraj	auction
ḥarīd	longnose parrotfish
ḥaṭab	firewood
ḥawṭa	topshell
ḥawwāt (pl. *ḥawwātīn*)	fisherman
ḥazīn	a sad sea song
hidra	sea cucumber
hinnām seyf	straight stem post
ḥizb al-baḥr	litany of the sea
hōk or *hūk*	white woollen linen material
ḥumūla	weight capacity
hūrī	see 'winged' *hūrī*
hūrī (pl. *hawārī* or *hawārā*)	dugout canoe imported from the west coast of India; double-ended, planked coastal boat, mostly paddled by oars but occasionally rigged with a sail

hūrī bil-lawḥ	planked *hūrī*
hūrī khashab	generic term for a wooden dhow
hūrī lis-sibāq	Jizani racing *hūrī*; double-ended, narrow-hulled with straight, slightly raked stem and stern posts, stepped with a mast
ḥūrī maḥfūr	dugout *hūrī*
hūrī mālikī	Sudanese planked, round-bottomed *hūrī* with raked stem and stern posts, propelled by an outboard engine, oars and/or a sail
'ibrī	Djiboutian term for *'obrī*
'īda	cord
'idda (pl. *'idad*)	reed trap used in fishing
'imāma	turban
'imāma dabwānī	turban with Indian weave
imlā	command to 'go right'
'irn	wood used to tan hides
ismūt	humpback red snapper
izīrī	long worms
jabāna	coffee pot
jāh	Polaris, the North Star
jalab	fishing line
jalba (pl. *jalbāt*)	Eritrean fibreglass boat
jalīla or *jawla* or *thaqqāla*	(stone) weight
jammāl (pl. *jammāla*)	camel driver
janūb or *janūbiyya*	south-south-east wind
jāriya al-maṭbakh	kitchen domestic
jāriya as-sarīr	concubine
jarrāḥ	see *barrāḥ*
jawla	see *jalīla*
jawsh	a single diving trip
jazwa	team of crew members
jelabiyya	long garment worn by Egyptians and Sudanese
jinn or *ginn* pl. *junūn* or *gunūn*)	genie; spirit
jōsh or *jowsh*	see *gōsh*
jūnya	see *gūnya*
jurād al-baḥr	prawns

jurdī (pl. *jarādī*)	single-masted Hijazi deep-sea, double-ended or transom-stern vessel with a crescent piece at the stem head; characterized by an upper curved bow and a straight stern post (also known as *jurdī-sanbūk*); operated by an inboard engine
kānūn	see *tannūr*
kassib	command to tie the luff rope
kayla (pl. *kaylāt*)	a dry measure
kerrānī	quartermaster; clerk
khabaṭ	finger protector
khām	raw material
khamsīn	strong summer wind
kharmāya or *khumkhuma*	snapper
kharṭūm	nose-clip
khashab	generic term for a wooden vessel
khayṭ tīl	type of linen
khōr (pl. *akhwār*)	bay, inlet or lagoon
khumsī	five-day working week
killāb	one- to four-pronged grapnel
kīs (pl. *akyās*)	jute sack used for various foodstuffs
kotia or *kūtiyya* (pl. *kawātī* or *kūtiyyāt*)	deep-sea vessel that is almost identical to the *ghanja* but with a backward-pointing parrot's head on the stem head; associated with Kuwait and Bahrain
kōws	the south-west monsoon
kukyān	spider conch; trocas; topshell
kurmush	sea biscuit
kushrān or *kusharān*	small grouper; hexagonal-spotted grouper
kūt	type of sweater
kūtiyya	see *kotia*
kuttāb	Qur'ānic primary school
lakhu	large conch shell
lanch or *lansh* (pl. *lanchāt* or *lanshāt*)	generic term for a metal trawler
lansh-sanbūk	single-masted, medium-sized, transom-stern Sudanese trading and fishing vessel with a low bow and prow, characterized by a slightly curved stem post and powered by an inboard engine

līf	fibre
liḥam	see *luḥam*
likiz	comb shell
lubba	the crew's small breakfast after dawn prayers
luḥam or *liḥam*	venus comb shell
lukhum	shark(s)
mabrad	type of linen
ma'dāl (pl. *ma'ādalī*)	pole fitted to the side of a racing *hūrī* that the sailor sits on to counterbalance the force of the wind
ma'dan (pl. *ma'ādin*) or *mazra' al-lu'lu'*	pearling bed
ma'diyya (pl. *ma'ādī*)	Hijazi ferryboat
madyūn	in debt
maflaka	knife used to open oyster shells
maghārib	stars marked westward on a compass
maghīb	the setting of a star
magwām	see *nāẓūr*
mahadi	hybrid Djiboutian vessel with a *za'īma-sanbūk*'s prow and an *'obrī*'s poop
maḥṣūl	income
maḥzam (pl. *maḥāzim*)	waistband; belt
majrā (pl. *majāri*)	a ship's course
mann (pl. *amnān*)	unit of weight
markab	see *merkeb*
marsā (pl. *marāsī*)	iron anchor
masāfa (pl. *masāfāt*)	distance
masāra (pl. *masārāt*)	sea route
masbaḥa (pl. *masābiḥ*)	prayer (or worry) beads
maslī	butter from grazing livestock
maṭāli'	stars marked eastward on a compass
maṭla'	the rising of a star
ma'ūn (pl. *mawā'in*)	large earthenware water container
mawwāl (pl. *mamāwīl* or *mawwālāt*)	sea shanty
mazra' al-lu'lu'	see *ma'dan*
merkeb or *markab* (pl. *marākib*)	generic term for a deep-sea vessel
mersā	natural bay with a creek for anchorage

mgabbil (pl. *mgabblīn*)	sailing south
mīfa	tall cylindrical container used for bread making
mirwāṣ	double-sided drum
miṣriyya	hot, dry north-north-westerly wind
mithgāl (pl. *mathāgīl*)	unit of weight
mīzān	balance
mōsem	season
mōsem el-ghōṣ	pearl diving season
mōsem eṣ-ṣeyf	summer season
mōsem eṣ-ṣīd	northern Red Sea fishing season
mōsem es-sijān	southern Red Sea fishing season
mōsem esh-shitā	winter season
mu'allim (pl. *mu'allimīn*)	deep-sea navigator; dhow builder
mugaddam (pl. *mugaddamīn*)	boatswain
mugāyada	verbal trading agreement
mughrāf	mariner's cup
munaddiḥ or *munaddaḥ*	lookout
murābiṭ (pl. *murābiṭīn*)	holy man
murjān	blueskin seabream
mushrāg	sailing eastbound
muskū	pine timber
mustarid	sailing westbound
mutallij (pl. *mutallijīn*)	fisherman responsible for the icebox on board the dhow
naḥḥām (pl. *naḥḥāma*)	singer of sea shanties
nahīd	seashells
(bidūn) nahr	flat-bottomed dugout
(bin-)nahr	the round-shaped bottom of planked *hūrī*
nājil	roving coral grouper
najjār (pl. *najjāra*)	carpenter
nākhōda (pl. *nawākhid* or *nawākhida*)	captain in the southern Red Sea region
nākhōda al-baḥr	captain at sea
nākhōda al-barr	harbourmaster
naqrazān	tambourine with cymbals
naṣfa	half of a diver's income
na'sh	the Great Bear

nasr or *nasr aṭ-ṭāyir*	Altair, the Flying Eagle
nawraz	seagull(s)
nawrī	Saudi flat-bottomed cargo transport vessel used in harbours
nayrūz	new year (maritime calendar)
nāẓūr or *magwām*	glassed-bottom metal box used by shell collectors to view the seabed
nishāra	woodchips
nūra	mixture of fat or shark liver oil and gypsum or lime that is smeared on the outside of a dhow's hull
'obrī (pl. *'abārī* or *'obriyāt*)	single-masted Yemeni double-ended cargo and fishing vessel, characterized by a straight stem post and stern post raking aft; propelled by an inboard engine
pothi	Indian term for pilot's manual
qawqa' (pl. *qawāqi'*)	generic term for a shell
qilw	alkaline solution used to wash clothes
qishr or *gishr*	coffee made from coffee-bean husks
quffa or *guffa* (pl. *qufaf* or *gufaf*)	date-palm-fibre basket
qumārī	a variety of turtle dove
qūṣayra (pl. *qūṣayrāt*)	palm-leaf basket; a dry measure
quṭṭ ar-rubbān	redmouth grouper
quyāsa	Sudanese fishing boat
ragīg	slave(s)
ragīṣ	sea song of joy and happiness
raḥā	grinding stone
rājiḥ (pl. *rawājiḥ*)	rigging
ramas (pl. *ramasāt*)	Sudanese flat-bottomed fishing and cargo vessel with a slightly raked stem post, a straight aft post and an outboard engine that is often propelled by a single sail or oars; also a Yemeni raft made of logs with cross-timbers; also a Farasani term for a wooden or polysterene float
raml (pl. *rimāl*)	sand
ramlī	sandy bed
rang or *buhya* or *bōya* or *būya*	paint that is applied to the outside of a vessel
rayyes (pl. *rayyesīn*)	captain in the northern Red Sea region
rayyes al-baḥr	sea captain

rayyes al-barr	harbourmaster
rīḥ (pl. *aryāḥ*)	wind
rīḥ guddāmnā	wind against us
rīḥ jānibnā	wind to the side of the boat
rīḥ shadīd	violent wind
rīḥ warānā	wind behind us
rijāl al-ma'ādī	ferry boatmen in the Hijaz
rubbān (pl. *rabābina*)	coastal navigator
rubyān	prawns in the southern Red Sea region
rudūd	summer north-north-east wind
rugāg	unleavened bread
rukhum or *wada'*	tiny shells
sa'af an-nakhīl	palm-tree branches
sabkha	flat coastal plain covered with salt due to flooding and subsequent evaporation
sabra	lump of lead or a stone
ṣadaf (pl. *aṣdāf*)	large shell
ṣaddāf or *ṣaddāfī*	Saudi term for a shell-collecting canoe
or *ṣaddāfa* (pl. *ṣaddāfī*)	fishing dugout; also an Eritrean double-ended flat-bottomed planked boat with upright posts or a keeled boat with raked posts, propelled by oar or sail
ṣafīḥa (pl. *ṣafāyiḥ*)	can; jerrycan
ṣaghīr or *walad*	cabin boy in the northern Red Sea region
sagīfa	awning
ṣāḥib al-aṣābi' (*pl. aṣḥāb al-aṣābi'*)	Chinese and Indian technique using a number of fingers to calculate the latitude of a ship
ṣāḥib (pl. *aṣḥāb*) *ad-daffa*	helmsman in the northern Red Sea region
ṣāḥib (pl. *aṣḥāb*) *al-baḥr*	captain
sāḥil (pl. *sawāḥil*)	anchorage; coastline
sāhil or *suhayl*	South Star, Canopus
sahm (pl. *ashima*)	share (dividend; percentage)
ṣaḥwa (pl. *ṣaḥāwī*)	fishing net
sā'iya (pl. *sawā'ī*)	long, narrow-hulled vessel
sakūna or *sukūna* (pl. *sakāyin*)	square-stern cargo vessel, similar to an Adeni *sanbūk*, with a curved bow and a transom-stern overhang; also a generic Egyptian term for a cargo vessel

salāf	advanced loan
salām	safe journey
salūna	crew's soup
samak (pl. *asmāk*)	fish
ṣamgh	gum
samn or *saman*	clarified butter
samn (or *saman*) *barrī*	fat from sheep's milk
samr or *samar* or *sumur*	species of acacia
sanbūk (pl. *sanābīk* or *sanābik* or *sanbūkāt*)	generic term for a double-ended or square-stern dhow; also a deep-sea Adeni trading vessel with a scimitar-shaped bow, a transom stern with an overhang and one or two masts
sanjar	a fleet of dhows
saranjī	boatswain
sarēdān or *sureydān*	firebox used for cooking on a dhow
sarong	knee-length sailor's garment
ṣawram	land and sea breezes
sayāl	species of acacia
ṣayyādī	generic term for a coastal fishing dhow
ṣayyādiyya	Egyptian and Sudanese fishermen's basic diet (fish, rice and bread)
seyf al-baḥr	outer stem post
ṣghayyir or *walad*	cabin boy in the southern Red Sea region
sha'āb or *shu'āb*	reef
sha'āb (*marjāniyya*)	coral reef
sha'ābī	coral reef bed
shabaka (pl. *shabak*)	fishing net
shaḥam or *shaḥm*	animal fat
shalmān (pl. *shalāmīn*)	dhow's frame
shamāl	north-westerly wind
shaṭṭa	pepper
shaṭṭiyya (pl. *shaṭāṭī* or *shaṭṭṭiyāt*)	transom-stern Sudanese fishing vessel with curved upper bow, powered by an outboard engine, sailed or paddled by oars
sha'ūr	emperor; redspot emperor
shaw	system for calculating the weight of pearls
shawāl (pl. *shawālāt* or *shiwāl*)	large sack

shawara (pl. *shawarāt*)	net
sheikh (pl. *shuyūkh*)	person in charge; chief
sheikh ad-dallālīn	overseer of auctioneers
sheikh al-ḥawwāta	overseer of fishermen
sherm	deep, narrow inlet
shikka	fish strung together in twos, fives or tens
shirā' (pl. *ashri'a*)	lateen or settee sail
shirwī	tuna
shu'āb	see *sha'āb*
shūna (pl. *shūnāt* or *shuwan*)	granary
shūra	species of mangrove
ṣidriyya	sailor's or fisherman's waistcoat
simsimiyya	wooden (or wooden and tin), round, rectangular or square five-string musical instrument
sinamāka	medicinal herb used to treat diarrhoea
suhayl	see *sāhil*
sukkān (pl. *sukkānāt*) or *daffa*	rudder
sukkānī or *sukūnī*	helmsman in the southern Red Sea region
sukūna	see *sakūna*
sulamānī	milkfish
sulfa	see *tagdima*
sumur	see *samr*
sunnāra (pl. *sanānīr*)	fishing hook
surati	thick cloth from Surat on the north-west coast of India
sureydān	see *sarēdān*
ṭabbākh (pl. *ṭabbākhīn*)	cook
ṭabla (pl. *ṭablāt*)	open-ended drum
tagdima or *sulfa*	advance payment
taghlīq al-baḥr	see *ghalq al-baḥr*
ṭaḥḥān (pl. *ṭaḥḥānīn*)	bread maker
ṭaḥīniyya or *ṭaḥāniyya*	sesame-seed and sugar cake
ṭalḥ	species of acacia
tallāja (pl. *tallājāt*)	icebox in which caught fish are stored
tanaka (pl. *tanakāt*)	bucket; can; cylinder; tank
tannūr or *kānūn*	oven
ṭāka (pl. *ṭākāt*)	roll of cloth

ṭarbūsh (pl. *ṭarābīsh*)	hat (with a tassel) made of cloth or felt
thaqqāla	see *jalīla*
thawb Abdallāh Khān	woman's dress
thurmān	see *farmān*
ṭihār	deep blue sea
ṭīn	clay
ṭīnī	clay seabed
tūna	shark mackerel
turābī	dusty wind(s)
turbāl	waterproof bag
tureyya	the Pleiades
twayna	giant grouper
'ūd	lute
'umg (pl. *a'māg*)	depth
umsiyya (pl. *umsiyyāt*)	evening gathering
'ushārī	Egyptian cloth; muslin
wada'	see *rukhum*
walad	see *ṣaghīr or ṣghayyir*
wāsṭī	large sail
wazīf	dried and salted fish
'winged' *hūrī*	single-masted Yemeni fishing vessel with a straight raked stem post characterized by two projecting fins at the large transom stern and powered by one or two outboard engines
yahomm	sailing with the wind
za'īma (pl. *za'āyim* or *za'īmāt*) or *za'īma-sanbūk*	single- or double-masted Adeni deep-sea, double-ended or transom-stern cargo or fishing vessel characterized by an upper curved bow and raised upper stern, powered by an inboard engine
zām (pl. *azwām*)	three-hour watch
zanbīl (pl. *zanābil*)	palm-leaf basket
zārūk (pl. *zawārīk*)	Sudanese transom-stern fishing vessel with a straight raked stem post and two small fins projecting at the stern, propelled by an outboard engine, oars and/or a sail
zārūk (pl. *zarārīk* or *zārūkāt*)	single-masted Yemeni double-ended, narrow-hulled cargo and fishing vessel with straight stem and stern posts, powered by an inboard motor

zawāda	provision of food and water
zaynub	longtail tuna
ziyāra (pl. *ziyārāt*)	visit to a holy man's mausoleum
zubb al-baḥr	sea cucumber
ẓufur	operculum

APPENDIX I

Sail and rigging configuration of an Egyptian *gaṭīra* (drawing by Lilli Haar)

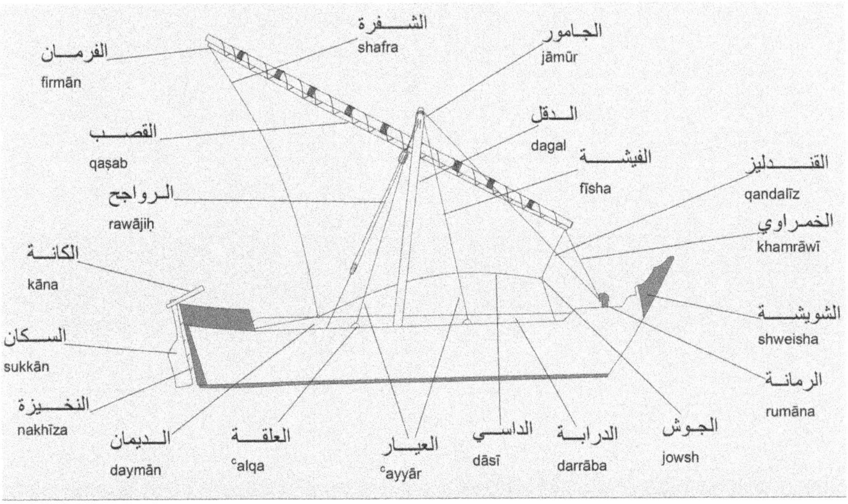

APPENDIX II

The yard and the sail (drawing by Lilli Haar)

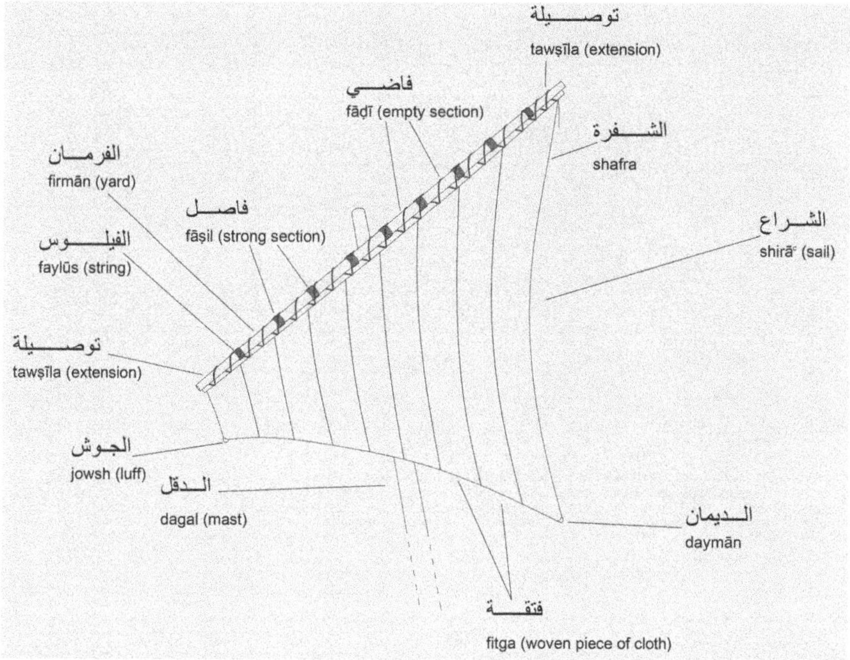

APPENDIX III

People interviewed during ethnographic fieldwork, Egypt, 2002–3.

Number	Name	Occupation	Age	Comments	Interview date
1	Mohammed Gaballah Musaid	Guide	20s		
2	Hany Hassan	Guide	20s		
3	Muhammad El Wafaa Hasan	Guide	30s		
4	Abu Muhammad El Wafaa Hasan	Former camel driver	66	Quseir; grandson of camel driver	31 March 2002, 23 March 2003
5	Ibrahim Ali Moosa	Master dhow builder	72	Quseir; from five generations of boat builders	31 March 2002
6	Atia Said Hussein	Fisherman	56	Quseir; from five generations of fishermen	31 March 2002
7	Abu Khalid		40s	Quseir; member of the ‘Ababda tribe	3 April 2002
8	Muhammed Saeed al-Sabbagh	Dhow builder	30	Quseir; originally from Rashid, near Alexandria; 15 years' experience in boat building	7 March 2003
9	Ali Hamza	Sea captain	65	Quseir; 35 years' experience at sea	8 March 2003
10	Abd Allah Abu Ghashin	Former camel driver	77	Quseir	8 March 2003
11	Shabhat Khaysha Hassan	Fisherman and assistant captain	55	Quseir	12 March 2003
12	Hasan Abd al-Qadir	Sea captain and fisherman	60	Idwa (near Faradir)	16 March 2003
13	Ramadan Abd Rabbih Hasan	Fisherman	55	Quseir	16 March 2003

14	Hasan Faraj al-Karim	Mariner	85–90	Guweih, north of Quseir	17 March 2003
15	Muhammad Mahmoud	Sea captain	50	Quft, River Nile	18 March 2003
16	Muhammad Khalifa	Former camel driver	75	Al-Awayna; member of the 'Amarawi tribe	22 March 2003
17	Jumaa Hamdan Muhammed Ahmed	Former camel driver	61	Al-Jabbara, Hayy al-Zahra, Quseir; son of a camel driver	23 March 2003
18	Mahmood Rahmat Allah	Fisherman	66	Member of the al-Qrijab (?) tribe from Al-Sheikh Malik	26 March 2003
19	Abu Al-Hamd Ahmed Khalil	Fisherman	65	Trombi	31 March 2003
20	Sayyid Ahmed Sayyid	Fisherman	45	Trombi	31 March 2003
21	Saad Ali Hasan	Sea captain	63	Mersa Alam	31 March 2003
22	Matar Fikri Muhammed Mustafa	Mariner	48	Mersa Alam	31 March 2003
23	Sayyid Ahmed Musa al-Barsi	Sea captain	58	Safaga; member of the 'Ababda tribe; spent his whole life at sea	4 April 2003

APPENDIX IV

People interviewed during ethnographic fieldwork, Egypt, 2004.

Number	Name	Occupation	Age	Comments	Interview date
1	Ahmed Nasser el Nimr	Guide	20s	Quseir	
2	Kamil Muhammad Abu Lubb al-Burri	Boatswain	68	Quseir; started life at sea at the age of 9	9 February
3	Abbas Muhammed Ali Daud	Sea captain; head of fisheries cooperative	81	Quseir; father and grandfather both experienced mariners	10 February
4	Ali Hussein Ahmed Ibrahim	Sea captain	53	Quseir; member of the Abu Hibaya tribe; father and grandfather both experienced mariners	11 and 12 February
5	Mahmud Saad Ibrahim	Sea captain	67	Al-Awayna; member of the ‘Ababda tribe	12 February
6	Seif el Din Hasan Mahmud	Boatswain	58	Quseir	17 February
7	Shadhli Ahmed Atallah	Boatswain	51	Quseir; started life at sea at the age of 11	18 February
8	Abd al-Hamid Hasan Hassan	Sea captain	67	Quseir; started life at sea at the age of 20	19 February
9	Duwi Toufiq Mahmud	Boatswain	64	Quseir	21 February
10	Hasan Mohammed Hamd Allah	Boatswain	55	Mersa Alam; member of the ‘Ababda tribe; started life at sea at the age of 12	22 February
11	Saad Abdallah Jouma	Former camel driver	40	Abu Tundura; member of the ‘Ababda tribe	22 February

12	Salah Baraka Muawwad	Fisherman	–	Mersa Alam	22 February
13	Ata Bishar Mhammed	Farmer and rope maker	43	Qale, Quft, River Nile	23 February
14	Atiya Saad Sikiyan Guta	Boat builder	59	Quseir	26 and 27 February
15	Ibrahim Ali Moosa	Master dhow builder	74	Quseir; previously interviewed in 2002; from five generations of boat builders	26 and 27 February

APPENDIX V

People interviewed during ethnographic fieldwork, Suakin, Sudan, 2004.

Number	Name	Occupation	Age	Comments	Interview date
1	Muhammad Hasan Mahmud	Guide	50	Guard at entrance to the island town	
2	Muhammad Abu al-Hasan al Shadhli	Sea captain	85	50 years' fishing experience	23 November
3	Muhammad Nour Saleh Othman	Dhow builder	42	Of Nigerian origin	23 November
4	Salim Girithli	Sea captain and fisherman	50	40 years at sea	23 November
5	Hussein Abd al-Hamid Abd Allah	Former sea captain and fisherman	120 (?)	Formerly lived on the island town	24 November and 6 December
6	Ali Said	Former sea captain	56	Of Eritrean origin; 30 years' experience as a conch trader; former pearl diver	27 November
7	Hashim Muhammad Ahmed	Sea captain and fisherman	54	35 years at sea	28 November
8	Isa Muhammad Ahmed	Sea captain and fisherman	43	30 years at sea	28 November
9	Mohammed Abdallah Ahmed *aka* Ra'is Mohammadayn	Dhow builder	50s	Originally from Port Sudan; 35 years' experience	29 November and 5 December
10	Hussein Ibrahim Muhammad *aka* Hussein Baloum	Master dhow builder	72	Originally from Port Sudan; 56 years' experience	29 November and 1 December
11	Hashim Mohammad Nour Manninay	Dhow builder	30	Learned the trade from his father	29 November

12	Hammad Tokulia Augan	Head of fisheries	46	From Jibal al-Nubia	1 December
13	Mudassir Mousa Othman Mohammed *aka* Takrouni Fallati	Dhow builder	44	Of Nigerian origin; apprentice under Hussein Baloum	2 December
14	Muhammed Idrees	Conch diver	35	16 years' experience	2 December
15	Hamid Hammad Jubouri	Conch diver			2 December
16	Hamid Idrees	Sea captain	54	Conch diver; former pearl diver; about 30 years at sea	4 December
17	Salim Salman Salim	Conch diver	45		4 December
18	Hashim Abd Salim Garmushi	Former sea captain	52	Of Hadhrami origin; 24 years at sea; now runs a restaurant in El Geif	4 December
19	Anur Abdallah	Blacksmith	56	From Tokar; works in the souq	5 December
20	Khalil Tahir Nour al-Din	Sea captain and fisherman	54	33 years at sea	7 December
21	Muhammed Muslih Saleh	Conch diver and fisherman	31		8 December

APPENDIX VI

People interviewed during ethnographic fieldwork, the Hijaz, Saudi Arabia, 2007.

Number	Name	Occupation	Age	Comments	Interview date
1	Awad al-Subhi	Guide	60	Superintendent, Yanbu al-Bahr Heritage Department; former teacher	
2	Ibrahim Khalil al-Sharif	Guide	–	El Wejh	
3	Rashid al-Balaw	Guide	–	El Wejh	
4	Abdallah al-Qahtani	Guide	–	Ummlejj	
5	Muawwid Abd al-Raheem Mirbas	Former dhow builder	101	Yanbu al-Bahr; father and grandfather both dhow builders	12 May
6	Ali Hamid al-Zimi	Dhow builder	48	Yanbu al-Bahr	12 May
7	Ibrahim Abu Atayiq	Dhow owner	60	Yanbu al-Bahr	12 May
8	Ali Rayyes	Fisherman		Yanbu al-Bahr	12 May
9	Marzuq Muhammad al-Ilaj	Fisherman	38	Ummlejj	14 May
10	Fahad Nahham	Former sailor	60s	Yanbu al-Bahr; singer	15 May

APPENDIX VII

People interviewed during MARES ethnographic fieldwork, Yemen, 2009.

Number	Name	Occupation	Age	Comments	Interview date
1	Salah al-Mansoori	Guide	30s	Sana'a	
2	Dr Raja BaTawil	Director	50s	General Organization of Antiquities and Museums, Aden	7 February
3	Hasan Salih Shihab	Boat researcher; maritime historian	76	Aden	7 and 8 February
4	Muhammed al-Ghaili	Former dhow builder	65	Of Hadhrami origin, residing in Dokka, Aden; 30 years' experience as a carpenter in Hadhramaut and Ma'alla, Aden	7 and 9 February
5	Hafiz Umar Awad	Fisherman	35	Seera, near Aden	9 February
6	Ahmad Qahtan	Fisherman	60s	Seera; from several generations of fishermen	9 February
7	Ibrahim Muhammad Abduh al-Anbari	Former dhow builder	60s	Of Khokha origin, residing in Aden; 40 years' experience as a carpenter in Khokha	10 February
8	Ali Ibn Ali Salim	Dhow builder	36	Kheesa, Bureiqa, near Aden; trained as a carpenter by his father	10 February
9	Mohammed Ali Abdallah al-Najjar	Former dhow builder	90	Fuqum near Aden; from several generations of dhow builders	10 February
10	Mohammad Ali Humaidan	Fisherman	45	Khor al-Ghureirah	12 February
11	Abd Allah Humaidan	Fisherman	23	Khor al-Ghureirah	12 February
12	Basim Ali Bin Ali	Fisherman	19	Khor al-Ghureirah	12 February
13	Abd Allah Ghalib Humaidan	Fisherman	22	Khor al-Ghureirah	12 February

14	Mohammad Ahmed Zaid al-Anbari	Sea captain and dhow owner	60s	Khor al-Ghureirah	12 February
15	Abdo Umar Bulghaith	Former dhow builder	46	Khor al-Ghureirah; descended from generations of carpenters	13 February
16	Anonymous	Sea captain	60s	Khor al-Ghureirah	13 February
17	Said Mohammad Alaiwa	Former boatswain	60s	Mokha; first at sea at the age of 20	15 February

APPENDIX VIII

People interviewed during MARES ethnographic fieldwork, Djibouti, 2009.

Number	Name	Occupation	Age	Comments	Interview date
1	Ali Chehem Mohamad *aka* Ali Aref	Guide	40s	Djibouti City	
2	Mohamed Yousouf	Guide	20s	Djibouti City	
3	Muhammad Hummid Ali	Mariner	80	Port de Pêche, Djibouti City; of Yemenite origin	9 October
4	Dr Abdirachid Mohamed Ismael	Lecturer; linguist	40s	University of Djibouti; Somali dialectology; oral history	10 October
5	Said Ahmed Warsama	Folklorist	–	Djibouti City	10 October
6	Kamil Hassan	Director	50s	Djibouti City; official in Ministry of Higher Education	10 October
7	Nabil Abdalla Ahmed	Fisherman	–	Ancienne Pêcherie, Djibouti City	12 October
8	Awad Mohammed	Fisherman	–	Djibouti City; part-time	12 October
9	Yasin Muhammad	Mariner	48	Djibouti City; father and uncle both conch and oyster divers	12 October
10	Aqib Abdalla	Sea captain	–	Port de Pêche, Djibouti City	12 October
11	Ziyad Ahmed Khizari *aka* Tazan	Mariner	50s	Port de Pêche, Djibouti City	12 and 13 October
12	Adawa Hassan	Historian	–	Djibouti City; research into the Horn of Africa	12 October
13	Dr Abdilaahi Omar Bouhi	President	50s	University of Djibouti	13 October
14	Adam Osman	Historian	–	Djibouti City; African studies	13 October
15	Houmed Barkat Siradj	Local historian	55	Tadjourah; Président de Majlis	15 October
16	Hadjdj Idrees Habawita	Sea captain	75	Tadjourah	16 October
17	Mohamed Salem Omar	Mariner	79	Tadjourah	16 October
18	Mohamed Billah	Sea captain	62	Tadjourah; 50 years at sea	17 October
19	Abou Bakar Habib	Mariner	76	Tadjourah	17 October

20	Ali Hadj	Fisherman	65	Tadjourah	17 October
21	Houmed Maki	Local historian	–	Tadjourah; regional councillor	18 October
22	Ibrahim Ishak	Local historian	–	Tadjourah; former senior police officer	18 October
23	Ahmed Muhammad al-Gumaani	Master dhow builder	59	Rassali near Tadjourah; of Yemenite origin	18 and 19 October
24	Ahmed Youssef Mohamed	Fisherman	60	Tadjourah	18 October
25	Ibrahim Abou Bakar	Dhow owner	50s	Tadjourah	19 October
26	Ibrahim Omar Ali	Director of fisheries cooperative	–	Obock	20 October
27	Ahmed Jaber Ali	Fisherman	45	Obock; of Yemenite origin; part-time dhow builder	21, 22, 24 and 26 October
28	Mohamed Moola	Dhow owner	45	Obock	21 October
29	Youssef Mohamed Isa	Fisherman	70	Obock; 53 years at sea	21 October
30	Abdou Suleiman	Sea captain	60	Obock; 47 years at sea	21, 22 and 23 October
31	Sadek Yakoub Abdalla	Sea captain	55 (?)	Obock	22 October
32	Youssef Omar Mohamed	Sea captain	77	Obock; originally from Khor Angar; many years' experience at sea	22 and 24 October
33	Ruqayya Hassan Mahalla	Wife of Abdalla Darwish	83	Obock; deceased husband sea captain; both of Yemenite origin	23 October
34	Abdalla Ibrahim Odeni	Carpenter	79	Obock	24 October
35	Ali Ahmed Jaber	Fisherman	24	Obock; son of Ahmed Jaber Ali	24 October
36	Houmed-Gaba Maki Ibrahim	Former sea captain and historian of material culture	76	Djibouti City	27 October
37	Ahmed Darar Djibril	Directeur de pêche	–	Centre de Pêche, Djibouti City	28 October
38	Ibrahim Omar Ali	Director of fisheries cooperative	–	Djibouti City	28 October
39	Nabil Dorani	TV Producer	–	Djibouti City; produced *Les boutres* documentary	28 October

APPENDIX IX

People interviewed during MARES ethnographic fieldwork, Jizan and Farasan Islands, Saudi Arabia, 2010.

Number	Name	Occupation	Age	Comments	Interview date
1	Abdo Mohammed Isa Aqili	Guide	46	Muharraq, Greater Farasan; Saudi Commission for Tourism and National Heritage employee; fisherman; part-time pearl diver	
2	Dr Faisal Al-Toumaihi	Guide	30s	Curator of the Sabiyah Archaeological Museum, Jizan	
3	Ibrahim Ahmed Bilghaith	Master dhow builder	55	Jizan	10 January; 11 and 12 May
4	Abdu Ibrahim Bilghaith	Dhow builder	32	Jizan; son of Ibrahim	10 January; 11 and 12 May
5	Majid Ibrahim Bilghaith	Dhow builder	30	Jizan; son of Ibrahim	10 January; 11 and 12 May
6	Ibrahim Abdalla Muftah	Local historian and ethnographer	70	Greater Farasan; author of books on the archipelago	11 January; 25 May
7	Muhammad Isa Ali Muzaffar	Local historian and folklorist	40s	Greater Farasan; primary school teacher	12 January
8	Suleiman Mohammad Ali Baloos	Pearl merchant	35	Greater Farasan; father was a pearl diver	12 January; 21 May
9	Sheikh Muhammad Hadi Al Rajhi	Pearl merchant	50s	Greater Farasan; father was a pearl merchant	13 January; 14 May

10	Najib Abd Allah Hamudi	Fisherman	60s	Jizan	11 May
11	Ahmed Mohammed Shahhar	Fisherman	56	Jizan	11 and 12 May
12	Ibrahim Mousa Ahmed	Fisherman	60s	Jizan; singer; former pearl diver and shell collector	13 May
13	Muhammad Hadrami Abdo	Dhow builder	50s	Jizan; assistant dhow builder to Ibrahim Bilghaith; model dhow maker	13 May
14	Ala Allah Abdo Hasan Mujawir	Retired	45	Muharraq, Greater Farasan; father was a dhow builder	15 May
15	Abd Allah Ibrahim Hasan	Fisherman	60s	Greater Farasan; singer	15 May
16	Muhammad Al-Mahdi	Local historian and folklorist	32	Khutub, Segid Island; primary school teacher; interested in material culture	16 May
17	Othman Humuq	Local government employee; folklorist	41	Khutub, Segid Island	16 May
18	Yahya Muhammad Ali Tami	Fisherman	76	Khutub, Segid Island; 60 years' experience at sea	16 May
19	Sheikh Muhammad Abd Allah Al-Rajhi	Sheikh of Khutub	79	Khutub, Segid Island; former pearl diver and fisherman	16 May
20	Munawwar Aqili	Fisherman	75	Harat as-Sulm, Greater Farasan; former pearl diver	17 May
21	Ali Khalifa Ali Hammed Damri	Former pearl diver	90s	Muharraq, Greater Farasan; remembers King 'Abd al-'Azīz's visit to the island	17 May
22	Sheikh Muhammad Isa Muhammad Aqili	Former pearl diver	76	Greater Farasan; father was a pearl diver	18 May
23	Muhammad Abd Allah Said Al-Hussayyal	Fisherman	69	Khutub, Segid Island; part-time pearl diver; started diving at a very young age	22 May

24	Ali Hasan Hammud Sharif	Sea cucumber diver	49	Khutub, Segid Island; part-time pearl diver	22 May
25	Mohammed Abdalla Ahmed Nasib	Former pearl diver	74	Muharraq, Greater Farasan; father was a pearl diver	22 May
26	Mohammad Abdalla Mohammad Abbas	Large shell collector	70s	Qummah Island; former pearl diver	23 May
27	Aqil Isa Hamadi Mohammad	Fisherman	70s	Qummah Island; former pearl diver	23 May
28	Muhammad Uthman Mahmud Hanas	Conch and sea cucumber diver	70s	Sayer, Segid Island; former pearl diver; father was a shell collector	24 May
29	Sheikh Yahya Ibrahim Bin Ibrahim al-Najdi al-Tamimi	Former sea captain and dhow owner	70s	Harat al-Khazzan, Greater Farasan; father was a pearl merchant	24 May

APPENDIX X

People interviewed during MARES ethnographic fieldwork, Eritrea, 2011.

Number	Name	Occupation	Age	Comments	Interview date
1	Muhammad-Nour Muhammad Al Hasan	Guide	40s	Massawa; Department of Fisheries, Ministry of Marine Resources employee	
2	Yohannes Gebreyesus	Guide	30s	Director, National Museum, Massawa	
3	Mathewos Gerray	Guide	20s	National Museum, Massawa, employee	
4	Tsega-Hobtay Keleta	Researcher	20s	Ethnographer with an interest in material culture	17 February
5	Tsegai Medin	Archaeologist	30s	Director, coordinator with l'Orientale (Napoli) excavation at Adulis	17 and 19 February
6	Fatima Muhammed Said	Potter	60s	Afta	19 February
7	Haleema Omar Muhammed	Potter	40s	Afta	19 February
8	Abdallah Yasin Othman	Farmer	69	Afta	19 and 21 February
9	Ismail Khaled Omar	Farmer	76	Zula	19 February
10	Umar Ali Din	Fisherman	–	Zula	22 February
11	Idrees Daud Ali	Fisherman	50	Zula; deputy to Hasan Madani, head of fisheries	22 February
12	Ahmed Zabib Usman	Former harbour porter	65	Zula; worked at Massawa	22 February
13	Hajj Abid Ebeid Agil	Cattle herder	65	Wadagi area; living in tent; member of the Rashayda tribe	22 February
14	Ahmed Suwaylin Ayesh	Cattle herder	50	Wadagi area; living in tent; member of the Rashayda tribe	22 February

15	Farih Gaas Mu'min	Fisherman	63	Wadagi area; living in tent; member of the Afar tribe; former sailor	22 February
16	Hamid Suleiman Hamid	Dhow builder	50	Tuwaled, Massawa	23 February
17	Ali Suleiman Hamid	Dhow builder	48	Tuwaled, Massawa; brother of Hamid	23 February
18	Isa Muhammed	Fisherman		Sigalat Lamba, Massawa; originally from Dihil Island, Dahlak Archipelago	24 February
19	Usman Ali Ahmed	Dhow owner and fisherman	62	Sigalat Lamba, Massawa; originally from Diese Island, Dahlak Archipelago	26 February
20	Abdo Muhammed Abdulla	Fisherman	50	Sigalat Lamba, Massawa; originally from Dihil Island, Dahlak Archipelago	26 February
21	Idrees Iribi Idrees	Mariner	65	Massawa	26 February
22	Ahmed Muhammed Saad	Former pearl merchant	85	Massawa	26 February
23	Siraj Muhammed Siraj	Eco-marine culture researcher	41	Massawa; originally from Bori, south-east of Zula	28 February
24	Muhsin Saud Muhsini	Sea captain	43	Edaga, Trtr, north of Sigalat Lamba; member of the Rashayda tribe	1 March
25	Bilal Muhammad Ge'der	Fisherman	45	Edaga, Trtr, north of Sigalat Lamba	1 March
26	Hammuda Abdalla Baghit	Fisherman	71	Massawa	1 March

APPENDIX XI

People interviewed during ethnographic fieldwork, the Hijaz and Tihama, Saudi Arabia, 2013.

Number	Name	Occupation	Age	Comments	Interview date
1	Awwad Bin Bakhit Bin Hilal Al-Rada'i Al-Juhuni *aka* Abu Hilal	Fisherman	60s	Yanbu al-Bahr; first went to sea at the age of 13; singer	24 and 25 March
2	Naji Muhammad Abdalla Al-Humi	Fisherman	61	Yanbu al-Bahr; father and grandfather were both fishermen	25 March
3	Kuleib Hamid AlAbsi	Fisherman	–	Yanbu al-Bahr; first went to sea at the age of 11	25 March
4	Abd al-Muhsin al-Khuwaishi	Shop owner	69	Yanbu al-Bahr	25 March
5	Abdallah Al-Dahi	Shop owner	61	Yanbu al-Bahr; former maritime border inspector	25 March
6	Abd al-Karim Khalil Khayaya	Fisherman	52	Ummlejj; former trader	26 March
7	Muhammad Hamid Alsinani	Folklorist	–	Ummlejj; municipal council employee	26 March
8	Hamdan Abd al-Marwani	Fisherman	40s	Ummlejj; father was a sailor on a cargo dhow	26 March
9	Salim Muhammad Awda al-Humidi	–	–	Ummlejj; singer	27 March
10	Juraybiyya Abdallah Hayit	–	–	Ummlejj; singer	27 March
11	Muhammad Bukhayyit Alsinani	Coal trader	92	Ummlejj; former mariner; first went to sea at the age of 6	27 March
12	Amin Alsanousi	Fisherman	65	Ummlejj; former captain on trading dhows	27 March
13	Ahmad Wusail al-Alati Aljuhni	Fisherman	62	Ummlejj; singer	27 March
14	Ali Muhammad Bakhit Alduraini	Fisherman	55	Ummlejj; singer	27 March
15	Muhammad Jumaa Abu Zayd Almarwati	Fisherman	60s	Ummlejj; singer	27 March

16	Abd al-Aziz al-Halwani	Dhow model maker	–	Ummlejj; workshop	27 March
17	Ahmad Muhammad Halwani	Higher education employee	–	Qunfudha; media	28 and 29 March
18	Abd Allah Hubaili	Higher education employee	–	Qunfudha; media	28 and 29 March
19	Muhammad Abd Allah Muhammad al-Abbadi	Former sailor	75	Qunfudha; first went to sea at the age of 10	29 and 30 March
20	Muhammad Darwish Sangur Sabban	Former mariner	90	Qunfudha	29 March
21	Abd al-Rahman Hamza Alshikhi al-Halwani	–	42	Qunfudha; singer	29 and 30 March
22	Abd Allah Ali Alsahari	–	52	Qunfudha; singer	30 March
23	Fuad Ahmad Abdalla Bukhari	Fisherman	54	Jeddah; former mariner	1 April
24	Hasan Muhammad Bin Salim Albishi	Fisherman	50	Jeddah; former mariner; first went to sea at a very young age	1 April
25	Hamdan Himeid Aljidaani	Fisherman	58	Jeddah; former sailor	1 April
26	Saad Khamis Muhammad Althaalabi	Fisherman	75	Jeddah; former sailor; first went to sea at the age of 8; uncle, former sea captain, 105, still alive at time of interview	1 April

NOTES

1 CULTURAL MEMORIES OF THE RED SEA

1. Interviewed on 24 May 2010.
2. Sheriff: *Dhow Cultures of the Indian Ocean*, p. 2.
3. Agius: *In the Wake of the Dhow*, p. 33.
4. Matsumoto and Juang: *Culture and Psychology*, p. 16.
5. https://www.nationalgeographic.org/encyclopedia/landscape/ (accessed 27 September 2017).
6. Tilley and Cameron-Daum: *An Anthropology of Landscape*, p. 5.
7. Ibid., p. 5.
8. Fagan: *Beyond the Blue Horizon*, p. 3.
9. Bāṭarfī: *Jidda, umm al-rakhā wa l-shidda*, p. 58.
10. Fagan: *Beyond the Blue Horizon*, p. 24.
11. http://www.dictionary.com/browse/cognitive (accessed 27 June 2017).
12. Westerdahl: 'The maritime cultural landscape', p. 5.
13. Ibid., pp. 5–14; Westerdahl: 'Fish and ships: Towards a theory of maritime culture', pp. 191–236.
14. Ibid., p. 212.
15. Ray: 'Maritime archaeology of the Indian Ocean', p. 11.
16. Westerdahl in Vaz Freire: 'Maritime cultural landscape: A new approach to the *Cascais* coastline', p. 145; see Van de Noort: *North Sea Archaeologists: A Maritime Biography*, p. 25.
17. Tuddenham: 'Maritime cultural landscapes, maritimity and quasi objects', pp. 8–11; Vaz Freire: 'Maritime cultural landscape: A new approach to the *Cascais* coastline', p. 145.
18. Tuddenham: 'Maritime cultural landscapes, maritimity and quasi objects', pp. 8–11; Vaz Freire: 'Maritime cultural landscape: A new approach to the *Cascais* coastline', p. 145.
19. Ibid., p. 145.
20. Sheriff: *Dhow Cultures of the Indian Ocean*, pp. 2, 23–25.
21. Rönnby: 'Maritime durées: Long-term structures in a coastal landscape', p. 67.

22. Ole Henrik Magga: 'Indigenous knowledge systems: The true roots of humanism', paper delivered at the World Library Congress: 71st IFLA General Conference and Council: 'Libraries: A voyage of discovery'.

2 'OUR LIFE ON THE SEA IS GONE BUT OUR STORIES WILL LAST FOREVER'

1. Bāṭarfī: *Jidda, umm al-rakhā wa l-shidda*, p. 58.
2. Translation by Yusuf Ali: *The Holy Qur-an*, vol. I, p. 489.
3. Sponsored by the GoldenWeb Foundation, Cambridge. MARES' original aim was to include the Arabian–Persian Gulf but it was, in its first year, modified to focus on the maritime activities of the peoples of the Red Sea.
4. Lucy Semaan graduated in 2014. Her thesis is titled 'The use of wood in boatbuilding in the Red Sea from antiquity until present times'.
5. Julian Jansen Van Rensburg conducted fieldwork among fishing communities on the island of Socotra. He graduated in 2013 and published a revised version of his thesis in 2016 under the title *The Maritime Traditions of the Fishermen of Socotra, Yemen*.
6. Interviewed on 23 October 2009.
7. Ricciardi: *The Voyage of the Mir-el-lah*, p. 62.
8. Employed by the Heritage Departments of the Saudi Commission for Tourism and National Heritage (SCTNH). Meetings held between 12 and 14 May 2007.
9. At the time, Fahad was a doctoral candidate at Exeter University. He gained his Ph.D. in 2015 and is now a researcher at the King Faisal Centre for Research and Islamic Studies in Riyadh. His thesis is titled 'The good, the bad and the ugly: Undocumented labour in Saudi Arabia: The case of Jeddah'. Meetings held between 28 and 30 March 2013.
10. Interviewed on 14 May 2007.
11. Personal communication from Shadia Taha (a Sudanese ethnographer), 8 July 2017.
12. Assmann: 'Canon and archive', pp. 97–8.
13. Agius, Cooper, Semaan, Zazzaro and Carter: 'Remembering the sea: Personal and communal recollections of maritime life in Jizan and the Farasan Islands, Saudi Arabia', p. 167.
14. Interviewed on 22 October 2009.
15. Interviewed on 1 March 2011.
16. Interviewed on 15 February 2009.
17. Interviewed on 13 February 2009.
18. Unless age was not provided by the informant, I always give the interviewee's age at the time of interview.
19. At the time of my early visits (2002 and 2003), the University of Southampton's archaeological team was undertaking fieldwork about 8 km north of the present town of Quseir in a place known as Myos Hormos during the Ptolemaic and Roman periods (third century BCE to third century CE), as Quseir during the Mamlūk period (twelfth–fifteenth century) and as Quseir al-Qadim to locals today. See Whitcomb and Johnson (eds): *Quseir al-Qadim 1978: Preliminary Report* and *Quseir al-Qadim 1980: Preliminary Report*; see also Peacock and Blue (eds): *Myos Hormos-Quseir Al-Qadim: Roman and Islamic Ports on the Red Sea*, vols I and II.

20. http://population.mongabay.com/population/egypt/360531/al-qusayr (accessed 14 December 2015).
21. Hillelson: ''Abābda', p. 1; see also Starkey: 'Travellers on the Red Sea coast between al-Quṣayr and Sawākin', pp. 75, 81.
22. The pilot visit was organized by the Saudi Commission for Tourism and National Heritage (SCTNH) together with Simon Woodward, architect, project director of the Red Sea towns. Earlier that year, Aylin Orbaşlı had submitted an outline detailing the objectives and methods for the conservation of historic buildings along the Hijazi coast to the SCTNH authorities. Her proposals related to four sea towns – Yanbu al-Bahr, Ummlejj, El Wejh and Dhuba – in order 'to maintain the[ir] historic fabric'; see Orbaşlı: 'The historic towns of Saudi Arabia's Red Sea coast: Tourism development and conservation', pp. 207–27.
23. Formerly my doctoral student, obtained his PhD in 2015, and now an assistant professor at the Islamic University in Medina; his revised thesis was published in 2016, see Alhazmi: *Maritime Terminology of the Saudi Arabian Red Sea Coast.*
24. http://www.google.co.uk/population+of+yanbu+al-bahr (accessed 5 January 2016).
25. http://www.citypopulation.de/SaudiArabia.html (accessed 8 December 2014).
26. On the invitation of the Cambridge McDonald Institute, I was asked to conduct an ethnographic study on the dhows as part of the Suakin project led by Laurence Smith of the institute and Michael Mallinson, an architect. The research team was conducting excavations in the ruined island town known as the Gezira. See Mallinson: 'Suakin 2003/4', pp. 90–5; Mallinson: 'Suakin: Paradigm of a port', pp. 159–72; Smith et al.: 'Archaeology and the archaeological and historical evidence for the trade of Suakin, Sudan', pp. 173–86; Phillips: 'Beit Khorshid Effendi: A "trader's" house at Suakin', pp. 187–99.
27. https://www.quandl.com/data/CITYPOP/CITY_SAWAKINSUAKINBHRSUDAN-Population-of-Sawakin-Suakin-BHR-Sudan (accessed 16 June 2018).
28. https://www.google.co.uk/population+in+aden (accessed 6 January 2016).
29. See Agius, Cooper, Van Rensburg and Zazzaro: 'The dhow's last redoubt? Vestiges of wooden boatbuilding traditions in Yemen', pp. 71–84; Agius, Cooper and Zazzaro: 'The maritime heritage of Yemen: A focus on traditional wooden "dhows"', pp. 143–57.
30. http://www.infoplease.com/country/djibouti (accessed 11 November 2015).
31. The Somalis, mainly settlers from neighbouring lands of former Somalia, form 59.01 per cent of the total population, followed by the Afars at 35.19 per cent; see http://www.cia.gov/library/publications/the-world-factbook/geos/dj.html. I am indebted to Mohamed Ismail Abdirachid for details of the ethno-population mix, information that can be found on the official National Department of Statistics website at http://djibouti.opendataforafrica.org/ (accessed 25 May 2017).
32. See Rouaud: 'Tadjurra', p. 71.
33. http://www.citypopulation.de/SaudiArabia.html (accessed 8 December 2014).
34. An additional aim of our field visit was to make a general survey of archaeological sites on Greater Farasan with a view to conducting a subsequent inquiry, comparing results with other Red Sea ports. See Cooper and Zazzaro: 'The Farasan Islands, Saudi Arabia: Towards a chronology of settlement', pp. 147–74.

35. See Semaan: 'The use of wood in boatbuilding in the Red Sea from antiquity until present times'.
36. https://www.google.co.uk/?gws_rd=ssl#q=population+in+Farasan+Islands (accessed 7 March 2016).
37. See Cooper and Zazzaro: 'The Farasan Islands, Saudi Arabia: Towards a chronology of settlement', pp. 147–8.
38. Part of this data-collection has been published in 2016; See Agius, Cooper, Semaan, Zazzaro and Carter, 'Remembering the sea: Personal and communal recollections of maritime life in Jizan and the Farasan Islands, Saudi Arabia', pp. 127–77.
39. The timing of our fieldwork to the islands was perfect as Rob was about to finish his book on the history of pearls in the Arabian–Persian Gulf from antiquity to the present day. See Carter: *Sea of Pearls: Seven Thousand Years of the Industry that Shaped the Gulf.*
40. http://thegpscoordinates.net/eritrea/massawa (accessed 11 January 2016).
41. Our fieldwork coincided with an archaeological dig at Adulis, south of Massawa, sponsored by the National Museum of Asmara under the directorship of Andrea Manzo of L'Orientale at the University of Napoli. See Zazzaro: *The Ancient Red Sea Port of Adulis and the Eritrean Coastal Region* and 'Adulis and the sea', pp. 151–70.
42. See Miran: *Red Sea Citizens: Cosmopolitan Society and Cultural Change in Massawa,* pp. 99–10; 134, 141, 240.
43. Information supplied by Ismail Khaled Omar on 19 February 2011.
44. Bāṭarfī: *Jidda, umm al-rakhā wa l-shidda.*
45. Al-Sayyid: *Malāmiḥ min tārīkh Yanbu'.*
46. Muftāḥ: *Farasān: al-nās, al-baḥr wa l-tārīkh.*
47. Ḍirār: *Tārīkh Sawākin wa l-baḥr al-aḥmar.*
48. Taha: *Attachment to Abandoned Heritage: The Case of Suakin.*

3 THE GEOGRAPHIC CONTEXT

1. These verses were found in a note among Henri R. Maurer's papers, now archived in the Alexandria Library of the Archaeological Society. Maurer was visiting or living in Egypt at some point between the 1920s and the 1940s.
2. http://www.newworldencyclopedia.org/entry/Red_Sea (accessed 18 September 2015).
3. http://world.bymap.org/Coastlines.html (accessed 24 August 2016).
4. Vine: *The Red Sea,* p. 15.
5. https://www.britannica.com/place/Red-Sea (accessed 26 August 2016).
6. Information gathered from Awad al-Subhi at Yanbu al-Bahr on 15 May 2007.
7. http://www.newworldencyclopedia.org/entry/Red_Sea (accessed 18 September 2015).
8. Siliotti: *Fishes of the Red Sea,* p. 7.
9. *Western Arabia and the Red Sea,* p. 170.
10. Ibid.
11. Wallin: *Travels in Arabia (1845 and 1848),* p. 109, fn.
12. Pesce: *Jiddah: Portrait of an Arabian City,* p. 102.
13. Becker [Beckingham]: 'Baḥr al-Ḳulzum', p. 931.
14. *Western Arabia and the Red Sea,* pp. 156–7.

15. Ibid., p. 154.
16. Weschenfelder: 'Beja in medieval Islamic geography and archaeology', p. 222.
17. Interviewed on 22 February 2004.
18. Buxton: *On Either Side of the Red Sea*, p. 4.
19. See Azab: 'Flood hazard between Marsa Alam-Ras Banas, Red Sea, Egypt', pp. 17–35.
20. Miran: 'Mapping space and mobility in the Red Sea region', p. 199.
21. See http://worldwildlife.org/ecoregions/at0112 (accessed 19 August 2014).
22. Schmid and Vine: *Saudi Arabian Red Sea*, p. 7.
23. McKinnon: *Arabia: Sand, Sea and Sky*, p. 58.
24. Siliotti: *Fishes of the Red Sea*, p. 11.
25. Vine: *The Red Sea*, p. 10.
26. PERSGA: 'The status of coral reefs in the Red Sea and Gulf of Aden', p. 5 (citing Sheppard and Sheppard: 'Corals and coral communities of Arabia'; Sheppard, Price and Roberts: *Marine Ecology of the Arabian Region: Patterns and Processes in Extreme Tropical Environments*).
27. Siliotti: *Fishes of the Red Sea*, p. 8.
28. McKinnon: *Arabia: Sand, Sea and Sky*, pp. 128, 145.
29. PERSGA: 'The status of coral reefs in the Red Sea and Gulf of Aden', p. 34 and 'Guidelines for compensation following damage to coral reefs by ship and boat grounding', p. 15.
30. Eltayeb: 'Review of the trochus fishery in Sudan', p. 5.
31. PERSGA: 'The status of coral reefs in the Red Sea and Gulf of Aden', p. 31.
32. PERSGA: 'Guidelines for compensation following damage to coral reefs by ship and boat grounding', p. 24.
33. PERSGA: 'The status of coral reefs in the Red Sea and Gulf of Aden', p. 3.
34. Ibid., pp. 31–7.
35. http://naturaldatabase.therapeuticresearch.com/nd/ (accessed 29 August 2016).
36. https://www.drugs.com/npp/coral.html (accessed 29 August 2016).
37. Greenlaw has provided architectural drawings of houses built of coral stone in Suakin with details of room distribution, building methods and woodwork typical of Ottoman and Egyptian houses of the time. See Greenlaw: *The Coral Buildings of Suakin*, pp. 8–12. Examples are still found in Massawa and Jeddah.
38. The Farasan Islands have at least two well-maintained examples of coral buildings: Munawwar Al Rifa'i's merchant's house, built in 1341/1921, with walls featuring intricate decoration and inscriptions; and the mosque built by the rich pearl merchant Ibrahim Al-Najdi in 1347/1928.
39. Pesce: *Jiddah: Portrait of an Arabian City*, p. 113.
40. Orbaşlı: 'The conservation of coral buildings on Saudi Arabia's northern Red Sea coast', p. 55.
41. Pesce: *Jiddah. Portrait of an Arabian City*, p. 113.
42. Vine: *The Red Sea*, p. 59.
43. Ibid., p. 56.
44. Ibid., p. 59.
45. PERSGA. 'Guidelines for compensation following damage to coral reefs by ship and boat grounding', p. 11.
46. PERSGA: 'The status of coral reefs in the Red Sea and Gulf of Aden', p. 8.

47. Ibid., p. 5.
48. Ibid., p. 3.
49. Ibid.; see also McKinnon: *Arabia: Sand, Sea and Sky*, p. 59.
50. http://www.unep.ch/regionalseas/main/persga/redrisk.html (accessed 26 August 2014).
51. PERSGA: 'Status of mangroves in the Red Sea and Gulf of Aden', pp. 19 and 22.
52. Ibid., pp. 27–8.
53. http://plantdiversityofsaudiarabia.info/Biodiversity-Saudi-Arabia/Vegetation/Farasan%20Islands.htm (accessed 8 December 2014) and http://www.arabiancamp.com/trips/farasanislands.html (accessed 8 December 2014); see also PERSGA: 'Status of mangroves in the Red Sea and Gulf of Aden', p. 30.
54. Sabkha: 'An area of coastal flats subject to periodic flooding and evaporation which result in the accumulation of aeolian clays, evaporites, and salts, found in North Africa and Arabia', https://en.oxforddictionaries.com/definition/sabkha (accessed 2 July 2017).
55. PERSGA: 'Status of mangroves in the Red Sea and Gulf of Aden', pp. 32, 35 and 37.
56. Ibid., pp. 39 and 41.
57. PERSGA: 'The status of coral reefs in the Red Sea and Gulf of Aden', p. 7.
58. http://www.unep.ch/regionalseas/main/persga/redrisk.html (accessed 26 August 2014).
59. PERSGA: 'The status of coral reefs in the Red Sea and Gulf of Aden', p. 7.
60. McKinnon: *Arabia: Sand, Sea and Sky*, p. 58.
61. PERSGA: 'The status of coral reefs in the Red Sea and Gulf of Aden', p. 6.
62. Siliotti: *Fishes of the Red Sea*, p. 8.
63. Ibid., p. 8.
64. Ibid., p. 17.
65. McKinnon: *Arabia: Sand, Sea and Sky*, p. 150.
66. http://www.unep.ch/regionalseas/main/persga/redrisk.html (accessed 26 August 2014).
67. PERSGA: 'Guidelines for compensation following damage to coral reefs by ship and boat grounding', p. 37.
68. PERSGA: 'Status of mangroves in the Red Sea and Gulf of Aden', p. 30.
69. PERSGA: 'The status of coral reefs in the Red Sea and Gulf of Aden', pp. 4–5; see also http://www.unep.ch/regionalseas/main/persga/redrisk.html (accessed 26 August 2014).
70. Ibid.
71. PERSGA: 'The status of coral reefs in the Red Sea and Gulf of Aden', p. 6.
72. Ibid.
73. Wehr: *A Dictionary of Modern Written Arabic*, p. 789.
74. Wellsted: *Travels in Arabia*, vol. II, pp. 244–5.
75. Morgan and Davies: *Red Sea Pilot*, p. 46.
76. Ibid.
77. *Western Arabia and the Red Sea*, p. 584.
78. Lane: *Arabic–English Lexicon*, vol. I, pp. 1086–7.
79. Morgan and Davies: *Red Sea Pilot*, p. 46.
80. Lane: *Arabic–English Lexicon*, vol. II, p. 1543.
81. *Western Arabia and the Red Sea*, p. 585.

82. Nawwab, Speers and Hoye: *Aramco and its World: Arabia and the Middle East*, p. 111.
83. Bloss, 'The story of Suakin' (1936), pp. 271–2; see also Salim: 'Field report: Suakin: On reviving an ancient Red Sea port city', p. 63.
84. *Western Arabia and the Red Sea*, p. 73.
85. Ibid., p. 585.

4 RED SEA CORRIDOR: THE EARLY MODERN PERIOD

1. One of the Egyptian prayer/sea songs that sailors perform while pulling their boats onto the shore; interview with Shadhli Ahmed Atalla on 18 February 2004.
2. Miran: *Red Sea Citizens: Cosmopolitan Society and Cultural Change in Massawa*, pp. 203–204.
3. Dubois: 'The Red Sea ports during the revolution in transportation', p. 59.
4. Raymond: 'A divided sea: The Cairo coffee trade in the Red Sea area during the seventeenth and eighteenth centuries', pp. 53–6.
5. André Raymond cited in Miran: *Red Sea Citizens: Cosmopolitan Society and Cultural Change in Massawa*, p. 203.
6. Lewis: *Levantine Adventurer: The Travels and Missions of the Chevalier d'Arvieux 1653–1697*, p. 20.
7. Van Der Meulen: *Faces in Shem*, p. xii.
8. Wick: *The Red Sea: In Search of Lost Space*, pp. 42, 47; see Foster: *England's Quest of Eastern Trade*, pp. 136, 184, 194, 196, 220, 235, 240, 288–94; Keay: *The Honourable Company: A History of the English East India Company*, pp. 73–85, 87–9, 95, 117–18, 104–105.
9. https://www.google.com/search?q=mocha+harbour+olfert+dapper (accessed 17 June 2018).
10. See Brouwer: *Al-Mukhā: Profile of a Yemeni Seaport as Sketched by Servants of the Dutch East India Company (VOC) 1614–1640*, p. 75.
11. See Sidebottom: *The Overland Mail*, p. 8; Sattin: *Lifting the Veil: British Society in Egypt*, p. 22.
12. Niebuhr: *Travels through Arabia and Other Countries in the East*, vol. I, pp. i–vii, 172, 176–7, 214.
13. Marlowe: *The Making of the Suez Canal*, p. 69.
14. Fowler: 'The fishes of the Red Sea', p. 113.
15. See Head: 'Introduction', in Edwards and Head (eds): *Key Environments: The Red Sea*, pp. 1–21.
16. Marlowe: *The Making of the Suez Canal*, pp. 62–77.
17. The road to Lesseps' success was not straight. On the engineer's character, John Marlowe (citing J. Charles-Roux) concluded: 'In order to succeed one must, like Lesseps, have "*le diable au corps*"'; see Marlowe: *The Making of the Suez Canal*, p. 77; see also Marshall: *Passage East*, p. 17.
18. Paine: *The Sea and Civilization: A Maritime History of the World*, p. 525.
19. Ibid.
20. Marshall: *Passage East*, p. 15.
21. *Western Arabia and the Red Sea*, p. 279.
22. Burckhardt: *Travels in Arabia*, pp. 426–35; *Travels of Ali Bey*, vol. II, pp. 163–78; Burton: *A Secret Pilgrimage to Mecca and Medina*, pp. 123–37.

23. See Hoskins: *British Routes to India*, pp. 117, 119, 187, 227.
24. Sidebottom: *The Overland Mail*, p. 73.
25. *Illustrated London News*, 18 December 1869, p. 609.
26. Minawi: 'Telegraphs and territoriality in Ottoman Africa and Arabia during the age of high imperialism', p. 573.
27. Sidebottom: *The Overland Mail*, p. 78.
28. Burton: *Arabia, Egypt, and India: A Narrative of Travel*, p. 70; Marshall: *Passage East*, p. 64.
29. Huber: *Channelling Mobilities*, p. 176; Marshall: *Passage East*, p. 64.
30. Huber: *Channelling Mobilities*, p. 176.
31. Rogers: *The Indian Ocean*, pp. 22–3.
32. *Western Arabia and the Red Sea*, p. 269.
33. Marshall: *Passage East*, p. 16. For almost 100 years, until the British left Aden in 1967, steamers 'increased the value of Aden' because of 'its coaling and oiling station'. In one year, 1939, Naval Intelligence reported that the port received 1,310 British steamers and 769 native craft – a total of 8,650,411 tons. See *Western Arabia and the Red Sea*, pp. 551, 553; see also Buxton: *On Either Side of the Red Sea*, p. 15.
34. Miran: *Red Sea Citizens: Cosmopolitan Society and Cultural Change in Massawa*, pp. 68–9.
35. http://www.medicinenet.com/cholera/page2.htm (accessed 11 May 2017).
36. Bouhdiba: 'Trans-national practices and sanitary risks in the Red Sea region', p. 226.
37. Burton: *Arabia, Egypt, India: A Narrative of Travel*, p. 86.
38. Issa: 'Dhows and epidemics in the Indian Ocean ports', pp. 63, 65–6.
39. Burton: *Arabia, Egypt, India: A Narrative of Travel*, p. 193.
40. Bouhdiba: 'Trans-national practices and sanitary risks in the Red Sea region', p. 226; Buxton: *On Either Side of the Red Sea*, p. 160.
41. Dubois: 'The Red Sea ports during the revolution in transportation', p. 64.

5 THE RED SEA SAILING DHOW

1. *The Periplus Maris Erythraei*, p. 283.
2. Fagan: *Beyond the Blue Horizon*, p. 61.
3. Crossland: *Desert and Water Gardens of the Red Sea*, p. 64.
4. Makin: *Red Sea Nights*, p. 182.
5. Ricciardi: *The Voyage of Mir-el-lah*, p. 56.
6. LeBaron Bowen: 'The dhow sailor', pp. 181, 197.
7. Klunzinger: *Upper Egypt: Its People and its Products*, pp. 299–300.
8. Villiers: 'Passage in a Red Sea dhow', p. 180.
9. Dubois: 'The Red Sea ports during the revolution in transportation', pp. 58–74.

6 ON BUILDING THE DHOW: SITES, SKILLS AND TECHNIQUES

1. See Bāṭarfī: *Jidda, umm al-rakhā wa l-shidda*, p. 67.
2. See Agius: *In the Wake of the Dhow* and *Seafaring in the Arabian Gulf and Oman*.
3. Agius, Cooper, Jansen Van Rensburg and Zazzaro: 'The dhow's last redoubt?', pp. 71–84; Agius: 'The Rashayda', pp. 169–216; Agius, Cooper and Zazzaro: 'The maritime heritage of Yemen', pp. 143–57; Agius, Cooper, Semaan, Zazzaro and Carter: 'Remembering the sea', pp. 127–77.

4. Hornell: 'A tentative classification of Arab sea-craft', p. 27.
5. Moore: 'Notes on "dhows"', p. 207.
6. Moore: 'Craft of the Red Sea and Gulf of Aden', p. 74.
7. Foster: *The Red Sea and the Adjacent Countries*, p. 177.
8. Niebuhr: *Travels through Arabia and Other Countries in the East*, vol. I, pp. 172, 176.
9. Burckhardt: *Travels in Arabia*, p. 23.
10. Hunter: *An Account of the British Settlement of Aden in Arabia*, p. 83.
11. See further details in Shihāb: *Al-marākib al-'arabiyya*, pp. 99, 137, 139.
12. Hunter: *An Account of the British Settlement of Aden in Arabia*, p. 83; see also Wilson: *The Native Craft*, p. 27.
13. Burton: *A Secret Pilgrimage to Mecca and Medina*, p. 118.
14. See Rouaud: 'Quelques termes arabes d'architecture navale en usage à Djibouti', p. 335.
15. Hornell: 'A tentative classification of Arab sea-craft', p. 15.
16. *Western Arabia and the Red Sea*, p. 531.
17. *Western Arabia and the Red Sea*, plate 282.
18. Stark: *East is West*, p. 9; see also Lewis: *Sand and Sea in Arabia*, p. 30.
19. Antonin Besse originally worked for a French company, Maison Bardey, which transported coffee from Hodeidah and Harar (in the southern mountains of Ethiopia) to Aden and ultimately Europe. The same company had employed Arthur Rimbaud (d. 1891) 24 years earlier. See Chateau, Nougarède and Bayle: *Les derniers boutres d'Aden*, n.p. Further information provided during interview with Antonin Besse Jr in Paris on 21 May 2009.
20. Interviewed on 10 January 2010.
21. Agius, Cooper, Semaan, Zazzaro and Carter: 'Remembering the sea', p. 136.
22. Crossland: *Desert and Water Gardens of the Red Sea*, p. 59.
23. See Agius: 'The Rashayda', 180–7; Taha: *Attachment to Abandoned Heritage: The Case of Suakin*, pp. 57–62.
24. Bloss: 'The story of Suakin, I', p. 249.
25. Personal communication from Michael Mallinson, 20 November 2004.
26. Perrier: *Les boutres de Djibouti*.
27. See ibid., p. 20; Pujo: 'Les boutres à Djibouti', p. 10.
28. Interviewed on 22 October 2009.
29. See Perrier: *Les boutres de Djibouti*, p. 26.
30. Shadia Taha learned that the Hadandawis were actively involved in dhow building long before the Rashaydas settled in Suakin (personal communication, 8 July 2017).
31. Personal communication from Lucy Semaan (researcher on the use of timber in sea craft on the Red Sea), 5 October 2012.
32. Interviewed on 20 November 2004; see also Agius: 'The Rashayda', pp. 178–9.
33. 'The forest department has been taking meticulous care to plant new teak-wood trees and eucalyptus trees to prevent deforestation' (http://www.wellingtonmalayalees.org.nz/, accessed 9 February 2014).
34. Antonin Besse Jr interviewed on 21 May 2009.
35. *Western Arabia and the Red Sea*, p. 531.
36. Kentley: 'Suakin and its fishermen', p. 30.
37. Ibid.
38. Moore: 'Craft of the Red Sea and Gulf of Aden, III', p. 142.

39. Interviewed on 9 February 2009.
40. Bāṭarfī: *Jidda, umm al-rakhā wa l-shidda*, p. 67.
41. Ibid., p. 66.
42. Interviewed on 26 March 2013.
43. Interviewed on 26 February 2004.
44. Pronounced with an uvular 'q' in the Gulf, rather than the velar 'k' of the Red Sea region.
45. I did not take notes during the interview, so I am quoting the master builder from memory. Unfortunately, I also cannot remember his name.
46. MS EUR. B69, British Library, f. 233r.
47. See Agius: *In the Wake of the Dhow*, pp. 49–51.
48. Makin: *Red Sea Nights*, p. 184.
49. Hugh Millar: 'Notes on Aden type Arab dhows' (MS in the library of St Antony's College, Oxford); see Footman: *Antonin Besse of Aden*, p. 94.
50. Hugh Millar: 'Notes on Aden type Arab dhows', fn. 38; Footman: *Antonin Besse of Aden*, pp. 94–5.
51. Wilson: *The Native Craft*, p. 5.
52. Agius, Cooper, Jansen Van Rensburg and Zazzaro: 'The dhow's last redoubt?', pp. 71–84; Agius, Cooper and Zazzaro: 'The maritime heritage of Yemen', pp. 143–57.
53. Wilson: *The Native Craft*, pp. 5–6.
54. Paine: *The Sea and Civilization: A Maritime History of the World*, p. 200.
55. Throckmorton: 'Reconstruction and conservation', p. 94.
56. Ibid.
57. Personal communication, 11 November 2010.
58. Personal communication from Tom Vosmer, 5 July 2002; see also Agius: *In the Wake of the Dhow*, pp. 135–6; Agius: *Classic Ships of Islam*, pp. 154–6, 161–8.
59. Interviewed on 10 February 2009.
60. Throckmorton: 'Reconstruction and conservation', p. 94.
61. Burton: *Personal Narrative of a Pilgrimage*, vol. I, p. 177.
62. Interviewed on 7 March 2003.
63. Interviewed on 31 March 2002.
64. Agius: *In the Wake of the Dhow*, pp. 145–66; Agius: *Seafaring in the Arabian Gulf and Oman*, pp. 39–42.
65. Ricciardi: *The Voyage of Mir-el-lah*, p. 56.
66. At least not before 2016. Personal communication from Michael Mallinson, 22 September 2016.
67. We described them as 'winged' because of their shape at the stern, which resembled a fish's fins.
68. Nougarède: 'Qualités nautiques des navires arabes', p. 95.

7 DOCUMENTING AND REMEMBERING OLD DHOWS

1. Interviewed on 22 October 2009.
2. Burnes: 'On the maritime communications of India, as carried on by the natives, particularly from Kutch, at the mouth of the Nidus', p. 25.
3. This chart Burnes acquired is probably related to a manual of nautical instructions. A whole genre of nautical manuals (*pothīs*) existed prior to this. The 'oldest known'

Indian coastline map is dated 1664 (personal communication from Himanshu Prabha Ray, 24 February 2016). Another (year uncertain) in the Delhi National Museum's *pothī* collection, which I viewed in 2014, includes information on dhow activity from Indian ports to the the Red Sea and South-East Asia (personal communication from Ashok B. Rajeshirke, 29 March 2016).

4. MS Asia S.4, Royal Geographical Society, London.
5. Burnes: 'On the maritime communications of India, as carried on by the natives, particularly from Kutch, at the mouth of the Nidus', p. 27.
6. Weismann: 'Depiction of Indo-Arabic ships on an eighteenth-century sea chart', pp. 425–34.
7. Agius, Cooper, Jansen Van Rensburg and Zazzaro: 'The dhow's last redoubt?', p. 80.
8. Al-Sayyid: *Malāmiḥ min tārīkh Yanbu'*, vol. I, p. 344.
9. Burckhardt: *Travels in Arabia*, p. 9.
10. Sim: *Desert Traveller: The Life of Jean Louis Burckhardt*, p. 274.
11. See Dubois: 'The Red Sea ports during the revolution in transportation', p. 63.
12. Moore: *Last Days of Mast and Sail*, p. 123, Figures 121–3.
13. Lane: *Arabic–English Lexicon*, vol. I, p. 367.
14. Moore: *Last Days of Mast and Sail*, pp. 123, 125, Figures 121–3; see also Hornell: 'A tentative classification of Arab sea-craft', p. 20.
15. Ibid., p. 35.
16. Agius: *In the Wake of the Dhow*, pp. 58–61.
17. See Cooper, Agius, Collie and Al-Naimi, 'Boat and ship engravings at al-Zubārah, Qatar', pp. 43–5.
18. Al-Sayyid: *Malāmiḥ min tārīkh Yanbu'*, vol. I, p. 344.
19. Burckhardt: *Travels in Arabia*, p. 22.
20. Klunzinger: *Upper Egypt: Its People and its Products*, pp. 294–5.
21. Moore: *Last Days of Mast and Sail*, p. 133.
22. *Travels of Ali Bey*, vol. II, p. 31.
23. Edye: 'Description of the various classes of vessels constructed and employed by the natives of the coasts of Coromandel, Malabar, and the Island of Ceylon for their coasting navigation', p. 11.
24. Cooper, Agius, Collie and Al-Naimi, 'Boat and ship engravings at al-Zubārah, Qatar', p. 45.
25. Science Museum, London (Cat. No. 1926-575); John P. Cooper and I are grateful to Charlotte Dixon (personal communication, 2 June 2014).
26. No. 232, ff. 5669–70, M. 215–16 (April 1808), Secret and Political Department Diaries, Gombroon Diaries, Centre for Documentation and Research, Abu Dhabi; see Agius: *In the Wake of the Dhow*, p. 19.
27. Al-Qasimi: 'Arab "piracy" and the East India Company encroachment in the Gulf 1797–1820', vol. II, p. 6a.
28. Edye: 'Description of the various classes of vessels constructed and employed by the natives of the coasts of Coromandel, Malabar, and the Island of Ceylon for their coasting navigation', p. 12.
29. See my discussion of different vessel types, nomenclatures, hull designs and dhow builders, Arabian migrants on the western coast of India and so on in Agius: *In the Wake of the Dhow*, pp. 186–7.

30. See Hornell: 'The sailing craft of western India', p. 219; Wiebeck: *Indische Boote und Schiffe*, p. 96; Dale: 'The Hadhrami diaspora in south-western India', pp. 181–2.
31. See Agius: *Classic Ships of Islam*, pp. 316–19.
32. Morton Nance: 'Fresh light on "terradas" and "gelves"', p. 38. These vessels were equipped at the stern with a rope-steering system, a feature that persisted until fairly recently; see Agius: *In the Wake of the Dhow*, pp. 80, 86, 98, 101, 105.
33. Moore: *Last Days of Mast and Sail*, p. 123.
34. See Moore: 'Craft of the Red Sea and Gulf of Aden, II', p. 99; Moore: *Last Days of Mast and Sail*, p. 126.
35. *Western Arabia and the Red Sea*, p. 251.
36. Leslau: *Concise Amharic Dictionary*, p. 201.
37. Kane: *Tigrinya–English Dictionary*, vol. II, p. 2181.
38. Lane: *Arabic–English Lexicon*, vol. I, pp. 438, 440; see also Dozy, *Supplément aux dictionnaires arabes*, vol. I, p. 204.
39. De Landberg: *Glossaire Daṯînois*, vol. I, p. 293; Dozy and Engelmann: *Glossaire des mots espagnols et portuguais dérivés de l'arabe*, p. 276.
40. http://www.thearchitecturestore.co.uk/Suakin/SuakinPeople&Trade.html (accessed 31 July 2017).
41. See Cooper: *The Medieval Nile*, p. 112.

8 THE *SANBŪKS* OF THE RED SEA

1. Interviewed on 16 March 2003.
2. The people of the Red Sea pronounce a final 'k', a voiceless velar stop, as opposed to the 'q' sound, uvular occlusive, that is often found further east, in the Arabian Gulf and Oman.
3. The list is long. Examples of different graphemic forms are in Agius: *In the Wake of the Dhow*, p. 85 and fn. 23, 24.
4. Al-Jawālīqī: *Kitāb al-mu'arrab*, pp. 177–9; see also Glidden: 'A comparative study of the Arabic nautical vocabulary from al-Aqabah, Transjordan', p. 71; Tabrīzī: *Burhān-e qāṭe'*, vol. II, p. 1170.
5. Löfgren suggests a Sanskrit source; see Piamenta: *A Dictionary of Post-Classical Yemeni Arabic*, vol. I, p. 243; Yule and Burnell: *Hobson-Jobson: A Glossary of Colloquial Anglo-Indian Words and Phrases*, p. 789.
6. Von Soden: *Akkadisches Handwörterbuch*, vol. II, p. 1022.
7. See Anāstās Mārī l-Kirmilī: 'Al-kalim al-yūnāniyya fī lughat al-'arabiyya', p. 68; Liddell and Scott: *A Greek–English Lexicon*, p. 1582.
8. Alian: *In Memory of the Sambuq*, p. 5.
9. De Landberg: *Glossaire Daṯînois*, vol. III, pp. 1985–6; Glidden: 'A comparative study of the Arabic nautical vocabulary from al-Aqabah, Transjordan', p. 71.
10. See Lane: *Arabic–English Lexicon*, vol. I, p. 1440.
11. *Al-Mu'jam al-wasīṭ*, vol. I, p. 455.
12. The full title is *Takmila wa l-dhayl wa l-ṣila li-kitāb tāj al-lugha wa ṣiḥāḥ al-'arabiyya* (Supplement to the Crown of the Language and the Correct [Word] of the Language).
13. Al-Zabīdī: *Tāj al-'arūs*, vol. XXV, p. 468; see Lane: *Arabic–English Lexicon*, vol. I, pp. 1299, 1440.
14. Alhazmi: *Maritime Terminology of the Saudi Arabian Red Sea Coast*, pp. 152–4.

15. Ibid., p. 151.
16. Al-Zabīdī: *Tāj al-ʿArūs*, vol. XXV, p. 468.
17. Al-Maqrīzī: *Kitāb al-mawāʿiẓ wa l-iʿtibār fī dhikr al-khiṭaṭ wa l-āthār* (1853), vol. II, p. 180.
18. *The Travels of Ibn Baṭṭūṭa*, vol. II, p. 413.
19. *Book of Duarte Barbosa*, vol. I, pp. 7, 9; *Three Voyages of Vasco da Gama*: pp. 75, 76, 79, 80, 109.
20. *The Commentaries of the Great Alfonso Dalboquerque*, vol. IV, p. 206.
21. Ibid.
22. See Al-Nakhīlī: *Al-Sufun al-islāmiyya ʿalā ḥurūf al-muʿjam*, p. 70.
23. *The Travels of Ludovico di Varthema*, p. 154.
24. *Western Arabia and the Red Sea*, p. 531.
25. Agius: *Classic Ships of Islam*, pp. 313–14.
26. Bardey: *Barr-Adjam: Souvenirs d'Afrique Orientale 1880–1887*, p. 209.
27. See Agius: *In the Wake of the Dhow*, pp. 111–12.
28. Kawatoko: *A Port City Site on the Sinai Peninsula: Al-Ṭūr*, pp. 60–1, plates 27–31.
29. Burton: *Personal Narrative of a Pilgrimage to Al-Madinah and Meccah*, vol. I, p. 188.
30. Ibid.
31. Klunzinger: *Upper Egypt: Its People and its Products*, pp. 294–5.
32. Wilson: *The Native Craft*, p. 50.
33. Crossland: *Desert and Water Gardens of the Red Sea*, pp. 60, 65.
34. Valentia: *Voyages and Travels to India, Ceylon, the Red Sea, Abyssinia and Egypt*, vol. II (1994), p. 30.
35. Wilson: *The Native Craft*, p. 50.
36. Moore: 'Notes on "dhows"', p. 207.
37. Ibid.
38. Helfritz: *The Yemen: A Secret Journey*, p. 16, plates 3a–3b.
39. Ibid., plates 3c–3d.
40. Hawkins: *The Dhow*, p. 56.
41. Interviewed on 15 May 2010.
42. Pâris: *Souvenirs de plans ou dessins de navires et de bateaux anciens ou modernes existants ou disparus*, part I, no. 57.
43. Personal communication, 24 February 2016.
44. Hawkins: *The Dhow*, p. 60.
45. Pujo: 'Les boutres à Djibouti', p. 10.
46. Hawkins: *The Dhow*, p. 79.
47. Moore: 'Notes on "dhows"', pp. 208–209.
48. See, e.g., Howarth: *Dhows*, p. 36.
49. McGrail: *Boats of the World*, p. 77.
50. Interviewed on 22 May 2010.
51. Interviewed on 25 March 2013.
52. Interviewed on 28 February 2011.
53. Interviewed on 16 March 2003.
54. PM 5222/15, National Maritime Museum.
55. Information provided by 66-year-old Seif el Din Hasan Mahmud, a boatswain from Quseir, who served at sea for 38 years after starting at the age of 12; interviewed on 17 February 2004.

56. Atia was 56 when I interviewed him on 31 March 2002.
57. Pâris: *Souvenirs de marine*, Figure 56.
58. Lane: *Arabic–English Lexicon*, vol. I, pp. 406–407.
59. Interviewed on 12 May 2007.
60. Interviewed on 12 March 2003 and 31 March 2002, respectively.
61. Interviewed on 12 May 2007.
62. Interviewed on 1 April 2013.
63. Hunter: *An Account of the British Settlement of Aden in Arabia*, p. 83.
64. Further details in Shihāb: *Al-marākib al-'arabiyya: ta'rīkhuhā wa anwā'uhā*, pp. 99, 137, 139.
65. Lane: *Arabic–English Lexicon*, vol. I, p. 1232.
66. Interviewed on 7 February 2009.
67. Interviewed on 28 February 2011.
68. Interviewed on 10 February 2009.
69. See Agius: *In the Wake of the Dhow*, pp. 51, 54.
70. Moore: 'Craft of the Red Sea and Gulf of Aden', p. 76; 'Craft of the Red Sea and Gulf of Aden, II', p. 99.
71. Hornell: 'A tentative classification of Arab sea-craft', p. 34.
72. Pujo: 'Les boutres à Djibouti', p. 11.
73. Jewell: *Dhows at Mombasa*, p. 42.
74. For further discussion, see Agius: *In the Wake of the Dhow*, p. 85.
75. SAD.621/2/33, Palace Green Library, Durham.
76. Jewell: *Dhows at Mombasa*, p. 49.

9 THE DHOW LANDSCAPE: THE NORTHERN AND SOUTHERN RED SEA

1. Interviewed on 9 February 2009; Ahmad used the term *hūrī*, a generic word for the traditional wooden boat in Yemen.
2. The *sanbūk*, *zārūk* and *gaṭīra*; see Pâris: *Souvenirs de plans ou dessins de navires et de bateaux anciens ou modernes existants ou disparus*, parts I–III.
3. Edye: 'Description of the various classes of vessels', pp. 1–14.
4. Hornell: *The Origins and Ethnological Significance of the Indian Boat Designs*, pp. 139–256; see also Hornell: 'A tentative classification of Arab sea-craft', pp. 11–40.
5. Moore: *Last Days of Mast and Sail*, p. ii.
6. Moore: 'Craft of the Red Sea and Gulf of Aden', pp. 73–6; 'Craft of the Red Sea and Gulf of Aden, II', pp. 98–104; 'Craft of the Red Sea and Gulf of Aden, III', pp. 136–42; *Last Days of Mast and Sail*.
7. Hornell: 'A tentative classification of Arab sea-craft', pp. 11–40.
8. LeBaron Bowen: 'Arab dhows of eastern Arabia', pp. 87–132; 'Primitive watercraft of Arabia', pp. 186–221; Hornell: *Water Transport: Origins and Early Evolution*; see also Agius: *In the Wake of the Dhow*.
9. Hawkins: *The Dhow: An Illustrated History of the Dhow and its World*; Villiers: *Sons of Sindbad: The Photographs*.
10. Perrier: *Les boutres de Djibouti: dessins, notes et croquis*.
11. Shihāb: *Al-Marākib al-'arabiyya: ta'rīkhuhā wa anwā'uhā*.
12. Interviewed on 4 April 2003.
13. Interviewed on 4 April 2003.

14. Alhazmi: *Maritime Terminology of the Saudi Arabian Red Sea Coast: A Lexical Semantic Study*, pp. 158–9.
15. Sūrat al-A'rāf ('The Heights'), 7: 64.
16. See Fraenkel: *Die Aramäischen Fremdwörter im Arabischen*, p. 212; see also Agius: *Classic Ships of Islam*, pp. 130–2.
17. Alhazmi: *Maritime Terminology of the Saudi Arabian Red Sea Coast: A Lexical Semantic Study*, pp. 159–60.
18. *Oxford English Dictionary*, vol. I, p. 982.
19. De Landberg: *Glossaire Daṯinois*, vol. III, p. 2436.
20. Interviewed on 27 February 2004.
21. See Agius: *In the Wake of the Dhow*, pp. 119–21. Though, elsewhere, they were from teak (Ar. *sāj*; Lat. *Tectona grandis*); see Jansen Van Rensburg: *The Maritime Traditions of the Fishermen of Socotra, Yemen*, pp. 115–16.
22. See Blue, Whitewright and Cooper: 'The ubiquitous *hūrī*', pp. 185–92.
23. Wilson: *The Native Craft*, p. 88; Glidden: 'A comparative study of the Arabic nautical vocabulary from al-Aqabah, Transjordan', p. 72.
24. See Agius: *In the Wake of the Dhow*, p. 121; *Classic Ships of Islam*, p. 123, fn. 73.
25. Wehr: *A Dictionary of Modern Written Arabic*, p. 470.
26. Lucy Semaan, personal communications, 9 December 2011 and 18 January 2014.
27. Personal communication, 3 February 2009.
28. Prados: 'Huris, sanbuqs and the boat builders of the Yemen', p. 50.
29. Interviewed on 7 February 2009.
30. Agius, Cooper, Jansen Van Rensburg and Zazzaro: 'The dhow's last redoubt?', p. 77.
31. Ibid., pp. 76–7.
32. Moore: 'Craft of the Red Sea and Gulf of Aden', pp. 136–42.
33. Lane: *Arabic–English Lexicon*, vol. I, p. 1232.
34. Agius: *In the Wake of the Dhow*, p. 52.
35. Hunter: *An Account of the British Settlement of Aden in Arabia*, p. 83.
36. Lane: *Arabic–English Lexicon*, vol. II, p. 1936.
37. Hawkins: *The Dhow*, p. 73.
38. See Shihāb: *Al-Marākib al-'arabiyya: ta'rīkhuhā wa anwā'uhā*, pp. 144–5.
39. Alhazmi: *Maritime Terminology of the Saudi Arabian Red Sea Coast: A Lexical Semantic Study*, p. 94.
40. Lane: *Arabic–English Lexicon*, vol. I, p. 1227. Note the Standard Arabic uvular 'q', which is equivalent to the Red Sea velar 'k'.
41. Al-Zabīdī: *Tāj al-'Arūs*, vol. XXV, pp. 394–5.
42. See Agius: *Classic Ships of Islam*, pp. 406–407, 423; *In the Wake of the Dhow*, p. 68.
43. De Landberg: *Glossaire Daṯinois*, vol. III, p. 1835.
44. Interviewed on 10 February 2009.
45. Aden (Random) Box, Serial No. 6: 78R7Aden 80.1, National Maritime Museum.
46. Prados: 'Huris, sanbuqs and the boat builders of the Yemen', pp. 50–6; 'Traditional fishing craft of the Tihamah and southwestern Arabian coast', pp. 89–115; 'Wooden boats of the Yemeni Tihamah', pp. 195–209.
47. For further details, see Agius, Cooper and Zazzaro: 'The maritime heritage of Yemen', pp. 147–8.
48. Agius, Cooper, Jansen Van Rensburg and Zazzaro: 'The dhow's last redoubt?', pp. 74–8.

49. Hornell: *The Origins and Ethnological Significance of the Indian Boat Designs*, pp. 147–8.
50. I am grateful to Chiara Zazzaro, who drew my attention to this generic usage in the Indian context; personal communication, 9 January 2018.
51. Interviewed on 9 February 2009.
52. http://www.madehow.com/Volume-2/Fiberglass.html (accessed 29 August 2012).
53. Personal communication, 15 May 2007.
54. Interviewed on 10 January and 11–12 May 2010.
55. Agius, Cooper, Jansen Van Rensburg and Zazzaro: 'The dhow's last redoubt?', pp. 76–7; Agius, Cooper and Zazzaro, 'The maritime heritage of Yemen', pp. 146–8.
56. Information provided by Ibrahim Al Duwairi, a folklorist, interviewed on 11 May 2010.
57. Interviewed on 24 May 2010.
58. Personal communication from Solène Marion de Procé, 24 October 2015.
59. Agius and Cooper: 'A preliminary investigation into the maritime heritage of Eritrea' submitted to the National Museum, Asmara, Eritrea, 3 March 2011.
60. Interviewed on 28 February 2011.
61. Interviewed on 23 February 2011.
62. Interviewed on 24 February 2011.
63. Interviewed on 27 February 2011.
64. Interviewed on 27 February 2011.
65. See Alhazmi: *Maritime Terminology of the Saudi Arabian Red Sea Coast: A Lexical Semantic Study*, p. 154.
66. See Agius: *Classic Ships of Islam*, pp. 172–3; see Alhazmi: *Maritime Terminology of the Saudi Arabian Red Sea Coast: A Lexical Semantic Study*, p. 155.
67. Information provided by Kamil Hassan, director of higher education, Djibouti, interviewed on 10 October 2009; another version is the Afar *doynik*, while Perrier suggests *doniki*; see Perrier: *Les boutres de Djibouti: dessins, notes et croquis*, p. 20.
68. Information provided by Kamil Hassan, Ali Chehem Mohamad, also known Ali Aref, our guide, and Mohamed Salem Omar, all from Tadjourah, interviewed on 10 and 16 October 2009.
69. Perrier: *Les boutres de Djibouti: dessins, notes et croquis*, pp. 51–79.
70. Ibid., p. 47.
71. Hawkins: *The Dhow*, p. 76.
72. Perrier: *Les boutres de Djibouti: dessins, notes et croquis*, pp. 46–7.
73. Ibid., p. 47.
74. Bāṭarfī: *Jidda, umm al-rakhā wa l-shidda*, p. 55.
75. *The Travels of Ibn Baṭṭūṭa*, vol. III, p. 728; vol. IV, pp. 849, 857.
76. Interviewed on 19 October 2009.
77. Interviewed on 19 October 2009.
78. Information provided by Ibrahim Abou Bakar of Tadjourah on 19 October 2009.

10 'OUR LIFE IS THE SEA: THE SHIP, THE COAST AND THE ANCHORAGE KNOW US'

1. Interviewed on 24 March 2013.
2. Makin: *Red Sea Nights*, p. 181.

3. Ibid.
4. See Villiers: 'Passage in a Red Sea dhow', pp. 173–4.
5. Waterhouse: *Gun Running in the Red Sea*, p. 20.
6. Serjeant: 'Maritime customary law off the Arabian coasts', p. 201.
7. Information on crews was provided by Ibrahim Ahmed Bilghaith, a dhow builder from Jizan, on 10 January, 11 and 12 May 2010; Ibrahim Mousa Ahmed, a former pearl diver and singer from Jizan, on 12 May 2010; Sheikh Muhammad Isa Muhammad Aqili, a former pearl diver from Farasan, on 18 May 2010; Mohammad Abdalla Mohammad Abbas and Aqil Isa Hamadi Mohammad, pearl divers from Qummah, on 23 May 2010; and Sheikh Yahya Ibrahim Bin Ibrahim al-Najdi al-Tamimi, a former pearl diver and *sanbūk* owner from Greater Farasan, on 24 May 2010.
8. Lane: *Arabic–English Lexicon*, vol. I, p. 996.
9. See Nadvī: *The Arab Navigation*, p. 6; see also Ferrand: 'L'élément persan dans les textes nautiques arabes', p. 203.
10. Interviewed on 22 October 2009.
11. Information provided by Hasan Faraj al-Karim on 17 March 2003.
12. Klunzinger: *Upper Egypt: Its People and its Products*, p. 295.
13. Information provided by Abou Bakar Habib of Tadjourah on 17 October 2009 and Ahmed Youssef Mohamed of Tadjourah on 18 October 2009.
14. Serjeant: 'Maritime customary law off the Arabian coasts', p. 201.
15. Clouet: 'La navigation au long cours yéménite de nos jours vers l'Afrique Orientale', p. 16.
16. Burton: *Personal Narrative of a Pilgrimage*, vol. I, p. 188.
17. Ovingdon cited in Foster: *The Red Sea and Adjacent Countries at the Close of the Seventeenth Century*, p. 179.
18. Villiers: 'Passage in a Red Sea dhow', p. 173.
19. Personal communication, 29 May 2015.
20. Interviewed on 22 February 2011.
21. Interviewed on 12 February 2004.
22. Burton: *A Secret Pilgrimage to Mecca and Medina*, p. 132.
23. Makin: *Red Sea Nights*, p. 190.
24. Clouet: 'La navigation au long cours yéménite de nos jours vers l'Afrique Orientale', p. 16.
25. Footman: *Antonin Besse of Aden*, p. 87.
26. Interviewed on 17 February 2004.
27. Interviewed on 17 May 2010.
28. Wehr: *A Dictionary of Modern Written Arabic*, pp. 747, 750.
29. Ibid., p. 747.
30. Information provided by Ali Hussein Ahmed Ibrahim, a *rayyes*, on 11 February 2004.
31. Interviewed on 12 May 2010.
32. *Travels of Ali Bey*, vol. II, p. 33.
33. Interviewed on 21 February 2004.
34. Interviewed on 15 February 2009.
35. Lane: *Arabic–English Lexicon*, vol. I, pp. 887–8.
36. Interviewed on 27 March 2013.

37. Al-Muqaddasī: *Aḥsan al-taqāsīm fī ma'rifat al-aqālīm*, p. 12.
38. Wehr: *A Dictionary of Modern Written Arabic*, p. 635.
39. Tibbetts: 'Arab navigation in the Red Sea', p. 333.
40. Recorded as 'head of sailors' in al-Zabīdī: *Tāj al-'arūs*, vol. II, p. 479.
41. Lane: *Arabic–English Lexicon*, vol. I, p. 1002.
42. See Agius: *Seafaring in the Arabian Gulf and Oman*, pp. 131–4, especially the discussion of this term on p. 131.
43. Nougarède: 'Qualités nautiques des navires arabes', p. 109.
44. Badr Aḥmad Sālim al-Kasādī collected a number of narratives from the elders about their seafaring past; see al-Kasādī: *Abṭāl mansiyyūn min rabābina l-milāḥa l-baḥriyya l-'arabiyya*.
45. MS 82.263, National Museum, New Delhi. Information provided by Himanshu Prabha Ray, personal communicaton, 26 February 2016, and Ashok B. Rajeshirke, personal communications, 29 March and 14 April 2016.
46. *The Commentaries of the Great Alfonso Dalboquerque*, vol. IV, p. 26.
47. Burckhardt: *Travels in Arabia*, pp. 23, 431.
48. Valentia: *Voyages and Travels to India, Ceylon, the Red Sea, Abyssinia and Egypt in the Years 1802–1806*, vol. II (1994), p. 211.
49. Niebuhr: *Travels through Arabia*, vol. I, p. 216.
50. Information provided by Ali AlGhabban, interviewed on 18 January 2010.
51. Shihāb: *Al-Milāḥa l-falakiyya 'inda l-'arab*, pp. 68–76; see Agius: *Classic Ships of Islam*, p. 198.
52. Nadvī: *The Arab Navigation*, p. 110.
53. Interviewed on 1 March 2011.
54. Shihāb: *Al-Marākib al-'arabiyya, tārīkhuhā wa anwā'uhā*, p. 344.
55. See Klunzinger: *Upper Egypt: Its People and its Products*, pp. 301–302; see also Agius: *Seafaring in the Arabian Gulf and Oman*, pp. 156–7.
56. Interviewed on 22 October 2009.
57. Interviewed on 9 October 2009.
58. Ricciardi: *The Voyage of Mir-el-lah*, p. 91.
59. Interviewed on 7 February 2009.
60. Interviewed on 12 February 2009.
61. Interviewed on 12 February 2009.
62. Wehr: *A Dictionary of Modern Literary Arabic*, p. 42.
63. Shafiq: *Seafarers of the Seven Seas*, pp. 110–11.
64. Lewis: *Sand and Sea in Arabia*, p. 73.
65. Footman: *Antonin Besse of Aden*, p. 87.
66. Information provided by Antonin Besse Jr, interviewed on 21 May 2009.
67. Interviewed on 24 March 2013.
68. Interviewed on 9 January 2010.
69. Clouet: 'La navigation au long cours yéménite de nos jours vers l'Afrique Orientale', p. 17.
70. Klunzinger: *Upper Egypt: Its People and its Products*, p. 295.
71. Interviewed on 30 March 2013.
72. Villiers: 'Passage in a Red Sea dhow', p. 173.
73. Makin: *Red Sea Secrets*, p. 182.
74. See Treat: *Pearls, Arms, and Hashish*, pp. 136–7.

75. Makin: *Red Sea Secrets*, p. 182.
76. Interviewed on 10 February 2004.
77. Interviewed on 17 October 2009.
78. Interviewed on 12 February 2009.
79. Villiers: 'Passage in a Red Sea dhow', p. 174.
80. Interviewed on 15 February 2009.
81. Wehr: *A Dictionary of Modern Written Arabic*, pp. 551, 554.
82. Villiers: 'Passage in a Red Sea dhow', p. 176.
83. Makin: *Red Sea Nights*, p. 185.
84. Villiers: 'Passage in a Red Sea dhow', p. 177.
85. Information provided by Muhammad Bukhayyit Alsinani, Ummlejj, on 27 March 2013.
86. Clouet: 'La navigation au long cours yéménite de nos jours vers l'Afrique Orientale', p. 15; Villiers: 'Passage in a Red Sea dhow', p. 176.
87. Interviewed on 12 January 2010.
88. Yule and Burnell: *Hobson-Jobson: A Glossary of Colloquial Anglo-Indian Words and Phrases*, p. 796.
89. Villiers: 'Passage in a Red Sea dhow', p. 175.
90. Serjeant: 'Maritime customary law off the Arabian coasts', p. 199.
91. Cutting from the *Uganda Argus* (1963), n.p. (courtesy of Carol Whitaker).
92. Clouet: 'La navigation au long cours yéménite de nos jours vers l'Afrique Orientale', p. 17; Lesourd: 'Notes sur les nawakhid, navigateurs de la mer', p. 347.
93. Wehr: *A Dictionary of Modern Written Arabic*, p. 292.
94. Interviewed on 31 March 2003
95. See Dozy: *Dictionnaire détaillé des noms des vêtements chez les arabes*, p. 340; Lane: *Arabic–English Lexicon*, vol. II, p. 2459.

11 ON BOARD THE DHOW: EATING, RESTING AND ENTERTAINMENT

1. Interviewed on 15 May 2010.
2. Interviewed on 17 February 2004.
3. LeBaron Bowen: 'The dhow sailor', p. 172.
4. *Travels of Ali Bey*, vol. II, p. 32.
5. Burton: *Personal Narrative of a Pilgrimage*, vol. I, p. 188.
6. Niebuhr: *Travels through Arabia*, vol. I, pp. 213–14.
7. LeBaron Bowen: 'The dhow sailor', p. 190.
8. Burton: *A Secret Pilgrimage to Mecca and Medina*, p. 125.
9. Burckhardt: *Travels in Arabia*, p. 426.
10. *Travels of Ibn Jubayr* (1952), p. 65; al-Maqrīzī: *Kitāb al-mawāʿiẓ wa l-iʿtibār fī dhikr al-khiṭaṭ wa-l-āthār* (2002), vol. I, p. 551.
11. See Sim: *Desert Traveller*, p. 275.
12. Ibid.
13. Niebuhr: *Travels through Arabia*, vol. I, p. 219.
14. LeBaron Bowen: 'The dhow sailor', p. 173.
15. Villiers: 'Passage in a Red Sea dhow', p. 177.
16. Interviewed on 21 February 2004.
17. Burckhardt: *Travels in Arabia*, p. 427.

18. Makin: *Red Sea Nights*, p. 186.
19. Ala Abdo Hasan Mujawir, a boat model maker from Muharraq village, interviewed on 15 May 2010; the Sheikh of Khutub village, Muhammad Abd Allah Al Rajhi, a former pearl diver and fisherman, interviewed on 16 May 2010; Sheikh Muhammad Isa Muhammad Aqili, a former pearl diver from Greater Farasan Island, interviewed on 18 May 2010; and Ali Hasan Hammud Sharif, a former pearl diver and fisherman from Khutub, interviewed on 22 May 2010.
20. Van Der Meulen: *Faces in Shem*, p. 101.
21. See Kemp: *The Oxford Companion to Ships and the Sea*, p. 85.
22. Interviewed on 16 May 2010.
23. Wehr: *A Dictionary of Modern Written Arabic*, p. 470.
24. Interviewed on 8 January 2010.
25. Wehr: *A Dictionary of Modern Written Arabic*, p. 133.
26. See Burckhardt: *Travels in Arabia*, p. 427.
27. See Foster: *The Red Sea and Adjacent Countries at the Close of the Seventeenth Century*, p. 160.
28. Interviewed on 18 May 2010.
29. Burckhardt: *Travels in Arabia*, p. 429.
30. Niebuhr: *Travels through Arabia*, vol. I, p. 166.
31. Interviewed on 1 March 2011.
32. Interviewed on 17 February 2004.
33. Burton: *A Secret Pilgrimage to Mecca and Medina*, pp. 124, 129, 132.
34. Information provided by the governor of the Farasan Islands, Muhandas Abd al-Rahman Bin Muhammad Abd Al Haqq, interviewed on 13 January 2010; see also Muftāḥ: *Farasān: al-nās, al-baḥr wa l-tārīkh*, pp. 181–6 and https://www.marhaba.qa/traditional-games-of-qatar/ (accessed 7 August 2017).
35. Interviewed on 21 May 2009.
36. Interviewed on 24 October 2009.
37. Interviewed on 15 May 2010.
38. De Monfreid: *Secrets of the Red Sea*, p. 53.
39. Recorded by Muhammad Alhazmi on 12 May 2015.
40. Recorded by Muhammad Alhazmi on 7 May 2010.
41. Interviewed on 13 May 2010.
42. Interviewed on 23 March 2003; see also Klunzinger: *Upper Egypt*, pp. 289–90.
43. Information provided by Muhammad Al-Mahdi, interviewed on 16 May 2010; see also Muftāḥ: *Farasān: al-nās, al-baḥr wa l-tārīkh*, pp. 97–9.

12 THIS DANGEROUS SEA

1. Interviewed on 21 February 2004.
2. See Lunde: 'João de Castro's *Roteiro do Mar Roxo* (1541)', p. 217, citing Cortesão and Albuquerque: *Obras completas de João de Castro*, vol. II, p. 281.
3. Villiers: 'Passage in a Red Sea dhow', pp. 173–4.
4. The name probably derives from a Southern Arabian language, but this needs further investigation.
5. Morgan and Davies: *Red Sea Pilot*, p. 43.

6. See Yapp: 'The India Office Records as a source for the economic history of the Middle East', pp. 502, 503, 505.
7. For example: 'Figures show Somali pirates were responsible for 44% of 289 piracy incidents on world's seas in first nine months of 2010' (Alexandra Topping: 'Piracy in Somalia: Key facts', *Guardian*, 14 November 2010; available at https://www.theguardian.com/world/2010/nov/14/somalia-piracy-key-facts (accessed 22 September 2017).
8. See Agius: *In the Wake of the Dhow*, pp. 13–22, 58–66; *Classic Ships of Islam*, pp. 235–8.
9. See Morier: *A Second Journey through Persia, Armenia, and Asia Minor to Constantinople between 1810 and 1816*, pp. 27–8; Davies: *The Blood-Red Arab Flag: An Investigation into Qasimi Piracy 1797–1820*; Al-Qasimi: *The Myth of Arab Piracy in the Gulf.*
10. Howarth: *Dhows*, p. 113.
11. Makin: *Red Sea Nights*, p. 187.
12. Osgood: *Notes of Travel*, pp. 119–20.
13. MSS EUR B369/1 (1840–48), India Office Records, British Library, f. 237r–v.
14. Makin: *Red Sea Nights*, p. 187.
15. Ibid.
16. Niebuhr: *Travels through Arabia*, vol. I, p. 213.
17. Serjeant: 'Maritime customary law off the Arabian coasts', p. 200.
18. Colomb: *Slave-Catching in the Indian Ocean*, p. 39.
19. Interviewed on 22 March 2003.
20. De Monfreid: *Secrets of the Red Sea*, pp. 195–6.
21. *The Straits Times*, 15 November 1905, p. 6.
22. Lewis: *Sand and Sea in Arabia*, p. 74.
23. Damian Whitworth: 'This is the front line in the war with Somali pirates', *The Times*, 19 June 2010, p. 38.
24. Ibid.
25. Interviewed on 21 February 2004.
26. The other five articles of faith are belief in: Allāh, the angels, the holy books, the prophets and the Last Day of Judgement. See Gardet: 'Īmān', pp. 1170–4.
27. Damian Whitworth: 'This is the front line in the war with Somali pirates', *The Times*, 19 June 2010, p. 38.
28. See Gardet: 'Al-ḳaḍā' wa 'l-ḳadar', pp. 365–6.
29. See https://en.oxforddictionaries.com/definition/fate (accessed 28 April 2017).
30. Bāṭarfī: *Jidda, umm al-rakhā wa l-shidda*, p. 80.
31. Auchterlonie: *Encountering Islam: Joseph Pitts*, p. 183.
32. Burton: *A Secret Pilgrimage to Mecca and Medina*, pp. 129, 134–5.
33. *Travels of Ali Bey*, vol. II, p. 33.
34. Valentia: *Voyages and Travels to India, Ceylon, the Red Sea, Abyssinia and Egypt in the Years 1802–1806*, vol. III (1994), p. 301.
35. Wellsted: *Travels in Arabia*, vol. II, p. 109.
36. Ibid., p. 115.
37. MSS EUR B369/1, India Office Records, British, Library, ff. 232r–v, 233r–v.
38. De Monfreid: *Secrets of the Red Sea*, p. 286.
39. *Travels of Ali Bey*, vol. II, p. 33.
40. Lat. 25, 28N; Long. 37; see Wright: *A New and Comprehensive Gazetteer*, vol. III, p. 344.

41. *Travels of Ali Bey*, vol. II, pp. 34–5.
42. Interviewed on 17 October 2009.
43. Interviewed on 25 March 2013.
44. Bāṭarfī: *Jidda, umm al-rakhā wa l-shidda*, p. 59.
45. Ibid.
46. Muhammad Alhazmi, personal communication, 18 June 2015.
47. PERSGA: 'Guidelines for compensation following damage to coral reefs by ship and boat grounding', p. 14.
48. Ibid., p. 11.
49. Interviewed on 19 October 2009.
50. Extract from a panel describing the sinking of a ship off Belitung Island, Indonesia, in the exhibition 'The Lost Dhow: A Discovery from the Maritime Silk Route', Aga Khan Museum, Toronto, Canada, 13 December 2014–26 April 2015. See also Guy: 'Rare and strange goods', pp. 19–23, 39.
51. Makin: *Red Sea Nights*, pp. 182–3.
52. Interviewed on 26 October 2009.
53. Information collected on 11 February 2009.
54. See http://www.nytimes.com/2006/02/04/international/middleeast/04egypt (accessed 19 August 2014); http://www.imo.org/en/KnowledgeCentre/InformationResourcesOnCurrentTopics/InformationResourcesOnCurrentTopicsArchives/Documents/ (accessed 2 October 2017).
55. See *Tradewinds*, xviii/42 (19 October 2007), p. 43; see http://www.imo.org/en//Information/ResourcesOnCurrentTopicsArchives/Documents.pdf (accessed 18 November 2016).
56. See http://news.bbc.co.uk/1/hi/world/middle_east/4685576.stm (accessed 20 September 2017); see also http://www.imo.org/en/KnowledgeCentre/InformationResourcesOnCurrentTopics/InformationResourcesOnCurrentTopicsArchives/Documents/AL%20SALAM%20BOCCACCIO%2098%20_January%202010.pdf (accessed 20 September 2017).
57. Valentia: *Voyages and Travels to India, Ceylon, the Red Sea, Abyssinia and Egypt in the Years 1802–1806*, vol. III (1994), p. 337.
58. Ibid.
59. Wellsted: *Travels in Arabia*, vol. II, p. 246.
60. Wick: *The Red Sea: In Search of Lost Space*, p. 145.
61. Ibid., p. 137.

13 'YOU ONLY RIDE THE SEA IF YOU KNOW THE SEA': WINDS AND SAILS

1. Interviewed on 26 March 2013.
2. Sabini: *Armies in the Sand*, p. 49.
3. Interviewed on 20 October 2009.
4. Fagan: *Beyond the Blue Horizon*, p. 118.
5. J. Ovington in Foster: *The Red Sea and Adjacent Countries at the Close of the Seventeenth Century*, p. 179.
6. Makin: *Red Sea Nights*, p. 189.
7. See Agius: *Seafaring in the Arabian Gulf and Oman* and *Classic Ships of Islam*.
8. Tibbetts: *Arab Navigation in the Indian Ocean*, p. 243.

9. Ibid., pp. 7, 243.
10. Ibid., p. 231; see Facey: 'Sailing the Red Sea', pp. 110–11, 114.
11. Breen: 'Towards an archaeology of Early Islamic ports in the Western Red Sea coast', p. 313, discussing J. Whitewright: 'How fast is fast?', pp. 77–88.
12. Ole Henrik Magga: 'Indigenous knowledge systems: The true roots of humanism', paper delivered at the World Library Congress: 71st IFLA General Conference and Council: 'Libraries: A voyage of discovery'.
13. For example, al-Quṭāmī's *Dalīl al-muḥtār fī 'ilm al-biḥār* (*Guide to Surroundings in the Nautical Science*) draws upon 'European methods'; see Norie: *A Complete Set of Nautical Tables*.
14. Serjeant: 'Maritime customary law off the Arabian coasts', pp. 197–8.
15. See Alain Clouet's discourse on the myth of Arab navigation in 'La navigation au long cours yéménite de nos jours vers l'Afrique Orientale', p. 13.
16. Whitewright: 'Sailing with the *mu'allim*', p. 149.
17. MS Asia S.4, Royal Geographical Society, London.
18. For further discussion on the use of lateen/settee and square sails with reference to Islamic sources, see Agius: *Classic Ships of Islam*, pp. 210–14.
19. Whitewright: 'The potential performance of ancient Mediterranean sailing rigs', p. 2.
20. Personal communication from Julian Whitewright, 28 February 2017; see also Whitewright: 'The potential performance of ancient Mediterranean sailing rigs', pp. 7, 9, 10, 14.
21. Paine: *The Sea and Civilization: A Maritime History of the World*, p. 201.
22. Personal communication, 28 February 2017.
23. *Travels of James Bruce through Part of Africa*, p. 79.
24. Ibid., p. 82.
25. Personal communication from Julian Whitewright, 28 February 2017.
26. Interviewed on 10 February 2009.
27. Personal communication from Julian Whitewright, 28 February 2017.
28. Information provided by Ahmed Jaber Ali of Obock, Djibouti, interviewed on 22 October 2009.
29. Fagan: *Beyond the Blue Horizon*, p. 130.
30. Nougarède: 'Qualités nautiques des navires arabes', p. 102.
31. Paine: *The Sea and Civilization: A Maritime History of the World*, p. 201.
32. Interviewed on 21 May 2009.
33. Fagan: *Beyond the Blue Horizon*, p. 130.
34. Cited in Foster: *The Red Sea and Adjacent Countries at the Close of the Seventeenth Century*, pp. 109–10.
35. Cited in ibid., p. 47.
36. Cited in ibid., p. 19.
37. Niebuhr: *Travels through Arabia*, vol. I, p. 242.
38. Hornell: 'A tentative classification of Arab sea-craft', p. 14.
39. Information provided by Ibrahim Muhammad al-Anbari, interviewed on 10 February 2009.
40. Information provided by Sheikh Muhammad Al-Rajhi, interviewed on 16 May 2010; see Wehr: *A Dictionary of Modern Written Arabic*, p. 215.
41. Interviewed on 11 and 12 May 2010.

42. Hunter: *An Account of the British Settlement of Aden in Arabia*, p. 85.
43. Interestingly, the root radicals √b.r.d. also occur in *burda*, the prophet's outer garment; see Wehr: *A Dictionary of Modern Written Arabic*, p. 51.
44. Interviewed on 26 March 2013.
45. Information provided by Ibrahim Ahmed Bilghaith, interviewed on 10 January 2010.
46. Burton: *Personal Narrative of a Pilgrimage to Al-Madinah and Meccah*, vol. I, p. 178.
47. Information provided by Ibrahim Ahmed Bilghaith, interviewed on 10 January 2010.
48. Interviewed on 19 February 2004.
49. Information provided by Ali Said of Suakin, interviewed on 27 November 2004, and Muhammad al-Abbadi of Qunfudha, interviewed on 30 March 2013.
50. Interviewed on 24 May 2010.
51. Information provided by Hasan Mohammed Hamd Allah, interviewed on 22 February 2004.
52. Interviewed on 23 February 2004.
53. Information provided by Muhammed-Nour Muhammad Al Hasan, interviewed on 1 March 2011, and Abdo Mohammed Isa Aqili, interviewed on 10 January 2010, both of whom acted as guides for the MARES team.
54. Observed on 5 December 2004.
55. Klunzinger: *Upper Egypt: Its People and its Products*, p. 294.
56. Hunter: *An Account of the British Settlement of Aden in Arabia*, p. 85.
57. Hornell: 'A tentative classification of Arab sea-craft', p. 13.
58. Interviewed on 10 January 2010.
59. Agius: 'Medieval Qalhat', pp. 173–220.
60. Tibbetts: *Arab Navigation in the Indian Ocean*, p. 368.
61. Edwards and Head: 'Climate and oceanography', p. 48.
62. Morgan and Davies: *Red Sea Pilot*, p. 29.
63. Valentia: *Voyages and Travels to India, Ceylon, the Red Sea, Abyssinia and Egypt in the Years 1802–1806*, vol. III (1994), p. 353.
64. Wellsted: *Travels in Arabia*, vol. II, p. 470.
65. Ibid.
66. Tibbetts: *Arab Navigation in the Indian Ocean*, p. 326.
67. *Western Arabia and the Red Sea*, p. 156; Morgan and Davies: *Red Sea Pilot*, p. 27.
68. 'Journal of a voyage into the Red Sea', MS, Lyndon Estate, p. 13.
69. De Monfreid: *Hashish*, p. 268; Klunzinger: *Upper Egypt: Its People and its Products*, p. 298.
70. *Western Arabia and the Red Sea*, p. 156; Morgan and Davies: *Red Sea Pilot*, p. 27.
71. Lesourd: 'Notes sur les nawakhid, navigateurs de la Mer Rouge', pp. 348–9.
72. Interviewed on 10 February 2009.
73. Interviewed on 26 February 2011.
74. De Monfreid: *Hashish*, pp. 71, 138.
75. Information provided by Muhammad Abd Allah Abbadi of Qunfudha, interviewed on 9 March 2013.
76. Interviewed on 22 February 2011.
77. Valentia: *Voyages and Travels to India, Ceylon, the Red Sea, Abyssinia and Egypt in the Years 1802–1806*, vol. III (1994), p. 295.

78. Makin: *Red Sea Nights*, p. 188.
79. *The Periplus Maris Erythraei*, p. 283.
80. Lesourd: 'Notes sur les nawakhid, navigateurs de la Mer Rouge', p. 349.
81. Thomas: *Arabia Felix*, p. 122.
82. Interviewed on 31 March 2003.
83. Interviewed on 31 March 2003 and 11 February 2004.
84. Interviewed on 17 October 2009.
85. Interviewed on 27 October 2009.
86. Nougarède: 'Qualités nautiques des navires arabes', p. 119.
87. See Tibbetts: *Arab Navigation in the Indian Ocean*, pp. 364, 368; see Agius: *Seafaring in the Arabian Gulf and Oman*, pp. 191–6.
88. Tibbetts: 'Arab navigation in the Red Sea', p. 326; see also Whitewright: 'The potential performance of ancient Mediterranean sailing rigs', pp. 11–12.
89. McMaster: 'The ocean-going dhow trade to East Africa', pp. 15–16; see also Tibbetts: *Arab Navigation in the Indian Ocean*, p. 326.
90. *The Periplus Maris Erythraei*, p. 287, fn. 14.
91. Tibbetts: *Arab Navigation in the Indian Ocean*, p. 364.
92. Fagan: *Beyond the Blue Horizon*, p. 15.
93. De Monfreid: *Hashish*, p. 142.
94. Personal communication, 28 February 2017.
95. Fagan: *Beyond the Blue Horizon*, p. 15.
96. Burton: *Personal Narrative of a Pilgrimage to Al-Madinah and Meccah*, vol. I, p. 195.
97. Fagan: *Beyond the Blue Horizon*, p. 15.
98. Burton: *Personal Narrative of a Pilgrimage to Al-Madinah and Meccah*, vol. I, p. 195.
99. *The Itinerário of Jerónimo Lobo*, p. 87.
100. *The Periplus Maris Erythraei*, ch. 20.
101. De Monfreid: *Hashish*, p. 6.
102. Ibid.
103. Tibbetts: 'Arab navigation in the Red Sea', p. 325.
104. Tibbetts: *Arab Navigation in the Indian Ocean*, p. 419; see also Morgan and Davies: *Red Sea Pilot*, pp. 105–107.
105. See Lunde: 'João de Castro's *Roteiro do Mar Roxo* (1541)', p. 217, fn. 41.
106. Purchas: *Hakluytus Posthumus*, vol. VI, p. 269; see also Tibbetts: 'Arab navigation in the Red Sea', p. 413; Lunde: 'João de Castro's *Roteiro do Mar Roxo* (1541)', p. 217, fn. 41.
107. See Lunde: 'João de Castro's *Roteiro do Mar Roxo* (1541)', p. 217, citing Cortesão and Albuquerque: *Obras completas de João de Castro*, vol. II, p. 280; Purchas: *Hakluytus Posthumus*, vol. VI, p. 269; see also Morgan and Davies: *Red Sea Pilot*, pp. 152–5.
108. Lunde: 'João de Castro's *Roteiro do Mar Roxo* (1541)', p. 217, fn. 41.
109. Ibid.
110. See Morgan and Davies: *Red Sea Pilot*, pp. 124, 181–212.
111. Interviewed on 29 May 2015.
112. Information provided by 72-year-old Ibrahim Ali Moosa, interviewed on 30 March 2002; Muhammad Khalifa, in his 60s, interviewed on 22 March 2003; and 68-year-old Kamil al-Burri, interviewed on 9 February 2004.
113. MSS EUR A103, India Office Records, British Library, f. 45; Klunzinger: *Upper Egypt: Its People and its Products*, p. 298.

114. Becker and Beckingham: 'Baḥr al-Ḳulzum', p. 931.
115. Information provided by Ibrahim Ali Moosa, interviewed on 31 March 2002; Hasan Faraj al-Karim, in his late 80s, interviewed on 17 March 2003; 81-year-old Abbas Muhammad Ali Daud, interviewed on 10 February 2004; and 53-year-old Ali Hussein Ahmed Ibrahim, interviewed on 11 February 2004; see also Burckhardt: *Travels in Nubia*, p. 459; *Travels in Arabia*, p. 431.
116. See Ovington's report in Foster: *The Red Sea and Adjacent Countries at the Close of the Seventeenth Century*, p. 179; *The Suma Oriental of Tomé Pires and the Book of Francisco Rodrigues*, vol. I, p. 9; Niebuhr: *Travels through Arabia*, vol. I, pp. 235–6.
117. Klunzinger: *Upper Egypt: Its People and its Products*, p. 298.
118. Interviewed on 10 February 2004.
119. Interviewed on 29 May 2015.
120. Interviewed on 28 November 2004.
121. Interviewed on 27 November 2004.
122. Klunzinger: *Upper Egypt: Its People and its Products*, p. 299.
123. Interviewed on 10 February 2004.
124. Tibbetts: 'Arab navigation in the Red Sea', p. 326.
125. Lunde: 'João de Castro's *Roteiro do Mar Roxo* (1541)', p. 217, citing Cortesão and Albuquerque: *Obras completas de João de Castro*, p. 281; Purchas: *Hakluytus Posthumus*, vol. V, p. 269.
126. Clouet: 'La navigation au long cours yéménite de nos jours vers l'Afrique Orientale', p. 18; see also Moore: *Last Days of Mast and Sail*, p. 132.
127. Kemp: *The Oxford Companion to Ships and the Sea*, p. 853.
128. Moore: 'Craft of the Red Sea and Gulf of Aden, III', p. 136.
129. Interviewed on 31 March 2003.
130. Interviewed on 22 October 2009.
131. Personal communication, 27 February 2017.
132. Ibid.
133. Facey and Facey: *Oman: A Seafaring Nation*, p. 115; see also figure on p. 116.
134. Kemp: *The Oxford Companion to Ships and the Sea*, p. 929.
135. Ibid.
136. Interviewed on 22 February 2004.
137. Caption from Whitewright: 'Maritime technological change in the ancient Mediterranean', Figure 2–20; drawing from Moore: *Last Days of Mast and Sail*, Figure 105.
138. Interviewed on 21 October 2009.
139. Interviewed on 12 May 2010.
140. Clouet: 'La navigation au long cours yéménite de nos jours vers l'Afrique Orientale', p. 17.
141. Interviewed on 31 March 2003.
142. Footman: *Antonin Besse of Aden*, p. 95.

14 'WE SET FORTH WITH A FAVOURABLE WIND': THE RED SEA DHOW TRADE

1. Cited by Muhammad-Nour Muhammad Al Hasan, our guide, interviewed on 27 February 2011.

2. Serjeant: 'Maritime customary law off the Arabian coasts', p. 200.
3. Information provided by Ibrahim Ahmed Bilghaith, interviewed on 10 January 2010, and Ibrahim Abdalla Muftah, interviewed on 13 January 2010; see also Agius: *Seafaring in the Arabian Gulf and Oman*, pp. 111–26.
4. Burckhardt: *Travels in Arabia*, p. 17.
5. Cutting from the *Uganda Argus* (1963).
6. Fagan: *Beyond the Blue Horizon*, p. 116.
7. Interviewed on 10 January 2010.
8. LeBaron Bowen: 'The dhow sailor', p. 173; Villiers: *Sons of Sinbad*, pp. 111, 143.
9. Interviewed on 10 January 2010.
10. Al-Sayyid: *Malāmiḥ min tārīkh yanbuʿ*, vol. I, p. 263; see also Serjeant: 'Maritime customary law off the Arabian coasts', pp. 203–204.
11. Interviewed on 27 November 2004.
12. The documents were found at the back of an excavated room; see Kawatoko: *A Port City on the Sinai Peninsula: Al-Ṭūr*, pp. 55–74.
13. The letters are now archived at the King Abdulaziz Foundation for Research and Archives in Riyadh; see Freitag: 'A twentieth-century merchant network centered on Jeddah: The correspondence of Muḥammad b. Aḥmad Bin Ḥimd'.
14. Quoted in Bāṭarfī: *Jidda, umm al-rakhā wa l-shidda*, p. 81.
15. Ibid., p. 80.
16. Interviewed on 27 March 2013.
17. Interviewed on 25 March 2013.
18. Interviewed on 11 May and 13 January 2010.
19. De Landberg: *Glossaire Daṯînois*, vol. III, p. 2500.
20. Serjeant: 'Maritime customary law off the Arabian coasts', p. 204.
21. Lesourd: 'Notes sur les nawakhid, navigateurs de la Mer Rouge', pp. 351–2; see Rouaud: 'Quelques termes arabes d'architecture navale en usage à Djibouti', pp. 337–8.
22. Information provided by 76-year-old Abou Bakar Habib, interviewed on 17 October 2009.
23. LeBaron Bowen: 'The dhow sailor', p. 198.
24. Interviewed on 16 October 2009.
25. Hawkins: *The Dhow*, pp. 84–5.
26. Hornell: 'A tentative classification of Arab sea-craft', pp. 11–40; see also LeBaron Bowen: 'Arab dhows of eastern Arabia', p. 101; Agius: *In the Wake of the Dhow*, p. 51.
27. *Travels of Ali Bey*, vol. II, p. 30.
28. Valentia: *Voyages and Travels to India, Ceylon, the Red Sea, Abyssinia and Egypt in the Years 1802–1806*, vol. III (1994), pp. 351–2.
29. *Travels of James Bruce through Part of Africa*, p. 75; Niebuhr: *Travels through Arabia*, vol. I, p. 165; Klunzinger: *Upper Egypt: Its People and its Products*, pp. 272–5.
30. Niebuhr: *Travels through Arabia*, vol. I, p. 165.
31. Craftsmen in Jerusalem make rosary beads, crucifixes and statues of saints from mother-of-pearl, while their counterparts in Mecca make prayer beads; see Burton: *Personal Narrative of a Pilgrimage to Al-Madinah and Meccah*, vol. I, p. 179.
32. Burckhardt: *Travels in Nubia*, pp. 439–40.
33. Burton: *Personal Narrative of a Pilgrimage to Al-Madinah and Meccah*, vol. I, p. 178.
34. Wallin: *Travels in Arabia (1845 and 1848)*, p. 295.

35. Kawatoko: *A Port City on the Sinai Peninsula: Al-Ṭūr*, pp. 55–6.
36. Denon: *Travels in Upper and Lower Egypt*, vol. II, p. 120.
37. Klunzinger: *Upper Egypt: Its People and its Products*, pp. 278–9, 281, 283–5, 286–9.
38. Klunzinger: *Upper Egypt: Its People and its Products*, p. 274.
39. MS Wilkinson dep. d. 48, Bodleian Library, Oxford, p. 122.
40. *Travels of James Bruce through Part of Africa*, p. 75.
41. Klunzinger: *Upper Egypt: Its People and its Products*, pp. 272, 286–7.
42. Interviewed on 10 February 2004.
43. Ghabbān: *Shamāl gharb al-mamlaka l-'arabiyya l-sa'ūdiyya*, pp. 166–7.
44. Interviewed on 23 March 2003.
45. Interviewed on 13 May 2007
46. Interviewed on 22 February 2004.
47. Interviewed on 17 February 2004.
48. Interviewed on 12 February 2004.
49. Wallin: *Travels in Arabia (1845 and 1848)*, pp. 298–9.
50. Burckhardt: *Travel in Arabia*, p. 230.
51. *Western Arabia and the Red Sea*, p. 539.
52. Wellsted: *Travels in Arabia*, vol. I, p. 191.
53. Interviewed on 27 March 2013.
54. Interviewed on 27 March 2013.
55. Interviewed on 26 March 2013.
56. *Western Arabia and the Red Sea*, p. 540.
57. Burckhardt: *Travels in Arabia*, p. 420.
58. Ibid.
59. Wellsted: *Travels in Arabia*, vol. I, p. 216.
60. Al-Sayyid: *Malāmiḥ min tārīkh yanbu'*, vol. I, pp. 263–4.
61. Interviewed on 25 March 2013.
62. Ghabbān: *Shamāl gharb al-mamlaka l-'arabiyya l-sa'ūdiyya*, p. 84.
63. Personal communication from Lucy Semaan, 15 May 2014, who drew my attention to *talḥ* (*Acacia hockii*); see Provençal: *The Arabic Plant Names*, p. 64. Hans Wehr lists it as *Acacia gummifera*; see Wehr: *A Dictionary of Modern Written Arabic*, p. 564.
64. Provençal: *The Arabic Plant Names*, p. 65.
65. Ghabbān: *Shamāl gharb al-mamlaka l-'arabiyya l-sa'ūdiyya*, p. 84.
66. Mustaller: 'Maricultural development and management of shallow water marine resources in the Sudanese Red Sea', p. 38.
67. Bruce: *Travels to Discover the Source of the Nile in the Years 1768–73*, vol. III, pp. 246–50; see also Helfritz: *The Yemen: A Secret Journey*, p. 88.
68. Poncet: *A Voyage to Ethiopia*, pp. 117–18.
69. Bruce: *Travels to Discover the Source of the Nile in the Years 1768–73*, vol. III, p. 250.
70. For details of the Ottoman administration, see Talhami: *Suakin and Massawa under Egyptian Rule 1865–1885*, pp. 40–1.
71. Valentia: *Voyages and Travels to India, Ceylon, the Red Sea, Abyssinia and Egypt in the Years 1802–1806*, vol. II (1994), p. 286.
72. Greenlaw: *The Coral Buildings of Suakin*, p. 14.
73. Ibid. It should be noted that Greenlaw's source for this information is unclear.
74. SAD.474/20/14, Palace Green Library, Durham.
75. Interviewed on 24 November 2004.

76. Interviewed on 24 November 2004.
77. Interviewed on 4 December 2004; confirmed by Hussein Abd al-Hamid Abd Allah, interviewed on 6 December 2004.
78. Interviewed on 24 November 2004.
79. Information provided by Rashayda elders to Muḥammad Ṣāliḥ Ḍirār and cited in Ḥasan: *The Arabs and the Sudan from the Seventh to the Early Sixteenth Century*, p. 219, fn. 2.
80. *The Commentaries of the Great Alfonso Dalboquerque*, vol. IV, p. 185.
81. Valentia: *Voyages and Travels to India, Ceylon, the Red Sea, Abyssinia and Egypt in the Years 1802–1806*, vol. II (1809), p. 86.
82. LeBaron Bowen: 'The dhow sailor', pp. 171–2; Stark: *East is West*, p. 9; Lewis: *Sand and Sea in Arabia*, p. 40.
83. Ibid.
84. 'Tony Besse', obituary, *The Times*, 16 December 2016, p. 57.
85. Interviewed on 11 January 2010; see also Muftāḥ: *Farasān: al-nās, al-baḥr wa l-tārīkh*, pp. 109–19.
86. LeBaron Bowen: 'The dhow sailor', pp. 171–2.
87. Martin and Martin: *Cargoes of the East*, p. 55.
88. Ibid., p. 51.
89. Ibid., pp. 108, 110–15.
90. Lewis: *Sand and Sea in Arabia*, p. 40.
91. Stark: *East is West*, p. 9.
92. *The Itinerário of Jerónimo Lobo*, p. 88.
93. Brouwer: *Al-Mukhā*, pp. 357–8.
94. Valentia: *Voyages and Travels to India, Ceylon, the Red Sea, Abyssinia and Egypt in the Years 1802–1806*, vol. II (1994), p. 363.
95. A + E Networks Corp Digital History, available at http://www.history.com/news/history-lists/ (accessed 31 March 2017).
96. Pesce: *Jiddah: Portrait of an Arabian City*, p. 102.
97. The Portuguese defeat was recorded in one of the epic *cantos* of De Camões: *The Lusíads*, Canto 9.3.
98. *The Itinerário of Jerónimo Lobo*, pp. 89–90.
99. Burckhardt: *Travels in Arabia*, pp. 9, 22.
100. Lefebvre: *Voyage en Abyssinie executé pendant les années 1839–1843*, vol. II, pp. 6–12; Ferret and Galinier: *Voyage en Abyssinie*, vol. I, ch. 10; both cited by Pesce: *Jiddah: Portrait of an Arabian City*, pp. 233–7.
101. See Semple: *A Silver Legend: The Story of the Maria Theresa Thaler*, pp. 51–90.
102. Bāṭarfī: *Jidda, umm al-rakhā wa l-shidda*, p. 55.
103. Ibid., p. 80.
104. See Burton: *Arabia, Egypt, India: A Narrative of Travel*, p. 93.
105. Burton: *Personal Narrative of a Pilgrimage to Al-Madinah and Meccah*, vol. I, p. 179.
106. Burckhardt: *Travels in Nubia*, p. 441.
107. LeBaron Bowen: 'The dhow sailor', pp. 171–2, 175.
108. 'Travels of Thomas Machell', MSS EUR B369/1, India Office Records, British Library, f. 217r.
109. *Travels of James Bruce through Part of Africa*, p. 111.

110. Valentia: *Voyages and Travels to India, Ceylon, the Red Sea, Abyssinia and Egypt in the Years 1802–1806*, vol. II (1809), pp. 18, 19.
111. Dubois: 'The Red Sea ports during the revolution in transportation', p. 62.
112. Interviewed on 22 February 2011.
113. Interviewed on 21 May and 14 May respectively. See Miran: *Red Sea Citizens*, pp. 99–106, 110, 134, 141, 240; see also Agius, Cooper, Semaan, Zazzaro and Carter: 'Remembering the sea', pp. 127–77.
114. Interviewed on 28 February 2011.
115. Interviewed on 25 February 2011.
116. Interviewed on 21 February 2011.
117. Interviewed on 26 February 2011.
118. Interviewed on 12 October 2009.
119. See PERSGA: 'Status of mangroves in the Red Sea and Gulf of Aden', p. 9.
120. Rouaud: 'Tadjurra', p. 71.
121. Interviewed on 16 October 2009.
122. Interviewed on 16 October 2009.
123. Interviewed on 16 October 2009.
124. Interviewed on 27 October 2009.
125. Interviewed on 17 October 2009.
126. Lesourd: 'Notes sur les nawakhid, navigateurs de la Mer Rouge', p. 346.
127. Ibid., p. 355.
128. Interviewed on 16 October 2009.
129. Interviewed on 18 October 2009.
130. Interviewed on 18 October 2009.
131. Interviewed on 12 February 2009.
132. Interviewed on 12 February 2009.
133. Pesce: *Jiddah: Portrait of an Arabian City*, p. 105.
134. Kay: *Saudi Arabia: Past and Present*, p. 39.

15 'WE SAIL WITH THE HOPE OF A GOOD CATCH': FISHING AND SHELL COLLECTING

1. Interviewed on 18 February 2004.
2. Steingass: *A Comprehensive Persian English Dictionary*, p. 1488.
3. http://www.red-sea.fishing/index.html (accessed 27 December 2016).
4. Al-Ḥarbī: *Al-Thaqāfa l-munākhiyya bayn al-ḍarūra l-ḥatmiyya wa l-aḥkām al-shar'iyya wa l-dirāsa l-taṭbīqiyya*, pp. 162–89.
5. Interviewed on 22 October 2009.
6. Interviewed on 24 March 2013.
7. Interviewed on 26 March 2003.
8. Interviewed on 24 March 2013.
9. Interviewed on 1 March 2011.
10. Interviewed on 4 April 2003.
11. Information provided by Shabhat Khaysha Hassan, interviewed on 12 March 2003; see also Abū Shūsha, Kalantan, al-Nāẓrī and al-Ghāmdī: *Asmāk min al-miyāh al-iqlīmiyya lil-mamlaka fī l-baḥr al-aḥmar*, pp. 137, 206, 211.

12. I had no access to official statistics about the fishing population. The figure of 600 was an estimate provided by Hammad Tokulia Augan, head of fisheries in Suakin, interviewed on 1 December 2004. In a 1976 census, there were 107 fishermen in Suakin out of a total of 376 along the whole Sudanese coast; see Kentley: 'Suakin and its fishermen', p. 164.
13. Information provided by Hammad Tokulia Augan, interviewed on 1 December 2004.
14. Interviewed on 25 March 2013.
15. Interviewed on 12 February 2009.
16. Interviewed on 9 February 2009.
17. Interviewed on 22 October 2009.
18. Interviewed on 22 October 2009.
19. Siliotti: *Fishes of the Red Sea*, p. 17.
20. Abū Shūsha, Kalantan, al-Nāẓrī and al-Ghāmdī: *Asmāk min al-miyāh al-iqlīmiyya lil-mamlaka fī l-baḥr al-aḥmar*, pp. 19–20; Siliotti: *Fishes of the Red Sea*, p. 17.
21. Interviewed on 12 January 2010.
22. Crossland: *Desert and Water Gardens of the Red Sea*, p. 68.
23. Kira Cochrane: 'What made the Red Sea sharks attack?', *Guardian*, 7 December 2010, available at http://www.theguardian.com/world/2010/dec/07/what-made-sharks-attack (accessed 13 August 2014).
24. *Al-Riyāḍ*, 29 May 1990.
25. Interviewed on 26 February 2011.
26. Detailed information on this festival is provided by Muftāḥ: *Farasān: al-nās, al-baḥr wa l-tārīkh*, pp. 120–31, who includes poetry and folklore traditions and customs; see also Hubaylī and Hubaylī: *Jazīrat Farasān: al-tārīkh wa l-siyāḥa*, pp. 111–24; for other details, see Gladstone: 'Unique annual aggregaton of longnose parrotfish', available at http://www.worldfishcenter.org/Naga/Naga25-3&4/pdf/NAGA_25no3n4_features_f.pdf (accessed 3 January 2014).
27. Interview with Ahmad Bakri and Ahmad Dawud in the Saudi newspaper *Al-Okaz*, available at http://www.saudigazette.com.sa/index.cfm?method=home.regcon&contentid (accessed 3 January 2014).
28. http://www.arabnews.com/node/410800 (accessed 6 July 2015).
29. Interviewed on 22 February 2011.
30. Interviewed on 24 October 2009.
31. Interviewed on 18 October 2009.
32. Interviewed on 21 October 2009.
33. See Abū Shūsha, Kalantan, al-Nāẓrī and al-Ghāmdī: *Asmāk min al-miyāh al-iqlīmiyya lil-mamlaka fī l-baḥr al-aḥmar*, p. 95.
34. Interviewed on 26 February 2011.
35. Interviewed on 1 March 2011.
36. Interviewed on 26 February 2011.
37. Moore: 'Craft of the Red Sea and Gulf of Aden, III', p. 141.
38. Agius, Cooper, Jansen Van Rensburg and Zazzaro: 'The dhow's last redoubt?', pp. 78, 80.
39. See Agius: *Classic Ships of Islam*, pp. 120–2.
40. Vine: *Red Sea Invertebrates*, p. 134.

41. Sharabati: *Red Sea Shells*, plate 3; Vine: *Red Sea Invertebrates*, p. 127; Agius, Cooper, Semaan, Zazzaro and Carter: 'Remembering the sea', p. 158.
42. http//www.enchantedlearning.com/cgifs/Conchbw.GIF (accessed 7 December 2009).
43. Information provided by Ali Said, interviewed on 27 November; Hammad Tokulia Augan, interviewed on 1 December; Hashim Abd Salim Garmushi, interviewed on 4 December 2004.
44. Information provided by Muhammad Idrees and Hamid Hammad Jubouri, interviewed on 2 December 2004; see also http://www.alibaba.com/showroom/trocas-shell.html and http://www.aliexpress.com/w/wholesale-trocas-shell-buttons.html (accessed 28 November 2013).
45. Suakin was renowned for its pearling industry in the early eighteenth century; see Poncet: *A Voyage to Ethiopia*, pp. 117–18.
46. Both interviewed on 2 December 2004.
47. De Monfreid: *Hashish*, p. 15.
48. Eltayeb: 'Review of the trochus fishery in Sudan', p. 5.
49. Interviewed on 21 October 2009.
50. Vine: *Red Sea Invertebrates*, p. 205.
51. Information provided by Hammad Tokulia Augan, interviewed on 1 December 2004, and Hamid Idrees, interviewed on 4 December 2004.
52. Vine: *Red Sea Invertebrates*, p. 205.
53. Ibid.
54. Interviewed on 26 March 2013.
55. Anonymous government official, interviewed on 24 February 2011.
56. Interviewed on 25 February 2011.
57. See Agius, Cooper, Jansen Van Rensburg and Zazzaro: 'The dhow's last redoubt?', p. 75.
58. http://www.britannica.com/EBchecked/topic/652831/Yemen/45258/Agriculture-forestry-and-fishing (accessed 4 December 2014).
59. Interviewed on 31 March 2003.
60. Moore: 'Craft of the Red Sea and Gulf of Aden, III', p. 142.
61. Interviewed on 1 December 2004.
62. Anonymous dhow owner, interviewed on 20 November 2004; see also Serjeant: 'Maritime customary law off the Arabian coasts', p. 196.
63. Interviewed on 29 November 2004.
64. See Agius, Cooper, Semaan, Zazzaro and Carter: 'Remembering the sea', pp. 127–77.
65. Bosch and Bosch: *Seashells of Southern Arabia*, p. 83; Vine: *Red Sea Invertebrates*, p. 159.
66. Al-Mas'ūdī: *Murūj al-dhahab wa ma'ādin al-jawhar*, vol. I, p. 168.
67. Sharabati: *Red Sea Shells*, plate 41; Vine: *Red Sea Invertebrates*, p. 134.
68. Sharabati: *Red Sea Shells*, p. 73; Vine: *Red Sea Invertebrates*, p. 141.
69. Ibid., p. 140.
70. Sharabati: *Red Sea Shells*, pp. 93, 95; Vine: *Red Sea Invertebrates*, p. 140.
71. Sharabati: *Red Sea Shells*, plate 17; Vine: *Red Sea Invertebrates*, p. 140.
72. Sharabati: *Red Sea Shells*, plate 3; Vine: *Red Sea Invertebrates*, p. 127.
73. Sharabati: *Red Sea Shells*, plate 34; Vine: *Red Sea Invertebrates*, p. 145.

74. Information provided by Ibrahim Abdalla Muftah, interviewed on 11 January 2010, and Suleiman Mohammad Ali Baloos, interviewed on 12 January 2010.
75. Agius, Cooper, Semaan, Zazzaro and Carter: 'Remembering the sea', pp. 155–7.
76. Information provided by a number of fishermen. Interviews conducted between 1 and 6 February 2018.
77. Interviewed on 21 October 2009.
78. Interviewed on 17 May 2010; he remembers the days when King Ibn Saud (d. 1953) visited the islands.
79. Interviewed on 22 May 2010.
80. Interviewed on 21 May 2010.
81. Interviewed on 26 February 2011.
82. Interviewed on 18 May 2010.
83. Interviewed on 17 May 2010.
84. Interviewed on 22 May 2010.
85. Information on diving provided by Soleiman Baloos, interviewed on 12 January and 21 May 2010; Abdo Mohammed Isa Aqili, interviewed on 10 January and 11 May 2010; Munawwar Aqili, interviewed on 17 May 2010; Sheikh Muhammad Isa Muhammad Aqili, interviewed on 18 May 2010; Muhammad Abd Allah Said Al-Hussayyal, interviewed on 22 May 2010; and Mohammad Abd Allah Mohammad Abbas, interviewed on 23 May 2010.
86. Information provided by Suleiman Baloos, interviewed on 12 January 2010.
87. Makin: *Red Sea Nights*, p. 186; see also Crossland: *Desert and Water Gardens of the Red Sea*, p. 71.
88. http://www2.padi.com/blog/2015/10/31/9-facts-about-devil-rays/ (accessed 13 February 2018).
89. Makin: *Red Sea Nights*, p. 195.
90. See ibid., p. 196. I was unable to find further information about *dawls*.
91. Ibid., p. 195.
92. http://www.stylecraze.com/articles/benefits-of-guava-leaves-for-skin-hair-and-health/ (accessed 4 February 2014).
93. Information provided by Hamid Idrees and Mohammed Abdallah Ahmed, interviewed on 4 and 5 December 2004; see also Abū Shūsha, Kalantan, al-Nāẓrī and al-Ghāmdī: *Asmāk min al-miyāh al-iqlīmiyya lil-mamlaka fī l-baḥr al-aḥmar*, p. 239.
94. De Monfreid: *Hashish*, p. 17.
95. Other terms for the share system were *qism* and *nāyb*; see Kawatoko: *A Port City Site on the Sinai Peninsula: Al-Ṭūr*, pp. 62–3.
96. Ibid., p. 63.
97. Interviewed on 18 February 2004.
98. Interviewed on 31 March 2003.
99. See Serjeant: 'Maritime customary law off the Arabian coasts', p. 201.
100. Bent and Bent: *Southern Arabia*, p. 7.
101. For further details, see Agius, Cooper, Semaan, Zazzaro and Carter: 'Remembering the sea', pp. 162–6.
102. Ibid., pp. 165–7.
103. Interviewed on 18 May 2010.
104. Interviewed on 22 May 2010.

105. LeBaron Bowen: 'The dhow sailor', p. 194.
106. Ibid., p. 200.
107. Ibid., p. 201.
108. Donaldson: 'Erythraean ichthyophagi', p. 25.
109. See Alsharif: 'The good, the bad and the ugly'.
110. http://www.greenprophet.com/2012/04/parrot-fish-festival-red-sea/ (accessed on 3 January 2014).
111. Interviewed on 12 and 13 January and 14 and 21 May 2010.
112. See Agius: *Seafaring in the Arabian Gulf and Oman*, pp. 105–107.
113. LeBaron Bowen: 'The dhow sailor', p. 202.
114. Ibid., p. 201.

16 THE DHOW HUNT: THE SLAVE TRADE AND GUN RUNNING IN THE SOUTHERN RED SEA

1. Translation by Yusuf Ali, *The Holy Qur-an*, vol. I, p. 270 with some amendments.
2. A number of authors have attempted to tackle this labyrinthine topic in greater depth. See, for instance, Pankhurst: 'The Ethiopian slave trade in the nineteenth and early twentieth centuries', pp. 220–8; Ochsenwald: 'Muslim–European conflict in the Hijaz', pp. 115–26; Ewald: 'The Nile Valley system and the Red Sea slave trade 1820–1880', pp. 71–92, and 'Crossers of the sea', pp. 69–91; Moore-Harell: 'Slave trade in the Sudan in the nineteenth century and its suppression in the years 1877–80', pp. 113–28; Clarence-Smith: *Islam and the Abolition of Slavery*; Dubois: 'Un traite tardive en Mer Rouge méridionale', pp. 197–222; Zdanowski: *Slavery and Manumission*; Reilly: 'A well-intentioned failure', pp. 91–115; Huber: *Channelling Mobilities*, pp. 172–203.
3. Serels: *Starvation and the State*, pp. 140–1.
4. Colomb: *Slave-Catching in the Indian Ocean*, p. vii.
5. Miran: *Red Sea Citizens*, p. 16.
6. Colomb: *Slave-Catching in the Indian Ocean*, p. viii.
7. Huber: *Channelling Mobilities*, p. 180.
8. Ibid., p. 184; see also Burdett: *Slave Trade into Arabia*, vol. I, p. v.
9. See Hazell: *The Last Slave Market*, pp. 11, 26, 39, 50, 147, 223.
10. Sūrat al-Nisā' ('The Women'), 5: 92; Sūrat al-Balad ('The City'), 90: 13; translations in *The Holy Qur-an*, vol. I, p. 180; vol. II, p. 1739.
11. Sūrat al-Tawba ('Repentance'), 9: 60; translation in *The Holy Qur-an*, vol. I, p. 458.
12. Sūrat al-Mā'ida ('The Table Spread'), 5: 92; translation in *The Holy Qur-an*, vol. I, p. 270.
13. Interviewed on 23 March 2013.
14. Information provided by Muhammad Alhazmi (26 March 2013).
15. Hamilton: *The Princes of Zinj*, p. 202.
16. Hurgronje: *Mekka in the Latter Part of the 19th Century*, p. 21; see Huber: *Channelling Mobilities*, p. 180.
17. Osgood: *Notes of Travel*, p. 191.
18. Valentia: *Voyages and Travels to India, Ceylon, the Red Sea, Abyssinia and Egypt in the Years 1802–1806*, vol. III (1994), p. 328.
19. Tunstall: *Vanishing Kingdoms*, p. 87.

20. Information gathered by a former pearl diver on 23 May 2010.
21. Information gathered by a former sailor on 27 March 2013.
22. Londres: *Pêcheurs de perles*, p. 109.
23. Treat: *Pearls, Arms, and Hashish*, p. 126.
24. Ibid.
25. Londres: *Pêcheurs de perles*, p. 108.
26. Ewald: 'The Nile Valley system and the Red Sea slave trade 1820–1880', p. 78.
27. Moore-Harell: 'Slave trade in the Sudan in the nineteenth century and its suppression in the years 1877–80', p. 121.
28. Makin: *Red Sea Nights*, p. 259.
29. Simon: *Slavery*, pp. 58–9.
30. Zdanowski: *Slavery and Manumission*, p. 77, cited by Reilly: 'A well-intentioned failure', p. 94.
31. See Moore-Harell: 'Slave trade in the Sudan in the nineteenth century and its suppression in the years 1877–80', p. 118.
32. Ibid., p. 121.
33. Colomb: *Slave-Catching in the Indian Ocean*, p. 65.
34. Burdett: *Slave Trade into Arabia*, vol. III, pp. 489–93.
35. Burton: *Arabia, Egypt and India*, p. 92.
36. See Huber: *Channelling Mobilities*, p. 188, fn. 48 and 49.
37. Burdett: *Slave Trade into Arabia*, vol. IV, pp. 701–707.
38. R/20/A 3994, Perim, 25 October 1916, Cpt Henri De Monfreid, India Office Records, British Library, ff. 139, 140, 178.
39. R/20/A 3994, Aden, 10 March 1917, Cpt Henri De Monfreid, India Office Records, British Library, f. 178.
40. Colomb: *Slave-Catching in the Indian Ocean*, p. 70.
41. *The Graphic*, 22 March 1902, p. 397 (courtesy of University of Exeter Special Collections).
42. Coupland: *East Africa and its Invaders*, p. 188.
43. Tunstall: *Vanishing Kingdoms*, p. 87.
44. *The Graphic*, 22 March 1902, p. 397 (courtesy of University of Exeter Special Collections).
45. Makin: *Red Sea Nights*, p. 262.
46. *The Graphic: Supplement*, 25 April 1874, p. 404 (courtesy of University of Exeter Special Collections).
47. Treat: *Pearls, Arms, and Hashish*, pp. 131–2.
48. Berlioux: *La traite orientale*, p. 215.
49. Young to Jones cited in Reilly: 'A well-intentioned failure', p. 100.
50. Toledano: *The Ottoman Slave Trade and its Suppression*, p. 34.
51. See Gerard DeGroot's review of Broich: *Squadron: Ending the African Slave Trade*, in *The Times*, 20 January 2018, Saturday Review, p. 16.
52. Hazell: *The Last Slave Market*, p. 148.
53. See Pujo: 'Les boutres à Djibouti', p. 9; Rouaud: 'Quelques termes arabes d'architecture navale', p. 337; see also Agius: *In the Wake of the Dhow*, pp. 22–4; *Seafaring in the Arabian Gulf and Oman*, pp. 13, 15, 51, 53, 80–1, 97, 104, 118, 121, 125–6, 180.

54. Hornell: 'A tentative classification of Arab sea-craft', pp. 24–5.
55. Hornell: *Water Transport*, p. 239.
56. Ibid., p. 240; Lewis: *Sand and Sea in Arabia*, p. 37.
57. De Monfreid: *Secrets of the Red Sea*, p. 221; information also provided by Antonin Besse Jr, interviewed on 21 May 2009.
58. De Monfreid: *Secrets of the Red Sea*, p. 221.
59. Devereux: *A Cruise in the 'Gorgon'*, pp. 129, 132.
60. Doughty: *Travels in Arabia Deserta*, vol. II, pp. 187, 189, 524.
61. Colomb: *Slave-Catching in the Indian Ocean*, p. 54.
62. See Miers: *Slavery in the Twentieth Century*, especially ch. 7.
63. Makin: *Red Sea Nights*, p. 259.
64. Osgood: *Notes of Travel*, p. 191.
65. De Monfreid: *Secrets of the Red Sea*, pp. 23–4.
66. Hawkins: *The Dhow*, p. 74.
67. Howarth: *Dhows*, p. 114.
68. FO 541/21, Captain Malcolm to the Earl of Northbrook, 12 November 1881, National Archives, cited in Huber: *Channelling Mobilities*, p. 195; see also Reilly: 'A well-intentioned failure', p. 106.
69. Ibid.
70. Huber: *Channelling Mobilities*, p. 196.
71. Ibid., p. 195.
72. Ibid., p. 183, fn. 31; Burdett: *Slave Trade into Arabia*, vol. I, p. ix.
73. Berlioux: *La traite orientale*, p. 215.
74. Waterhouse: *Gun Running in the Red Sea*, p. 13.
75. Hamilton: *The Princes of Zinj*, p. 100.
76. Makin: *Red Sea Nights*, p. 181.
77. Nicholl: *Somebody Else*, p. 183.
78. Waterhouse: *Gun Running in the Red Sea*, pp. 72–3.
79. Thomas: *Arabia Felix*, p. 142.
80. Footman: *Antonin Besse of Aden*, pp. 115–16.
81. Interviewed on 18 October 2009.
82. http://news.bbc.co.uk/1/shared/spl/hi/picture_gallery/04/africa_djibouti_fisherman/html/9.stm (accessed 28 May 2014).
83. Interviewed on 12 October 2009.
84. *The Periplus of the Erythraean Sea*, 8: 23, 31: 38, 36: 40.
85. Harris: *The Highlands of Aethiopia*, vol. II, p. 52.
86. *The Travels of Ibn Baṭṭūṭa*, vol. II, p. 373.
87. Burton: *First Footsteps in East Africa*, pp. 112–37, 233–53.
88. Fontrier: *Abu-Bakr Ibrahim, Pacha de Zeyla, marchand d'esclaves*, p. 52.
89. Interviewed on 15 October 2009.
90. Harris: *The Highlands of Aethiopia*, vol. I, pp. 53–4, vol. III, p. 305; see also Treat: *Pearls, Arms, and Hashish*, pp. 125–6. On the salt caravans, see, for example, Montillier: *Djibouti. Les caravaniers du sel.*
91. Interviewed on 16 October 2009.
92. Treat: *Pearls, Arms, and Hashish*, pp. 118–19.
93. Ibid., pp. 125–6.
94. Makin: *Red Sea Nights*, p. 257.

95. Nicholl: *Somebody Else*, pp. 272–82.
96. Interviewed on 15 October 2009.
97. Treat: *Pearls, Arms, and Hashish*, pp. 131–2.
98. Reilly: 'A well-intentioned failure', p. 101.
99. Hazell: *The Last Slave Market*, p. 157.
100. Reilly: 'A well-intentioned failure', p. 102.
101. Interviewed on 23 October 2009.
102. Makin: *Red Sea Nights*, p. 256.
103. Davis: *The Problem of Slavery in the Age of Revolution, 1770–1823*, pp. 343–468, cited in Huber: *Channelling Mobilities*, p. 172.
104. De Monfreid: *Secrets of the Red Sea*, p. 263.
105. *Western Arabia and the Red Sea*, p. 351.
106. Londres: *Pêcheurs de perles*, p. 109.

17 THE DHOW, THE COAST AND THE SEA: INTERACTING WITH NATURE, THE SPIRITS AND THE SUPERNATURAL

1. See Burton: *A Secret Pilgrimage to Mecca and Medina*, p. 132.
2. Hornell: 'Survivals of the use of *oculi* in modern boats', pp. 289–321; 'Boat *oculi* survivals', pp. 339–49; Myers: 'Little Aden folklore', pp. 177–233; LeBaron Bowen: 'Maritime superstitions of the Arabs', pp. 5–48; 'Origin and diffusion of *oculi*', pp. 262–91; Serjeant: 'Maritime customary law off the Arabian coasts', pp. 195–207; Johnstone: 'Folklore and folk literature', pp. 7–25; Naumkin: *Island of the Phoenix*; 'Myth, gender and eroticism in Socotran folklore', pp. 189–94; Smith: 'Magic, *jinn* and the supernatural in medieval Yemen', pp. 7–18. See also my recent contribution to the subject: Agius: 'Red Sea folk beliefs', pp. 131–61.
3. See Nicolini: 'Some thoughts of the magical practice of the *zār* along the Red Sea in the Sudan', p. 160.
4. Sūrat Yūsuf ('[The Story of] Joseph'), 12: 64; see Lane: *An Account of the Manners and Customs of the Modern Egyptians*, vol. I, p. 377.
5. Cited in Foster: *The Red Sea and Adjacent Countries at the Close of the Seventeenth Century*, pp. 19, 73.
6. See Morton Nance: 'Terradas and talismans', pp. 8 and 10.
7. Proverbs 23: 6.
8. Sūrat al-Qalam ('The Pen'), 68: 51; see *The Holy Qur-an: Text, Translation and Commentary*, vol. II, p. 1594, fn. 5633.
9. See LeBaron Bowen: 'Primitive watercraft of Arabia', p. 200; 'Maritime superstitions of the Arabs', p. 24; Moore: 'Notes on "dhows"', p. 205; Hornell: 'Boat *oculi* survivals', pp. 339–49; 'Survivals of the use of *oculi* in modern boats', pp. 289–321.
10. Hornell: *Water Transport*, p. 285 seq.
11. Ettinghausen: 'The man-made setting', p. 68.
12. See Perrier: *Les boutres de Djibouti*, pp. 104–109.
13. Agius: 'Decorative motifs on Red Sea boats', pp. 101–10.
14. See Agius: *In the Wake of the Dhow*, p. 36; see also Foster: *Landscape with Arabs*, p. 180.
15. See Guiley and Imbrogno: *The Djinn Connection*.

16. Sūrat al-Jinn ('The Spirits'), 72: 1–28; Sūrat al-Ḥijr ('The Rocky Tract'), 15: 27; Sūrat Sabā ('[The City] of Sabā'), 34: 41; Sūrat al-Aḥqāf ('Winding Sand-Tracts'), 46: 29–32.
17. Sūrat al-Raḥmān ('[God] Most Gracious'), 55: 15. See *The Holy Qur-an: Text, Translation and Commentary*, vol. II, p. 1474 and fn. 5182.
18. *The Holy Qur-an: Text, Translation and Commentary*, vol. II, p. 1474, fn. 5182.
19. Wehr: *A Dictionary of Modern Written Arabic*, p. 138.
20. Sūrat al-An'ām ('Cattle'), 6: 6 and Sūrat al-Ṣāffāt ('Those Ranged in Ranks') 37: 159.
21. *The Holy Qur-an: Text, Translation and Commentary*, vol. I, p. 319, fn. 929.
22. Al-Shāfa'ī: *Al-Silāḥ wa l-'udda fī tārīkh Bandar Judda*, pp. 53–4.
23. Thomas: *Arabia Felix*, p. 44.
24. Interviewed on 9 and 10 February 2004.
25. Interviewed on 14 May 2010.
26. Thomas: *Arabia Felix*, pp. 117–18.
27. Ibid.
28. Myers: 'Little Aden folklore', p. 215.
29. Burton: *A Secret Pilgrimage to Mecca and Medina*, pp. 124, 129, 132.
30. Nicolini: 'Some thoughts of the magical practice of the *zār* along the Red Sea in the Sudan', p. 159.
31. De Montfreid: *Secrets of the Red Sea*, p. 48.
32. Interviewed on 22 October 2009.
33. Interviewed on 29 May 2010.
34. Interviewed on 22 October 2009.
35. Myers: 'Little Aden folklore', p. 198.
36. Ibid., p. 220.
37. Cited by G. Rex Smith in *A Traveller in Thirteenth-Century Arabia*, p. 136, fn. 5.
38. Serjeant: 'Maritime customary law off the Arabian coasts', p. 199.
39. Burckhardt: *Travels in Arabia*, p. 429.
40. Ibid.
41. See al-Nuwayrī l-Iskandarānī: *Kitāb al-ilmām bil-iᶜlām) fī mā jarat bihi l-aḥkām*, vol. II, p. 232; see also Agius: *Classic Ships of Islam*, p. 161.
42. Spilka and Ladd: *The Psychology of Prayer*, pp. 172–3.
43. Ladd and McIntosh: 'Meaning, God, and prayer', p. 29; see also Spilka and Ladd: *The Psychology of Prayer*, p. 171.
44. Burton: *Personal Narrative of a Pilgrimage to Al-Madinah and Meccah*, vol. I, p. 194.
45. See Conrad: 'Islam and the sea', p. 152.
46. *The Travels of Ibn Baṭṭūṭa*, vol. I, pp. 25–6.
47. Sūrat al-Naḥl ('The Bee'), 16: 14.
48. Interviewed on 17 October 2009.
49. Capps: 'The psychology of petitionary prayer', pp. 130–41.
50. Spilka and Ladd: *The Psychology of Prayer*, p. 173.
51. Ibid.
52. Schoff: 'Cinnamon, cassia and Somaliland', p. 260.
53. Nalesini: 'Sacred places and beings of the Red Sea littoral societies', p. 80.
54. Moreman: 'Rehabilitating the spirituality of pre-Islamic Arabia', p. 142.
55. Burckhardt: *Travels in Arabia*, p. 429.
56. Burton: *A Secret Pilgrimage to Mecca and Medina*, pp. 124, 129, 132.
57. De Monfreid: *La perle noire*, p. 36.

58. Ibid., p. 38.
59. Klunzinger: *Upper Egypt: Its People and its Products*, p. 104.
60. Agius: '"Leave your homeland in search of prosperity"', pp. 370–2, 378–9.
61. An example of such holy men's tombs is the Haji Ali Dargah, a mausoleum with windswept domes and minarets on a small island that is connected to the mainland by a causeway in south Mumbai. Here, people of various faiths pay their respects to Haji Ali – the protector of seafarers. Visitors donate food that is then distributed to the poor.
62. Merchant: 'Reinventing Eden', p. 158.
63. De Monfreid: *Secrets of the Red Sea*, p. 290; see also Treat: *Pearls Arms and Hashish*, pp. 252–3.
64. Stone: 'Notes on the crafts, customs and local industries of the north Yemen Tihāmah', p. 121, fn. 79.
65. Auchterlonie: *Encountering Islam*, p. 184.
66. Crossland: *Desert and Water Gardens of the Red Sea*, p. 37.
67. Doyle: *Lone Dhow*, p. 27.
68. Not to be confused with the Egyptian Sheikh al-Shadhili, discussed earlier.
69. See Walls: *Preservation of Monuments and Sites*.
70. Myers: 'Little Aden folklore', pp. 193–4.
71. Ibid., p. 195.
72. Fagan: *Beyond the Blue Horizon*, p. 14.
73. Rouaud: 'Tadjurra', p. 71.
74. Foster: *Landscape with Arabs*, p. 177.

18 CULTURAL IDENTITIES OF A RED SEA LANDSCAPE: RECOLLECTIONS AND REFLECTIONS

1. Translation from *The Holy Qur-an: Text, Translation and Commentary*, vol. II, p. 1088.
2. Bāṭarfī: *Jidda, umm al-rakhā wa l-shidda*, p. 58.
3. Assmann: 'Canon and archive', p. 106.
4. http://www.dictionary.com/browse/cognitive (accessed 1 June 2017).
5. Miran: 'Mapping space and mobility in the Red Sea region', p. 207.
6. Ibid., p. 208.
7. Ibid., p. 208.
8. See Lesourd: 'Notes sur les nawakhid, navigateurs de la Mer Rouge', p. 347.
9. Ibid.
10. A discussion on the criteria early lexicographers applied to decide what fits the Arabic mould is in Agius: *Arabic Literary Works as a Source of Documentation for Technical Terms of the Material Culture*, pp. 123–9.
11. See Alhazmi: *Maritime Terminology of the Saudi Arabian Red Sea Coast*, pp. 151–70.
12. Ibid., ch. 9.
13. Interviewed on 21 October 2009.
14. Interviewed on 10 January and 11 May 2010.
15. Interviewed on 16 May 2010.
16. Interviewed on 12 May 2007.
17. Aylin Orbaşlı has investigated 'coral stone conservation' and adaptation using 'traditional repair techniques' to renovate these buildings; see Orbaşlı:

'The conservation of coral buildings on Saudi Arabia's northern Red Sea coast', p. 51.

18. Information provided by Muhammad Alhazmi, written communication, 20 November 2017.
19. Greenlaw: *The Coral Buildings of Suakin*, p. 10.
20. *Travels of James Bruce, through Part of Africa, Syria, Egypt and Arabia into Abyssinia to Discover the Source of the Nile*, p. 75.
21. See Le Quesne: *Quseir*, p. 37 seq.
22. Breen: 'Towards an archaeology of early Islamic ports on the Western Red Sea coast', p. 315.
23. Bouhdiba: 'Trans-national practices and sanitary risks in the Red Sea region', p. 226.
24. See Wehr: *A Dictionary of Modern Written Arabic*, p. 172.
25. Interviewed on 16 May 2010.
26. *Travels of Ibn Jubayr*, p. 68.
27. Lane: *Arabic–English Lexicon*, vol. II, p. 2532.
28. Ibid., p. 2534.
29. See Regourd: 'Arabic language on documents on paper', pp. 339–41.
30. See Davies: *Bernard von Breydenbach and his Journey to the Holy Land*; I am grateful to Marita Koornwinder, who drew my attention to this information, personal communication, 3 June 2004.
31. Assmann: 'Canon and archive', p. 99.
32. Muftāḥ: *Farasān, al-nās wa l-tārīkh*, pp. 120–31.
33. Ibid., p. 65.
34. See Agius, Cooper, Semaan, Zazzaro and Carter: 'Remembering the sea', pp. 134, 171.
35. Sūrat al-mā'ida ('The Table Spread') 5: 99; translation in *The Holy Qur-an: Text, Translation and Commentary*, vol. I, p. 273.
36. See, e.g., Bent and Bent: *Southern Arabia*, p. 9.
37. Nicolini: 'Some thoughts on the magical practice of the *zār* along the Red Sea in the Sudan', p. 160.
38. Munif: *Cities of Salt*.
39. See Al-Sarrani: 'From soil to oil', pp. 20–3.
40. Tuddenham: 'Maritime cultural landscapes, maritimity and quasi objects', p. 8.
41. Agius, Cooper, Semaan, Zazzaro and Carter: 'Remembering the sea', p. 173.
42. Interviewed on 17 May 2010.

BIBLIOGRAPHY

Abū Shūsha, Ṭalāl, Manṣūr Kalantan, Ḥusayn al-Nāẓrī and Yāsir al-Ghāmdī, *Asmāk min al- miyāh al-iqlīmiyya lil-mamlaka fī l-baḥr al-aḥmar* (Riyadh, 1432/2011).

Admiralty Sailing Directions. Red Sea and Gulf of Aden Pilot (London, 2015; eighteenth edition).

Agius, Dionisius A., *Arabic Literary Works as a Source of Documentation for Technical Terms of the Material Culture* [Islamkundliche Untersuchungen No. 98] (Berlin, 1984).

Agius, Dionisius A., 'Medieval Qalhat: Travellers, dhows and stone anchors in south-east Oman', in *Archaeology of Seafaring: The Indian Ocean in the Ancient Period*, ed. H.P. Ray (Delhi, 1999), pp. 173–220.

Agius, Dionisius A., *In the Wake of the Dhow: The Arabian Gulf and Oman* (Reading, 2002; second edition 2010).

Agius, Dionisius A., '"Leave your homeland in search of prosperity": The ostrich egg in a burial site at Quseir al-Qadim in the Mamluk period', in *Egypt and Syria in the Fatimid, Ayyubid and Mamluk Era*, ed. U. Vermeulen and J. Van Steenbergen (Leuven, 2005), pp. 355–79.

Agius, Dionisius A., *Seafaring in the Arabian Gulf and Oman: The People of the Dhow* (London, 2005).

Agius, Dionisius A., 'Decorative motifs on Red Sea boats: Meaning and identity', in *Natural Resources and Cultural Connections of the Red Sea: Proceedings of Red Sea Project III*, ed. J. Starkey, P. Starkey and T. Wilkinson [Society for Arabian Studies Monograph No. 5] (Oxford, 2007), pp. 101–10.

Agius, Dionisius A., *Classic Ships of Islam: From Mesopotamia to the Indian Ocean* (Leiden, 2008).

Agius, Dionisius A., 'The Rashayda: Ethnic identity and dhow activity in Suakin on the Red Sea coast', *Northeast African Studies* [special issue], 12/1 (2012), pp. 169–216.

Agius, Dionisius A., 'Red Sea folk beliefs: A maritime spirit landscape', *Northeast African Studies* [special issue], 17/1 (2017), pp. 131–61.

Agius, Dionisius A., John P. Cooper, Julian Jansen Van Rensburg and Chiara Zazzaro, 'The dhow's last redoubt? Vestiges of wooden boatbuilding traditions in Yemen', *Proceedings of the Seminar for Arabian Studies*, 40 (2010), pp. 71–84.

Agius, Dionisius A., John P. Cooper and Chiara Zazzaro, 'The maritime heritage of Yemen: A focus on traditional wooden "dhows"', in *Ships, Saints and Sealore: Cultural*

Heritage and Ethnography of the Mediterranean and the Red Sea, ed. D.A. Agius, T. Gambin and A. Trakadas (Oxford, 2014), pp. 143–57.

Agius, Dionisius A., John P. Cooper, Lucy Semaan, Chiara Zazzaro and Robert Carter, 'Remembering the sea: Personal and communal recollections of maritime life in Jizan and the Farasan Islands, Saudi Arabia', *Journal of Maritime Archaeology*, 11/2 (2016), pp. 127–77.

Alhazmi, Muhammad Zafer, *Maritime Terminology of the Saudi Arabian Red Sea Coast: A Lexical Semantic Study* (Berlin, 2016).

Ali, Abdullah Yusuf, see *The Holy Qur-an: Text, Translation and Commentary*.

Ali Bey, see *Travels of Ali Bey*.

Alian, Mohamed, *In the Memory of the Sambuq: Record of a Way of Life* (Ruwi, 2006).

Alsharif, Fahad, 'The good, the bad and the ugly: Undocumented labour in Saudi Arabia: The case of Jeddah', Ph.D. thesis, University of Exeter (2015).

Anāstās Mārī l-Kirmilī, 'Al-kalim al-yūnāniyya fī lughat al-'arabiyya', *Al-Mashriq*, 3 (1900), pp. 63–8.

Assmann, Aleida, 'Canon and archive', in *Cultural Memory Studies: An International and Interdisciplinary Handbook*, ed. A. Erll and A. Nünning (Berlin, 2010), pp. 97–108.

Auchterlonie, Paul, *Encountering Islam: Joseph Pitts: An English Slave in 17th-Century Algiers and Mecca* (London, 2012).

Azab, M.A., 'Flood hazard between Marsa Alam-Ras Banas, Red Sea, Egypt', in *Fourth Environmental Conference* [Faculty of Science, Zagazig University] (Zagazig, 2009), pp. 17–35.

Barbosa, Duarte, see *Book of Duarte Barbosa*.

Bardey, Alfred, *Barr-Adjam: Souvenirs d'Afrique Orientale 1880–1887* (Paris, 1981).

Bāṭarfī, Khālid Muḥammad, *Jidda, umm al-rakhā wa l-shidda* (Jeddah, 1418/1997).

Becker, Carl H. [Charles F. Beckingham], 'Baḥr al-Ḳulzum', in *Encyclopaedia of Islam*, volume I (Leiden, 1960; second edition), pp. 931–3.

Bent, Theodore and Mrs Theodore Bent, *Southern Arabia* (London, 1900; new edition Reading, 1994).

Berlioux, Étienne-Félix, *La traite orientale: Histoire des chasses à l'homme organisées en Afrique depuis quinze ans pour les marchés de l'Orient* (Paris, 1870).

Bloss, John F.E., 'The story of Suakin, I', *Sudan Notes and Records*, 19/2 (1936), pp. 271–300.

Bloss, John F.E., 'The story of Suakin, II', *Sudan Notes and Records*, 19/2 (1937), pp. 247–80.

Blue, Lucy, Julian Whitewright and John P. Cooper, 'The ubiquitous *hūrī*: Maritime ethnography, archaeology and history in the Western Indian Ocean', in *Ships and Maritime Landscapes: Proceedings of the Thirteenth International Symposium on Boat and Ship Archaeology*, ed. J. Gawronski, A. van Holk and J. Schokkenbroek (Elde, 2017), pp. 185–92.

Book of Duarte Barbosa, trans. M. Longworth Dames, volumes I–II (London, 1918–21).

Bosch, Donald and Eloise Bosch, *Seashells of Southern Arabia* (Dubai, 1989).

Bouhdiba, Sofiane, 'Trans-national practices and sanitary risks in the Red Sea region: The case of the pilgrimage to Mecca', in *Connected Hinterlands: Proceedings of Red Sea Project IV*, ed. L. Blue, J.P. Cooper, R. Thomas and J. Whitewright [British Foundation for the Study of Arabia Monograph No. 8] (Oxford, 2009), pp. 225–8.

Braudel, Fernand, *The Mediterranean and the Mediterranean World in the Age of Philip II*, trans. S. Reynolds, volumes I–II (New York, 1972).

Braudel, Fernand, *The Mediterranean and the Mediterranean World in the Age of Philip II*, trans. S. Reynolds, volumes I–III (London, 2000).

Breen, Colin, 'Towards an archaeology of early Islamic ports on the western Red Sea coast', *Journal of Maritime Archaeology* [special issue], 8/2 (2013), pp. 311–23.

Broich, John, *Squadron: Ending the African Slave Trade* (London, 2017).

Brouwer, C.G., *Al-Mukhā: Profile of a Yemeni Seaport as Sketched by Servants of the Dutch East India Company VOC 1614–1640* (Amsterdam, 1997).

Bruce, James, *Travels to Discover the Source of the Nile in the Years 1768–73*, volumes I–III (London, n.d.).

Bruce, James, see *Travels of James Bruce*.

Burckhardt, Johann Ludwig, *Travels in Nubia* (London, 1819).

Burckhardt, Johann Ludwig, *Travels in Arabia* (London, 1829).

Burdett, Anita L.P. (ed.), *Slave Trade into Arabia*, volumes I–IX (Slough, 2006).

Burnes, Alexander, 'On the maritime communications of India, as carried on by the natives, particularly from Kutch, at the mouth of the Nidus', *Journal of the Royal Geographical Society of London*, 6 (1836), pp. 23–9.

Burton, Isabel, *Arabia, Egypt, India: A Narrative of Travel* (Cambridge, 1879).

Burton, Richard F., *Personal Narrative of a Pilgrimage to Al-Madinah and Meccah*, volumes I–II (London, 1893; new edition New York, 1964).

Burton, Richard F., *First Footsteps in East Africa* (Köln, 2000).

Burton, Richard F., *A Secret Pilgrimage to Mecca and Medina* (London, 2004).

Buxton, E.N., *On Either Side of the Red Sea* (London, 1895).

Capps, D., 'The psychology of petitionary prayer', *Theology Today*, 39/2 (1982), pp. 130–41.

Carter, Robert, *Sea of Pearls: Seven Thousand Years of the Industry that Shaped the Gulf* (London, 2012).

Chateau, Christiane, Paul Nougarède and L.M. Bayle, *Les derniers boutres d'Aden* (Paris, 1963).

Chaudhuri, Kirti N., *Trade and Civilisation in the Indian Ocean: An Economic History from the Rise of Islam to 1750* (New Delhi, 1985).

Clarence-Smith, William Gervase, *Islam and the Abolition of Slavery* (London, 2006).

Clouet, Alain G., 'La navigation au long cours yéménite de nos jours vers l'Afrique Orientale', *Pount: Bulletin de la Société d'Études de l'Afrique Orientale*, 12 (1973), pp. 13–18.

Colomb, Philip Howard, *Slave-Catching in the Indian Ocean: A Record of Naval Experiences* (London, 1873; new edition 1968).

The Commentaries of the Great Alfonso Dalboquerque, trans. W. De Gray Birch, volumes I–IV (London, 1875–84).

Conrad, Lawrence L., 'Islam and the sea: Paradigms and problematics', *Al-Qantara*, 23/1 (2002), pp. 123–54.

Cooper, John P., *The Medieval Nile: Route, Navigation and Landscape in Islamic Egypt* (Cairo and New York, 2014).

Cooper, John P., Dionisius A. Agius, Tom Collie and Faisal Al-Naimi, 'Boat and ship engravings at al-Zubārah, Qatar: The *dāw* exposed?', *Proceedings of the Seminar for Arabian Studies*, 45 (2015), pp. 35–47.

Cooper, John P. and Chiara Zazzaro, 'The Farasan Islands, Saudi Arabia: Towards a chronology of settlement', *Arabian Archaeology and Epigraphy*, 25/2 (2014), pp. 147–74.
Cortesão, A. and L. Albuquerque (eds), *Obras completas de João de Castro*, volume II (Coimbra, 1971).
Coupland, Reginald, *East Africa and its Invaders: From the Earliest Times to the Death of Sayyid Said in 1856* (Oxford, 1938; new edition New York, 1965).
Crossland, Cyril, *Desert and Water Gardens of the Red Sea: Being an Account of the Natives and the Shore Formations of the Coast* (Cambridge, 1913; new edition 2010).
D'Alboquerque, see *The Commentaries of the Great Alfonso Dalboquerque.*
Da Gama, Vasco, see *Three Voyages of Vasco da Gama and his Viceroyalty.*
Dale, Stephen, 'The Hadhrami diaspora in south-western India: The role of the Sayyids of the Malabar Coast', in *Hadhrami, Traders, Scholars and Statesmen in the Indian Ocean, 1750s–1960s*, eds U. Freitag and W.G. Clarence-Smith (Leiden, 1997), pp. 75–184.
Davies, Charles, *The Blood-Red Arab Flag: An Investigation into Qasimi Piracy 1797–1820* (Exeter, 1997).
Davies, Hugh William, *Bernard von Breydenbach and his Journey to the Holy Land* (Utrecht, 1483–4; new edition 1968).
Davis, David B., *The Problem of Slavery in the Age of Revolution, 1770–1823* (Oxford and New York, 1999).
De Camões, Luís Vaz, *The Lusíads*, trans. Landeg White (Oxford, 1997).
De Landberg, Le Comte, *Glossaire Daṯînois*, ed. K.V. Zetterstéen, volumes I–III (Leiden, 1920–42).
De Monfreid, Henry, *Secrets of the Red Sea*, trans. Helen Buchanan Bell (London, 1934).
De Monfreid, Henry, *Hashish: The Autobiography of a Red Sea Smuggler*, trans. Helen Buchanan Bell (New York, 1973).
De Monfreid, Henry, *La perle noire* (Paris, 2009).
Denon, Vivant, *Travels in Upper and Lower Egypt, during the Campaigns of General Bonaparte*, trans. F. Blagdon, volumes I–II (London, 1802; new edition 1986).
Devereux, William Cope, *A Cruise in the 'Gorgon'* (London, 1968).
Di Varthema, Ludovico, see *The Travels of Ludovico di Varthema*
Ḍirār, Muḥammad Ṣāliḥ, *Tārīkh Sawākin wa l-baḥr al-aḥmar* (Khartoum, 1408/1988).
Donaldson, William James, 'Erythraean ichthyophagi: Arabian fish-eaters observed', *New Arabian Studies*, 5 (2000), pp. 7–32.
Doughty, Charles M., *Travels in Arabia Deserta*, volumes I–II (London, 1888; new edition 1943).
Doyle, Adrian Conan, *Lone Dhow* (London, 1963).
Dozy, Reinhart, *Dictionnaire détaillé des noms des vêtements chez les arabes* (Amsterdam, 1845; new edition Beirut, n.d.).
Dozy, Reinhart, *Supplément aux dictionnaires arabes*, volumes I–II (Leiden and Paris, 1967; third edition).
Dozy, Reinhart and Willem Herman Engelmann, *Glossaire des mots espagnols et portuguais dérivés de l'arabe* (Leiden, 1869).
Dubois, Colette, 'The Red Sea ports during the revolution in transportation', in *Modernity and Culture from the Mediterranean to the Indian Ocean*, eds L. Tarazi Fawaz and C.A. Bayly (New York, 2002), pp. 58–74.

Dubois, Colette, 'Un traite tardive en Mer Rouge méridionale: La route des esclaves du Golfe de Tadjoura (1880–1936)', in *Traites et esclavages en afrique oriental et dans l'océan indien*, eds H. Médard, M.-L. Derat, T. Vernet and M.-P. Ballarin (Paris, 2013), pp. 197–222.

Edwards, Alasdair and Stephen Head, 'Climate and oceanography', in *Key Environments: Red Sea*, eds A. Edwards and S. Head (Oxford, 1987), pp. 45–69.

Edye, John, 'Description of the various classes of vessels constructed and employed by the natives of the coasts of Coromandel, Malabar, and the Island of Ceylon for their coasting navigation', *Journal of the Royal Asiatic Society*, 1 (1835), pp. 1–14.

Eltayeb, Mohamed Mustafa, 'Review of the trochus fishery in Sudan', *Trochus Information Bulletin*, 11 (September 2004), pp. 5–7.

Ettinghausen, Richard, 'The man-made setting: Islamic art and architecture', in *The World of Islam: Faith, People and Culture*, ed. B. Lewis (London, 1976), pp. 57–88.

Ewald, Janet J., 'The Nile Valley system and the Red Sea slave trade 1820–1880', *Slavery and Abolition*, 9/3 (1988), pp. 71–92.

Ewald, Janet J., 'Crossers of the sea: Slaves, freedmen, and other migrants in the northwestern Indian Ocean, *c.*1750–1914', *American Historical Review*, 105/1 (2000), pp. 69–91.

Facey, William, 'The Red Sea: The wind regime and location of ports', in *Red Sea Trade and Travel in the Red Sea Region: Proceedings of the Red Sea Project 1*, eds P. Lunde and A. Porter [Society for Arabian Studies Monograph No. 2] (Oxford, 2004), pp. 7–17.

Facey, William, 'Sailing the Red Sea', in *The Principles of Arab Navigation*, eds A.R. Constable and W. Facey (London, 2013), pp. 97–114.

Facey, William and Michael Rice Facey, *Oman: A Seafaring Nation* (Muscat, 1979).

Fagan, Brian, *Beyond the Blue Horizon: How the Earliest Mariners Unlocked the Secrets of the Oceans* (London, 2012).

Ferrand, Gabriel, 'L'élément persan dans les textes nautiques arabes des XVe et XVIe siècles', *Journal Asiatique*, 204 (1924), pp. 193–257.

Fontrier, Marc, *Abou-Bakr Ibrahim, Pacha de Zeyla, marchand d'esclaves: Commerce et diplomatie dans le Golfe de Tadjoura* (Paris, 2003).

Footman, David, *Antonin Besse of Aden* (Basingstoke and Oxford, 1986).

Foster, Donald, *Landscape with Arabs: Travels in Aden and South Arabia* (London, 1969).

Foster, William, *England's Quest of Eastern Trade* (London, 1933).

Foster, William (ed.), *The Red Sea and Adjacent Countries at the Close of the Seventeenth Century* (Lichtenstein, 1967).

Fowler, Henry W., 'The fishes of the Red Sea', *Sudan Notes and Records*, 26/1 (1945), pp. 113–37.

Fraenkel, Siegmund, *Die Aramäischen Fremdwörter im Arabischen* (Leiden, 1886; new edition Hildesheim, 1962).

Freitag, Ulrike, 'A twentieth-century merchant network centered on Jeddah: The correspondence of Muḥammad b. Aḥmad Bin Ḥimd', *Northeast African Studies* [special issue], 17/1 (2017), pp. 101–29.

Gardet, Louis, 'Īmān', *Encyclopaedia of Islam*, volume III (Leiden, 1971; second edition), pp. 1170–4.

Gardet, Louis, 'Al-ḳaḍā' wa 'l-ḳadar', *Encyclopaedia of Islam*, volume IV (Leiden, 1990; second edition), pp. 365–7.

Al-Ghabbân, Alî Ibrâhîm, *Les deux routes syrienne et égyptienne de pèlerinage au nord- ouest de l'Arabie Saudite*, volumes I–II (Cairo, 2011).
Ghabbān, 'Alī Bin Ibrāhīm, *Shamāl gharb al-mamlaka l-'arabiyya l-sa'ūdiyya* (Riyadh, 1413/1993).
Glidden, Harold W., 'A comparative study of the Arabic nautical vocabulary from al-Aqabah, Transjordan', *Journal of the American Oriental Society*, 62 (1942), pp. 68–72.
Greenlaw, Jean-Pierre, *The Coral Buildings of Suakin* (London, 1975; new edition 1995).
Guiley, Rosemary Ellen and Philip J. Imbrogno, *The Djinn Connection: Unveiling the Hidden Agendas of Genies* (Woodbury, MN, 2011).
Guy, John, 'Rare and strange goods: International trade in ninth century Asia', in *Shipwrecked: Tang Treasures and Monsoon Winds*, eds R. Krahl, J. Guy, J. Keith Wilson and J. Raby (Washington, DC, 2010), pp. 19–34.
Hamilton, Genesta, *The Princes of Zinj: The Rulers of Zanzibar* (London, 1957).
Al-Ḥarbī, Sāmī Sulaymān, *Al-Thaqāfa l-munākhiyya bayn al-ḍarūra l-ḥatmiyya wa l-aḥkām al-shar'iyya wa l-dirāsa l-taṭbīqiyya* (Jeddah, 1432/2011).
Harris, William Cornwallis, *The Highlands of Aethiopia*, volumes I–III (London, 1844).
Ḥasan, Yusuf F., *The Arabs and the Sudan from the Seventh to the Early Sixteenth Century* (Khartoum, 1967; new edition 1973).
Hawkins, Clifford W., *The Dhow: An Illustrated History of the Dhow and its World* (Lymington, 1977).
Hazell, Alastair, *The Last Slave Market* (London, 2012).
Head, Stephen M., 'Introduction', in *Key Environments: The Red Sea*, eds A.J. Edwards and S.M. Head (Oxford, 1987), pp. 1–21.
Helfritz, Hans, *The Yemen: A Secret Journey*, trans. M. Heron (London, 1958).
Hillelson, S, "Abābda', in *Encyclopaedia of Islam*, volume I (Leiden, 1960; second edition), pp. 1–2.
The Holy Qur-an: Text, Translation and Commentary, trans. A. Yusuf Ali, volumes I–II (Cambridge, MA, 1946).
Hornell, James, 'The origins and ethnological significance of the Indian boat designs', *Memoirs of the Asiatic Society of Bengal*, 7/3 (1920), pp. 139–256.
Hornell, James, 'Survivals of the use of *oculi* in modern boats', *Journal of the Royal Anthropological Institute of Great Britain and Ireland*, 53/2 (1923), pp. 289–321.
Hornell, James, 'Boat *oculi* survivals: Additional records', *Journal of the Royal Anthropological Institute of Great Britain and Ireland*, 68/2 (1938), pp. 339–49.
Hornell, James, 'A tentative classification of Arab sea-craft', *Mariner's Mirror*, 28/1 (1942), pp. 11–40.
Hornell, James, 'The sailing craft of western India', *Mariner's Mirror*, 32/4 (1946), pp. 195–217.
Hornell, James, *Water Transport: Origins and Early Evolution* (Cambridge, 1946).
Hoskins, Halford Lancaster, *British Routes to India* (London, 1928; new edition 1966).
Howarth, David, *Dhows* (London, 1977).
Hubaylī, Munā Bint Muḥammad Aḥmad and Laylā Bint Muḥammad Aḥmad Hubaylī, *Jazīrat Farasān: Al-tārīkh wa l-siyāḥa*, rev. and ed. F. Al-Ḥarbī (Jizan, 1431/2009).
Huber, Valeska, *Channelling Mobilities: Migration and Globalisation in the Suez Canal Region and beyond 1869–1914* (Cambridge, 2013).

Hunter, Captain F.M., *An Account of the British Settlement of Aden in Arabia* (London, 1877).

Hurgronje, Christiaan Snouck, *Mekka in the Latter Part of the 19th Century: Daily Life, Customs and Learning: The Moslims of the East-Indian Archipelago*, trans. J.H. Monahan (Leiden, 2007).

Ibn al-Mujāwir, Jamāl al-Dīn, see *A Traveller in Thirteenth-Century Arabia.*

Ibn Baṭṭūṭa, Abū 'Abd Allāh Muḥammad, see *The Travels of Ibn Baṭṭūṭa.*

Ibn Jubayr, Abū l-Ḥasan Muḥammad, see *Travels of Ibn Jubayr.*

Ibn Mājid, Aḥmad, see Tibbetts, Gerald R., *Arab Navigation in the Indian Ocean*

Ibn Shahriyār, Buzurg, *Kitāb 'ajā'ib al-Hind (Livre des merveilles de l'Inde)*, Arabic text ed. P.A. Van der Lith, trans. L. Marcel Devic (Leiden, 1883–6).

Ibn Shahriyār, Buzurg, *The Book of the Wonders of India*, ed. and trans. G.S.P. Freeman-Grenville (London and The Hague, 1981).

Issa, Amina A., 'Dhows and epidemics in the Indian Ocean ports', *Ziff Journal*, 3 (2006), pp. 63–70.

The Itinerário of Jerónimo Lobo, trans. D.M. Lockhart, ed. M.G. Da Costa, introduction and notes C.F. Beckingham (London, 1984).

Jansen Van Rensburg, Julian, *The Maritime Traditions of the Fishermen of Socotra, Yemen* (Oxford, 2016).

Al-Jawālīqī, Abū Manṣūr Mawhūb b. Aḥmad b. Muḥammad, *Kitāb al-mu'arrab min al-kalām al-a'jamī 'alā ḥurūf al-mu'jam*, ed. A.M. Shākir (Tehran, 1389/1969).

Jewell, John A., *Dhows at Mombasa* (Nairobi, 1969).

Johnstone, Thomas Muir, 'Folklore and folk literature', *Arabian Studies*, 1 (1974), pp. 7–25.

Kane, Thomas Leiper, *Tigrinya–English Dictionary*, volume II (Springfield, IL, 2000).

Al-Kasādī, Badr Aḥmad Sālim, *Abṭāl mansiyyūn min rabābina l-milāḥiyya l-baḥriyya l-'arabiyya*, rev. M. 'Alawī Bāhārūn (Abu Dhabi, 2012).

Kawatoko, Mutsuo, *A Port City Site on the Sinai Peninsula: Al-Ṭūr: The 13th Expedition in 1996 – a Summary Report* (Tokyo, 1998).

Kay, Shirley, *Saudi Arabia: Past and Present* (London, 1979).

Keay, John, *The Honourable Company: A History of the English East India Company* (London, 1993).

Kemp, Peter (ed.), *The Oxford Companion to Ships and the Sea* (Oxford, 1976; new edition 1992).

Kentley, Eric George, 'Suakin and its fishermen: A study of economic activities and ethnic groupings in a Sudanese port', Ph.D. thesis, University of Hull (1988).

Klunzinger, Carl Benjamin, *Upper Egypt: Its People and its Products* (New York, 1878; new edition 2000).

Kunitzsch, P., 'Al-Manāzil', in *Encyclopaedia of Islam*, volume VI (Leiden, 1991; second edition), pp. 374–6.

Ladd, Kevin L. and Daniel N. McIntosh, 'Meaning, God, and prayer: Physical and metaphysical aspects and social support', *Religion and Culture*, 11/1 (2008), pp. 23–38.

Lane, Edward, *An Account of the Manners and Customs of the Modern Egyptians*, volumes I–II (London, 1842).

Lane, Edward W., *Arabic–English Lexicon*, volumes I–II (Cambridge, 1984).

LeBaron Bowen, Richard Jr., 'Arab dhows of eastern Arabia', *American Neptune*, 9/1 (1949), pp. 87–132.

LeBaron Bowen, Richard Jr., 'The dhow sailor', *American Neptune*, 11/3 (1951), pp. 161–203.
LeBaron Bowen, Richard Jr., 'Primitive watercraft of Arabia', *American Neptune* 12/3 (1952), pp. 186–221.
LeBaron Bowen, Richard Jr., 'Maritime superstitions of the Arabs', *American Neptune* 15/1 (1955), pp. 5–48.
LeBaron Bowen, Richard Jr., 'Origin and diffusion of *oculi*', *American Neptune* 17/4 (1957), pp. 262–91.
Le Quesne, Charles, *Quseir: An Ottoman and Napoleonic Fortress on the Red Sea Coast of Egypt* (Cairo, 2007).
Leslau, Wolf, *Concise Amharic Dictionary* (Addis Ababa, 2002).
Lesourd, Michel, 'Notes sur les nawakhid, navigateurs de la mer rouge', *Bulletin de l'Institut Fondamental de l'Afrique Noire*, 22/1–2 (1960), pp. 346–53.
Lewis, Norman, *Sand and Sea in Arabia* (London, 1938).
Lewis, W.H., *Levantine Adventurer: The Travels and Missions of the Chevalier d'Arvieux 1653–1697* (New York, 1963).
Liddell, Henry George and Robert Scott, *A Greek–English Lexicon*, rev. H. Stuart and R. McKenzie (Oxford, 1843; revised ninth edition 1940; reprint 1953).
Lobo, Jerónimo, see *The Itinerário of Jerónimo Lobo*
Londres, Albert, *Pêcheurs de perles* (Dijon-Quetigny, 1931; new edition 2008).
Lunde, Paul, 'João de Castro's *Roteiro do Mar Roxo* (1541)', in *Connected Hinterlands: Proceedings of Red Sea Project IV*, eds L. Blue, J.P. Cooper, R. Thomas and J. Whitewright [Society for Arabian Studies Monograph No. 8] (Oxford, 2009), pp. 211–24.
McGrail, Seán, *Boats of the World: From the Stone Age to Medieval Times* (Oxford, 2001; new edition 2004).
McKinnon, Michael, *Arabia: Sand, Sea and Sky* (London, 1990).
McMaster, D.N., 'The ocean-going dhow trade to East Africa', *East African Geographical Review*, 6 (1966), pp. 13–24.
Makin, William J., *Red Sea Nights* (London, 1932).
Mallinson, Michael, 'Suakin 2003/4', *Sudan Archaeological Research Society Bulletin*, 8 (2004), pp. 90–5.
Mallinson, Michael, 'Suakin: Paradigm of a port', in *Navigated Spaces, Connected Spaces: Proceedings of Red Sea Project V*, eds D.A. Agius, J.P. Cooper, A. Trakadas and C. Zazzaro [British Foundation for the Study of Arabia Monograph No. 12] (Oxford, 2012), pp. 159–72.
Al-Maqrīzī, Taqī l-Dīn Abū l-'Abbās Aḥmad b. 'Alī b. 'Abd al-Qādir, *Kitāb al-mawā'iẓ wa l-i'tibār fī dhikr al-khiṭaṭ wa l-āthār*, ed. M.Q. al-'Adawī, volumes I–II (Bulaq, 1269/1853).
Al-Maqrīzī, Taqī l-Dīn Abū l-'Abbās Aḥmad b. Alī b. 'Abd al-Qādir, *Kitāb al-mawā'iẓ wa l-i'tibār fī dhikr al-khiṭaṭ wa l-āthār*, ed. F. Sayyid, volumes I–IV (London, 2002).
Marlowe, John, *The Making of the Suez Canal* (London, 1964).
Marshall, Ian, *Passage East*, commentary J. Maxtone-Graham (Charlottesville, VA, 1997).
Martin, Esmond Bradley and Chryssee Perry Martin, *Cargoes of the East: The Ports, Trade and Culture of the Arabian Seas and Western Indian Ocean* (London, 1972).
Al-Mas'ūdī, Abū l-Ḥasan 'Alī b. al-Ḥusayn, *Murūj al-dhahab wa ma'ādin al-jawhar*, ed. Y.A. Dāghir, volumes I–IV (Beirut, 1269/1983).
Matsumoto, David and Linda Juang, *Culture and Psychology* (Pacific Grove, CA, 1996).

Merchant, Carolyn, 'Reinventing Eden: Western culture as a recovery narrative', in *Uncommon Ground: Rethinking the Human Place in Nature*, ed. W. Cronon (London, 1996), pp. 133–59.
Miers, Suzanne, *Slavery in the Twentieth Century: The Evolution of a Global Problem* (Walnut Creek, CA, 2003).
Minawi, Mostafa, 'Telegraphs and territoriality in Ottoman Africa and Arabia during the age of high imperialism', *Journal of Balkan and Near Eastern Studies*, 18/6 (2017), pp. 567–87.
Miran, Jonathan, *Red Sea Citizens: Cosmopolitan Society and Cultural Change in Massawa* (Bloomington, IN, 2009).
Miran, Jonathan, 'Mapping space and mobility in the Red Sea region, *c.*1590–1950', *History Compass*, 12/2 (2014), pp. 197–216.
Montillier, Philippe, *Djibouti: Les caravaniers du sel* (Vétraz-Monthoux, 2000).
Moore, Alan, 'Craft of the Red Sea and Gulf of Aden', *Mariner's Mirror*, 6/3 (1920), pp. 73–6.
Moore, Alan, 'Craft of the Red Sea and Gulf of Aden, II', *Mariner's Mirror*, 6/4 (1920), pp. 98–104.
Moore, Alan, 'Craft of the Red Sea and Gulf of Aden, III', *Mariner's Mirror*, 6/5 (1920), pp. 136–42.
Moore, Alan, *Last Days of Mast and Sail* (Oxford, 1925; new edition Newton Abbot, 1970).
Moore, Alan, 'Notes on "dhows"', *Mariner's Mirror*, 26/2 (1940), pp. 205–13.
Moore-Harell, Alice, 'Slave trade in the Sudan in the nineteenth century and its suppression in the years 1877–80', *Middle Eastern Studies*, 34/2 (1998), pp. 113–28.
Moreman, Christopher M., 'Rehabilitating the spirituality of pre-Islamic Arabia: On the importance of the *kahin*, the *jinn*, and the tribal ancestral cult', *Journal of Religious History*, 41/2 (2017), pp. 137–57.
Moresby, Robert and T. Elwon, *Sailing Directions for the Red Sea* (New York, 2015; first published by the British Admiralty, nineteenth century).
Morgan, Elaine and Stephen Davies, *Red Sea Pilot* (Huntingdon, 2002).
Morier, James, *A Second Journey through Persia, Armenia, and Asia Minor to Constantinople between 1810 and 1816* (London, 1818).
Morton Nance, Robert, 'Terradas and talismans', *Mariner's Mirror*, 4/1 (1914), pp. 3–13.
Morton Nance, Robert, 'Fresh light on "terradas" and "gelves"', *Mariner's Mirror*, 6/2 (1920), pp. 34–9.
Muftāḥ, Ibrāhīm 'Abd Allāh, *Farasān: Al-nās, al-baḥr wa l-tārīkh* (Jeddah, 1426/2005).
Al-Mu'jam al-wasīṭ, eds I. Muṣṭafā, A. al-Zayyāt, Ḥ. 'Abd al-Qādir, M. al-Najjār and 'A.-Q. al-Salām Hārūn, volumes I–II (Cairo, 1379–80/1960–1).
Munif, Abdelrahman, *Cities of Salt*, trans. P. Theroux (New York, 1987).
Al-Muqaddasī, Muḥammad b. Aḥmad, *Aḥsan al-taqāsīm fī ma'rifat al-aqālīm*, ed. M.J. Goeje [Bibliotheca Geographorum Arabicorum No. 3] (Leiden, 1906).
Al-Muqaddasī, Muḥammad b. Aḥmad, *The Best Divisions for Knowledge of the Regions*, trans. B.A. Collins and M.H. Alta'i (Reading, 2001).
Mustaller, Michael, 'Maricultural development and management of shallow water marine resources in the Sudanese Red Sea', *Journal of the Faculty of Marine Science*, 2 (1982), pp. 37–43.
Myers, Oliver H., 'Little Aden folklore', *Bulletin de l'Institut Français d'Archéologie Orientale*, 44 (1947), pp. 177–233.

Nadvī, Syed Sulaimān, *The Arab Navigation* (Lahore, 1386/1966).
Al-Nakhīlī, Darwīsh, *Al-Sufun al-islāmiyya 'alā ḥurūf al-mu'jam* (Cairo, 1394/1974).
Nalesini, Oscar, 'Sacred places and beings of the Red Sea littoral societies', in *Navigated Spaces, Connected Places: Proceedings of Red Sea Project V*, eds D.A. Agius, J.P. Cooper, A. Trakadas and C. Zazzaro [British Foundation for the Study of Arabia Monograph No. 12] (Oxford, 2012), pp. 77–84.
Nash, Harriet, Dionisius A. Agius, Ali M. Al-Mahrooqi and Said Al-Yahyai, 'Stars used by fishermen in Oman', *International Journal of Nautical Archaeology*, 46/1 (2017), pp. 179–91.
Naumkin, Vitaly V., *Island of the Phoenix: An Ethnographic Study of the People of Socotra* (Reading, 1993).
Naumkin, Vitaly V., 'Myth, gender and eroticism in Socotran folklore', *Proceedings of the Seminar for Arabian Studies*, 31 (2001), pp. 189–94.
Nawwab, Ismail I., Peter C. Speers and Paul F. Hoye, *Aramco and its World: Arabia and the Middle East* (Washington, DC, 1981).
Nicholl, Charles, *Somebody Else: Arthur Rimbaud in Africa 1880–1891* (London, 1997).
Nicolini, Beatrice, 'Some thoughts of the magical practice of the *zār* along the Red Sea in the Sudan', in *People of the Red Sea: Proceedings of Red Sea Project II*, ed. J.C.M. Starkey [Society for Arabian Studies Monograph No. 3] (Oxford, 2005), pp. 157–62.
Niebuhr, Carsten, *Travels through Arabia and Other Countries in the East*, trans. R. Heron, volumes I–II (Edinburgh, 1792; new edition Reading, 1994).
Norie, John William, *A Complete Set of Nautical Tables* (London, 1803).
Nougarède, M.P., 'Qualités nautiques des navires arabes', in *Océan indien et méditerranée* [Travaux du Sixième Colloque International d'Histoire Maritime et du Deuxième Congrès de l'Association Historique Internationale de l'Océan Arabe] (Paris, 1964), pp. 95–122.
Al-Nuwayrī l-Iskandarānī, Muḥammad b. Qāsim, *Kitāb al-ilmām bil-i'lām fī mā jarat bihi l-aḥkām wa l-umūr al-maqḍiyya fī waq'at al-Iskandariyya*, volumes I–VII (Hyderabad, 1388–96/1968–76).
Ochsenwald, William: 'Muslim–European conflict in the Hijaz: The slave trade controversy, 1840–1895', *Middle Eastern Studies*, 16/1 (1980), pp. 115–26.
Orbaşlı, Aylin, 'The conservation of coral buildings on Saudi Arabia's northern Red Sea coast', *Journal of Architectural Conservation*, 15/3 (2009), pp. 49–64.
Orbaşlı, Aylin, 'The historic towns of Saudi Arabia's Red Sea coast: Tourism development and conservation', in *Human Interaction with the Environment in the Red Sea*, eds D.A. Agius, E. Khalil, E.M.L. Scerri and A. Williams (Leiden, 2017), pp. 207–27.
Osgood, Joseph B.F., *Notes of Travel or, Recollections of Majunga, Zanzibar, Muscat, Aden, Mocha, and Other Eastern Ports* (Salem, MA, 1854).
Paine, Lincoln, *The Sea and Civilization: A Maritime History of the World* (London, 2015).
Pankhurst, Richard, 'The Ethiopian slave trade in the nineteenth and early twentieth centuries: A statistical inquiry', *Journal of Semitic Studies*, 9/1 (1964), pp. 220–8.
Pâris, François Edmond, *Souvenirs de marine* (Paris, 1882; new edition 2013).
Pâris, François Edmond, *Souvenirs de plans ou dessins de navires et de bateaux anciens ou modernes existants ou disparus*, parts I–III (Paris, 1882; new edition Grenoble, 1975).
Peacock, David and Lucy Blue (eds), *Myos Hormos – Quseir Al-Qadim: Roman and Islamic Ports on the Red Sea*, volume I: *Survey and Excavations 1999–2003* (Oxford, 2006).

Peacock, David and Lucy Blue (eds), *Myos Hormos – Quseir Al-Qadim: Roman and Islamic Ports on the Red Sea*, volume II: *Finds from the Excavations 1999–2003* (Oxford, 2011).

The Periplus of the Erythraean Sea, trans. and ed. G.W.B. Huntingford (London, 1980).

The Periplus Maris Erythraei, trans. L. Casson (Princeton, NJ, 1989).

Perrier, Henri, *Les boutres de Djibouti: Dessins, notes et croquis* (Djibouti, 1994).

PERSGA, 'Status of mangroves in the Red Sea and Gulf of Aden', *PERSGA Technical Series*, 11 (2004), pp. 1–61.

PERSGA, 'Guidelines for compensation following damage to coral reefs by ship and boat grounding', *PERSGA Technical Series*, 15 (2009), pp. 1–53.

PERSGA, 'The status of coral reefs in the Red Sea and Gulf of Aden: 2009', *PERSGA Technical Series*, 16 (2010), pp. 1–100.

Pesce, Angelo, *Jiddah: Portrait of an Arabian City* (Napoli, 1976).

Phillips, Jacke, 'Beit Khorshid Effendi: A "trader's" house at Suakin', in *Navigated Spaces, Connected Spaces: Proceedings of Red Sea Project V*, eds D.A. Agius, J.P. Cooper, A. Trakadas and C. Zazzaro [British Foundation for the Study of Arabia Monograph No. 12] (Oxford, 2012), pp. 187–99.

Photographies d'Arabie: Hedjaz 1907–1917 (Paris and Riyadh, 1999).

Piamenta, Moshe, *A Dictionary of Post-Classical Yemeni Arabic*, volumes I–II (Leiden, 1990–1).

Pires, Tomé, see *The Suma Oriental of Tomé Pires*

Poncet, Charles-Jacques, *A Voyage to Ethiopia* (London, 1709).

Prados, Edward, 'Huris, sanbuqs and the boat builders of the Yemen', *Woodenboat*, 131 (1996), pp. 50–6.

Prados, Edward, 'Traditional fishing craft of the Tihamah and southwestern Arabian coast', *American Neptune*, 56 (1996), pp. 89–115.

Prados, Edward, 'Wooden boats of the Yemeni Tihamah', *Nautical Research Journal*, 43/4 (1998), pp. 195–209.

Provençal, Philippe, *The Arabic Plant Names of Peter Forsskål's Flora Aegyptiaco-Arabica* (Copenhagen, 2010).

Pujo, Jean-Marie, 'Les boutres à Djibouti: Une survivance de l'âge de la voile', *Pount*, 2 (1967), pp. 9–15.

Purchas, Samuel, *Hakluytus Posthumus, or Purchas his Pilgrimes: Contayning a History of the World in Sea Voyages and Lande Travells by Englishmen and Others*, volumes I–XX (Glasgow, 1905–7).

Al-Qasimi, Sultan Muhammad, 'Arab "piracy" and the East India Company encroachment in the Gulf 1797–1820', Ph.D. thesis, University of Exeter (1985).

Al-Qasimi, Sultan Muhammad, *The Myth of Arab Piracy in the Gulf* (Abingdon, 2006; second edition).

Al-Quṭāmī, 'Īsā, *Dalīl al-muḥtār fī 'ilm al-biḥār* (Kuwait, 1384/1964).

Ray, Himanshu Prabha, 'Maritime archaeology of the Indian Ocean', in *Oxford Research Encyclopedia of Asian History*, February 2017, pp. 1–27. Online: http://asianhistory.oxfordre.com/view/10.1093/acrefore/9780190277727.001.0001/acrefore-9780190277727-e-27 (accessed 27 May 2018).

Raymond, André, 'A divided sea: The Cairo coffee trade in the Red Sea area during the seventeenth and eighteenth centuries', in *Modernity and Culture from the*

Mediterranean to the Indian Ocean, eds L. Tarazi Fawaz and C.A. Bayly (New York, 2002), pp. 46–57.
Regourd, Ann, 'Arabic language documents on paper', in *Myos Hormos – Quseir Al-Qadim: Roman and Islamic Ports on the Red Sea*, volume II: *Finds from the Excavations 1999–2003*, eds D. Peacock and L. Blue (Oxford, 2011), pp. 339–44.
Reilly, Benjamin J., 'A well-intentioned failure: British anti-slavery measures and the Arabian Peninsula, 1820–1940', *Journal of Arabian Studies*, 5/2 (2015), pp. 91–115.
Ricciardi, Lorenzo, *The Voyage of Mir-el-lah* (New York, 1980).
Rogers, Stanley, *The Indian Ocean* (London, 1932).
Rönnby, Johan, 'Maritime durées: Long-term structures in a coastal landscape', *Journal of Maritime Archaeology*, 2/2 (2007), pp. 65–82.
Rouaud, Alain, 'Quelques termes arabes d'architecture navale en usage à Djibouti', in *Mélanges linguistiques offerts à Maxime Rodinson par ses élèves*, ed. C. Robin (Paris, 1985), pp. 335–41.
Rouaud, Alain, 'Tadjurra', in *Encyclopaedia of Islam*, volume X (Leiden, 2000; second edition), pp. 71–2.
Sabini, John, *Armies in the Sand: The Struggle for Mecca and Medina* (London, 1981).
Salim, Abdel Rahim, 'Field report: Suakin: On reviving an ancient Red Sea port city', *Traditional Dwellings and Settlements Review*, 8/2 (1997), pp. 63–74.
Al-Sarrani, Abeer Abdulaziz, 'From soil to oil: The resistance of the environment in the *Cities of Salt*', *International Journal of Comparative Literature and Translation Studies*, 3/4 (2015), pp. 20–6.
Sattin, Anthony, *Lifting the Veil: British Society in Egypt 1768–1956* (London, 1988).
Al-Sayyid, Ṣāliḥ Bin 'Abd al-Laṭīf 'Alyān, *Malāmiḥ min tārīkh Yanbu'*, volumes I–II (Yanbu al-Bahr, 1425/2004).
Schmid, Hagen and Peter Vine, *Saudi Arabian Red Sea* (Mainz, n.d.; fifth revised edition).
Schoff, Wilfred H., 'Cinnamon, cassia and Somaliland', *Journal of the American Oriental Society*, 40 (1920), pp. 260–70.
Semaan, Lucy, 'The use of wood in boatbuilding in the Red Sea from antiquity until present times', Ph.D. thesis, University of Exeter (2014).
Semple, Clare, *A Silver Legend: The Story of the Maria Theresa Thaler* (Manchester, 2005).
Serels, Steven, *Starvation and the State: Famine, Slavery, and Power in Sudan, 1883–1956* (New York, 2013).
Serjeant, Robert B., 'Maritime customary law off the Arabian coasts', in *Sociétés et compagnies de commerce en orient et dans l'Océan Indien*, ed. M. Mollat (Paris, 1970), pp. 195–207.
Al-Shāfa'ī, 'Abd al-Qādir b. Aḥmad b. Muḥammad b. Faraj, *Al-Silāḥ wa l-'udda fī tārīkh Bandar Judda* (Port Said, n.d.).
Shafiq, Suhanna, *Seafarers of the Seven Seas: The Maritime Culture in the* Kitāb 'Ajā'ib al- Hind *by Buzurg Ibn Shahriyār (d. 399/1009)* (Berlin, 2013).
Sharabati, Doreen, *Red Sea Shells* (London, 1984).
Sheppard, Charles R. and Anne L.S. Sheppard, 'Corals and coral communities of Arabia' *Fauna of Saudi Arabia*, 12 (1991), pp. 3–170.
Sheppard, Charles, Andrew Price and Callum Roberts, *Marine Ecology of the Arabian Region: Patterns and Processes in Extreme Tropical Environments* (London, 1992).
Sheriff, Abdul, *Dhow Cultures of the Indian Ocean. Cosmopolitanism, Commerce and Islam* (London, 2010).

Shihāb, Ḥasan Ṣāliḥ, *Al-Marākib al-'arabiyya: ta'rīkhuhā wa anwā'uhā* (Kuwait, 1407/1987).

Shihāb, Ḥasan Ṣāliḥ, *Al-Milāḥa l-falakiyya 'inda l-'arab* (Kuwait, 1421/2001).

Sidebottom, John K., *The Overland Mail* (London, 1948).

Siliotti, Alberto, *Fishes of the Red Sea* (Cairo, 2002).

Sim, Katharine, *Desert Traveller: The Life of Jean Louis Burckhardt* (London, 1969).

Simon, Kathleen, *Slavery* (London, 1930).

Smith, G. Rex, 'Magic, jinn and the supernatural in medieval Yemen: Examples from Ibn al- Muǧāwir's 7th/13th century guide', *Quaderni di Studi Arabi*, 13 (1995), pp. 7–18.

Smith, L.M.V., M.D.S. Mallinson, J.S. Phillips, A.H. Adam, A.I. Said, H. Barnard, C.P. Breen, G. Breen, D. Britton, W. Forsythe, J. Jansen Van Rensburg, T. McErlean and S. Porter, 'Archaeology and the archaeological and historical evidence for the trade of Suakin, Sudan', in *Navigated Spaces, Connected Spaces: Proceedings of Red Sea Project V*, eds D.A. Agius, J.P. Cooper, A. Trakadas and C. Zazzaro [British Foundation for the Study of Arabia Monograph No. 12] (Oxford, 2012), pp. 173–86.

Spilka, Bernard and Kevin L. Ladd, *The Psychology of Prayer: A Scientific Approach* (New York and London, 2013).

Stark, Freya, *East is West* (London, 1945; new edition 1947).

Starkey, Janet C.M., 'Travellers on the Red Sea coast between al-Quṣayr and Sawākin', in *People of the Red Sea: Proceedings of Red Sea Project II*, ed. J.C.M. Starkey [Society for Arabian Studies Monograph No. 3] (Oxford, 2005), pp. 75–86.

Steingass, F., *A Comprehensive Persian English Dictionary* (New Delhi, 1977).

Stone, Francine, 'Notes on the crafts, customs and local industries of the north Yemen Tihāmah', in *Studies on the Tihāmah: The Report of the Tihāmah Expedition 1982 and Related Papers*, ed. Francine Stone (Harlow, 1985), pp. 109–32.

The Suma Oriental of Tomé Pires and the Book of Francisco Rodrigues, trans. and ed. A. Cortesão, volumes I–II (London, 1944).

Tabrīzī, Muḥammad Ḥusayn, *Burhān-e qāṭe'*, volumes I–IV (Tehran, 1402/1982).

Taha, Shadia, *Attachment to Abandoned Heritage: The Case of Suakin* [BAR International Series No. S2477] (Oxford, 2013).

Talhami, Ghada H., *Suakin and Massawa under Egyptian Rule 1865–1885* (Wahsington, DC, 1979).

Thomas, Bertram, *Arabia Felix: Across the Empty Quarter of Arabia* (London, 1932).

The Thousand and One Nights, trans. E.W. Lane, ed. E.S. Poole, volumes I–III (London, 1838; new edition 1979–81).

Three Voyages of Vasco da Gama and his Viceroyalty: From the Lendas da India *of Gaspar Correa*, trans. H.E.J. Stanley (London, 1869).

Throckmorton, Peter, 'Reconstruction and conservation: The shipwright's art', in *Histroy from the Sea: Shipwrecks and Archaeology*, ed. P. Throckmorton (London, 1987), pp. 92–100.

Tibbetts, Gerald Randall, 'Arab navigation in the Red Sea', *Geographical Journal*, 127/3 (1961), pp. 322–34.

Tibbetts, Gerald Randall, *Arab Navigation in the Indian Ocean before the Coming of the Portuguese Being a Translation of* Kitāb al-fawā'id fī uṣūl al-baḥr wa l-qawā'id *of Aḥmad b. Mājid al-Najdī* (London, 1971; new edition 1981).

Tilley, Christopher and Kate Cameron-Daum, *An Anthropology of Landscape* (London, 2017).

Toledano, Ehud R., *The Ottoman Slave Trade and its Suppression: 1840–1890* (Princeton, NJ, 1982).
A Traveller in Thirteenth-Century Arabia: Ibn al-Mujāwir's Tārīkh al-mustabṣir, trans. and ed. with revisions and annotations by G. Rex Smith (London, 2007).
Travels of Ali Bey in Morocco, Tripoli, Cyprus, Egypt, Arabia, Syria, and Turkey between the Years 1803 and 1807, volumes I–II (London, 1816; reprint Frankfurt am Main, 1995).
The Travels of Ibn Baṭṭūṭa A.D. 1325–1354, trans. with revisions and notes H.A.R. Gibb, volumes I–IV (London, 1958–2000).
Travels of Ibn Jubayr, trans. R.J.C. Broadhurst (London, 1952; reprint 2004).
Travels of James Bruce through Part of Africa, Syria, Egypt and Arabia into Abyssinia to Discover the Source of the Nile (Edinburgh, 1839).
The Travels of Ludovico di Varthema, trans. J. Winter Jones, ed. G.P. Badger (London, 1863).
Treat, Ida, *Pearls, Arms, and Hashish: Pages from the Life of a Red Sea Navigator, Henri De Monfreid* (London, 1930).
Tuddenham, David B., 'Maritime cultural landscapes, maritimity and quasi objects', *Journal of Maritime Archaeology*, 5/1 (2010), pp. 5–16.
Tunstall, John, *Vanishing Kingdoms* (Cape Town, 1966).
Valentia, George Viscount, *Voyages and Travels to India, Ceylon, the Red Sea, Abyssinia and Egypt in the Years 1802–1806*, volumes I-III (London, 1809); volumes I-IV (New Delhi, 1994; new edition).
Van de Noort, Robert, *North Sea Archaeologists: A Maritime Biography 10,000 BC–AD 1500* (Oxford, 2011).
Van Der Meulen, Daniel, *Faces in Shem* (London, 1961).
Vaz Freire, Jorge, 'Maritime cultural landscape: A new approach to the Cascais coastline', *Journal of Maritime Archaeology*, 9/1 (2014), pp. 143–57.
Villiers, Alan, *Sons of Sinbad* (New York, 1940).
Villiers, Alan, 'Passage in a Red Sea dhow', *Mariner's Mirror*, 40/3 (1954), pp. 171–82.
Villiers, Alan, *Sons of Sindbad: The Photographs*, introduction W. Facey, Y. Al-Hijji and G. Pundyk (London, 2006).
Vine, Peter, *The Red Sea* (London and Jeddah, 1985).
Vine, Peter, *Red Sea Invertebrates* (London, 1986).
Von Soden, Wolfram, *Akkadisches Handwörterbuch*, volumes I–III (Wiesbaden, 1959–81).
Wallin, Georg August, *Travels in Arabia (1845 and 1848)* (Cambridge, 1979).
Walls, Archibald G., *Preservation of Monuments and Sites: Architectural Survey of Mocha* (Paris, 1981).
Waterhouse, Francis A., *Gun Running in the Red Sea* (London, 1935).
Wehr, Hans, *A Dictionary of Modern Written Arabic*, ed. J.M. Cowan (Wiesbaden, 1966).
Weismann, Norbert, 'Depiction of Indo-Arabic ships on an eighteenth-century sea chart', *Mariner's Mirror*, 98/4 (2012), pp. 421–35.
Wellsted, James Raymond, *Travels in Arabia*, volumes I–II (Graz, 1978).
Weschenfelder, Petra, 'Beja in medieval Islamic geography and archaeology', in *Navigated Spaces, Connected Places: Proceedings of Red Sea Project V*, eds D.A. Agius, J.P. Cooper, A. Trakadas and C. Zazzaro [British Foundation for the Study of Arabia Monograph No. 12] (Oxford, 2012), pp. 221–8.

Westerdahl, Christer, 'The maritime cultural landscape', *International Journal of Nautical Archaeology*, 22/1 (1992), pp. 5–14.

Westerdahl, Christer, 'Fish and ships: Towards a theory of maritime culture', *Deutches Schiffahrtsarchiv Wissenschaftliches Jahrbuch des Deutchen Schiffahrtsmuseums*, 30 (2008), pp. 191–236.

Western Arabia and the Red Sea [Geographical Handbook Series No. BR527] (Oxford and Cambridge, 1946).

Whitcomb, Donald S. and Janet H. Johnson (eds), *Quseir al-Qadim 1978: Preliminary Report* (Cairo, 1979).

Whitcomb, Donald S. and Janet H. Johnson (eds), *Quseir al-Qadim 1980: Preliminary Report* [American Research Center in Egypt No. 7] (Malibu, CA, 1982).

Whitewright, Julian, 'How fast is fast? Technology, trade and speed under sail in the Roman Red Sea', in *Natural Resources and Cultural Connections of the Red Sea: Proceedings of Red Sea Project III*, eds J. Starkey, P. Starkey and T. Wilkinson [Society for Arabian Studies Monograph No. 5] (Oxford, 2007), pp. 77–88.

Whitewright, Julian, 'Maritime technological change in the ancient Mediterranean: The invention of the lateen sail', Ph.D. thesis, University of Southampton (2008).

Whitewright, Julian, 'The potential performance of ancient Mediterranean sailing rigs', *International Journal of Nautical Archaeology*, 40/1 (2011), pp. 2–17.

Whitewright, Julian, 'Sailing with the *mu'allim*: The technical practice of Red Sea sailing during the medieval period', in *Navigated Spaces, Connected Places: Proceedings of Red Sea Project V*, eds D.A. Agius, J.P. Cooper, A. Trakadas and Chiara Zazzaro [British Foundation for the Study of Arabia Monograph No. 12] (Oxford, 2012), pp. 147–56.

Wick, Alexis, *The Red Sea: In Search of Lost Space* (Oakland, CA, 2016).

Wiebeck, E., *Indische Boote und Schiffe* (Rostock, 1987).

Wilson, N.F.J., *The Native Craft: A General Description of the Native Craft Visiting Bombay Harbour and Particulars as to Their Survey, Registry, Measurement and Lighting* (Bombay, 1909).

Wright, G.N., *A New and Comprehensive Gazetteer*, volumes I–IV (London, 1836).

Yapp, Malcolm Edward, 'The India Office Records as a source for the economic history of the Middle East', in *Studies in the Economic History of the Middle East from the Rise of Islam to the Present Day*, ed. M.A. Cook (London, 1970), pp. 501–13.

Yule, Henry and Arthur C. Burnell, *Hobson-Jobson: A Glossary of Colloquial Anglo-Indian Words and Phrases*, ed. W. Crooke (Sittingbourne, 1994).

Al-Zabīdī, Muḥammad Murtaḍā, *Tāj al-'arūs*, volume II, ed. 'A. Hiālī, rev. 'A.-A. al-'Alāīlī and 'A.-S. Aḥmad Farrāj (Kuwait, 1386/1966); volume XXV, ed. M. Ḥijāzī (Kuwait, 1409/1989); volume XXIX, ed. 'A-F. al-Ḥilū, rev. A. Mukhtār 'Umar and Kh. 'Abd al-Karīm Jum'a (Kuwait, 1418/1997).

Zazzaro, Chiara, *The Ancient Red Sea Port of Adulis and the Eritrean Coastal Region* [British Archaeological Report No. S2569] (Oxford, 2013).

Zazzaro, Chiara, 'Adulis and the sea', in *Human Interaction with the Environment in the Red Sea*, eds D.A. Agius, E. Khalil, E.M.L. Scerri and A. Williams (Leiden, 2017), pp. 151–70.

Zdanowski, Jerzy, *Slavery and Manumission: British Policy in the Red Sea and the Persian Gulf in the First Half of the 20th Century* (Reading, 2013).

INDEX

References to illustrations and maps are in italics

'Ababda (tribe), 14, 160, 196
Abbadi, Muhammad Abd Allah, 107
Abbas, Muhammad Abd Allah, 211
Abd al-Qadir, Hasan, 74, 75
Abdalla, Sadek Yaqoub, 179, 211
Abd Allah, Hussein Abd al-Hamid, 164–5
Abdallah, Mohammed Ali, 90
Abd Allah, Muhammad, 105–6
Abdo, Muhammad Hadrami, 51
Abdul Raouf Khalil Museum, 226, *228*
Abou Bakar, Ibrahim, 96, 130
Abu Atayiq, Ibrahim, 76
Abu Hilal, 176, 178
Abu Ramad (Egypt), 150
abū-samaka (double-ended), 49, 81
Abu Zulayma (holy man), 214
accidents (at sea), 104, 107, 115, 124, 126, 128–33, 147–8
  see also safety
Aden (Yemen)
  cargo boats, 70, 78
  fibreglass boats, 54, 86
  folk beliefs, 211–12
  Indians in, 51
  interviews, 19
  jinn, 211–12
  migration, 51
  monuments, 228
  Parsees in, 51
  passengers, 114
  Portugal, 65–6
  shipbuilding, 49–51, 53, 54, 55, 62–3, *73*, *74*, 77–8, 88
  slave-trafficking, 198
  steamships, 41
  trade, 154, 166–7
  Valentia, Viscount, 116
admirals, 100
Admiralty Sailing Directions, 133, 144
Afar (tribe), 21, 96, 202, 203
afreets, 201
agents (commercial), 155, 169, 177, 188, 190
Agig (Sudan), 165
Ahmadi, Muhammad Saad al-, 4
Ahmed, Ibrahim Moosa, 102, 122, 152
Ahmed, Usman Ali, 141, 181, 186

Aidhab (Sudan), 67, 115
Akil, Mohammad, 125
Alaiwa, Said Mohammad, 13, 102, 108, *111*
Alexandria (Egypt), 56
algae, 27, 31
AlGhabban, Ali, 100, 106, 146, 147
Alhazmi, Muhammad, 17, 121, 122
Ali, Ahmed Jaber, 134, 181, 222
Ali, Atia Said Hussein, 75, *77*
Ali, Idrees Daud, 100, 141
Ali, Muhammed Hummid, 105
Ali Bey, pseudonym of Domènec Badia i Leblich
- cabins, 114
- *dāw*, 62
- helmsman, 128
- lookout, 102, 128
- steamships, 38
- storms, 129
- Suez, 157
- written sources, 3

Allāh, 127–8, 212–13, 216–17, 219, 228
Al-Sa'īdī (name of ship), 129
Al Salam Boccaccio (name of ship), 131–2
Alsanousi, Amin, 162
Alsinani, Muhammad Bukhayyit, 103, 156, 162
Alsinani, Muhammad Hamid, 54
amīr al-baḥr see admiral
amulets, 12, 217
Anbari, Ibrahim Muhammad, 56, 136, 141
Anbari, Mohammad Ahmed Zaid al-, 106, 108, 173, 179
anchorages, 33–4, 44, 102, 104, 146
anchors, 102, 107, 139, 179
anchovies, 181–2
animals
- cargo, 131, 159–60, 162, 165, 166, 171, 173, 202
- folk-beliefs, 201, 214

apprentices, 100
Aqaba (Jordan), 128, 132
Aqili, Abdo Mohammed Isa, 210
Aqili, Mohammed Isa, 93
Aqili, Muhammad Isa Muhammad, 119, 186, 191
Aqili, Munawwar, 232
Arabian Nights, 209, 217
Arabic, 9–10, 25, 27, 107, 221–2
archives, 232
art, 209, 226, *227*, *228*
Assab (Eritrea), 41, 145, 171, 173, 202, 211
Atalla, Shadhli Ahmed, 188, 189
auctions, 26, 177–8, 179
Augan, Hammad Tokulia, 184
Austin, Samuel, 160, *161*
Awaini, Ahmed al-, 179
awnings, 114
Aydarūs (legendary figure), 216
Azab, M.A., 29
azyab (wind), 141–2, 143, 144, 176, 199–200

Bab el-Mandeb, 28, 39, 43, 59, 67, 124, 143, 145
Badia i Leblich, Domènec *see* Ali Bey
Baghit, Hammuda Abdalla, 119, 181
baghla (type of ship)
- India, 49, 62
- Klunzinger, C., 58
- Kuwait, 78, 157
- Lingeh, *170*
- Machell, T., 125
- transom sterns, 55
- Wellsted, J., 128

baḥḥār see sailors
Bahrain, 56, 138, 157, 192
bailing out (water), 107
Balaw, Rashid al-, 10, 159
ballast, 130–1, 156, 200
Baloos, Soleiman Mohammad Ali, 209, 171, 179, 286, 192
Bangladeshis, 191
Banī Zarānik (tribe), 125
Al-Baraka (name of ship), 172
Barsi, Sayyid Ahmed Musa al-, 84, 177
baskets, 179, 187
Basra (Iraq), 143, 154, 169, 173, 216
Bāṭarfī, Khālid Muḥammad, 26, 169
Bayri, Alam Bughri, 95
bedding, 114–15
Bedouin, 119, 125, 160, 178, 206, 210, 224
Berbera (Somalia), 36, 59–60, 131, 170, 173
Berlioux, Étienne Félix, 201
Besse, Antonin, Jr., 119, 137
Besse, Antonin, Sr., 51, 53, 106, 114, 157, 166, 202
Bible, 207
bibliography *see* written sources
bil-gadaḥ (square-sterned), 49
Bilghaith, Ibrahim, 51, 91–2, 139, 155, 156, 223
Bin Ḥimd, Muḥammad bin Aḥmad, 155
biodiversity, 31–2
birds, 33
boatmen, 169
boats (types of)
  abū-samaka, 49, 81
  baghla
    India, 49, 62
    Klunzinger, C., 58
    Kuwait, 78, 157
    Lingeh, *170*
    Machell, T., 125
    transom sterns, 55
    Wellsted, J., 128
  bil-gadaḥ, 49
  bōt, 84, 88
  būtī, 96
  caravel, 67, 72
  dangī, 177
  dāw, 61–2
  doonik, 96
  falūka, 56, 74, 84–5, 92, 93, 150, 177, 189
  galba, 62–3, 94
  gārib, 92
  gaṭīra, 74–5, 76, 77, 80, 139, 189, *248, 249*
  ghanja, 49, 62, 68, 78
  ghuweirī, 90
  hūrī, 91
    dugout boats, 49, 95, 102, 170, 177, 181, 195
    Farasan Islands, 93, 186–7
    ferries, 87, 155
    fishing boats, 94, 102, 177, 181, 191
    Gulf, 87
    Hornell, J., 90–1
    Khokha, *91*
    lifeboats, 45
    Obock, 181
    Oman, 87
    pearling, 187
    planks, 57, 86–7, 102, 177
    racing boats, 92, 138, 223
    Safaga, 177
    sails, 138
    share-system, 189
    Sigalat Lamba, 94
    transom stern, 57

Tuwaled, 93
Yanbu al-Bahr, 86
hūrī-khashab, 96
jalba, 94
jurdī-sanbūk, 75–7, 80, 86, 88, 96
kotia, *68*
lanch, 85, 169
lansh-sanbūk, *57*, 86, 183
ma'diyya, 96
mahadi, 96, *208*
merkeb, 96
nawrī, 85, 156
'obrī, 76, 88, *89*, 92, 93, 96, *127*, 172
quyāsa, 63–5, *64*
ramas, 87, 95, 182, 186
ṣaddāfa, 94–5, 177, 186
sā'iya, *60–1*, *81*
sakūna, 70
sanbūk
Burton, R., 68, 100, 114
coffee, 70
design, 67–72, 80–1, 92
Djibouti, 52
Eritrea, 171
Farasan Islands, 73–4, 187
ferries, 84
Gulf, 79–82, *81*
Jizan, 51, 92
jurdī, 76
Khor al-Ghureirah, 88
Klunzinger, C., 68
Kuwait, 54
lexicography, 66–7
Luheyya, 1
Moore, A., 69, 88
Obock, 204
Oman, 79–81
pearling, 70–1, 187
Port Sudan, *80*
Quseir, 54
safety, 45
Sheikh Mansoor, 46, 70, *75*
Sigalat Lamba, 94
Tadjourah, 172
transom sterns, 69, *70*, 74, 80, 92
Villiers, A., 46, 70
written sources, 67–8
shaṭṭiyya, 86–7
za'īma-sanbūk, 49, 77–9
accidents, 131
Djibouti, 131
Hornell, J., 79
Jizan, 91–2
jurdī, 76
Khor al-Ghureirah, 69, 88
Moore, A., 78, 79
Ras Ali, 97
Tadjourah, 172
tonnage, 78, *156*
tourism, 96
transom sterns, 77, 79, 92
Tuwaled, 93
zārūk-sanbūk, 90
cargo boats, 89, 130
Djibouti, 130
drug smuggling, 202
fishing boats, 180
Hornell, J., 200
Khor al-Ghureirah, 88
Monfreid H. de, 200
Obock, 200
overloading, 130
pirates, 127
Ras Ali, 96
slave-trafficking, 89, 127, 200–1, 203
Suakin, 85, 86–7
Tadjourah, 93, 130
tourism, 96

Tuwaled, 93, 130
Villiers, A., 100, 109
see also cargo boats, dugout boats, ferries, fibreglass boats, fishing boats, lifeboats, metal-hulled boats, pearling, pilgrims, pleasure boats, racing boats, replica boats, shipbuilding, steamships
boatswain, 101–3, 188
bōt (type of boat), 84, 88
Brett, Lieutenant J., 70, *72*, 81
Brouwer, C.G., 167
Bruce, James, 136, 157, 159, 163, 170, 225
Budgin, John, 146
buildings, 30, *31*, *164*, *165*, 223–4
Bukhari, Abd al-Hamid, 127–8
Bukhari, Fuad Ahmed Abdallah, 77
Burckhardt, Johann Ludwig
Bedouin, 119, 158
burials, 116
corpses, 116
dāw, 62
jinn, 212
leather, 158
overcrowding, 61, 115
pilots, 104
Quseir, 115
saints, 214
sā'iya, 61
shipbuilding, 49
steamships, 31
Suez, 49, 162
tombs, 214
water, 115
written sources, 3
Yanbu al-Bahr, 119, 162
burials (at sea), 116
Burnes, Sir Alexander, 59
Burri, Kamil Muhammad Abu Lubb, 210
Burton, Isabel, 41, 197
Burton, Richard
Abū Zulayma, 214
cabins, 114
Harar, 202
Jeddah, 100
jinn, 211
pilgrims, 68, 114, 115, 169
saints, 214
sanbūk, 68, 100, 114
shipbuilding, 56
spices, 169
steamships, 38
storms, 128
Suez, 56, 100, 158
timber, 50
trade, 158
Tur, 128
winds, 144
written sources, 3
būtī (type of ship), 96
Buxton, E.N., 29
Buzara, Muhammad Said, 164

cabin-boys, 109
cabins, 114–15
calendar, 175–6, 181, 219
camels *see* animals; caravans
Cape Guardafui (Somalia), 126, 141
captain (ship's), 99–109, 117, 119
boatswain, 101–2
cabin-boys, 109
cargo, 99
clothes, 109
contracts, 155
convoys, 153–4
debt, 189–91
discipline, 99–100, 109

fishing boats, 99, 172
food, 117
helmsman, 102–3
greetings, 153–4
navigation, 100–4, 135
overloading, 130
passengers, 99, 130
pearling, 99, 103
pilots, 103–5
sailors, 106–8
share-system, 188–91
storms, 118, 130, 131, 147–8
storytelling, 119
Villiers, A., 108
water, 119
caravans, *17*, 119, 155, 160, 162, 163, 171, 219
caravel (type of ship), 67, 72
careening, 107–8, 144
cargo, 147, 156–7
animals, 131, 159–60, 162, 165, 166, 171, 173, 202
captain, 99
cloth, 70, 138, 166, 169, 171, 173
clothing, 154, 162, 164–5, 166, 170, 171, 173
coal, 156, 160
coffee, 36, 70, 158, 160, 162, 166, 167, *168*, 170, 173
dates, 143, 154, 162, 166, 171, 173, 216
dried fish, 163, 166
firewood, 172
foodstuffs, 41, 154, 159, 162–3, 164–5, 170, 171, 172–3
frankincense, 36, 70, 167, 170
gold, 36, 103
grain, 36, 157–9, 162, 170–1, 173
iron, 162, 171, 172
ivory, 36, 167, 165, 171
leather, 158
oil, 166
porcelain, 165
rice, 36, 156–7, 162, 165, 166, 169, 173
spices, 169, 170
timber, 164–5, 166
cargo boats, 47, 54, 99, 154–5
Aden, 70, 78
Basra, 143
Dhuba, *161*
Djibouti City, 8
Farasan Islands, 117
gaṭīra, 75
Mocha, 21
'obrī, 88
overloading, 130
pirates, 125
Quseir, 70
storms, 129–30
Suakin, 52
Suez, 43
tonnage, 156–7
Ummlejj, 162
Yanbu al-Bahr, 77
zārūk, 89, 130
carpenters, 49, 54, 56, 108
Carter, Robert, 23
Castro, João de, 124, 145, 147
cattle *see* animals
caulking, 57, *58*, 108
celestial navigation *see* navigation; stars
charts, 45, 59–60, *60*, 100, 101, 136, 199
see also dīra
China, 165, 167
see also Far East
Chodoc (name of ship), 126
cholera, 41, 225

clams, 187
clerks, 99
climate, 28–9
cloth, 70, 138, 166, 169, 171, 173
clothes (on board ship), 109–11, *110*, *111*
clothing (as cargo), 154, 162, 165, 166, 170, 171, 173
Clouet, Alain, 101, 107, 109, 149
coal, 40, 156, 160, 201
coffee, 29
  Burton, R., 158
  caravans, 160
  cargo, 36, 70, 158, 160, 162, 166, 167, *168*, 170, 173
  East India Company, 167
  Essex, 125
  food, 117
  Mocha, 21, 35, 70, 125, 166, 167, *168*, 170, 173
  sanbūk, 70
  Suez, 158
  Valentia, Viscount, 167
  Yanbu al-Bahr, 162
Colomb, Philip H., 126, 193, 194, 197
colours, 208–9
compasses, 45, 100, 105, 146
  see also dīra
Conant, John Edward, 140
conch shells, 182, 186–7
construction techniques, 55–8
contracts, 155
convoys, 126, 153, 186
cooks, 108, 117, 188
cooking (on board ship), 116–17
Cooper, John P., 8, 13, 19, 22–4, 48, 70–1, 93, 97, 119
co-operatives, 2, 113–4
coral, 29–31, 128, 145, 147, 219
corpses, 116
Coupland, Reginald, 197
Crossland, Cyril, 3, 68, 69, 215
crustaceans *see* shellfish
cultural identity, 218–19
cultural landscape, 4–6, 41, 82, 219, 225–32
currency, 169
customs duties, 155
  see also taxes

Dahi, Abd Allah, 156
Dahlak Archipelago (Eritrea), 22, 24–5, 171, 186–7, 219–20
dallāl see agents
Damri, Ali Khalifa Ali Hammed, 186
dancing, 120–2, 180, 231
Daniel, William, 207
dangī (type of boat), 177
dates (fruit), 143, 154, 162, 166, 171, 173, 216
Daud, Abbas Muhammed Ali, 146–7, 159, 210
Davies, Stephen, 124, 132
dāw (type of boat), 61–2
debt, 189–91
decks, 45, 49, 114
De Monfreid, Henri *see* Monfreid, Henri de
Denmark, 37
Denon, Vivant, 158
Description de l'Égypte, 65
design, 53–4, 67–72, 80–1, 92, 96
  see also hulls, transom sterns
Dhofar, 125, 170, 210
Dhuba (Saudi Arabia), 30, 132, 146, 154, 159, 160, *161*, 224
diesel engines, 45, 86, 92, 152, 174, 184
dīra (navigational instrument), 99, 104, *105*
  see also compasses

Ḍirār, M.S., 20
discipline, 99–100, 102, 108, 109
diving, 179, 183, 185–8, 190–1
Djibouti (state)
  coral, 30
  fishing boats, 191–2
  government policies, 184
  Hadhramis in, 220
  mangroves, 32
  routes, 144
  sanbūk, 52
  shell collecting, 183
  shipbuilding, 25, 50, 52, 58, 96
  transom stern, 71
  Yemenis in, 50, 52
  za'īma, 131
  zārūk, 130
Djibouti City, 8, 21, 25, 41, 88, 95–6, 130, 144, 172–3
dolphins, 187
Donaldson, William J., 191
doonik (type of boat), 96
Doughty, Charles, 200
dried fish, 163, 166
drug smuggling, 201, 202
Dubois, Colette, 42, 46
dugongs, 33
dugout boats, 49, 87, 95, 102, 170, 177, 181, 195
Duruni, Abd al-Aziz, 164

East Africa, 53, 78, 165, 166
East India Company (British and Dutch), 3, 21, 36, *37*, 41, 62, 134, 167
Edfu (Egypt), 160
Edye, John, 62, 82
Egypt, government, 52–3, 84, 94, 196, 201
Egyptians, 51, 92, 164
Ehrenberg, C.G., 37
Eltayeb, Mohamed Mustafa, 183
El Wejh (Saudi Arabia), 33
  grain, 157
  interviews, 10, 17–18
  pilgrims, 146, 160, 162
  quarantine stations, 225
  Quseir, 226
  routes, 43, 144, 146, 157
  saints, 214
  tombs, 214
Elwon, J., 132
environment, 30, 34, 192, 219
equipment (for fishing), 177, 180, 181
Essex (name of ship), 125
Eritrea, *23*, 24–5, 171–2 180–1, 182, 183–4, 205, 220
Eritreans, 131, 192, 205
Ethiopia, 171, 172–3, 195, 196, 200, 201, 202–4
Ethiopians, 192
ethnography, 6, 135
  Arabic, 8–9, 9–10, 25
  cultural identity, 218–19
  cultural landscape, 4–6, 41, 82, 219, 225–32
  definition of, 7–8
  fieldwork, 8, 193–4, 218–19
  interviews, 8–26
    Aden, 19
    Arabic, 9–10, 25
    Djibouti City, 21
    El Wejh, 10, 17–18
    Farasan Islands, 8, 22–3
    Jeddah, 25–6
    Jizan, 22
    Khokha, 9, 14, 21
    Khor al-Ghureirah, 8, 21
    literacy, 10
    Massawa, 13, 24–5

memory, 12–13
Mersa Alam, 14–15
Mocha, 13, 21
Obock, 9, 13, 21
occupations (of interviewees), 15, 21
Qunfudhah, 11, 25–6
Quseir, 11, 14–15
Safaga, 8, 14
security, 11
Suakin, 8, 18
Tadjourah, 8, 9, 21
Ummlejj, 10, 17, *18*
Yanbu al-Bahr, 10, 17
slave-trafficking, 193–4
written sources, 5–6, 26
Ettinghausen, Richard, 208
eunuchs, 195–6
evil eye, 2–7–8, 217
see also oculus
Ewald, Janet, 196

Fagan, Brian, 4, 144
falūka (type of boat), 56, 74, *84*, 85, 92, 93, 150, 177, 189
Far East, 182
see also China, Japan
Farāhīdī, al-Khalīl al-, 85
Farasan Islands (Saudi Arabia), *22*
birds, 33
coral, 30
festivals, *180*, 192, 223, 230
fibreglass boats, 93
folk beliefs, 210–11
food, 117, 223
hūrī, 93, 186–7
interviews, 8, 22–3
jinn, 8, 210–11
kurmush, 117, 223
mangroves, 32
museums, 228
music, 120
parrotfish, 180, 230
pearling, 47, 70–1, 171, 185–92, 219–20, 212
sanbūk, 73–4, 187
sharks, 189
shell collecting, 185–9
shipbuilding, 92
tourism, 210, 228
farming, 23, 106–7, 178
Fateh el-Rahman (name of ship), 197
Fatḥ al-Khayr (name of ship), *170*
faybar-sanbūk see fibreglass boats
Ferret, Pierre Victor, 169
ferries, 52
accidents, 130, 131–2
boatmen, 169
Dhuba, 132
Djibouti City, 172
falūka, 84
hūrī, 87, 155
lansh, 169
ma'diyya, 86
metal-hulled boats, 85
nawrī, 156
Obock, 172
'obrī, 172
Quseir, 14
Safaga, 14, 85
sanbūk, 84
steamships, 26
Suakin, 84
Tadjourah, 172
festivals, *180*, 192, 230–1
fibreglass boats, 90–5, 97
Aden, 54, 88
environment, 34
Dhuba, 160
Djibouti, 184

Eritrea, 94, 183–4
falūka, 92–3
Farasan Islands, 93
fishing boats, 52–3, 183–4, 191
government policies, 9, 52–3, 94, 184
Jizan, 92
Khor al-Ghureirah, 90
Massawa, 183
shipbuilding, 17, *18*, 47, 52–3, 54, 58, 90–2, 183, 191, 222–3
Suakin, 52–3, 86
Ummlejj, 17, *18*, 85
Yanbu al-Bahr, 86
Yemen, 9, 184
fieldwork, 8, 193–4, 218–19
firewood, 75, 172
Fīrūzabādī, Muḥammad bin Ya'qūb al-, 67
fish, 26, 30, 32–3, 77–9, 180–1, 187–8, 231
see also anchovies, dried fish, jellyfish, parrotfish, sardines, sharks
fishing boats, 2, 47, 85, 107
anchovies, 181–2
Bangladeshis, 191
baskets, 179
calendar, 175, 181
captain, 99, 177
co-operatives, 2, 183–4
dangī, 177
Djibouti, 191–2
Egypt, 184
equipment, 177, 180, 181
falūka, 74, 177
fibreglass boats, 52–3, 183–4, 191
hūrī, 91, 102, 177, 181, 191
Jeddah, 178–9
Jizan, 51
Khokha, 182
Khor al-Ghureirah, 179
Massawa, 181, 182, 183–4
Obock, 181
'obrī, 88
parrotfish, 180
Quseir, 176
Safaga, 85
sails, 175–6, 180–1
sardines, 181
sharks, 108, 177
shikka, 179
Suakin, 86, 178
Sudan, 177
Ummlejj, 162
winds, 175–6, 180–1
Yanbu al-Bahr, 77
zārūk, 180
food (on board ship), 109, 116–18, 129, 231
foodstuffs (as cargo), 41, 154, 159, 162–3, 164–5, 170, 171, 172–3
see also dates, grain, rice
Footman, David, 101
Forsskål, Peter, 37
forts, 75, *77*, *161*, 224, 224–5, 226
France, 38, 41, 194, 186–7, 202
frankincense, 36, 70, 167, 170
Freire, Jorge Vaz, 5
Freitag, Ulrike, 155

Galinier, Joseph Germain, 169
galba (type of boat), 62–3
gārib (type of boat), 92
Garmushi, Hashim Abd Salim, 165
gaṭīra (type of boat), 74–5, 76, *77*, 80, 139, 189, *248*, *249*
geography, 27–34
Ghaili, Muhammed al-, 54, 88
ghanja (type of boat), 49, 62, 68, 78
ghuweirī (type of boat), 90

Goddard, David, 56
Godoria (Eritrea), 205
gold, 36, 163
government policies
  Djibouti, 184
  Egypt, 52–3, 184
  Eritrea, 94–5, 182, 183–4
  India, 53
  Sudan, 52, 53, 184
  Yemen, 9, 184
grain, 36, 157–9, 162, 170–1, 173, 225
Great Britain, 36–42, 167, 211
  gun-running, 201–2
  slave-trafficking, 194, 196–201, 204
  trade, 201–2
  see also Royal Navy
great powers, 36–42, 171
Greater Farasan *see* Farasan Islands
Greeks, 56
greetings, 153–4
guides (nautical), 132–3, 134–5, 144
Guillain, Antoine, 61
Gulf (Arabian-Persian), 41, 79–81, *80*, 87, 171, 222, 231
Gumaani, Ahmed Muhammad al-, 96
gun-running, 47, 52, 89, 127, 166, 200–2, 204
guns, 126, 194
Guta, Atiya Saad Sikiyan, 85

Habib, Abou Bakar, 108, 129, 143, 173, 213
Hadandawa (tribe), 12, 18, 52, 182, 211, 221, 231
Hadi bin Hasan, 73
Hadhramaut, 51, 54, 167, 170, 173, 205
Hadhramis, 62, 78, 164, 220–1
Hamd Allah, Hasan Mohammed, 150
Hamdan, Jumaa, 159
Al-Hami (Yemen), 103, 135
Hamid, Ali Suleiman, 93
Hamid, Hamid Suleiman, 93
Hamilton, Genesta, 195
Hammed, Ali Khalifa Ali, 101
Hamra Island (United Arab Emirates), 129
Hanas, Muhammad Uthman Mahmud, 92
hand-tools, 52, 56–7, 222
Ḥaqmī (tribe), 21
Harar (Ethiopia), 173, 202
Ḥarbī, Sāmī Sulaymān al-, 175
harbour master, 99, 131
Harrigan, Peter, 22
Harris, William Cornwallis, 202
Hasan, Abd Allah Ibrahim, 120
Hasan, Muhammad El Wafaa, 122
Hasan, Muhammad-Nour Muhammad, 94, 171–2, 183–4
Hasan, Saad Ali, 150, 152
Hassan, Abd al-Hamid Hasan, 138
Hassan, Shabhat Khaysa, 77
Hawabita, Idrees, 172, 183
Hawkins, Clifford W., 3, 71–2, 83, 96, 157
Hazell, Alastair, 204
heat, 28, 39, 114, 115, 119, 201
Hedab, Muhammad-Nour, 228
Helfritz, Hans, 69–70
helmsman, 102, 103, 128
Hemprich, F., 37
Hijazis, 76, 142, 178, 196, 221
Al-Ḥijāziyya (poem), 135
Ḥizb al-Baḥr (religious poem), 212–13
Hodeidah (Yemen), 30, 88, 125, 128, 166–7
  shipbuilding, 49–50, 70, 78
  slave-trafficking, 200

Hornell, James, 48–9
  folk beliefs, 207
  hūrī, 90–1
  India, 82–3, 139
  oculus, 207
  rope, 139
  shipbuilding, 50, 82–3
  tonnage, 157
  trade, 139
  written sources, 3
  za'īma, 79
  zārūk, 200
hospitals, 225
Howarth, David, 125
Huber, Valeska, 39
hulls, 48–9, 53–4, 55–8, 68–72, 80–1, 89, 92, 96
Humaidan, Mohammed Ali, 173
Humi, Naji Muhammad Abdallah, 162
Humuq, Othman, 117, 225
Hunter, F.M., 3, 49, 89
Hurghada (Egypt), 30, 85, 147, 160
Hurgronje, Christiaan Snouck, 195
hūrī (type of boat), *91*
  dugout boats, 49, 95, 102, 170, 177, 181, 195
  Farasan Islands, 93, 186–7
  ferries, 87, 155
  fishing boats, 94, 102, 177, 181, 191
  Gulf, 87
  Hornell, J., 90–1
  Khokha, *91*
  lifeboats, 45
  Obock, 181
  Oman, 87
  planks, 57, 86–7, 102, 177
  pearling, 187
  racing boats, 92, 138, 223
  Safaga, 177
  sails, 138
  share-system, 189
  Sigalat Lamba, 94
  transom stern, 57
  Tuwaled, 93
  Yanbu al-Bahr, 86
hūrī-khashab (type of boat), 90
Hussayyal, Muhammad Abd Allah Said al-, 186
Hydrographic Office (United Kingdom), 144

Ibn Baṭṭūṭa, Abū 'Abd Allāh Muḥammad, 67, 96, 202
Ibn Jubayr, Abū l-Ḥasan Muḥammad, 115, 225
Ibn Mājid, Aḥmad, 101, 134–5, 140, 144, 145
Ibn Saud, King of Saudi Arabia, 205
Ibn Ṭūlūn, Ahmad (sea battle by), 67
Ibrahim, Ali Hussein Ahmed, 142
Ibrahim, Houmed-Gaba Maki, 143, 173
Ibrahim, Mahmud Saad, 160
'ibrī see 'obrī
ice boxes, 177, 178
Idrees, Idrees, Iribi, 181
Idrees, Muhammed, 183
Al-Idrīsī, Abū 'Abd Allāh Muḥammad al-, 172
Ilaj, Marzuq Muhammad al-, 11
illnesses, 41, 187, 225
Imam, Ahmed, 129–30
incense-burning, 209, 225
India
  government policies, 53
  Hadhramis in, 62
  Hornell, J., 82–3

kotia, *68*
migration, 51, 164, 221
shipbuilding, 49–51, 62, 82–3, 118
trade, 2, 35–6
Aden, 154
clothing, 162, 164–5, 166
East India Company, 3, 21, 36, *37*, 41, 62, 134, 167
foodstuffs, 154, 162, 164
rice, 165
rope, 139
Suakin, 170
sea cucumbers, 183
Suez, 158
timber, 52, 57, 164
Indians, 51, 164, 221
insurance, 127
interpreters, 198
interviews
Aden, 19
Arabic, 9–10, 25
Djibouti City, 21
El Wejh, 10, 17–18
Farasan Islands, 8, 22–3
Jeddah, 25–6
literacy, 10
Jizan, 22
Khokha, 9, 14, 21
Khor al-Ghureirah, 8, 21
Massawa, 13, 24–5
memory, 12–13
Mersa Alam, 14–15
Mocha, 13, 21
Obock, 9, 13, 21
occupations (of interviewees), 15, 21
see also Appendix III-XI
Qunfudhah, 11, 25–6
Quseir, 11, 14–15
Safaga, 8, 14
security, 11
Suakin, 8, 18
Tadjourah, 9, 21
Ummlejj, 10, 17, *18*
Yanbu al-Bahr, 10, 17
Iran, 170
see also Persia
iron, 162, 171, 172
Ishak, Ibrahim, 173, 202
islands, 33, 145–6, 225
see also Dahlak, Farasan, Hamra, Kamaran, Mait, Mayyun
Issa (tribe), 21, 202
Italy, 41, 171–2
ivory, 36, 163, 165, 171

Jaber, Ahmed, 52, 131, 152
Jaber, Ali Ahmed, 181
jalba see galba
Jansen van Rensburg, Julian, 8
janūbiyya (wind), 141–2, 143
Japan, 166, 169, 171
Java, 165, 166, 167, 169
see also South-East Asia
Jazan (Saudi Arabian province), 230
Jeddah (Saudi Arabia)
Abdul Rauf Khalil Museum, 226, *228*
Bowen, R. LeBaron, 170
Burckhardt, J.L., 168
coral, 30
fishing boats, 178–9
hospitals, 225
interviews, 25–6
migration, 221
pilgrims, 25–6, 36, 41, 43–4, 146, 167, 169, 195, 215, 221
pilots, 132
routes, 43, 68, 100, 144, 146, *148*, 150, 157
shipbuilding, 51, 54

slave-trafficking, 171, 195, 200
trade, 35–6, 41, 154–5, 158, 167–70, 171, 172, 174
jellyfish, 188
Jewell, John H.A., 79
jinn (spirits), 8, 12, 209–12, 214–15, 217
Jizan (Saudi Arabia), *24*
Egyptians in, 51
festivals, 230
interviews, 22
mangoes, 230
'obrī, 92
racing boats, 22, 92, 138, 223
sails, 138
sanbūk, 51, 92
shipbuilding, 51, 91–2
timber, 22
Yemenis in, 51, 92
za'īma, 91–2
Jouma, Saad Abdallah, 160
Jubouri, Hamid Hammad, 183
Juhuni, Awwad bin Bakhit al-, 98, 106
jurdī-sanbūk (type of boat), 75–7, 80, 86, 88, 96

Kamaran Island (Yemen), 32, 69, 226
Kawatoko, Mutsuo, 155
Kay, Shirley, 174
kerrānī see clerks
Khalifeh, Muhammed, 126
Khalil, Abu al-Hamd Ahmed, 184
khamsīn (wind), 140, 142
khatira see gaṭīra
Khayaya, Abd al-Karim, 54, 138, 162
Khayyat, Ahmad Ibrahim, 54
Khizari, Ziyad Ahmed, 172, 202
Khokha (Yemen), 9, 14, 21, 57, 91, 96, 182
Khor al-Ghureirah (Yemen), 8, *20*
fishing boats, 179
hūrī, 90
interviews, 5, 21
mangroves, 32
migrant-smuggling, 131
'obrī, 88, *89*
sanbūk, 88
trade, 173
za'īma, 69, 88
zārūk, 88
Khuwaishi, Abd al-Muhsin al-, 73, 129
Klunzinger, Carl
dāw, 62
grain, 158
Jeddah, 158
ostrich eggs, 214
pilgrims, 146
Quseir, 37–8, 45, 68
routes, 146
sailors, 107
saints, 214
safety, 45
sanbūk, 68
trade, 158
tombs, 214
written sources, 3
kotia (type of boat), 68
kurmush (type of sea-biscuit), 117, 223
Kuwait, 54–5, 78, 135, 157

lanch (type of boat), 85, 169
Landberg, Count Carlo de, 85
landmarks (coastal), 100–2, 124, 214, 225
Lane, E.W., 207
language, 107, 221–2
see also Arabic, *lingua franca*
lansh-sanbūk (type of boat), *57*, 86, 183
leaks, 45, 107, 188

Latin America, 181
leather, 158
LeBaron Bowen, Richard, 83
  Aden, 114
  debt, 191
  Jeddah, 170
  leaks, 45
  overcrowding, 115
  share-system, 191–2
  wages, 192
  women, 115–16
  written sources, 3
Lefebre, Théophile, 169
Le Masson (French engineer), 75, *76*
Lesourd, Michel, 156
Lesseps, Ferdinand de, 38
Lewis, Norman, 106, 126
lexicography, 66–7, 85, 90, 95, 222
lifeboats, 45, 116
Lingeh (Iran), 157, *170*
lingua franca, 107, 221
Litany of the Sea (religious poem), 212–13
literacy, 10, 101
Lith (Saudi Arabia), 30, 33, 200
Lobo, Jerónimo, 145, 168
log books, 99, 103
Londres, Albert, 196
lookout, 102, 124, 128, 188
Luheyya (Yemen), 1, 30, 49, 70, 167

Machell, Thomas, 55, 125, 128
ma'diyya (type of boat), 96
Magga, Ole Henrik, 6
magic, 12, 204, 217
  see also jinn
Mahalla, Ruqayya Hassan, 9, 204
mahadi (type of boat), 96, *208*
Mahdi, Muhammad al-, 122, 223
Mahmud, Duwi Toufiq, 102, 116, 127
Mahmud, Muhammad Hasan, 165
Mahmud, Seif el Din Hasan, 114, 119, 160
Mahrī, Sulaymān al-, 101, 135, 145
Mait Island (Somalia), 33, 215
Mājid bin Muḥammad, 135
Makin, William, 55, 96
  bailing out, 107
  clams, 187
  fish, 187
  gun-running, 201
  navigation, 100–1
  pirates, 125–6
  seamanship, 134
  water, 109
Makki, Sheikh, 203
Malkato (Eritrea), *23*, 25
mammals (marine), 33
mangoes, 230
mango wood, 86, 87
mangroves, 31–2, 165, 166
Maqdisī, Muḥammad bin Aḥmad al-, 103
Maqrīzī, Taqī l-Dīn Aḥmad al-, 115
MARES *see* Maritime Ethnography of the Red Sea Project
Maritime Ethnography of the Red Sea Project, 8, 11, 19, *24*, 48, 55, 83, 120, 185
marriage, 106, 221–2
marsā see mersā
Marwani, Hamdan Abd al-, 183, 186
Mashlīḥī (tribe), 21
Massawa (Eritrea)
  art, 226
  co-operatives, 183
  coral, 30
  fibreglass boats, 183
  fishing boats, 181, 182, 183–4
  interviews, 13, 24–5

Italy, 41
migration, 221
pilgrims, 172
routes, 43
shipbuilding, 50, 93
slave-trafficking, 200
steamships, 41
trade, 165, 170–2, 173
Valentia, Viscount, 171
water, 119
masts, 130, 136–7
Matbuli, Muhammad Said, 156, 169
Maurer, Henri R., 68, 69, *70*
Mayyun (Perim) Island (Yemen), 39, 96, 173, 181, 200
McGrail, Séan, 72
McMaster, D.N., 143
memory, 12–13, 72, 101, 227–8, 232
Merchant, Carolyn, 214
merchants, 129, 159, 164–5
buildings, 224
coffee, *168*
Jeddah, 155
Mocha, *168*
pearling, 192
pilgrims, 164
Suakin, 164, 223
Suez, 157
Tur, 68, 155, 158
Yanbu al-Bahr, 223
merkeb (type of boat), 96
mersā (bay), 31–2, 149
Mersa Alam (Egypt), 14–15, 30, 33–4, 36, 75, 160
metal-hulled boats, 34, 51, 85, 223
see also steamships
Meulen, Daniel van der, 36, 117
Mhammed, Ata Bishar, 139
mibkhara (building), 225
migrant-smuggling, 92, 131, 191–2, 205
migration, 219–20
Aden, 51
Bangladeshis, 91, 221
Djibouti, 50, 52
Egyptians, 51, 92, 163
Ethiopians, 192
Eritreans, 131, 192, 205
Greeks, 56
Gulf, 231
Hadhramis, 62, 164, 220–1
Hijazis, 221
Indians, 51, 164, 221
Jeddah, 221
Massawa, 221
Nigerians, 52
Oman, 203
Parsees, 51
Somalis, 131
Suakin, 52, 164
Yemenis, 21, 50, 51, 52, 92, 220
Millar, Hugh, 55
Miran, Jonathan, 194, 221
Mirbas, Muawwid Abd al-Raheem, 77
missionaries, 38
Mocha (Yemen), *37*
coffee, 21, 35, 70, 125, 166, 167, *168*, 170, 173
folk beliefs, 215, *216*
forts, 225
interviews, 13, 21
merchants, *168*
pirates, 125
saints, 215, *216*
shipbuilding, 49
slave-trafficking, 171, 195, 200
storms, 128
tombs, 215, *216*

trade, 35, 141, 166–7, 171, 172
winds, 143
Mohamed, Abdoulkader Houmed, 21
Mohamed, Ahmed Youssef, 181
Mohamed, Youssef Omar, 13, 105, 120, 179, 211
money, 129, 155–6, 169
see also currency, debt, share-system, wages
Monfreid, Henri de
Cape Guardafui, 126
coral, 145
drug-smuggling, 201
gun-running, 209
jinn, 211, 214
leaks, 107
music, 120–1
saints, 214–15, *216*
slave-trafficking, 197, 198–200, 201, 202–3
smells, 183
storms, 128–9
tombs, 214–15, *216*
trocas shells, 183
Warsangali, 126
written sources, 3
zārūk, 200
monsoon, 44, 143, 154
monuments, 228, *229*, *230*
moonlight, 145
Moore, Alan, 49, 83
carpenters, 54
dāw, 62
galba, 63
sā'iya, 61
sanbūk, 79, 88
written sources, 3
za'īma, 78, 79
Moosa, Ibrahim Ali, 54, 56, 77, 85
Moresby, Robert, *44*, 132
Morgan, Elaine, 124, 132
mosquitoes, 115
mother of pearl, 36, 158, 186
mu'allim see pilots
Muftāḥ, Ibrāhīm, 26, 156, 166, 180
mugaddam see boatswain
Muhammad, Abbas, 108
Muhammad, Hashim, 147
Muhammad, Hussein Ibrahim, 53, 184
Muhammed, Isa, 94
Muhsini, Muhsin Saud, 13, 104, 176
Mujawir, Abdo Hasan, 92
Mujawir, Ala Allah Abdo, 70
Mu'min, Farih Gaas, 180
munaddiḥ see lookout
Murābiṭ, Ḥasan, 214
Musaid, Mohammed Gaballah, 11
Muscat, 49, 125
museums, 226, *228*, 232
music, 119–22, *120*, 180, 230
Mustafa, Matar Fikri Muhammed, 110, 142, 188
Muwallad, Humaid Mani al-, 76, *78*
Muweilah (Saudi Arabia), 128, 146, 157, 159, 160, 225
Muzaffar, Mohammad Ahmad, 109, 187
Myers, O., 211, 216
Myos Hormos (Egypt), 278, note, 19

Najdi, Yahya Ibrahim al-, 138
Najjar, Mohammed Ali Abdallah al-, 78
nākhōda see captain
Nance, Robert Morton, 61, 63
Nasib, Mohammed Abdallah Ahmed, 73, 191
Nautical Tables, 135

navigation, 100–6, 124, 130, 135, 146, 232
see also charts, *dīra*, pilots, stars, winds
navigator *see* pilots
nawrī (type of boat), 86, 156
Netherlands, 36–7, 167
Nicholl, Charles, 203
Niebuhr, Carsten
Bedouin, 119
cabins, 115
grain, 157–8
Jeddah, 158
passengers, 115
pilots, 104
sails, 137–8
scientists, 37
shipbuilding, 49, 157–8
Suez, 49
trade, 157–8
Tur, 104
written records, 3
Nigerians, 52
Norie, John William, 135
nūra, 108
Nuwayrī l-Iskandarānī, Muḥammad bin Qāsim al-, 67

Obock (Djibouti)
buildings, 223
fishing boats, 181
interviews, 9, 13, 21
mangroves, 32
migrant-smuggling, 191–2
passengers, 95
posters, 226, *227*
routes, 173
sanbūk, 204
trade, 172
winds, 143
Yemenis in, 21, 50
zārūk, 200
'obrī (type of boat), 76, 88, *89*, 92, 83, 96, *127*, 172
occupations (of interviewees), 15, 21
see also Appendix III-XI
oculus, 207–9, *208*, 217
see also evil eye
oil (petroleum), 166, 191, 231
Oman, 79–81, 87, 135, 139, 154, 195, 202, 203, 222
Omar, Mohamed Salem, 157, 172, 173, 203
open sea, 219–20
oral history *see* fieldwork, interviews, memory
Orbaşlı, Aylin, 30, 91
Orne, Joseph, 125
Osgood, Joseph B.F., 3, 125, 195, 200
ostrich eggs, 207, 214
Othman, Abdallah Yasin, 171–2
Ottomans, 36–7, 163, 166, 168, 194, 197, 201, 225
overcrowding, 61, 115
overloading, 130, 131–2
Ovington, John, 3, 49, 100, 134
Oxford Companion to Ships and the Sea, 149
oysters, 116, 117–18, 231
see also mother of pearl, shell collecting

P & O *see* Peninsular and Oriental Steam Navigation Company
Paine, Lincoln, 136
Pappagallo, Linda, 192
Pâris, François-Edmond, 3, 69, *71*, 81, 82
parrotfish, 30, 180, 192, 230, 231

Parsees, 51
passengers, 8, 39, 99, 113–19, 122, 130–1, 147, 172
Peninsular and Oriental Steam Navigation Company, 39
pearling, 2, 6, 22, 23, 72
  captain, 99, 103
  Dahlak, 186–7, 219–20
  diving, 185–6, 190–1
  Eritrea, 47
  Farasan Islands, 47, 70–1, 171, 185–92, 219–20, 232
  food, 117
  Gulf, 171
  hūrī, 187
  Massawa, 171
  merchants, 192
  sails, 152
  sanbūk, 70–1, 187
  sharks, 179
  Suakin, 182
  trade, 171, 192
  wages, 189–91
  weighing, 189, *190*
people-smuggling *see* migrant-smuggling
Perim Island *see* Mayyun Island
Periplus of the Erythraean Sea, 145
Perrier, Henri, 3, 52, 53, 86
PERSGA *see* Regional Organization for the Conservation of the Environment of the Red Sea and Gulf of Aden
Persia, 138, 169
Pesce, Angelo, 28, 30, 174
pilgrims, 2, 15, 47, 85, 154–5, 157
  Agig, 165
  Burton, R., 68, *114*, 115, 158
  El Wejh, 146, 160, 162
  falūka, 84
  Jeddah, 25–6, 36, 41, 43–4, 146, 167, 169, 195, 215, 221
  Klunzinger, C., 146
  Massawa, 172
  merchants, 169
  Mersa Alam, 36
  pirates, 126
  Port Sudan, 52
  Quseir, 36, 146, 158–60, 225
  Safaga, 36, 44
  slave-trafficking, 195, 197
  steamships, 41, 44
  Suakin, 44, 52, 84, 163
  Suez, 36, 43
  Ummlejj, 162
pilots, 103–4, 132–3, 134–5, 144–5, 201
pirates, 62, 125–7, 166, *198*, 224
Pitts, Joseph, 128, 137, 215
place-names, 225–6
planks
  buildings, 223
  constuction techniques, 57, *58*
  hūrī, 57, 86–7, 102, 177
  Obock, 223
  ṣaddāfa, 95
  stitch planking, 68
  timber, 53
  Tuwaled, 94
plans, 53
pleasure boats, 84, 85
plumb-lines, 45, 103
poetry, 101, 121–2, 135, 209
police, 11
Poncet, Charles-Jacques, 118, 137, 163
porcelain, 165
Port Said (Egypt), *40*, 41
Port Sudan (Sudan), 34, 41, 50, 51–2, *80*, 130, 165, 215

portolans *see* charts
Portugal, 67, 164, 165–6, 168
posters, 226, *227*
Prados, Edward, 87, 88, 90
prawns, 92, 118, 231
predestination *see qadar*
prayer, 212–13, 214, 217
Pujo, Jean-Marie, 52, 71
Purchas, Samuel, 145

qadar (predestination), 127–8
Qahtan, Ahmad, 91, 179
Qahtani, Abdallah, 10
Qammash, Abdallah Mabruk, 92
qat (plant), 9, 29
quarantine stations, 225
quartermaster *see* clerks
Quft (Egypt), 29
Qunfudhah (Saudi Arabia), 11, 25–6
Qur'ān, 194, 207, 209–10, 212
Quseir (Egypt), 29
  Bruce, J., 136
  Burckhardt, J.L., 115
  caravans, *17*
  coral, 30
  ferries, 14
  fishing boats, 176
  folk beliefs, 214
  forts, 75, *77*, 225, 226
  interviews, 11, 14–15
  Klunzinger, C., 37–8, 45, 68
  monuments, 228, *229*
  ostrich eggs, 214
  pilgrims, 36, 146, 158–60, 225
  place-names, 226
  routes, 43, 144, 146–8, *148*, 150 152, 157
  sails, 138
  saints, 214
  sanbūk, 54
  shipbuilding, 52, 53, 54, 56, *70*, 75, *77*, 85
  tombs, 214
  tourism, 75, 85
  trade, 158–70
  transom sterns, 54
  water, 119, 158, 224
  winds, 140, 142–3, 146
quyāsa (type of boat), 60, *64*

Rabigh (Saudi Arabia), 76, *78*, 185
racing boats, 22, 92, 138, 223
al-Rāḍī family, 68, 155, 158, 188
Rahmat Allah, Mahmood, 176
rainfall, 38–9
Rajhi, Muhammad Hadi al-, 171, *190*, 192
Ramadan, 157
ramas (type of boat), 87, 95, 182, 186
Ras Ali (Djibouti), 96
Ras al-Khaimah (Arabian-Persian Gulf), 62
Ras Asir *see* Cape Guardafui
Ras Dawair (Egypt), 145–6
Ras Muhammad (Egypt), 146
Rashayda (tribe), 12, 18, 52, 126, 220
Ray, Himanshu Prabha, 5
rayyes see captain
Red Sea Pilot, 124, 132
reefs, 29–31, 128, 145, 147, 219
Regional Organization for the Conservation of the Environment of the Red Sea and Gulf of Aden, 30, 130
replica boats, 75, 76, *77*, *78*, 86, 92
Ricciardi, Lorenzo, 105
rice, 36, 156–7, 162, 165, 166, 169, 173
rigging, 8, 49, 102, 107, 108, 136–7, 139, 150, *248*, *249*
  see also sails

Rimbaud, Arthur, 201, 202
rock shrines, 213–14, 217
Rönnby, Johan, 6
rope, ropemaking, 107, 137, 138–9
Rouaud, Alain, 3, 156
routes, 43–4, 144–8, *148*
  Bab el-Mandeb, 39, 58, 67
  charts, 59–60
  Dhuba, 146
  Djibouti, 144
  El Wejh, 43, 144, 146, 157
  Jeddah, 43, 68, 100, 144, 146, *148*, 150, 157
  Massawa, 43
  Muweilah, 146, 157
  Obock, 173
  Quseir, 43, 144, 146–8, *148*, 150 152, 157
  steamships, 39
  Suakin, 43
  Suez, 43, 68, 100, 144, 157
  trade, 154, 157
  Yanbu al-Bahr, 43, 146, 157
Royal Marines, 126, *127*
Royal Navy, 126, 166, 193, 196–202
rubbān see pilots
Rüppell, E., 37
Ruwaysi, Naji, 121

Saad, Ahmed Muhammad, 179
Saad, Mahmud, 100
ṣabā, (wind), 142, 143
Sabbagh, Mohammed Saeed al-, 56
Sabini, John, 134
ṣaddāfa (type of boat), 94–5, 177, 186
Safaga (Egypt)
  accidents, 42
  coral, 30
  ferries, 14, 85
  fishing boats, 85
  hūrī, 177
  interviews, 14
  pilgrims, 14, 36, 44
  sails, 8
  shipbuilding, 52, 85
  steamships, 44
  tourism, 85
safety, 45, 115, 130, 131, 147–8
  see also accidents
Safi, Umar as-, 164
Ṣaghānī, al-Ḥasan bin Muḥammad al-, 67
ṣaghīr see cabin-boys
ṣāḥib ad-daffa see helmsman
Said, Ali, 147, 155
Sā'īda bin Ju'ayya, 67
sailcloth, 137–8
Sailing Directions for the Red Sea, 132–3
sailmaking, 138
sailors, 106–12, 119–23, 188
sails, *46, 141, 248, 249*
  boatswain, 102
  diesel engines, 86
  fishing boats, 171
  gaṭīra, 248, 249
  lansh-sanbūk, 86
  masts, 136–7
  Niebuhr, C., 137–8
  pearling, 152
  Persia, 138
  Quseir, 138
  Safaga, 8
  sailcloth, 138
  sailors, 107
  sailmaking, 138
  tacking, 151
  wearing, 150–1
saints, 214–17
sā'iya (type of boat), 60–1, 81

al-Salif (Yemen), 19, 90, 167, 171, 181
sakūna (type of boat), 70
salinity, 28
Salt, Henry, 132
saranjī see boatswain
sanbūk (type of boat)
  Burton, R., 68, 100, 114
  coffee, 70
  design, 67–72, 80–1, 92
  Djibouti, 52
  Eritrea, 171
  Farasan Islands, 73–4, 187
  ferries, 84
  Gulf, 79–81, *81*
  Jizan, 51, 92
  jurdī, 76
  Khor al-Ghureirah, 88
  Klunzinger, C., 68
  Kuwait, 54
  lexicography, 66–7
  Luheyya, 1
  Moore, A., 69, 88
  Obock, 204
  Oman, 79–81
  pearling, 70–1, 187
  Port Sudan, *80*
  Quseir, 54
  safety, 45
  Sheikh Mansoor, 46, 70, *75*
  Sigalat Lamba, 94
  Tadjourah, 52
  transom sterns, 69, *70*, 74, 80, 92
  Villiers, A., 46, 70
  written sources, 67–8
sardines, 181
Sayyid, Ṣāliḥ Bin 'Abd al-Laṭīf 'Alyān al-, 26, 61
scientists, 37–8
sea-chests, 109, 155
sea cucumber, 182, 183
seagrass, 31, 32
seamanship, 45, 128, 134
sea shanties, 8, 13, 17, 26, 119–22, *120*, 180, 231
seaweed, 32
seaworthiness, 55
  sea also accidents, overcrowding, overloading, safety
security, 11
Semaan, Lucy, 8, 48, 87
Serjeant, Bob, 109, 126, 135, 212
sghayyir see cabin-boys
Shahhar, Ahmed Mohammed, 138
Shādhilī, Abū l-Ḥasan al-, 212–3
Shādhilī, 'Alī bin 'Umar al-, 215, *216*
shamāl (wind), 140, 143, 144, 146, 149, 151, 165, 199
share-system, 188–91, 192
Sharif, Ali Hasan Hammud, 187
Sharif, Fahad al-, 11
Sharif, Ibrahim al-, 10, 159
sharks, 32–3, 57, 168, 177, 179, 187, 199
sharm see sherm
Sharm el-Sheikh (Egypt), 179
shaṭṭiyya (type of boat), 86–7
Sheikh ad-Dallālīn, 179
Sheikh Mansoor (name of ship), 46, 70, *75*
Sheikh Said (Yemen), 96–7
shellfish, 23, 231
  see also oysters, prawns
shell collecting, 8, 86–7, 163, 182–3, 185–8, 192
sherm (creek), 32, 149
Shihāb, Ḥasan Ṣāliḥ, (author and interviewee), 3, 78, 83, 105–6
shikka (string of fish), 179

shipbuilding
Aden, 49–51, 53, 54, 55, 62–3, 70, *73*, *74*, 88
Alexandria, 56
Bahrain, 56
Burckhardt, J.L., 49
Burton R., 56
carpenters, 49, 54, 56, 108
caulking, 57, *58*
construction techniques, 55–8
design, 53–4, 67–72, 80–1, 92, 96
diesel engines, 92, 152, 154
Djibouti, 25, 50, 52, 58, 96
Farasan Islands, 92
fibreglass boats, 17, *18*, 47, 52–3, 54, 58, 90–2, 183, 191, 222–3
Gulf, 79–81, *80*, 222
hand-tools, 52-, 56–7
Hodeidah, 49–50, 70, 78
Hornell, J., 50, 82–3
hulls, 48–9, 53–4, 55–8, 68–72, 80–1, 89, 92, 96
India, 49–52, 62, 82–3, 118
Jeddah, 51, 54
Jizan, 51, 91–2
Khokha, 57, 96
Kuwait, 54–5
Luhayya, 51, 70
Massawa, 50, 93
metal-hulled boats, 34, 51, 85, 223
Mocha, 49
Muscat, 49
Niebuhr, C., 49, 157–8
Oman, 79–81, 222
Port Sudan, 50, 51–2, *80*
Quseir, 52, 53, 54, 56, *70*, 75, *77*, 85
replica boats, 75, 76, *77*, *78*, 86, 92
Safaga, 52, 85
Sheikh Said, 86–7
Suakin, 12, 50, 51–3, *57*, *58*, *64*, 65, 86–7, 222
Suez, 49, 56
Tadjourah, 52
timber, 51, 52, 53, 57, 91, 93
Tuwaled, 25, 93, *94*, 95
Ummlejj, 85
Yanbu al-Bahr, 52, 76–7, *78*, 85–6
Yemen, 200
ships, types of *see* boats, types of, steamships
ship's biscuit *see kurmush*
ship's boat *see hūrī*
shipwrecks *see* accidents
Sigalat Lamba (Eritrea), 25, 93–4
Sim, Katharine, 115
simsimiyya (musical instrument), 120
Siradj, Houmed Barkat, 202–3
Siraj, Siraj Muhammed, 73, 78, 93, 171
Siyan, Muhammad as-, 164
slaves (treatment of), 195–6
slave-trafficking, 12, 38, *198*, *199*
Djibouti, 9, 47, 193, 200, 202
Ethiopia, 195, 196, 200, 202–4
ethnography, 193–4
fieldwork, 193–4
Great Britain, 194, 196–202, 204
Hadhramaut, 205
Hodeidah, 200
hūrī, 195
Ibn Saud, 205
interpreters, 198
Jeddah, 171, 195, 200
Lith, 200
Makin, W., 198, 204
Massawa, 200
Mocha, 171, 195, 200
Monfreid, H. de, 197, 198–200, 201, 202–3
Obock, 204

'obrī, 127
Oman, 202
pilgrims, 195, 197
pirates, 125
Royal Navy, 166, 196–202
Steamships, 201
Tadjourah, 202–3
Valentia, Viscount, 195
zārūk, 89, 127, 200–1
smells, 45, 116, 183
smuggling *see* gun-running, migrant-smuggling, slave-trafficking
Somali (language), 21
Somalia (state), 125–7, 131
Somalis, 205
songs *see* sea shanties
sources *see* written sources
Southampton University, 278, note, 19
South-East Asia, 53, 138, 167, 169, 171
see also Java
Sri Lanka, 62
Stark, Freya, 51, 167
stars, 13, 164–7, 141, 146–7, 175–6, 219, 232
steamships, *40*
accidents, 124, 131–2
Aden, 41
Ali Bey, 38
Burton, R., 38
Dubois, C., 42, 46
ferries, 26
France, 41
Great Britain, 39, 41
Italy, 41
Jeddah, 41
Klunzinger, C., 41
Massawa, 41
Mocha, 41
passengers, 39
Peninsular and Oriental Steam Navigation Company, 39
pilgrims, 41, 44
routes, 39, 41
Royal Navy, 201
Safaga, 44
slave-trafficking, 201
Suakin, 34, 41, 44
Suez Canal, *40*
tourism, 39
stitch-planking, 68
storms, 128–32, 140, 142, 147–8, 219
storytelling, 119
Suakin (Sudan)
buildings, *164, 165*, 223
diving, 182, 187
Egyptians in, 164
falūka, 84
ferries, 84
forts, 224–5
Hadhramis in, 164
India, 170
Indians in, 164
interviews, 8, 18
magic, 12
merchants, 223
migration, 52, 164
Nigerians in, 52
pearling, 182
pilgrims, 44, 52, 84, 163
rope, 139
routes, 43
sails, 138
shell collecting, 8, 182–3, 192
shipbuilding, 12, 50, 51–3, *57*, *58*, *64*, 65, 86–7, 222
steamships, 34, 41, 44
telegraph, 39
trade, 34, 41–2, 163–5, 171
Valentia, Viscount, 163

water, 115, 224
zārūk, 85, 86–7
Subhi, Awad al-, 10, 223
Sudan, 52, 53, 177, 220
Suez (Egypt)
Ali Bey, 157
Bruce, J., 57
Burckhardt, 49, 162
Burton, R., 56, 100, 158
coffee, 173
grain, 158
India, 158
merchants, 157
Niebuhr, C., 49, 157–8
pilgrims, 36, 43
routes, 43, 68, 100, 144, 157
shipbuilding, 49, 56
trade, 157–8, 165, 169
Valentia, Viscount, 157
Suez Canal, 38–9, *40*, 42, 46, 166, 201
sukkānī see helmsman
sukūnī see helmsman
Suleiman, Abdou, 52, 150, 181, 186
Sur (Oman), 154, 216

Taalibballa (name of ship), 173
ṭabbākh see cooks
tacking (sailing technique), 149, 150–2, *151*
Tadjourah (Djibouti)
ferries, 172
folk beliefs, 215, 217
gun-running, 202
interviews, 8, 9, 21
jinn, 217
overloading, 130
passengers, 8
saints, 215
sanbūk, 52, 130
shipbuilding, 52
slave-trafficking, 202–3
tombs, 215
trade, 172–3
za'īma, 172
zārūk, 131
Taha, Shadia, 26
ṭahhān see cooks
talismans *see* amulets
taxes, 53, 155, 166–7, 184, 194, 225
teak, 53, 170
telegraph, 39
terrorism, 126
Thomas, Bertram, 202, 210
Tigrinya (language), 25
timber, 8, 91
Burton, R., 50
cargo, 165, 166
costs, 53, 57, 93, 157
East Africa, 53, 166
India, 52, 53, 164–6
Jizan, 22
South-East Asia, 53
see also mango wood, teak
toilet boxes, 116
tombs, 214–7, 225
tonnage, 52, 78, 156–7
tools *see* equipment, hand-tools
tourism, 33, 118, 231
coral, 31
Dhuba, 160
falūka, 56, 85
Farasan Islands, 210, 228
jinn, 210
Mersa Alam, 15
Quseir, 75, 85
Ras Ali, 96
Safaga, 85
Sharm el-Sheikh, 179
steamships, 39
Suez Canal, 39

za'īma, 96
zārūk, 96
trade, 31–42, 47, 153
Aden, 166–7
Basra, 143, 154, 169, 173, 216
Burton, R., 158
China, 165, 167
East Africa, 53, 78, 165, 166
East India Company, 3, 21, 36, *37*, 41, 62, 134, 167
El Wejh, 162
Ethiopia, 167, 173
Far East, 182
Great Britain, 163–4
India, 2, 35–6
Aden, 154
clothing, 162, 164–5, 166
East India Company, 3, 21, 36, *37*, 41, 62, 134, 167
foodstuffs, 154, 162, 164
rice, 165
rope, 139
Suakin, 170
sea cucumbers, 183
Suez, 158
Java, 165, 166, 167, 169
Jeddah, 35–6, 41, 154–5, 158, 167–70, 171, 172, 174
Jizan, 155
Klunzinger, C., 158
Khor al-Ghureirah, 173
Latin America, 181
Massawa, 165, 170–2, 173
Mocha, 25, 41, 166–7, 171, 172
Niebuhr, C., 157–8
Obock, 172
Ottomans, 36–7, 163, 169
Persia, 169
Port Sudan, 165
Quseir, 158–60
routes, 154, 157
South-East Asia, 167, 169, 171
Suakin, 34, 41–2, 163–5, 171
Suez, 157–8, 165, 169
Suez Canal, 38–9, *40*, 42
Tadjourah, 172–3
Tur, 68, 155, 158
Ummlejj, 162
Valentia, Viscount, 167
Vietnam, 78, 106
winds, 153–4, 156
Yanbu al-Bahr, 162–3
transom sterns
baghla, 55
bōt, 84
design, 71–2
Djibouti, 71
ghanja, 62
hūrī, 57
jurdī, 76
lansh-sanbūk, 86
Quseir, 54
sā'iya, 60
sanbūk, 69, *70*, *74*, 80, 92
Taalibballa, 173
za'īma, 77, 79, 92
tribal warfare, 194
trocas shells, 182–3, 186–7
Tuddenham, David Berg, 5
Tunstall, Irene, 195, 197
Tunstall, John, 195, 197
Tur (Egypt), 63, 68, 104, 128, 155, 158, 188, 225
turbans, 109–10, *110*, *111*
Turkey, 51, 92
turtles, 33, 117
Tuwaled (Eritrea), 25, 93–4, *94*, 95

Ubayd, Umar Uthman, 164
'ūd (musical instrument), 121

Ummlejj (Saudi Arabia), 10, 17, *18*, 30, 162, 225, *230*
Usman, Ahmed Zabib, 171

Valentia, George Annesley, Viscount
Aden, 166
coffee, 167
East India Company, 167
Massawa, 171
pilots, 104, 132
slave-trafficking, 195
storms, 142
Suakin, 163
Suez, 157
trade, 167
winds, 128, 132, 140, 142
written sources, 3
Van Der Meulen, Daniel *see* Meulen, Daniel van der
Varthema, Ludovico de, 67
verses *see* poetry
Vietnam, 78, 106
Villiers, Alan, 98, 124
captain, 108
discipline, 108
sanbūk, 46, 70
Sheikh Mansoor, 46, 70
smells, 116
water, 109
written sources, 3
zārūk, 100, 109

wages, 99, 104, 188–91, 192
Wallin, Georg August, 28, 158, 160
Warsangali (tribe), 126
watches (on board ship), 108
water, 102, 109, 115, 118–19, 158, 224
Waterhouse, Francis, 98, 201
wearing (sailing technique), 149–51, *149*
weighing (of pearls), 189, *190*
Weismann, Norbert, 60
Wellsted, James R., 3, 128, 132, 140, 160, 162
Westerdahl, Christer, 5
Whitewright, Julian, 135, 136, 144, 150
Wick, Alexis, 133
Wilson, N.J.F., 3, 55, 68, 69
winds, 219
azyab, 141–2, 143, 144, 176, 199–200
Bab el-Mandeb, 143
Burton, R., 144
fishing boats, 175, 180–1
janūbiyya, 141–2, 143
khamsīn, 140, 142
Mocha, 143
Monfreid H. de, 140, 144
monsoon, 44, 143, 154
Obock, 143
Quseir, 140, 142–3, 146
Ras Dawair, 145–6
ṣabā, 142, 143
shamāl, 140, 143, 144, 146, 149, 151, 165, 199
storms, 140, 147–8
tacking, 151
Tadjourah, 143
trade, 153–4, 156
Valentia, Viscount, 128, 132, 140, 142
wearing, 149–50
women, 9, 115–16, 122, 185
wood *see* firewood, mango wood, teak, timber
woodchips, 55
wrecks *see* accidents
written sources, 3, 5–6, 26, 52–3, 67–8

Yanbu al-Bahr (Saudi Arabia), 33, *44*
  buildings, *31*, 223
  Burckhardt, J.L., 49, 116, 162
  coffee, 162
  coral, 30
  dāw, 61
  hospitals, 225
  hūrī, 86
  interviews, 10, 17
  jinn, 212
  merchants, 223
  museums, 230
  music, 230
  replica boats, *78*
  routes, 43, 146, 157
  shipbuilding, 52, 76–7, *78*, 85–6
  trade, 162–3
Yaḥyā, Imam of Yemen, 125–6
Yemen, 9, 184, 200, 203, 204
Yemenis, 21, 50, 51, 52, 92, 220

Zabayda (tribe), 126
Zabīdī, Muḥammad Murtaḍā al-, 85
Za'īliyya, Aḥmad bin Aḥmad, 216
za'īma-sanbūk (type of boat), 49, 77–9
  accidents, 131
  Djibouti, 131
  Hornell, J., 79
  Jizan, 91–2
  jurdī, 76
  Khor al-Ghureirah, 69, 88
  Moore, A., 78, 79
  Ras Ali, 96
  Tadjourah, 172
  tonnage, 78, *156*
  tourism, 96
  transom sterns, 77, 79, 92
  Tuwaled, 93
zārūk-sanbūk (type of boat), 90
  cargo boats, 89, 130
  Djibouti, 130
  drug smuggling, 202
  fishing boats, 180
  Hornell, J., 200
  Khor al-Ghureirah, 88
  Monfreid H. de, 200
  Obock, 200
  overloading, 130
  pirates, 127
  Ras Ali, 96
  slave-trafficking, 89, 127, 200–1, 203
  Suakin, 85, 86–7
  Tadjourah, 93, 130
  tourism, 96
  Tuwaled, 93, 130
  Villiers, A., 100, 109
Zazzaro, Chiara, 8, 19, *20*, 22, 48, 97
Zeilah (Somalia), 131, 170, 173, 202, 204, 215